Home Maintenance

Home Maintenance

3rd Edition

by Tom Kraeutler
and James Carey and
Morris Carey, Jr.

A Wiley Brand

Home Maintenance For Dummies®, 3rd Edition

Published by: **John Wiley & Sons, Inc.**, 111 River Street, Hoboken, NJ 07030-5774, www.wiley.com

For general information on our other products and services, please contact our Customer Care Department within the U.S. at 877-762-2974, outside the U.S. at 317-572-3993, or fax 317-572-4002. For technical support, please visit https://hub.wiley.com/community/support/dummies.

Wiley publishes in a variety of print and electronic formats and by print-on-demand. Some material included with standard print versions of this book may not be included in e-books or in print-on-demand. If this book refers to media that is not included in the version you purchased, you may download this material at http://booksupport.wiley.com. For more information about Wiley products, visit www.wiley.com.

Library of Congress Control Number: 2024940754

ISBN: 978-1-394-24107-1 (pbk); 978-1-394-24109-5 (ebk); 978-1-394-24108-8 (ebk)

SKY10087146_100824

Contents at a Glance

Table of Contents

Introduction

Your home is like a superhero in your life, the caped crusader against decay, pests, and everyday wear and tear. It's your fortress, and it deserves all the love and protection you can give it! It's also the largest investment that you'll ever make in your life. So, it makes good sense to do everything you can to maintain it.

In addition to protecting the structural integrity of your home, regular maintenance will make it more comfortable, safer, and more energy efficient. And don't forget that a well-cared-for home stands out in the neighborhood, and that's worth something — a bigger price tag when it comes time to sell, or simply the satisfaction of knowing that you're in charge of your home and not vice versa.

Get ready for a rollercoaster ride of home-maintenance fun. Buckle up as we dive into the world of preserving your castle's integrity, boosting comfort and energy efficiency, and standing tall in the neighborhood with a well-cared-for abode.

Home Maintenance For Dummies, 3rd Edition, is your trusty sidekick, packed with tips and tricks to keep your home shining like a beacon of pride and satisfaction. Enjoy the adventure!

About This Book

Like most *For Dummies* books, *Home Maintenance For Dummies*, 3rd Edition, is a reference, meaning that it was written with the expectation that you would *not* read it from cover to cover over a couple of sittings. Instead, consider it one of the most important reference tools in your home-maintenance arsenal — like your prized hammer or power drill that you pick up and use whenever necessary.

Each chapter is divided into sections, and each section offers instructions on a different home maintenance task, like

>> How to fix those pesky floor squeaks

>> What to do when you know you've got a leak but you don't know where it's coming from

- » What cleaning solution is the best for removing mildew

- » How to easily maintain those confusing machines that keep you comfortable, like your furnace, boiler, air conditioner, and water heater

- » How to prevent a flooded basement and how to fix it if your last fix didn't work

- » How to reduce your energy costs while improving your comfort — all at once

- » How to decide whether to do it yourself or hire a contractor

Who needs this book? Everyone — no matter if your home is new or, like mine, was built in the last century! Seriously, if your home is an apartment, condo, single-family house, flat, co-op, cave, or hut; if you rent, own, or borrow; if your habitat is old, new, or somewhere in between, this book is for you.

Conventions Used in This Book

To help you navigate through this book and make maintenance as easy as possible, I've set up a few conventions:

- » *Italics* are used for emphasis and to highlight new words or terms that I define.

- » **Boldface** indicates the actionable part of numbered steps.

In addition to these standard conventions, whenever a task takes more than a few tools, I'll provide a list so that you can gather everything you need before you start to work.

What You're Not to Read

This book is written so that you can easily find information and easily understand what you find. And although I'd like to believe that you want to pore over every last word between the two yellow-and-black covers, I actually make it easy for you to identify skippable material — the stuff that, although interesting and related to the topic at hand, isn't essential for you to know. This text appears in *sidebars*, which are the shaded boxes that appear here and there throughout the book. They share personal stories and observations, but they aren't necessary reading.

Foolish Assumptions

You know what they say about the word *assume*. In any event, I've made the following assumptions about you:

>> You care about the appearance and condition of your home and, hence, its value.

>> You're not a home-improvement fanatic, nor are you particularly handy — you don't need to be.

>> You have a song in your heart, a smile on your face, and an insatiable desire to see your home be the best that it can be.

>> You don't have a warehouse full of tools and you're interested in getting only the tools you need. A few tools are of infinite value when it comes to home maintenance. However, the most complicated tool that you'll need is a cordless drill/driver for sinking a screw here and there. The tools that you'll find yourself needing most often are a scrub brush, a paintbrush, and plenty of patience.

>> You're the type who always seeks help when needed and always puts safety first when attempting a home-maintenance endeavor.

How This Book Is Organized

The chapters of this book are divided into the following parts so that you can easily find just the information that you're looking for.

Part 1: Home Maintenance and You

This part introduces you to the benefits of home maintenance and to the major systems and components in your home. You can also find a series of lists to help you keep your home-maintenance tasks organized. Follow this schedule, and your home will love you for it.

Even though you don't have to read this book from cover to cover, I strongly recommend that you check out the three chapters in this part so that you have a clear understanding of what parts of your home require maintenance and why you should pay attention to them.

Part 2: The Energy Envelope

Your home's envelope consists of all its exterior surfaces and associated components like windows and doors. And don't forget the attic, roof, basement, and foundation. For you to be comfortable inside your home, its exterior must be secure and in sound condition. Turn to this part to discover how easily you can maintain your home's exterior.

Part 3: Key Systems — Plumbing and HVAC (Heating, Ventilation, and Air Conditioning)

Nothing is scarier than hearing a noise that wasn't there before emanating from mechanical equipment: a popping sound in the water heater, a faucet that suddenly sounds like it's running on a flat tire, or a screeching racket inside the deepest, darkest part of your furnace. If you want to prevent or repair these elements of your home, check out this part.

Part 4: Inside Home Sweet Home

This part contains information on the stuff that you come into contact with on a day-to-day basis within your home, such as the walls, ceilings, floors, interior doors, cabinets, countertops, and appliances, to name a few. If you never venture into another part of this book, and you accomplish most of the tasks contained in this part, you'll be light-years ahead of the home-maintenance curve. Part 4 helps you patch walls, quiet floors, unstick doors, cure cabinet woes, and fix fireplaces. And, as an added bonus, you'll find out how to keep your home and yourself safe and secure. If this book could be compared to a meal, this part would definitely be the main course.

Part 5: Out in the Great Wide Open

If Part 4 contains all the stuff that you see everyday *in* your home, Part 5 is all about what you (and others) can see *outside* your home, such as walkways, paths, patios, decks, and driveways. Think that the interior of your home takes a beating? Consider the abuse that your wood deck, concrete patio, or metal porch railing is subject to from constant exposure to sunlight, rain, wind, and snow. Wood oxidizes, cups, and cracks; concrete expands, contracts, chips, and cracks; and metal can become a full-blown science experiment when covered with rust. Fortunately, Part 5 is chock-full of money-saving and time-tested tips and recipes that will tame even the most ferocious home-maintenance predator in your great wide open.

Part 6: The Part of Tens

In this part, you'll find ten cleaning solutions you can make yourself. Not only will these recipes save you all kinds of money, but you'll actually know what's in the products you're using. You'll also find out about the ten home-maintenance skills you need to keep your home in tip-top shape, plus ten smart home products that I think will add value and convenience to your home ownership experience.

Icons Used in This Book

Some information in this book is so important that it's emphasized by placing little pictures (called *icons*) next to certain points. Here's what the icons mean:

REMEMBER

This icon flags text that's important and not to be forgotten.

TIP

The Tip icon represents your basic good idea or trick-of-the-trade. It's what you wish somebody told you before you found out the hard way. I'm that somebody.

WARNING

Kidding aside for this icon. I use this icon to steer you clear of things *not* to do! It points out dangers and health hazards you should be aware of.

Beyond the Book

In addition to the pages you're reading right now, this book comes with a free access-anywhere cheat sheet that offers a number of home-maintenance-related pearls of wisdom. To get this cheat sheet, visit www.dummies.com and type **home maintenance for dummies cheat sheet** in the Search box.

Where to Go from Here

This book is organized so that you can go wherever you want to find complete information. Did your roof spring a leak? Head to Chapter 5. Need to replace a toilet? Chapter 8 is for you. If you're not sure where you want to go, you can start with Part One — it gives you all the basic info you need, including vital safety guidelines and a home-maintenance plan to follow; plus, it points you to places where you can find more detailed information. You can also use the index to look up specific topics or the table of contents for broader categories. Or, simply let your fingers do the walking until you find a topic that inspires you, and let the games begin! This book makes for great armor — just don't get it wet!

1

Home Maintenance and You

See why maintenance matters to your health and your wallet.

Get a handle on how your house systems work, and how to keep them working.

Put together a workable home maintenance plan.

Chapter 1

Home Maintenance: What It Is and Why It Matters

I grew up in a house that was built by my great-grandfather way back in 1886, and I'm proud to say that it's where my wife and I raised three children and still call home today. Luckily for me, my ancestors must have been pretty handy over the years, taking on painting, plumbing, roofing, and a billion other tasks. Or so it seemed.

However, maintenance is not reserved for older homes. Home maintenance should begin the day the house is completed and continue for as long as the structure exists. But please don't think that you've signed up for years of drudgery. Home maintenance needs shift by house age, and modern building materials perform better than those used in years past. In this chapter, I show you how home maintenance can be fast, easy, and even fun — and how it can save you money in the long run.

Keeping Up with Upkeep

Some homeowners think of maintenance as a challenge, something to take on, overcome, and, with luck, complete. Some see it as a learning experience, looking to master new skills and, in the process, improve their home. Some get into the Zen of it, finding enlightenment in knowing — and truly understanding — the inner workings of their dwellings. And some focus on the bottom line, seeing maintenance as the preservation and enhancement of their huge home investment. Most just want their homes to look nice and work well.

Personally, I find home maintenance projects to be good therapy, minus the therapist and comfy couch. Completing always leaves me with a sense of accomplishment. If that's you, pull up an empty spackle bucket and sit yourself down for an enjoyable read about the world of home maintenance.

From little to big

As you approach maintenance, you have to stay on top of your to-do list to keep little problems from becoming big trouble. It's smart to keep everything looking good, and keeping your home's systems working efficiently also makes financial sense.

REMEMBER

Maintenance is not about big, time-consuming, and expensive projects. In fact, one of the most effective and worthwhile tasks — painting a room — requires only a couple of gallons of paint, a $15 brush, and a $5 paint roller. Changing the furnace filter takes two minutes. Caulking a drafty window frame is a five-minute, $5 job. Doing these little things, and doing them continuously or as needed, makes a huge difference in the appearance, comfort, and efficiency of your home.

Over time, there will be more little projects than big ones. My advice: Do the little ones yourself. Most of them are easy to do. You'll save money, your home will look and work better, and you'll feel as though you've accomplished something. You'll also build skills as you go and become more empowered to take on larger jobs.

Medium-size projects — like adjusting a sticking exterior door or replacing a toilet — need to be evaluated on a case-by-case basis. To decide whether to do them yourself or hire a pro, ask yourself these questions:

>> Do I have the right skills and knowledge?

>> Do I have the necessary tools?

>> Do I have the time?

If you have to say no to any one of these questions, you need to think hard before taking on the job. You may be better off hiring a pro.

Which brings us to the big projects, things like replacing the roof, leveling a floor, or pouring a new driveway. Unless you have some really awesome skills, solid experience, and know-how, as well as a workshop full of tools, hiring a pro is best. You may think you know how to build a deck, even if you've never done it before. However, there are people who build decks every day, people who know how to do the job right. It's worth the cost of hiring a contractor to be satisfied with the end product.

Many of the folks who listen to my *Money Pit* radio show or podcast are homeowners who've taken on projects that are way beyond their expertise, require the purchase of expensive tools, and take much longer than expected. And they're not calling to share how wonderful the projects have gone. They need help putting things back together or advice on how to find someone who can get the monkeys off their backs, so to speak. Don't get caught in this trap. Be smart. Know your limitations.

TIP

I once had a caller to my show ask for help with a plumbing project — after his fifth trip to the hardware store. He figured if he could get a project done in less than five trips, it was worth it before calling a pro! While I don't share his viewpoint, the key takeaway is that your time has a value, and you can waste a whole lot it if a seemingly simple project gets the best of you!

The chapters in Parts 2 through 5 contain many of the most common small and medium-size maintenance tasks that you can tackle yourself. And when a task really should be left to a pro, I tell you that, too.

From inside to outside

Homes are complicated. They have many components and systems that need to be monitored and maintained. (See Chapter 2.) Inside, the systems include plumbing, electrical, and heating/air conditioning. Plus, you've got the foundation, structural framing, walls, floors, appliances, countertops, cabinets, sinks, bathtubs, fireplaces, and more to care for. It sounds like a lot (and it is), but you can find all the details you need in Parts 2, 3, and 4.

Outside, the components that require attention include windows and doors, roof, chimney, garage door, concrete, masonry, and siding. The key thing to know about problems on the outside of your home is that if you don't attend to them, they can become problems on the *inside,* too. That's why I devote entire sections of Chapters, 5, 6 and 16 to helping you prevent and address problems outside.

Benefiting from a Little TLC

There are five major benefits to maintaining your home well:

» Improved safety

» Increased comfort

» Enhanced home value

» Money savings

» Energy efficiency

Here's what this list tells you: that home maintenance literally pays off. To put it another way, these five big benefits prove that an ounce of prevention really is worth a pound of cure. And, as you'll soon discover, those are words to live by when it comes to your home.

To your health (and safety)

A poorly cared-for home is not just an aesthetic problem — it can hurt you:

» A poorly maintained furnace can leak deadly carbon monoxide gas, a leading cause of poisoning deaths in the United States.

» A smoke detector with a dead battery doesn't work — it's literally playing with fire.

» A clogged gutter can lead to cracked foundations, flooded basements, and the growth of toxic mold.

» An air-conditioning system that fails in the heat of summer or a furnace that takes a hiatus in the worst of winter can lead to extreme indoor temperatures, which can be dangerous.

» A rotted subfloor can result in an unexpected visit to the floor below — complete with bumps, cuts, bruises, and maybe a trip to the hospital.

Simple home maintenance can prevent these disasters and make your house a safer place to live for you and your family. For example, replacing your smoke detector with a new ten-year model that never needs a new battery takes 15 minutes and could prevent you from losing your home, a pet, or a loved one, not to mention years of those annoying low-battery chirps!

REMEMBER

YOU GET WHAT YOU PAY FOR

Here's the first rule of home-maintenance materials: Buy the best that you can afford. Doing so gives your home maximum benefit and protection. If you buy inferior materials, you'll likely be doing the job over again soon. Worse yet, you may end up spending a hefty sum to make repairs that otherwise wouldn't be needed had you spent a little more upfront. Not a bad proposition if you enjoy spending all your free time and spare change fixing up your home.

So how do you spell safety when it comes to your home?

M-A-I-N-T-E-N-A-N-C-E!

Comfort: You'll miss it if it's gone

Your house contains a number of systems and components that make it a comfortable place to live. (See Part 2.) Most people take the comfort systems in their house for granted. They don't think about them until one of the systems breaks down. And then the result is a distinct *lack* of comfort.

For example, your home's electrical system powers lights, your refrigerator, your water heater, and your washer and dryer, among other things. You may not think about your electrical system when you turn on lights, grab a cold can of soda from the fridge, take a hot, relaxing shower, or fold your freshly laundered clothes, but if that electrical system breaks down, you'll quickly realize how much of your day-to-day comfort depends on it.

REMEMBER

Because many of the systems found in houses these days have motors and moving parts, they're especially vulnerable to wear and tear that, without preventive maintenance, could result in major inconvenience — and, at least at my house, lots of swearing.

Money in the bank

Preventing a problem is almost always less expensive than making repairs after a problem occurs. And it's always less expensive to fix a little problem before it becomes big trouble.

Avoiding more expensive repairs

Here's how the ounce-of-prevention thing works: The metal flashing that surrounds a chimney can be the source of a nasty roof leak if it's not maintained. The $150 it costs to have a roofer reflash the chimney is a fraction of the hundreds or thousands of dollars you would spend to repair water damage to ceilings, walls, and flooring.

Gaps in siding and trim around windows and doors allow cold drafts and moisture to make their way into the wood skeleton of your home. Aside from driving up utility bills, the moisture produces rot that, in turn, weakens the structural elements in your home, and provides a veritable smorgasbord for structural pests like termites and other wood ravagers, as well as creating a breeding ground for dangerous mold. These small gaps can result in thousands of dollars' worth of repairs and, if left unrepaired long enough, can actually lead to the demise of your home. The flip side: Spend five minutes and $10 to caulk the trim around a window. Your home will love you for it, and you'll love yourself for saving so much of your hard-earned cash.

Increasing efficiency

Most people know that the more efficiently a mechanical device works, the less it costs to operate. A well-tuned automobile engine, for example, delivers far better fuel efficiency than a clunker. The same holds true with many of the machines that you have around your home. Your furnace is a great example. An annual service by an HVAC (Heating, Ventilation and Air Conditioning) technician keeps the burners at peak efficiency. Along with a clean furnace filter, the furnace operates more efficiently, consumes less energy, and is less susceptible to breakdowns.

REMEMBER

Energy savings equal money savings. Keeping the appliances in your home running efficiently also helps the environment — a major benefit for yourself and the planet.

Many times, improving efficiency requires the replacement of the system or appliance in question. A brand-new refrigerator is twice as efficient as one just seven years old. A new tankless water heater is significantly cheaper to operate than the tank-style water heater you've been using. Your 15-year-old air-conditioning system? Terribly wasteful! New ones feature more environmentally friendly refrigerants and must meet significantly tougher efficiency standards. The repair-versus-replace decision is complicated when it comes to appliances and energy-consuming systems. You need to consider whether it's worth repairing an old, inefficient unit and whether the new one will pay for itself (and how long that will take). The handy chart in Chapter 14 will help guide that decision.

ROOTS: A HAMMER, NAILS, AND BLOCK OF WOOD

Precocious. That's as good a word as any to describe me as a youngster. I had a habit of always getting into things I shouldn't, until one day my parents figured out the perfect way to keep me busy. They pulled out a hammer, nails, and a block of wood. There I sat on the back porch of our house gleefully driving nails into wood, and the rest, as they say, was history.

I was blessed to have parents who knew which end of the hammer to hold. Whether by osmosis or DNA, I picked up skills and learned the value of taking care of our family home from those very early days forward. But I know that's rarely the case today for many young homeowners, who rely on YouTube, Instagram, TikTok, or Home and Garden TV, where every project comes out perfectly — every time — or conveniently gets edited out long before you hit the Play button. Regardless of whether you consider yourself a capable do-it-yourselfer or not, I promise to show you the tips and tricks I've learned over the years to maintain your home — and help make sure you don't become a do-it-TO-yourselfer!

Maintaining and increasing your home's value

If you're like most people, your home is the single largest investment of your lifetime. Besides just wanting a roof over your head, you may have also made this investment with the hopes of making some money on it when you sell the house. Thus, it makes good sense (and big bucks) to keep your home in tip-top shape.

As a former professional home inspector, I can tell you that homes with curb appeal sell faster and for more money than those with a worn, poorly maintained exterior. Conversely, a poorly maintained home can be a real eyesore and worth significantly less than its well-maintained counterpart. Even if you don't intend to sell your home in the near future, maintaining your home is key to maintaining your initial investment.

Ready-Set-Go!

Now that you have an idea of what it is about your home that needs to be maintained and why it's important to do so, you can use the information in this book to charge forward to tackle projects that have been on your to-do list. Keep in mind that when it comes to project order, you should crawl before you walk and walk before you run. So as not to become discouraged or end up with a mess on your hands, I suggest that you attempt smaller, more doable projects first. This approach gives you the opportunity to get comfortable using tools and materials you may not be so familiar with.

TIP

Callers to my radio show are often folks who've recently moved into a home and are charged up to take on a dozen or more projects — all at the same time! My advice? S-L-O-W D-O-W-N. Not only is it hard to manage many projects at once, but it's also smart to live with what you have for a little while. One of two things will happen: You'll either get used to the way things are and save a whole bunch of money by not doing the project, or the desire to make the change will persist and you'll ultimately get the project done, but at a more manageable pace. Either way, you can't lose.

REMEMBER

Safety first! Always have the right tools and equipment for the job and never be in a hurry. Haste makes waste and is a recipe for potential injury and poor results. I suggest that you have a look at Chapter 3 for suggestions on what projects to take on first and the basic tools that you'll need to accomplish most home-maintenance projects. Start with small projects and work your way up the ladder — literally and figuratively — to more-complex projects. With time and experience, you'll grow increasingly comfortable and confident wielding a hammer in one hand and a caulking gun in the other.

When all's said and done, the idea is to protect your home, save money, and have fun in the process. Who knows? You may just find that you like this home maintenance stuff. Let the adventure begin!

Chapter 2

Getting to Know Your House and Its Systems

H ome maintenance reminds me a lot of the *Monopoly* board game. Both involve a bit of a gamble with real estate. In the game, dice decide your destiny. A favorable roll can turn you into a real-estate baron. On the other hand, the wrong combination can land you straight in the pokey!

Each time you postpone a maintenance task, you're rolling the dice with your home's structural and aesthetic integrity as well as its value. Plus, although it isn't very likely that failing to keep up your home will have you doing the jailhouse rock, sadly, there are occasions when such negligence can be dangerous and result in tremendous damage for which you can conceivably be held liable — not to mention the personal loss that you could suffer.

In this chapter, I show you that your home is more than just four walls and a roof; it is actually made up of a group of systems and fixtures, all of which need your loving care and attention from time to time. I introduce you to each of these systems, which I describe in greater detail throughout this book.

The Exterior: It's Nice to Fool Mother Nature

Every area of a home needs ongoing maintenance, but some areas require more care than others. At the top of the "needy" list is a home's exterior. The exterior is subject to constant deterioration thanks to the forces of Mother Nature — the sun, wind, and rain. Consequently, it's no accident that you may find yourself spending a majority of your home-maintenance time on the exterior.

The following sections discuss the elements of a home's exterior that will, from time to time, require maintenance.

Your home's infrastructure: The foundation and floor frame

The foundation (which I discuss in detail in Chapter 4) is a key component of a home's infrastructure. The other key component of the infrastructure is the floor frame, also covered in detail in Chapter 4. Together, these two components support the walls, roof, and other structural elements of your home.

The foundation

Your home's foundation, whether it's a basement, a crawlspace, or a concrete slab, is the element of construction that helps a home stay put. A level foundation can usually contribute to a level floor, windows and doors that operate smoothly, and the absence of cracks in walls and ceilings. For homes with basements, the foundation also holds back earth and limits the intrusion of unwanted water.

While you'd expect anything called a foundation to be stable, they're not. Foundations move and shift based on the grading around the home, as well as the roof drainage and even the type of soil. Maintaining your foundation means taking steps to manage these external conditions to keep it from moving, settling, cracking, or shifting. But stabilizing a foundation does not require the work of bulldozers or jackhammers that you might expect. Not all cracks are concerning, and surprisingly simple tasks like sealing cracks before they spread and stopping moisture from collecting along the perimeter go a long way toward stopping foundation movement.

The floor frame

The floor frame consists of floor joists (beams which typically rest on girders) and the subfloor. The joists and girders travel horizontally and both rest on the foundation. The subfloor consists of boards or panels that are fastened to the joists. Finish flooring (carpet, vinyl, hardwood, and so on) is installed above the subfloor.

The floor frame is notorious for the maddening creaks and squeaks that occur when traipsing across it. Aside from the fact that floor squeaks can drive you nuts, they're considered a sign of inferior construction, which can lower your home's perceived value. Although this can be true, the reality is that even the best-built homes can suffer from a squeak now and again. Thus, silencing squeaks is the most common maintenance task when it comes to the floor frame. You can find all the information you need to successfully carry out this task in Chapter 4.

Roofing and siding: Your home's protective coat

Most people think of siding as either vinyl or wood, but professionals use the term to describe a wider class of materials — whatever can be used as a finished, protective coat on the exterior walls of your home, such as vinyl, brick, wood, stucco, or a composite siding.

Siding is, by design, expected to stand up to the forces of nature, keeping wind, water, and all sorts of weather out of the walls it protects. That's why maintaining your siding is key. Vinyl can loosen, wood siding can split, and stucco can crack. You'll discover that exterior wall maintenance is all about preserving the integrity of the siding.

Think of the roof as the fifth wall of your house. It's subject to all the same forces that siding is, and then some. Like siding, rain and sun are a roof's biggest enemies. Maintenance on your roof isn't much different from what you do to maintain your siding. So, I combine roofing and siding in Chapter 5.

Keeping a roof clean of unsightly moss or algae is another common maintenance task. Metal flashing at vents, chimneys, skylights, valleys, and other critical areas most prone to leak, often requires attention to prevent water intrusion. And although not officially a part of the roof, gutters and downspouts are essential when it comes to managing water around your home and, when well maintained, can prevent everything from a roof leak to a severely flooded basement or crawl-space. Keeping gutters clean and spouts secured and extended away from the house count among the most common gutter and spout-related maintenance tasks.

Windows, exterior doors, and insulation

Like siding, windows and doors keep the forces of nature out, while allowing you a clear view of the exterior from the comfort of the interior. But unlike siding, windows and doors are designed to provide light, ventilation, and access, which means they come with moving parts that need to be maintained! Insulation provides a key role as well, keeping you comfortable year-round.

Windows and doors

Windows and doors are frequently among the most maintenance-intense elements, primarily because, unlike siding and roofing, windows and doors have moving parts that suffer from wear and tear. What's more, in most homes, windows and doors are also responsible for the majority of energy loss.

Water leaks, drafts, and condensation are a few of the most common window-related maintenance issues. As for doors, a touch of lubrication to hinges and hardware, shimming a hinge, and adjusting a strike plate or door bottom can be the saving grace to any door.

Chapter 6 offers tips on these window- and door-maintenance tasks.

REMEMBER

An out-of-level floor can make doors and windows tough to operate and can be the cause of cracks in walls over windows and doors. If you're tired of patching cracks and wrestling with doors and windows, head to Chapter 4. Out-of-level floors have virtually nothing to do with the floor itself and almost everything to do with the foundation and soil that support it. I'll share tips to help you stabilize that settlement and avoid further window or door follies!

Insulation

Insulation is like a nice, warm blanket on a cold winter's night. It can make all the difference when it comes to comfort and energy efficiency. Insulation can typically be found in the attic, exterior walls, and between the floor beams above crawlspaces and basements. There are all kinds of insulation, ranging from fiberglass to mineral wool to spray foam. Over time, some types of insulation can settle, becoming more compact and less effective. That's the bad news. The good news is that in Chapter 7, I show you what you can do about it.

Walkways, patios, and driveways

Walks and patios are to a home's exterior what halls and entertaining areas are to a home's interior. Can you imagine directing a houseguest down a hall with an uneven walking surface or trying to entertain a group of people in a room with chunks of carpet, tile, or hardwood missing? Doing so would inevitably result in a twisted ankle or a nasty fall — talk about putting a damper on a party! Why, then, would you be any less attentive to the condition of the walking and entertaining surfaces outside your home?

In the grand scheme of things, chances are good that the walks, paths, patios, and steps that surround your home are subject to as much traffic as, or more traffic than, many spaces within your home. In addition to the safety aspects of an uneven step, loose patio brick, or cracked walkway, these and other paved areas, such as a driveway or carport, can have a tremendous influence on the overall appearance (the "curb appeal") of your home. Accordingly, they should be given the same degree of attention when it comes to home maintenance.

Paths, patios, and other paved areas typically consist of concrete, brick, stone, or asphalt. None of these materials is immune to the need for periodic maintenance. Uneven surfaces, cracks of varying proportion, potholes, and staining are conditions that cry out for attention. Ironically, the need for many of these repairs can be prevented down the road with ongoing maintenance. For example, a driveway remains more resilient and water-resistant and, hence, is less likely to crack when a sealer is periodically applied.

TIP

If your driveway looks like a truck stop or your front walk has holes the size of the Grand Canyon, you can clean 'em, patch 'em, seal 'em, or even stain or paint 'em using the information found in Chapter 17.

Decks

Decks are perhaps the most popular outdoor place for rest, relaxation, or entertainment in a house. They're most commonly made from wood, composite, or vinyl and take the brunt of everything Mother Nature can throw at them. For this reason, they need regular maintenance and a review to make sure they're safe. For wood decks, the walking surface, steps, and railings need to be stained to protect them from cracking brought on by an intense baking from the sun. Vinyl and composite decks won't need staining but can pick up super-slippery moss or algae that needs to be cleaned. And all decks need a structural review to make sure they're safe and secure for your family and the 40 friends you want to invite over for a big summer BBQ blowout! Chapter 18 is chock-full of information that you can use to make your deck safe, sound, and the envy of your neighborhood.

Fences

Fences, like decks, come in all shapes, sizes, and materials. Wood, steel chain-link, ornamental iron, vinyl, and the new kid on the block, composite fencing, are the materials that are most widely used. In spite of the vast array of material choices, most fences are constructed of wood, including wood posts, wood framing, and wood fence boards (or pickets).

Regardless of the material used to construct it, keeping a fence plumb (upright); preventing posts, framing, and fence boards from deteriorating or being ravaged by pests; keeping fence boards securely attached to the framing; and taking the sag out of a gate are the items that can be found on most homeowners' checklists. Chapter 18 tells you all about these tasks, and more.

Retaining walls

If your home is built on anything other than a flat lot, you may know that a retaining wall holds back earth that would otherwise come crashing through to your home or yard. You can also use a retaining wall to expand the "usable" area of a property that slopes by terracing the steeper hills.

Although more and more retaining walls are being constructed of interlocking decorative blocks that need little maintenance, lots of residential, garden-variety retaining walls are constructed of wood posts and wood landscape ties (large beams that can be stacked to hold back the earth). As it should be clear by now, wood needs a lot of attention to remain sturdy and effective. The information in Chapter 18 about maintaining retaining walls can add years to the life of your retaining wall.

The Interior: Your Home's Insides

As with the exterior of your home, basic elements of the interior require maintenance from time to time. The following sections help you identify these elements and the ongoing maintenance they require.

The plumbing system

Of all of a home's systems, the plumbing system is likely the most demanding when it comes to maintenance. Leaking pipes, clogged drains, and a gurgling water heater are just a few of the many plumbing-related maintenance challenges that pop up.

Let me be the first to tell you that Chapters 7, 8, and 9 are all wet. That's because they focus on running water in the home. In these chapters, you can find out how to locate and shut off your main water valve, keep your water heater happy, and care for wells and water softeners, as well as a bunch of other stuff.

Although the plumbing system is one of the most maintenance-intensive, it really isn't particularly complex. Even beginners can easily perform the most common plumbing maintenance tasks: cleaning, lubricating, adjusting, and replacing worn parts. Make your plumber jealous by reading all about these simple maintenance tasks in Chapters 7, 8, and 9.

Pipes and water heaters

Indoor plumbing is one of the marvels of the last hundred years. It can also be the scourge of humankind when it isn't operating quite right: banging or rattling pipes, water pressure that has been reduced to a trickle, and shower temperatures that fluctuate like the stock market — one minute it's nice and hot and the next you're playing freeze-out. On top of all that, dealing with plumbing odors from drains, pipes, water heaters, or toilets can be one stinky problem. Yikes!

Armed with the proper tools and the information in Chapter 8, all your water woes will soon be behind you. There, I tell you how to replace a clogged pipe, fix a leaking pipe, increase water pressure, and track down dreaded stinky plumbing odors. Who could ask for more?

When it comes to the water heater, what's on most people's minds is how long it'll last before it conks out. What most people don't understand is that, with a little care and maintenance, they can double the life of their water heater — really! In Chapter 7, you find out that a little sediment removal from the bottom of the tank, replacement of a metal rod known as a sacrificial anode, and replacement of a broken dip tube (yes, there is such a thing) will keep your water heater going long after others have failed. And, as an added bonus, your utility bill will drop, and you'll get a good night's sleep if your water heater stops rumbling in the middle of the night.

Fixtures

Sinks, faucets, toilets, tubs, and showers are the working end of your plumbing system and need cleaning and maintenance to keep the flow going.

Sinks take a beating from hard water and toothpaste leftovers, so it's key that you keep them clean. Shower heads can get clogged, resulting in a less-than-invigorating morning wake-up. And toilets, in particular, have valves that wear out and can be easily replaced. Chapter 8 offers straightforward guidance on everything you need to know.

The drain, waste, and vent system

Chapter 9 discusses two essential elements of a plumbing system: running water and plumbing fixtures. Where does all the running water produced by faucets and all the waste produced by people and collected by fixtures go? Thankfully, it ends up in your on-site septic system or a municipal sewer system. The key is to get it from the fixture (tub, shower, sink, toilet, and so on) to one of these locations as quickly and as easily as possible.

The part of the plumbing system that performs this very important task is the drain, waste, and vent system. The drain and waste system uses gravity to carry wastewater and solid material to your home's main sewer line, located in the basement, in the crawlspace, or under the concrete slab.

The vent system prohibits dangerous sewer gases from making their way into your home. A *trap*, or water door, at each fixture accomplishes this chore by being full of water at all times. You're probably familiar with the chrome or plastic U-shaped pipe under your kitchen sink. What you may not know is that the same configuration exists below your bathtub and shower and is an integral part of the design of every toilet in your home.

If the foul odors don't make it into your home, where do they go? They're carried out vent pipes that are connected to drainpipes and go through the roof. The vents also serve another important function: they equalize pressure in the drain and waste system that facilitates drainage and prevents the siphoning of water from the traps.

What can go wrong? Plenty! Toilets, tubs, showers, and sinks can back up and cause chaos. What's more, slow-running drains and the foul odor that accompanies them can drive you nuts. Don't wait another moment. Set yourself and your drains free with the information in Chapters 7, 8, and 9. Don't waste another moment, because all your plumbing problems will soon be down the drain.

The heating, cooling, and ventilating systems

Heating, ventilation, and air conditioning (HVAC) — without these systems, our homes would be little more than the caves that primitive civilizations once occupied. How important are these systems? You tell me. Try turning off your heating system in the dead of winter or your air-conditioning system when a heat wave sends the mercury soaring above 90 degrees. It's no wonder that these systems are routinely referred to as "comfort systems" by heating and air-conditioning professionals. After all, their mission is to provide comfort, regardless of the climate or weather conditions.

There's more to a home-comfort system than heating and air conditioning, of course. Studies show that most Americans spend more than 90 percent of their time indoors, so the quality of the indoor air has as much to do with health as it does comfort. That's where ventilation comes in. Without adequate ventilation, heat, humidity, air pollutants, and odors can build up inside a home, causing serious health problems.

You can read about all these systems and find out how to maintain them in Chapter 10.

Heating

Home heating systems come in various shapes, sizes, and configurations and are fueled by a host of different types of energy, including natural gas, oil, electricity, propane, wood, coal, and even the sun. The two most common heating systems are *forced air* (where air is heated by a furnace and distributed throughout the home by a series of ducts) and *hydronic* (where water is heated by a boiler and distributed throughout the house as hot water or steam to radiators). Somewhat less desirable is electric resistance heat, most commonly in the form of electric baseboard radiators or an all-electric furnace, which is undoubtedly the most expensive way to heat a house. If electricity is the only fuel available to you, higher-efficiency heat pumps are a better option. On top of all these is solar, which can supplement your heating system by generating electricity or heating hot water. One thing that all the systems have in common, regardless of the style or the energy that powers them, is their need for periodic maintenance.

As heating systems have become more efficient, there is less DIY maintenance needed. That said, it's more important than ever that you arrange for professional service to keep the systems running safely and at peak efficiency. The more efficient a system, the less it costs to operate, the less energy it uses, and the longer it lasts. In Chapter 10, I review the to-dos for heating system maintenance, explain what you can do yourself, and tell you what you'll need a pro to handle.

Air conditioning

In 1902, Dr. Willis Carrier invented refrigerant air conditioning. Concerned that his new invention would receive a cool reception, he staged a boxing match to showcase this never-before-used technology. Although boxing remains a popular sport, it can't begin to compare to the phenomenon that air conditioning has become. Today, the U.S. Energy Information Administration reports that 88 percent of U.S. households use air conditioning, and two-thirds use central air conditioning, with the remainder chilling out with the help of portable air-conditioning units. That's a lot of cooling!

All air conditioners, whether window- or wall-mounted units or whole-house central air-conditioning systems, operate on the same principle. A fan sucks warm indoor air across a series of cool coils that contain a refrigerant. The cooled air is then blown back into the room. Amazingly, the refrigerant absorbs the heat and then exhausts it outdoors through another system of coils and fans.

The maintenance requirements for a home cooling system don't differ dramatically from those of its heating counterpart. In many cases, the systems are connected, sharing the same ductwork, blower, or other components. Cleaning, lubricating, and keeping the refrigerant level up are the most common maintenance tasks associated with a cooling system. (Many of these tasks should be performed by a professional, depending on what kind of system you have.) Maintain your cool by checking out Chapter 10.

Ventilation systems

There are two types of ventilation: passive and active. The former uses physics and natural air currents, while the latter incorporates some type of energized mechanical device. Passive systems can include a mechanical device so long as it isn't energized. Roof vents, ridge vents, gable wall vents, or soffit vents are examples of passive attic ventilation.

Mechanically powered exhaust fans (like those you'd find in your kitchen or bathroom) are active means of improving ventilation, reducing indoor humidity, removing pollutants, and improving indoor air quality. For newer, well-built homes that are sealed to avoid as many drafts as possible, a type of ventilation system known an Energy Recovery Ventilator (ERV) is often necessary to keep the home supplied with enough fresh air to maintain a healthy indoor environment while not losing energy in the process. ERVs work by expelling stale indoor air and replacing it with fresh outdoor air. What makes ERVs unique is their ability to recover the temperature of the expelled air, effectively pre-cooling or pre-warming the incoming outdoor air. This process conserves energy that would otherwise be required to heat or cool the air from scratch.

Here, again, basic maintenance tasks, like filter replacement and cleaning, are DIY projects you can tackle, while other more involved tasks need to be scheduled with a pro. After you read Chapter 10, you can breathe easy knowing that you can keep your home's ventilation system — and the people it serves — healthy.

Interior walls and ceilings

For the purposes of home maintenance, there isn't much that you can do to maintain interior wall structure, per se. It's the material that is on the interior walls that requires attention now and then. The same goes for the ceiling.

Drywall is the most common finish for walls and ceilings in homes built since the 1950s. Before that time, plaster was the material of choice for interior walls.

Although drywall is a time- and cost-efficient building material, it doesn't have the rigidity and resistance to damage that plaster does. By the same token, maintaining drywall is a heck of a lot easier than keeping plaster in shape. A nick here, a gouge there, a hole here, and a crack there — these are, without doubt, common sights on the walls and ceiling of almost any home. They're often the result of a doorknob crashing through the wall, a shift in the earth, foundation settlement, and the ever-present roughhousing by little ones.

TIP

Cracks in drywall and plaster are often a cause of great concern, especially among new homeowners who imagine their home sweet home is about to crumble! In the 20 years I spent as a professional home inspector, I rarely found a home that did not have cracks. Wall and ceiling cracks are very common, and not all cracks are concerning. Most are the result of normal expansion, contraction, or settlement of the building. Unfortunately, most homeowners (and even some pros) don't really know how to repair cracks so they don't come back year after year. In Chapter 11, you can find out how to patch these problems once and for all.

Patching holes and cracks in walls and ceilings, cleaning grit and grime, and painting are by far the most frequent maintenance tasks that folks encounter with their walls and ceilings. Cleaning, patching, and painting — it's all in Chapter 11.

Floors and interior doors

Floors. You can't live with 'em, and you can't live without 'em! Maintenance-starved floors can be summed up in three words: *squeaky, creaky,* and *dirty.* Sounds more like the members of a punk-rock group than a list of maintenance woes.

As for interior doors, they're important elements in your home — particularly when they're located at the entrance to a bedroom or bathroom, if you get my drift. Do they close easily and securely? Do they stay open without the need for rocks or paperweights in their paths?

Floors

Floors get the most wear and tear of anything in a home. Cleaning is the single most effective means of cutting down on the deterioration of a floor. Frequent vacuuming and spot-cleaning can more than double a carpet's life span. And if you're looking for a way to keep the finish on your vinyl plank and hardwood flooring looking good, the answer is as close as a broom and dustpan. The grit and grime underfoot that you track into your home acts like sandpaper that can turn a rich finish into a work in progress. The same holds true with ceramic tile with grimy grout and other types of flooring. Chapter 12 explains that when it comes to flooring, cleanliness is next to godliness.

Are squeaks in your floor driving you over the edge? Worried they signal the need for a big repair? Stop right there. Squeaks are, without a doubt, one of the most common home-maintenance issues and rarely signal a structural problem. Good news! Quieting a squeaking floor isn't brain surgery. Better news: I tell you how to do it in Chapter 4.

Doors

Open, close; open, close; slam shut! Interior doors get more than their share of use, and the accompanying wear and tear. Maintenance is minimal. Door hinges can become loose, which can make a door really hard to open or close; doors can stick, or alignment between a latch and strike plate can shift and prevent a door from being securely closed; a pocket door can be jammed in its pocket; and it seems like sliding wardrobe doors are always coming off their tracks. So, if your home is experiencing some of these common door dilemmas, I suggest that you open the door to Chapter 12 for help on how to solve these problems once and for all. Door, er, case closed!

Cabinets and countertops

Cabinets and countertops are like your home's furniture, just built-in. Aside from occasionally tightening a screw here or there, the biggest maintenance challenge that faces each of them is cleaning. Grit and grime from cooking and sticky fingers are the most common cleaning challenges with these fixtures. The cleaning means and methods vary from finish to finish, as you can read about in Chapter 13.

Aside from keeping your cabinets looking good, cabinet doors, like interior doors, have hinges and hardware that, from time to time, need lubricating and adjusting, as do the cabinet drawer glides and hardware. After you read Chapter 13, your cabinets will, indeed, be like other fine furniture in your home.

In days gone by, countertops in most homes were made of plastic laminate and, to a lesser extent, ceramic tile. Today, countertops have come a long way. An array of solid surface materials are now all the rage, along with natural options including stone like quartz, granite, and marble. Ceramic tile has remained a strong contender, especially for backsplash walls, and even plastic laminate is enjoying renewed interest.

Scratches in plastic laminate; dirty, cracked, or mildew-laden grout; and stains on natural stone tops are among the most common complaints that folks have about their counters. Accordingly, Chapter 13 offers solutions to all these problems and then some.

Appliances

A well-maintained appliance is both energy efficient and safe. In Chapter 14, I tell you how to maintain your cooktop, oven, range hood, microwave, dishwasher, refrigerator, freezer, washing machine, and clothes dryer to keep them working safely for years to come. Plus, you'll find out how to cut appliance energy costs without giving up any of the convenience they provide.

Fireplaces: Traditional and gas

Today, a traditional brick fireplace is rarely used as a primary source of home heating due to its poor efficiency. Even newer, pre-fabricated metal fireplaces, while more common today, aren't designed to be the primary heating source for a home. Nevertheless, fireplaces remain popular because they provide a cozy atmosphere and romantic appeal. More than any other element of a home, a fireplace represents warmth and comfort.

Not all fireplaces are created equal. Fireplaces built 100 years ago were constructed of solid stone or brick. After World War II, the fireplace became more of a decorative feature than a viable source of heat. Consequently, solid stone and brick were replaced by less pricey variations, such as a wood stove, free-standing metal fireplace or "zero-clearance" prefabricated models, so called because they could be installed in a home with zero inches of clearance between the outside of the fireplace body and a combustible wall. The latter is a far less costly way to incorporate a fireplace into a home's design and has been used almost exclusively in new construction over the last 20 years as a means of trimming building costs.

Cozy and romantic as it may be, a poorly maintained fireplace can be one of your home's most deadly elements. If you have a fireplace, following the advice in Chapter 15 is imperative. Regardless of the age or style of construction of your fireplace, you have to follow certain maintenance routines to ensure that the fireplace is safe.

The firebox, glass doors, screen, damper, spark arrestor, flue, and chimney require ongoing maintenance. Although all aspects of a fireplace are important, the integrity of the firebox and flue are of prime importance. *Creosote*, a byproduct of burning wood, can collect on the interior of a flue and, when ignited, can erupt into a raging and dangerous inferno. Consequently, one of the most important fireplace-related maintenance tasks is cleaning to prevent creosote buildup.

Gas fireplaces are also an option, either as using a gas burner inside a traditional brick fireplace or available as a prefabricated, zero-clearance fireplace. Fireplaces with gas burners inside traditional brick chimneys should have a device that prevents the damper from closing. In all cases, gas fireplaces need to be cleaned and the flame adjusted yearly. (Follow the manufacturer's specifications) for the prefab units.)

Also, you should know that prefab gas fireplaces are available as "vented" (meaning the exhaust gases vent to the outside) or "unvented," (also called "ventless," meaning the exhaust gas vents back into your house). I much prefer vented gas fireplaces for safety reasons. Although the unvented are never supposed to release a harmful level of carbon monoxide, I simply don't feel comfortable using one due to safety concerns. And it's not just me! Ventless gas fireplaces are illegal in Canada, as well as in several states and cities.

In any case, be absolutely sure your home is protected by carbon monoxide detectors. You should have one on every level of the house, plus one outside every bedroom.

In addition to regular chimney inspection and cleaning, cleaning and adjusting the glass doors and screen, cleaning and lubricating the damper, and making sure the spark arrestor is in tip-top shape are the most common preventive maintenance tasks.

Feel like a cup of hot chocolate around the fire? Check out Chapter 15 first! It may save your house — and your life!

Your home-safety systems

Repairing a leaking roof, quieting a squeaking floor, or making sure that your heating and cooling system is operating at peak performance are important and beneficial tasks. However, in the grand scheme of all things home, nothing is more important than making sure that your home is safe.

Home sweet home to most people consists of comfy surroundings and handsome finishes — cabinets, counters, flooring, and appliances. Yet the "bones" of a home consist of a complex system of pipes, wires, and ducts, which, often without warning, can go haywire and reduce your home to rubble.

A small electrical short can result in a disastrous house fire, and a poorly burning gas appliance that is not properly vented can produce deadly carbon monoxide.

REMEMBER

If you don't have smoke detectors and carbon-monoxide alarms, install them! If you do and they aren't operating properly, fix them! A little maintenance can go a long way when it comes to smoke detectors and carbon-monoxide alarms. Vacuum them regularly, test them often, and replace the batteries at least once a year or as needed.

TIP

Have you ever been annoyed by the incessant chirping of a smoke detector warning that a battery change is due? Today's smoke (as well as carbon-monoxide) detectors come with built-in 10-year batteries. They're designed to work for a full decade, then be discarded and replaced. No more chirps and a full 10 years of protection make replacing your old detectors with these modern marvels a worthwhile project.

The dangers associated with fire and carbon monoxide are clear. Less obvious is the devastating effect that a malfunctioning garage door or garage-door opener can have on you or someone in your home. Small children and pets can be seriously injured or killed by a malfunctioning system. Is the auto-reverse (anti-crush) function working properly? Does your system have electronic sensor beams, and are they doing their job?

Another concern for keeping your home safe relates to personal safety and security from prowlers and unwanted visitors. Have you stopped setting your burglar alarm due to repeated false alarms? The false alarms may be something as simple as a loose contact at a window or door, or a failing backup battery.

Throughout this book, you can find out about maintenance tasks that will keep your systems running efficiently and safely to prevent disaster. In Chapter 16, I focus on some of the top safety issues and specific steps that you can take that can save your home, your life, and the lives of your family should disaster strike.

When it comes to home maintenance, maintaining your home-safety systems is job number one!

Chapter 3

Creating Your Home Maintenance Plan

When people think about owning a home, they picture warm summer afternoons relaxing on the patio, not a hot afternoon fixing the fence around it. Fortunately, there are far more fun days than workdays. But don't kid yourself: There will be work to do. Of course, I think it's the fun kind of work, and I'm not alone. Many people get a great deal of enjoyment from maintaining and improving their homes.

Not a do-it-yourselfer? Not buying the work-as-fun concept? Let's talk money, instead. Maintenance is the work required to protect and maintain what is probably your single largest investment — your home. It's not optional. If it's not done (by you or by a professional), your home and its systems will slowly deteriorate, operate less and less efficiently, look worse, and, ultimately, lose real value, and may even become unsafe. So, with those negative outcomes in mind, I'm sure you'll agree that maintenance is necessary.

This chapter helps you prioritize your home-maintenance tasks and provides home-maintenance schedules you can follow. And if you're not a do-it-yourselfer? Well, I tell you how to find a pro, too.

Creating Your What-to-Tackle List

Out of the enormous universe of potential projects, which ones are the most important and when should you do them? Let's talk about priorities. By setting priorities, you make sure that your most critical and financially sensible projects get done first. This may seem to be the obvious approach, but you'd be surprised by how many low-priority jobs get done before truly necessary projects.

I understand how that happens. Do-it-yourselfers are eager to get going, so they begin with whatever comes to mind first. And homeowners frequently confuse what they *want* to do with what they *need* to do. Sure, installing a pretty new granite countertop is a lot more "fun" than shoring up a crumbling foundation wall, but it won't be any fun when the kitchen starts sliding into the backyard.

To help set priorities, it's helpful to divide maintenance jobs into three categories:

>> **Musts** are anything that threatens health and safety, violations of fire or building codes, structural weaknesses, and other critical needs.

>> **Shoulds** are anything that cuts utility bills, reduces maintenance costs, or prevents a large repair in the future.

>> **Coulds** are anything related to improving appearance and function.

For example, removing a dangerously obsolete (and probably overloaded), 60-year-old fuse box and replacing it with a modern circuit-breaker box (and more amperage for today's higher power demands) is, without question, a must. Reducing heating and cooling costs by adding another layer of attic insulation is a should. And wallpapering the bathroom is a could. *Voilà!* Intelligent priorities!

Musts: Ensuring safety and health

"Safety first" is more than a slogan. In all cases, safety and health issues are your number-one priorities. Don't even think about doing anything else until you do the following:

>> Install smoke detectors and carbon-monoxide detectors everywhere they should be installed — in bedrooms, in hallways, and on every level of your home.

>> Purchase and install appropriate fire extinguishers for the kitchen, garage, and workshop.

>> Replace all old and faulty electrical wiring. If your home was built before 1950, have the electrical system checked to make sure it isn't dangerously overloaded by the much higher power needs of a modern family, as well as properly grounded.

>> Install ground fault circuit interrupters (GFCIs) on all outlets within 4 feet of a sink, on all exterior and garage outlets, and on all electrical fixtures over showers and bathtubs.

>> Install or repair exterior lighting for safety and security (aesthetics is just a bonus). Add motion detector lighting for added security.

>> Clean out the dryer duct and replace the lint-catching flexible duct with a smooth, rigid duct.

>> Replace old, unsafe appliances.

>> Have the furnace professionally inspected, serviced, and repaired (or replaced) as necessary.

>> Test for lead and asbestos and perform any necessary abatement.

>> Repair unsecure or wobbly handrails.

>> Install a child-safe, auto-reversing garage door opener.

>> Replace any non-tempered sliding-glass doors and shower doors.

>> Apply non-slip decals to the bottom of every bathtub.

>> Eliminate mold and take steps to prevent regrowth.

>> Replace or reinforce failing foundation components and broken or sagging structural members.

>> Make any improvements — installing grab bars and ramps, widening doors, changing door levers, and so on — that are necessary to improve the safety of elderly or physically challenged people in your home.

It just makes sense to do these things before any others. After all, they're the tasks and projects that prevent fire, injury, and failure. It's hard to make a good argument for wallpapering the bathroom before completing tasks like these.

Shoulds: Reducing costs and preventing problems

Jobs that save energy and reduce utility costs come next. If you're looking to save big money and make your home significantly more efficient and eco-friendlier, you should do the following tasks:

- » Add attic insulation.
- » Insulate heating and cooling ducts.
- » Seal gaps around doors, windows, and pipes.
- » Caulk around window and door frames, both inside and outside.
- » Install weatherstripping on exterior doors and windows.
- » Insulate hot-water pipes.
- » Replace old toilets with modern, water-saving toilets.
- » Schedule yearly furnace/boiler and air-conditioning service.
- » Replace an old "gas-guzzling" furnace or power-gobbling air conditioner.
- » Enhance attic and crawlspace ventilation.
- » Replace old appliances with today's highly efficient Energy Star–rated appliances.
- » Take steps to protect against termites and other structural pests.
- » Replace energy-inefficient single-pane windows with new Energy Star–rated double- or triple-pane windows.
- » Repair dripping faucets and constantly running toilets.

Doing things that prevent future problems is literally putting money in the bank. It's smart to fix a small problem before it can become a bigger, more expensive repair. If you want to do all you can to avoid trouble tomorrow, do these things:

- » Seal any exterior gaps, including in siding and trim and around windows, doors, and pipes.
- » Paint the exterior.
- » Maintain and repair the roof and flashings.
- » Monitor the condition of bathtub caulk and grout and replace as necessary.
- » Find and stop foundation, crawlspace, or basement seepage.
- » Regularly clean and repair gutters, extend downspouts away from the foundation, and regrade the soil so water is directed away from the home.

>> Repair driveway, walkway, and patio deterioration, and seal cracks.

>> Repair exterior cracks as soon as possible.

>> Trim bushes and trees away from the house.

>> Tuck-point (replace loose mortar) between brick and concrete block as necessary.

>> Repair or replace leaking shower or tub walls.

Did you notice something about these projects? Most of them are about preventing water damage. The fact is, water and moisture are the number-one enemies of your home. Doing the jobs in this list, even if you do nothing else, will go a long way toward protecting your home's systems, structure, and value.

Coulds: Improving appearance and function

Many of the projects in this category are simple, inexpensive fixes or cleaning tasks that require what our parents called "elbow grease" — jobs like the following:

>> Patching holes in wallboard

>> Tightening up door hinges

>> Shining up a kitchen sink

>> Cleaning cabinets

>> Getting rid of mildew

Others are cosmetic improvements such as these:

>> Painting the interior

>> Installing crown molding

>> Putting in a new entry door

>> Refinishing wood flooring

>> Installing new carpet

>> Adding a skylight

>> Replacing cabinet and drawer pulls

>> Installing new door hardware

And still others are practical, functional improvements such as these:

>> Replacing an old, tired cooktop or dishwasher

>> Replacing shower tile

>> Replacing a worn-out garage door

>> Adding cabinet accessories like a pull-out rack

>> Installing garage or basement storage shelves

>> Installing wardrobe organizational systems

Putting together your maintenance plan

After you know how to prioritize your tasks, it's time to make your maintenance plan:

1. **Grab your phone or a notepad and go through your home top to bottom and end to end, writing down everything you see that needs to be done. Use the lists in this chapter to help you get organized.**

   TIP

   Be realistic. A 300-item list isn't going to get done. Focus on what you can do in the next six months. Promise yourself you'll make another plan at the end of the six months, and then do it.

2. **Mark each item with an M (for *must*), an S (for *should*), a C (for *could*), or an L (for *later*); then prioritize within those main categories by putting a number by the letter: M1, M2, M3, and so on.**

   Take a few minutes to make yourself a clean, easy-to-follow plan with every task or project listed in order of priority. Save the *later* tasks to a separate list and add them to your next plan.

Done. Now get to work — and try to have fun!

Setting a Smart Home-Maintenance Schedule

Maintenance performed regularly and on schedule provides optimum longevity and helps prevent potential breakdowns or malfunctions. Beyond maintenance procedures for operational sake, the primary (and most important) reason for checking, inspecting, and constantly tuning up your home is to ensure maximum safety for you, your family, and your friends.

Every home is different, so feel free to pick and choose from the following checklists. Whether you live in a typical suburban house, a condominium, a town house, a high-rise apartment, a farmhouse, or a palatial country estate, you're sure to find many items that pertain to your home.

TIP

Save manufacturers' instructions and product manuals for maintenance instructions and cleaning tips. If you don't have them, you can probably find them online at the manufacturers' websites. Also get in the habit of stapling receipts for your purchases to the manuals. This way you'll always know when the product was purchased, which is especially helpful if you need to file a warranty claim.

Things to do annually

Make these tasks part of your annual schedule:

>> Check for and repair weak or squeaky floors (Chapter 4).

>> Repair insulation, weatherstripping, and air leaks (Chapter 6).

>> Pressure-wash and repaint/stain wood fencing and check for rot (Chapter 18).

>> Inspect decks for secure attachment to your house, missing flashing, cracked/split boards, rusted fasteners, weak railings, and other key structural elements (Chapter 18).

>> Inspect and test your landscape irrigation system.

>> Clean and check irrigation anti-siphon valves and backflow-prevention devices.

>> Check and clean water-heater burners, tank, and flue (Chapter 7).

>> Clean or replace electric water-heater elements (Chapter 7).

>> Clean toilet siphon jets (Chapter 8).

>> Ensure that the tub overflow is secure to avoid a leak at the tub (Chapter 8).

>> Bleed radiators to release trapped air that prevents radiators from getting hot (Chapter 10).

>> Have a professional inspect and clean the fireplace and chimney (Chapter 15).

>> Fill cracks, gouges, and nail pops in wallboard (Chapter 11).

>> Repair sagging plaster at ceilings (Chapter 11).

>> Scrub and touch up the paint on walls, ceilings, and cabinets (Chapter 11).

>> Check and adjust the oven temperature (Chapter 14).

- » Check and replace appliance lights (Chapter 14).

- » Clean refrigerator-door gaskets and lubricate the hinges (Chapter 14).

- » Vacuum refrigerator condenser coils (Chapter 14).

- » Seal and protect tile and grout (Chapter 8).

- » Vacuum the dust off smoke alarms and carbon-monoxide detectors (Chapter 16).

- » Check flexible gas-line connections at appliances (Chapter 16).

- » Have your home inspected for termites or other structural pests (Chapter 18).

- » Have a professional check your septic tank and pump out solids as necessary (Chapter 9).

Things to do seasonally

With different seasons come different tasks. Use the following to keep your main-tenance up to date throughout the year.

Spring

Every spring, do these tasks:

- » Check gutters and downspouts for debris; extend spouts at least 4 feet from the foundation (Chapter 5).

- » Check for *efflorescence* (white, powdery mineral residue), fungus, and mold in the crawlspace or basement (Chapter 4).

- » Pressure-wash and repair exterior siding (Chapter 5).

- » Inspect the exterior walls and roof for winter and seasonal storm damage (Chapter 5).

- » Inspect the attic for signs of roof leaks (Chapter 5).

- » Clean algae or moss from the roof (Chapter 5).

- » Caulk and patch all exterior cracks and openings (Chapter 5).

- » Caulk window trim and door frames (Chapter 6).

- » Wash and repair holes and tears in window and door screens (Chapter 6).

- » Adjust sticking doors (Chapter 12).

- » Tighten and lubricate doorknobs, locks, and latches (Chapter 12).

>> Clean and preserve (or paint/stain) your wood deck (Chapter 18).

>> Replace the batteries in your irrigation controller and adjust the watering time.

>> Clean, adjust, lubricate, and tighten sprinkler heads.

>> Trim shrubs away from any air-conditioning compressors by at least 12 inches.

>> Check for and replace damaged sprinkler-head risers.

>> Clean and degrease exterior concrete surfaces (Chapter 17).

>> Clean stained plumbing fixtures (Chapter 8).

>> Clean faucet aerators (Chapter 8).

>> Clean air-conditioning compressor fins and have your air conditioner serviced (Chapter 10).

>> Clean lint from the dryer duct and from the interior of the dryer housing (Chapter 14).

>> Inspect the washing-machine water-supply hoses (Chapter 14).

>> Lubricate door hinges and drawer glides (Chapter 13).

Fall

Every autumn, do these tasks:

>> Check gutters and downspouts for debris (Chapter 5).

>> Water-test the roof and flashings for leaks (Chapter 5).

>> Check attic insulation. Add more as needed (Chapter 6).

>> Repair (tuck-point) mortar joints around masonry surfaces (Chapter 4).

>> Check for efflorescence, fungus, and mold in the crawlspace or basement (Chapter 4).

>> Prepare for and prevent roof ice dams (Chapter 5).

>> Look for loose shingles, siding, trim, or anything else that could become airborne in a winter storm (Chapter 5).

>> Caulk and patch all exterior cracks and openings (Chapter 5).

>> Caulk window trim and door frames (Chapter 6).

>> Check the condition of heat-duct and water-pipe insulation (Chapter 6).

>> Check decks for secure attachment to your house, missing flashing, cracked/split boards, rusted fasteners, weak railings, and other key structural elements (Chapter 18).

>> Clean exterior concrete surfaces (Chapter 17).

>> Seal and protect all concrete and masonry surfaces (Chapter 17).

>> Schedule a pre-season cleaning and service of the furnace (Chapter 10).

>> Open and adjust the fireplace damper (Chapter 15).

>> Clean and adjust the fireplace screen and doors (Chapter 15).

>> Check the condition of the chimney spark arrestor (Chapter 15).

>> Clean the lint from the dryer duct and from the interior of the dryer housing (Chapter 14).

>> Inspect the washing-machine water-supply hoses (Chapter 14).

>> Lubricate door hinges and drawer glides (Chapter 13).

Winter

Winterize your home by doing these things:

>> Insulate water lines to prevent freezing (Chapter 6).

>> Winterize your pool or spa.

>> Turn off hose bibb valves and drain hose spigots.

>> Turn off and drain your sprinkler system.

>> Have a professional drain or insulate sprinkler system backflow-prevention devices.

>> Install storm windows and doors (Chapter 6).

>> Clean and store all garden tools for the winter.

>> Clean, wrap, and store all garden furniture for the winter.

>> Thin major trees and shrubs prior to winter to allow sunshine through during the cold months.

Things to do monthly

Every month, do these tasks:

» Check water-purification and water-softener filters (Chapter 7).

» Clean and freshen your drains (Chapter 9).

» Degrease and freshen your disposal using disposer cleaning tablets (Chapter 9).

» Clean and replace furnace and air-conditioner filters (Chapter 10).

» Check the steam system safety valve and steam gauge (Chapter 10).

» Check the water level of your steam system (Chapter 10).

» Clean the filter on the interior of wall-mounted heat pumps (Chapter 10).

» Check air intakes for insect blockages and debris (Chapter 10).

» Clean the range-hood filter (Chapter 14).

» Clean your appliances (Chapter 14).

» Remove and clean range burners (Chapter 14).

» Wash and rinse the clothes-dryer lint screen (Chapter 14).

» Inspect, clean, and lubricate at least one major appliance per the manufacturer's instructions (Chapter 14).

» Clean and brighten tile and grout (Chapter 8).

» Deep-clean all types of flooring (Chapter 12).

» Inspect fire-extinguisher pressure gauges (Chapter 16).

» Test smoke-detector sensors and alarms (Chapter 16).

» Test carbon-monoxide detectors (Chapter 16).

» Test the auto-reverse safety feature on garage-door openers (Chapter 16).

Shutting-down checklist

If you're leaving for an extended period of time, shut down your house by doing these tasks:

» Turn off the well pump or close the water-main valve (Chapter 7).

» Open outside faucets and wrap with a towel or cloth.

» Disconnect all liquid-propane gas tanks and safely store them away from the house.

» Wrap all liquid-propane regulator valves in plastic to prevent corrosion.

- » Stop mail, newspaper, and magazine delivery.

- » Arrange for a neighbor to occasionally check your property.

- » Alert local police that you'll be gone.

- » Arrange to have the lawn mowed or the snow shoveled.

- » If the electricity will remain on, put the lights on timers.

- » Remove valuables or place them out of sight.

- » Draw the drapes and blinds to prevent people from seeing that you're not home.

- » Open all faucets.

- » Drain flexible spray hoses in sinks and hand-held showers.

- » Use a plunger to push water out of all p-traps in sinks, tubs, toilets, and so on (Chapter 8).

- » Turn off and drain the water heater (Chapter 7).

- » Turn off washing-machine inlet hoses; remove the hoses and let them drain.

- » Unplug all electric appliances and electronics, both big and small.

TIP

If your home (or vacation home) is located in a cold climate, leave the heat set no lower than 60 degrees. If you lower the temperature more, you'll risk moisture damage from humidity buildup in the house.

If you're in an unusually hot climate, be sure to do the following:

- » Leave the air conditioner on and turn the thermostat up to 85 degrees.

- » Leave toilet lids open to prevent condensation and mold.

- » Place a tablespoon of mineral oil in toilet bowls, tub/shower drains, sink drains, and the dishwasher tub to slow evaporation and keep seals moist.

Other periodic maintenance tasks

Here are additional maintenance tasks that need to be done periodically:

- » If your refrigerator is more than 10 years old, defrost and clean it every two months (Chapter 14).

- » If you use your stovetop range often:

    - Inspect electrical plug-in burner tips for grease or corrosion weekly (Chapter 14).

    - Clean the removable gas burners weekly (Chapter 14).

- » Run the dishwasher at least once a week to keep seals moist and prevent leaks and eventual failure (Chapter 14).

- » Check and replace all failed exterior light bulbs.

- » Make sure that emergency shut-off wrenches are present at gas and water locations (Chapters 7, 10, and 16).

- » Replace smoke detectors if they're more than 10 years old (Chapter 16).

- » Review shut-off procedures for electric, gas, and water mains (Chapters 7, 10, and 16).

- » Replace smoke alarm and carbon-monoxide detector batteries yearly or replace detectors with 10-year battery units (Chapter 16).

- » Test the backup battery on your burglar alarm at least twice a year (Chapter 16).

Paying Attention to Safety

Working around the house can be especially satisfying. It can also be extremely dangerous. Having the right safety gear (and using it) and practicing good work habits can prevent an otherwise pleasurable experience from becoming a nightmare.

REMEMBER

The Boy Scout motto is "Be prepared." It should also be your motto when it comes to tackling home projects:

- » **Know where the power, water, and gas shut-offs are, and how to use them.** Try them all at least once so you know if they're difficult to turn or hard to reach. You don't want to be figuring it out during an emergency!

- » **Know where a fire extinguisher is.** Even better, keep a small one in your tool bucket. Fire is a possibility whenever you're working with torches, heat guns, electricity, or power tools, or when you're doing demolition. You never know what'll happen, and you want to be ready if you have a close encounter of the flaming kind.

Wearing the right clothing and safety gear

No one expects to look fashionable when doing chores, but there's more to what you wear when you're tackling home maintenance than being comfortable. Make sure you do the following:

>> **Always wear safety glasses!** And they go on your eyes, not on your head or in your pocket!

>> **Wear gloves when you can.** Handling small screws and little parts is difficult with gloves on, but you can protect your hands most of the time — especially when using power tools or working with anything that can cut, puncture, scratch, burn, or squash your hands.

>> **Always wear protective footwear.** Work boots are best. Absolutely no flip-flops or sandals. A dropped tool or falling two-by-four will truly and terribly hurt your tootsies.

>> **Tie back your hair.** You really don't want it to get caught up in a drill or saw. Be safe and put it up in a ponytail.

>> **Wear a shirt with short sleeves or sleeves that can be rolled up or buttoned snugly at the wrist.** Flowing sleeves are a lovely look for a garden party, and an oversized sweatshirt may be comfy, but they may get tangled in power tools, catch on corners, snag tools, and even catch fire.

Following safe work habits

If you don't work smart, the chances that you'll either hurt yourself or damage your home are significantly increased. Do the following to stay safe while you work:

>> **Never work alone on dangerous projects, on ladders, or on the roof.** It's always good to have someone to help maneuver big materials, steady the ladder, or call an ambulance.

>> **Use the right tool for the job.** Using a tool for something other than its intended use is asking for trouble. No wrench/hammers or screwdriver/drills! Remember that keeping your tools sharp and clean will produce superior-quality results. Plus, sharp and clean tools are safer to use.

>> **Protect your work area.** A dropped hammer will mess up the floor. A spilled gallon of paint will take hours to clean up. Why risk damaging your home or its contents? Remove everything that doesn't need to be in your work area; cover

whatever remains and every inch of the floor with drop cloths. A good-quality reusable canvas drop cloth will pay for itself many times over in preventing damage.

>> **Work neatly and eliminate tripping hazards.** Keep your work area — especially the floor — free of tools, extension cords, and supplies. Put tools you aren't using in your bucket or out of the way. Bring in only the materials you need at the moment. Remove anything you no longer need for the job.

>> **Follow basic ladder-safety rules.** Don't overreach. Position your ladder properly and on a stable surface. Never use a bucket or chair instead of a stepladder.

>> **Keep a phone nearby while you're working.** If you break your leg falling off the ladder, you'll have to crawl only a few feet to summon help!

Choosing DIY or Going Pro: Know When to Call for Backup

Some jobs are either too big or too hard to do yourself, and there's no shame in hiring a pro to do them. But how do you know when you need to outsource a maintenance project? Simple! When you'll be in over your head. When you're crunched for time. When you don't have the specialized tools needed. When you won't be happy with your results. When you don't have the energy. When you don't want to be bothered. When the task requires specialized expertise.

Bottom line: If the job is going to be a pain in the butt and will exceed your skill/experience level, you're better off hiring someone who will do it right in a reasonable amount of time.

TIP

With that in mind, I think the jobs best left to experienced, expert pros include the following:

>> Furnace, boiler, and air-conditioner service and repair

>> Major electrical or plumbing work

>> Lead and asbestos testing and abatement

>> Major mold remediation (larger than 10 square feet)

>> Chimney cleaning and repair

>> Foundation and structural repairs

>> Window replacement

>> Roof replacement

>> Treatment for termites and other wood-destroying insects

>> Garage-door installation

Everything else, pretty much, is up to you.

Finding a pro

The best way to find a qualified, reliable professional is to get referrals from your relatives, friends, and neighbors. Period. End of discussion. Every other way is a complete crapshoot. So ask! If someone you know has had a good experience (not just an okay one) with a particular professional, add that person or company to your referral list.

Social media can also be a powerful way to find a local pro. For example, in my community there's a group page on Facebook where locals often report great (and not-so-great) experiences with local pros. Aside from social media, sites like ANGI (www.angi.com) publish verified reviews on contractors provided by their customers.

When you don't have a referral for a particular type of pro, improve the likelihood of a successful outcome by calling an established local company. Companies with roots in the community and a history of serving people in the community are unlikely to be unqualified hacks — they couldn't stay in business if they were. Plus, they'll be more familiar with homes like yours.

Check for licensing (where required), permits, and insurance. If you aren't sure what the licensing requirement is in your neck of the woods, check with your municipal and county offices. These folks can also tell you what type of insurance contractors are required to have and which permits you'll need.

TIP

When checking insurance coverage, always require a certificate be sent to you directly from the insurance carrier, not the contractor.

For most maintenance jobs, that's the majority of the information gathering you need to do. You're ready to move on to getting a price quote.

Getting a quote

If the job in question is really simple — such as a minor furnace service — the price is usually based on an hourly rate with a minimum service call or trip fee. The job isn't very complicated, and the price is based on a few hours of work. Often, such tasks are so inexpensive that it isn't worth getting lots of quotes — especially if you know that the company has a good reputation.

Comparing estimates for service work is simpler than tackling extensive rot repair or a roof replacement. For these larger maintenance projects, it's crucial to define the project's scope first. Then, ask professionals to provide a quote based on that scope and to estimate the time needed for completion. This ensures that all quotes cover the same scope of work and use similar-quality materials, allowing for a direct comparison ("apples-to-apples") between the professionals you're considering.

Selecting a pro

With quotes in hand (which inevitably vary widely in price), you're ready to assess the professionalism, skill, and experience of the pros in question and evaluate their estimates.

Even small maintenance projects require the same kind of investigation and reference checking as major remodeling projects. With your home and money at stake, you want to make absolutely sure that you've hired a reputable, professional, and qualified contractor.

TIP

Never make price the most important criteria — don't automatically choose the lowest bidder. Instead, all else being equal, you're usually better off selecting the contractor whose price is nearest the *average* of the bids.

Choose an individual or firm that you feel comfortable with. Home-maintenance projects involve a certain degree of closeness.

TIP

One final piece of advice: Never, ever, *ever* hire someone who comes uninvited to your door offering a "special deal" on driveway coating, roofing, carpet cleaning, and so on. These unsolicited visits almost always are scams, and the only thing they're going to do is take your money.

2

The Energy Envelope

Battle Mother Nature to protect your home from formidable foes like sun, wind, rain, and snow.

Focus on foundation, roof, siding, windows, and doors.

Maintain your home's energy envelope for comfort and safety.

Establish good maintenance practices to avoid costly repairs and keep the good vibes flowing.

IN THIS CHAPTER

» **Stopping cracks in the foundation**

» **Caring for brick, block, and concrete foundations**

» **Stopping basement floods forever**

» **Silencing squeaky floors**

» **Leveling uneven floors**

Chapter **4**

Foundation and Floor Frame Fundamentals

A sound and stable foundation is key to the structural integrity of the entire home upon which it is built. In this chapter, you find out how to care for this important component of your home. I show you how to preserve and protect your foundation from excessive settlement, keep small cracks from becoming bigger problems, and manage moisture around your home to keep your basement or crawlspace dry.

On top of that (literally!), I cover the floor frame. You find out how to silence the most annoying of floor framing issues — the dreaded floor squeak! Plus, I review how (and when) to level sagging floors and how to prevent fungus, rot, and termites from taking a bite out of your floor's structural integrity.

Focusing on the Foundation

The foundation is a home's underpinning. It supports the floor, wall, and roof structure. It helps keep floors level, basements dry, and (believe it or not) windows and doors operating smoothly. The foundation is also an anchor of sorts: It often travels deep into the ground, creating a structural bond between the house and the earth, which can be especially important if your home is built on anything other than flat ground or is in an area prone to earthquakes.

Interestingly, the origin of many leaks, squeaks, and cracks can be traced to the foundation. A foundation that's not graded properly or poorly waterproofed, for example, can result in excess moisture in a crawlspace or floods in the basement. Without adequate ventilation, this moisture can condense and lead to, at best, musty odors, leaks, and squeaks, and, at worst, rotted floor framing or toxic mold.

REMEMBER

Different types of foundations and different foundation materials exist. The foundation of your house may be a slab, a basement, or a crawlspace, and it may be made of poured-in-place concrete, brick, concrete block, or stone. With each of these configurations come a host of specific maintenance routines that can safeguard your home's integrity.

Types of foundations: Slabs, basements, and crawlspaces

The area below the main floor and within the foundation walls can consist of a concrete slab, a crawlspace, or a basement.

Almost all houses have one of the following foundations, and some have a combination — a slab in one area, for example, and a basement in another.

» **Slabs:** Slab is short for *concrete slab*. A slab floor (see Figure 4-1) is made of concrete poured directly onto the ground (poured in place). Slab floors are very rigid, so they don't give the way a wood floor does — which, unfortunately, makes them prone to cracking. Unlike wood, concrete floors never squeak and don't rot.

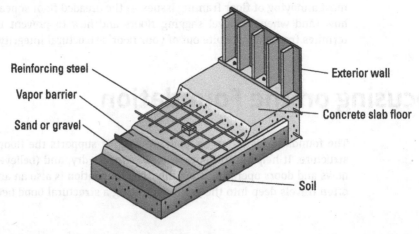

Reinforcing steel

Vapor barrier

Sand or gravel

Exterior wall

Concrete slab floor

Soil

FIGURE 4-1:
Concrete slab.

- » **Basements:** Today, basement walls are commonly constructed of concrete block or solid concrete (which is poured in place). In the past, basement walls were sometimes constructed of brick as well. Today, solid concrete is the preferred foundation material-of-choice for new construction, but, with proper engineering, concrete block is every bit as strong as solid concrete.

- » **Crawlspaces:** If you don't have a slab foundation, you have a wood-framed floor. And if you don't have a basement, the void between the ground and the underside of a wood-framed floor is known as the *crawlspace*. Crawlspaces are typically selected instead of a full basement to save money or when the home building site's water table is too high to allow a basement to be built without being underwater! The crawlspace provides access to run electricity and plumbing, and install insulation — but as the name implies, it's only accessible when you crawl!

Foundation materials

The most common foundation materials are solid concrete, brick, concrete block, and stone. Each has its own advantages and disadvantages, as the following list explains.

- » **Solid concrete (see Figure 4-2):** Solid concrete foundations are made of a mixture of cement, sand, rock or gravel, and water and are considered among the strongest of foundation materials. When poured into forms and left to dry, this pancake-batter-like blend becomes unbelievably rigid. Steel reinforcing bars are used within the concrete to create added strength. In some cases, concrete foundations are constructed of pre-cast concrete panels, made in a factory, and shipped to the building site for assembly. Factory-built concrete panels have gained in popularity because factories can build them more accurately and efficiently than can be done in the field.

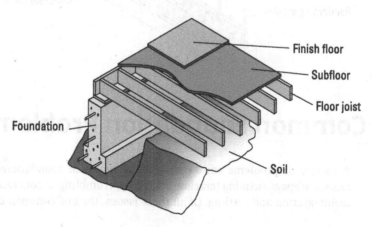

FIGURE 4-2:
Solid concrete.

>> **Concrete block (see Figure 4-3):** For well over a century, pre-cast concrete block, also called *cinder block*, was the preferred foundation material for a house. Concrete-block foundations were very popular because they were a standardized size and could be built by simply laying one block atop another. Unlike with brick, large holes within the blocks allow for steel reinforcing and mortar — both of which add strength to the finished wall. Each block is joined with mortar on all four sides.

>> **Brick:** Brick foundations aren't common today. Their strength is inferior to that of other foundation materials, because they normally don't contain steel reinforcing. Old brick foundations still exist, but they require a fair amount of ongoing maintenance, which I cover next.

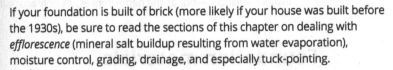

TIP

If your foundation is built of brick (more likely if your house was built before the 1930s), be sure to read the sections of this chapter on dealing with *efflorescence* (mineral salt buildup resulting from water evaporation), moisture control, grading, drainage, and especially tuck-pointing.

>> **Stone:** If a foundation is composed of massive chunks of granite, it is probably incredibly strong — the Egyptians proved that. Other than granite, though, just about every other kind of stone foundation can be compared to brick. And, like brick, stone foundations usually lack a key element — reinforcing steel — and need regular upkeep to maintain deteriorating mortar.

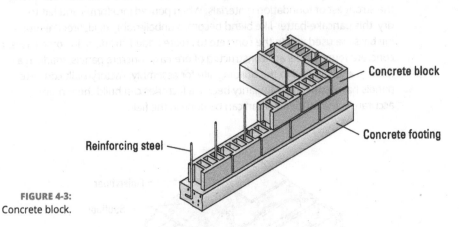

Concrete block

Concrete footing

Reinforcing steel

FIGURE 4-3:
Concrete block.

Fixing Common Foundation Problems

A variety of problems can occur with all types of foundations: efflorescence, cracks, seepage, *spalling* (cracking/chipping/crumbling of concrete/masonry), and disintegration and settling. Of all these issues, the one common unifying cause is water being where it's not supposed to be! Consider that water collecting around a foundation can

>> Make the soil weaker, leading to excessive settlement that can shift walls, doors, windows, and more.

>> Freeze in the winter, exerting pressure on the foundation wall and causing horizontal cracks known as *frost heave*.

>> Soak through and evaporate, leaving behind nasty mineral salt deposits known as *efflorescence*.

>> Soak through and under a foundation wall and flood a basement or crawlspace!

Fortunately, I tell you how to deal with all these problems in the following sections.

Cracking the code of foundation cracks

Foundations are rigid and tend to crack over time. Minor cracks, although unsightly, are not normally a cause for alarm. Major cracks, on the other hand, indicate substantial movement and can undermine your home's structural integrity. Therefore, you can't just ignore cracks in a foundation or concrete slab. Filling in these cracks and stopping them from spreading is essential to preventing serious structural issues in your foundation.

REMEMBER

If you've noticed cracks in your foundation, don't panic. Some number of cracks is normal. In fact, in the 20 years I spent as a professional home inspector, I rarely found a home that did not have cracks.

Cracks form for a number of reasons, including shrinkage or settlement, most frequently brought on by water intrusion, as described earlier. The key to knowing whether the crack is major or minor depends on a few factors.

>> **Size:** Hairline cracks or cracks that are up to ⅛ inch wide are rarely a cause for concern.

>> **Location:** The weakest part of any wall, including foundation walls, is around windows or doors. That's why foundation and drywall cracks often start from a window or door opening and shoot outward. Smaller cracks around windows or doors are no cause for alarm. However, cracks that form elsewhere — including horizontal cracks — are more of a concern (as are sets of mirror-image cracks on opposing walls). For example, if both the front and rear foundation walls have matching cracks, this may indicate that the end

foundation walls may have settled excessively and need further investigation by a licensed structural engineer.

>> **Type (active or static):** Many times, a crack will form once, perhaps from some initial settlement in early stages of a home's life, and never get any bigger — it will be *static*, in other words. If that's the case, I'd be a lot less concerned than if you had an *active* crack — one that gets bigger every year.

Minor cracks can be repaired by sealing them with a silicone caulk, or with a vinyl patch as outlined in the following section. Larger cracks should be examined by a structural engineer.

WARNING

Foundation crack diagnosis should only be done by a licensed structural or civil engineer. Many so-called foundation repair contractors simply do not have the education, skills, or credibility to diagnose and repair cracks. These contractors will often claim competency and use scare tactics to convince unknowing homeowners to hire them immediately for fear that their home is about to come crumbling down. Don't capitulate to these high-pressure salesmen. Take your time and hire a skilled professional engineer to (1) diagnosis the problem; (2) create a report that specifies the repair; and then (3) reinspect the finished repair to certify it was done correctly. Not only is this procedure important to make sure the work is done correctly, but it'll also be critical if you want to sell your house and the buyer wants to know what happened to the foundation wall.

Sealing cracks in concrete foundations and slabs

Even in the best of conditions, concrete moves a fraction of an inch here or there (although this doesn't always result in a crack). And, believe it or not, concrete expands on hot days and shrinks when the weather is cold!

Therefore, when patching cracks in concrete, you should use a product that gives a little. The more elastic the product, the less likely a crack will reappear. One of my preferred patching products for cracks that are wider than ⅛ inch is QUI-KRETE Concrete Repair, a vinyl concrete patch product, which comes premixed and available in either a squeeze or caulk tube.

To repair a small crack using caulking, follow these steps:

1. **Clean the area and get rid of any loose chips.**

   For cracks wider than ⅛ inch, use a small sledgehammer and a masonry chisel to chip away loose material and widen the crack to a minimum width of ¼ inch for horizontal and ½ inch for vertical cracks, as shown in Figure 4-4. Remove any loose material with a brush.

FIGURE 4-4:
Chipping away
loose material
in a crack.

2. **Cut the tip of the caulk tube and load into the caulk gun.**

3. **Insert the tip of the tube into the crack and slowly squeeze the handle to force the patch material into the crack.**

4. **Using a trowel, smooth out the concrete repair material to match the surface you're working on.**

   If the existing concrete surrounding the patch is rough, you can match the finish by sweeping it with a broom.

TIP

TIP

To repair large gaps (¼ inch or greater) in concrete (such as those between a concrete slab and foundation wall) that are not structural in nature and don't require advice from an engineer, use a self-leveling sealant. Also available in a caulk tube, this type of sealant flows easily and works well for filling large horizontal gaps in concrete surfaces.

To avoid wasting material that would otherwise fall deep into the gap or crack, partially fill the gap first with a *backer rod*, which allows the sealant to sit on top of the backer rod and just below the surface of the concrete.

Tuck-pointing brick and block foundations

Before the 1930s, bricks were used extensively to construct foundations. Today, however, if a foundation doesn't consist of solid concrete, it's probably constructed of concrete block. In either case, brick and block have one thing in common: They're both joined together using *mortar*, a combination of sand and cement.

Unfortunately, over time, mortar tends to deteriorate. Not only are cracked, loose, and eroded mortar joints unsightly, but they also diminish the integrity of the surface and can allow water to get behind the brick or block and cause major damage. You can avoid these problems by tuck-pointing the brick or block foundation, which means removing and replacing loose or missing mortar.

If the area is manageable, any do-it-yourselfer can easily perform the task by following these steps (shown in Figure 4-5). *Note:* If the cracked or deteriorating mortar is extensive — an entire foundation, wall, or wainscot — leave the tuck-pointing to professionals.

1. **Chip away cracked and loose mortar using a slim masonry chisel and a hammer; remove the existing material to a depth of approximately ½ inch.**

Be sure to wear safety goggles to avoid catching a piece of flying mortar in your eye. Use the masonry chisel slowly and carefully, to avoid damaging the surrounding brick. Clean out all the loose material and dust using a brush after you finish chiseling.

2. **Prepare your mortar and allow the mix to set for about five minutes.**

You can buy mortar premixed, or you can create your own batch using one part masonry cement and three parts fine sand. In either case, add enough water to create a paste — about the consistency of oatmeal. It's best to keep the mix a touch on the dry side. If it's too runny, it'll be weak and will run down the wall, making it difficult to apply.

3. **Brush the joints with fresh water.**

Doing so removes any remaining dust and prevents the existing mortar from drawing all the moisture out of the new mortar. Otherwise, the mortar can be difficult to apply and will most likely crack.

4. **Apply the mortar using a *pointing trowel* — a trowel whose blade looks surprisingly like a nice piece of pie.**

Force the mortar into the vertical joints first and remove the excess (to align with the existing adjacent mortar) using a *brick jointer* — a narrow and curved trowel that helps create a smooth and uniform finish. After all the vertical joints are filled in, tackle the horizontal ones.

Don't apply mortar in extreme weather conditions or temperatures that exceed those outlined by the mortar manufacturer because the mortar won't properly set up.

To clean excess mortar stains left behind on the brick, use a commercially available brick and mortar cleaner containing hydrochloric acid. Be sure to follow all safety precautions specified by the cleaner's manufacture, including safety glasses and full-face shield.

5. **A week or two later, after the mortar has had the opportunity to set up, apply a coat of high-quality acrylic or silicone masonry sealer to the entire surface (brick, block, or mortar).**

The sealer prevents water damage, which is especially important if you live in an area that gets particularly cold. Unsealed brick, block, and mortar absorb water, which freezes in cold weather. The water turns to ice and causes the material to expand and crack. Periodic sealing prevents this situation from occurring.

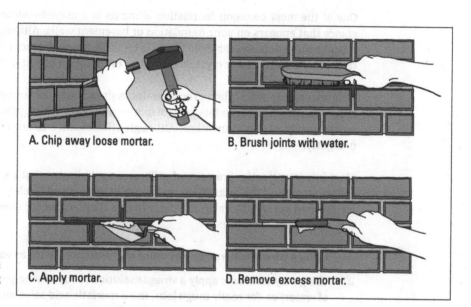

A. Chip away loose mortar.

B. Brush joints with water.

C. Apply mortar.

D. Remove excess mortar.

FIGURE 4-5: Tuck-pointing mortar joints.

Tackling spalling

Spalling — the chipping, cracking, and/or crumbling of brick, concrete, and mortar — occurs when water (a) gets into these materials and (b) freezes, expands, and breaks away small pieces of the surface. It's commonly seen on brick chimneys or concrete driveways and sidewalks, but it's also found on foundations walls, where water has been allowed to collect. Spalling can be worsened due to attack by salt. For example, if you've ever seen a sidewalk covered with chips and holes, you can bet somebody was de-icing it with rock salt, which destroyed the surface.

You can repair spalling with a vinyl acrylic latex concrete patch product. With concrete slabs, excessive spalling can be repaired using a concrete resurfacing product like QUIKRETE Re-Cap, which is specially formulated to stick to old concrete surfaces. For foundations, prevent spalling from happening in the future by applying a protective sealant, which helps to prevent salt air, water, and snow melt from attacking the foundation surface.

TIP

Make sure the sealer you use specifies that it is *vapor permeable*, which means that any moisture getting behind the sealer can evaporate out. Otherwise, that moisture can freeze, expand, and chip away the concrete or brick surfaces.

Is there a fungus among us? Dealing with efflorescence

One of the most common foundation ailments is a grayish-white powdery substance that appears on your foundation or basement walls. Although most people mistake these deposits for mold (mold is typically green or black), it's really *efflorescence*, a growth of salt crystals caused by evaporation of salt-laden water.

Efflorescence appears when ground water is drawn into the foundation and then evaporates, leaving behind its *mineral salts* — a grayish-white, powdery deposit — on the inside of the foundation. Although efflorescence is not destructive, it is unsightly.

Most importantly, the presence of efflorescence indicates that too much water is collecting around the foundation, most commonly caused by clogged, missing, or misdirected gutters. More on that later in this chapter, but for now, here's how to remove the efflorescence:

1. **Using a wire brush, remove as much of the efflorescence as you can.**

2. **Using a nylon brush, apply a vinegar solution (1 cup of vinegar in 1 quart of water) or, for really tough jobs, use a muriatic acid solution (1 cup of muriatic acid in 9 cups of water).**

   Muriatic acid is swimming pool acid. You can find it in swimming pool supply stores as well as many hardware stores and home centers.

WARNING

   Working with acid can be dangerous. Always wear safety goggles, rubber gloves, and protective clothing, and always have plenty of ventilation. Be sure to add the acid to the water in your bucket and not the other way around, as adding the water to the acid can produce a dangerous reaction. (Never mix acid in a metal bucket as it will cause the metal to erode — plastic is the way to go.)

3. **Let the solution you've applied stand for 10 to 15 minutes, but don't let it dry.**

4. **Thoroughly rinse the area with fresh water.**

   More than one application may be required to achieve the desired result.

TIP

Concrete block foundations in particular are very porous and *hygroscopic*, meaning that they just love to soak up water. Once you've cleaned away the efflorescence, and fixed the gutters or whatever other source was allowing water to collect around the foundation, it's a good idea to paint the inside of the foundation walls using a foundation wall paint like DRYLOK. Applying DRYLOK should be your last step — not your first. DRYLOK won't stop the walls from getting wet if the source of the moisture hasn't been fixed. What it will do is prevent or slow down any residual moisture that gets into the wall and stop it from evaporating and leaving more efflorescence behind.

Keeping Your Basement and Crawlspace Dry

The basement is one of the greatest untapped spaces in any home. Think about it — if you have a basement, it's like having an entire extra floor to do with what you wish. That is, however, unless it's a swimming pool!

Damp, leaking, or flooded basements (or crawlspaces) can severely diminish the value of a house. They can lead to a host of associated problems like mold, rotted floor structures, insect infestations, and more. Worse yet, the cost of fixing a wet basement will generally be in the tens of thousands!

Well, let's stop right there so I can let you in on a few facts about fixing floods:

» Most wet basements are blamed incorrectly on the home having a rising water table. This is usually not the case.

» The top cause of a wet basement or crawlspace is a lack of adequate roof and surface drainage. Clogged or misdirected gutters, along with grading that directs rainwater toward the house foundation, cause almost all below-grade water leakage.

» For years, so-called waterproofing companies have caused panic among homeowners by advising that a failure to install expensive sump pumps and drains will cause foundations to crack, and mold to take over. These high-pressure tactics could not be further from the truth and are simply an attempt to make a high-dollar sale on a system that's rarely needed.

» And the best news? Most wet basements can be fixed in a weekend using a few hundred dollars' worth of materials at most. I'll show you how.

Where basement leaks wait to happen: Start outside

In the 20 years I spent as a professional home inspector, it wasn't unusual for me to be asked to inspect a house that had a below-grade water problem. On one such occasion, a young couple had received five-figure estimates from multiple water-proofing companies along with a heaping helping of fear that the home would disintegrate if they didn't hire them. They'd called me to help them decide which five-figure-estimating company to hire.

With that in mind, I walked up to the house, glanced up, and immediately saw a series of 1- to 3-foot trees growing out of their insanely clogged gutters! Problem solved. Mike drop. Tom out!

Designing and cleaning gutters to keep water away

The primary reason that basements or crawlspaces leak, flood, or just get damp, is that the home does not have a properly functioning gutter system. There are several common gutter failures that I see.

>> **Clogged gutters:** The season is called Fall for a reason! Leaves, pine needles, and other tree droppings, along with the occasional tennis ball, regularly clog gutters. When that happens, gutters overflow, dumping all the rain that Mother Nature has to offer right along your foundation wall, where it has nowhere else to go but down and into your basement or crawlspace. (See Figure 4-6.)

>> **Too few downspouts:** For standard five-inch gutters, a home needs one downspout for every 600 to 800 square feet of roof surface. Stand back and stare up at your roof and try to estimate if your home has this. Be sure to include any gutters on second-floor roofs that drain to first-floor roofs on their way to the downspout. If you are moving more water than that, you'll need bigger gutters and spouts, or just more spouts.

>> **Downspouts discharging too close to the house:** Gutter installers have a really bad habit I'd like to break. They typically extend the downspout discharge about a foot, and then into a splash block, which runs it out another foot. If you have any indication that there's a water problem in your house, these need to be run out more like four to six feet.

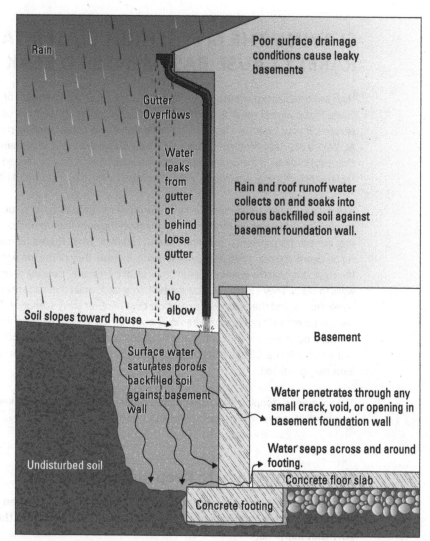

Rain

Gutter
Overflows

Water
leaks
from
gutter
or
behind
loose
gutter

No
elbow

Soil slopes toward house →

Surface water
saturates porous
backfilled soil
against basement
wall

Undisturbed soil

Poor surface drainage
conditions cause leaky
basements

Rain and roof runoff water
collects on and soaks into
porous backfilled soil against
basement foundation wall.

Basement

Water penetrates through any
small crack, void, or opening in
basement foundation wall

Water seeps across and around
footing.

Concrete floor slab

Concrete footing

FIGURE 4-6:
Clogged gutters
and grade sloping
toward the house
allow water to
collect and
leak into the
basement.

TIP

If your yard permits, one of the best ways to control roof drainage is to discharge downspouts into solid PVC plumbing pipes. These pipes should run underground and release water to the street or to another low-lying area. When making this improvement, be sure to pitch the pipe slightly toward the discharge point to avoid backups. Also, be sure the end of the pipe is visible. This way, you can access it for cleaning if a clog occurs.

Note: Don't attempt this with the soft, flexible black drainpipe that landscapers like to use around flower beds, because it's easily crushed and cannot be snaked clean like PVC plumbing pipe can.

SLAYING THE MYTH: HIGH WATER TABLES RARELY CAUSE BASEMENTS TO LEAK

High water tables are almost always blamed as the cause for basement or crawlspace leaks. That is almost never the case, and here's why. Water tables move slowly with the seasons. If your basement leaks consistently with heavy rain or melting snow, it is ALWAYS a drainage problem that is easily fixed, as I've explained elsewhere in this chapter. However, if the problem occurs seasonally, then it *may* be related to the water table, although in my experience, poor drainage is still a major contributing factor.

Interestingly, when consumers turn to waterproofing companies for solutions, these "professionals" somehow rarely seem to mention the easy fixes to outdoor drainage that correct this problem more than 9 out of 10 times. Why? There's no money to be made cleaning gutters and improving grading. Instead, they prime the panic button by talking about how the water will exert "hydrostatic pressure," causing your foundation walls to crack. They'll warn you about developing toxic mold that can spread to your whole house, and they'll dramatize a whole host of other scary scenarios. This is all to tee you up for a big quote to jackhammer out the floor of your basement and install drainage pipes and a new sump pump — all at a cost of tens of thousands of dollars. Not only is a system like this not needed, but it will do little to stop all the scary problems they predicted.

The solution to stopping a wet basement is simply water management. Keep the water away, and it'll never soak in and under your house.

Making the grade to keep water away

After leaking gutters, the second reason basements flood is when the soil around the house settles and prevents water from draining away from the house. Here's why that happens:

>> When a home with a basement or crawlspace is built, excavators dig a deep hole to allow the masons to start building a foundation. This hole is wider than the house so that contractors can access all sides to build the foundation.

>> As the home nears completion, the excavators return to backfill the soil around the house and — hopefully — grade it to slope away from the foundation walls.

>> As time marches on, however, that soil starts to settle and compact. The grade that initially was pitched to run away from the house, goes to flat and ultimately reverses to run water toward the house.

>> Once that happens, rainwater soaks into the soil around the foundation, and if it rains hard enough, it shows up in the basement as a leak or full-out flood.

Restoring a positive grade is not all that difficult. You'll need to add soil along the foundation perimeter and grade it to slope downward about 6 inches over the first 4 feet away from the foundation. For this project, you'll want to use clean fill dirt — not topsoil or mulch, which is too organic and will hold water instead of letting it drain.

Aside from maintaining a positive grade, be mindful of anything that traps water along the house, like brick, stone, or wood landscaping. If you are trying to fix a leak, you can't afford to have anything holding water too close to your house.

Paths and patios should slope away from the foundation, too. A path or patio that slopes *toward* the home discharges water into the basement or crawlspace.

TIP

Improving your gutters and site drainage are the two most effective ways to correct a leaking, damp, or musty basement. But of those two, gutter improvements are far and away much more important than grading improvements. In my 20 years as a professional home inspector diagnosing basement and crawlspace leaks, I've found that gutters cause 90 percent of the problem, with grading causing the rest. So, tackle your gutter fixes first. They are more likely to solve the problem (see Figure 4-7) and are actually a lot easier to do than hauling dirt to add around your foundation!

TAKE A WALK IN THE RAIN

If you really want to see why your house has water problems, do this. The next time you get a really heavy rain, throw on your rain gear, grab an umbrella, and take a walk around the outside of your house to see where all that water is going. Look at the roof and gutters to see if gutters or spouts are backing up or clogged. Look at the downspouts to see where all the water is being collected on your roof and where it is ending up. And look at your yard to see if water is being directed toward — instead of away from — your house. I promise this will be a real eye-opener and worth the soaking you'll get in the process! Just keep safety in mind and don't go out in high winds or during thunder and lightning.

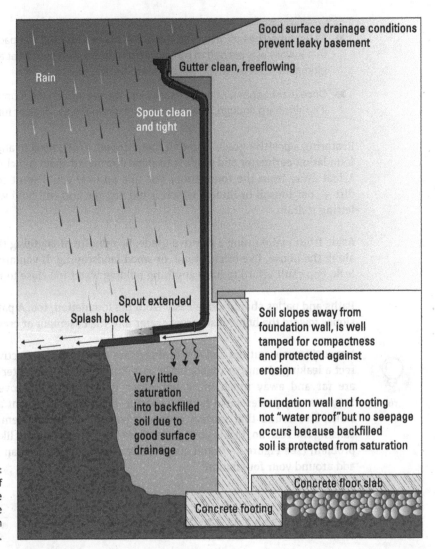

Good surface drainage conditions prevent leaky basement

Gutter clean, freeflowing

Rain

Spout clean and tight

Spout extended

Splash block

Soil slopes away from foundation wall, is well tamped for compactness and protected against erosion

Very little saturation into backfilled soil due to good surface drainage

Foundation wall and footing not "water proof" but no seepage occurs because backfilled soil is protected from saturation

Concrete floor slab

Concrete footing

FIGURE 4-7: Corrected roof and surface drainage prevents leaks in your basement.

Other sources of moisture under your home

Compared to outdoor drainage issues, other sources of basement leaks are rare — very rare. However, when they do happen, they can cause wet basement head-aches. So be observant and stay on top of maintenance with the following systems and appliances located close to (or in) your basement.

A musty or pungent odor usually accompanies efflorescence and excessive mois-ture. Accordingly, a good sniffer proves invaluable in investigating the problem. Here are common causes of moisture.

- **Sewage pipe backup:** If you live in an area prone to flooding, the danger of a sewage backup into your basement — and through every drain in your house — can be stopped short with a backflow preventer valve. Work with your plumber to install this disaster preventer.

- **Burst water pipe:** Water pipes that silently serve your home day in and day out can become raging geysers when windy, sub-zero temperatures find their way into the wall and floor cavities shared by your home's plumbing system, freezing water in your pipes, making them expand and burst.

- **A leaking toilet, tub, or valve located in the walls above the floor:** Although a leaking toilet is often visible from above the floor, most leaks must be searched out from below the floor. When it comes to finding the cause of a damp basement or crawlspace, leave no stone unturned.

- **Leaking washing machine:** Since many homes have laundry areas in their basements, it's not uncommon for these machines to break down, leading to an all-out flood.

- **Overwatering landscape surrounding the house:** Adjusting watering time, watering less often, installing an automatic timer, and adjusting sprinkler heads are the simplest means of solving this problem.

- **Leaking water heater:** Although a water heater may appear to get its job done without much fuss or attention, regular checks and maintenance are crucial to preventing and stopping leaks.

Basement water collection systems: The sump pump

The most common basement water collection system is the sump pump. Basement water is directed, via drainage trenches and/or sloped floors, to a recessed cavity in the floor known as a *sump*. The sump cavity is outfitted with a drainage pump that draws water in the sump and pumps it up and out of the basement (or in some cases, a crawlspace) to a safe discharge location. The sump pump is activated by a pressure switch or float valve; when the water in the sump rises, so does the valve or pressure switch, activating the pump. The pump continues to discharge water from the sump until the level drops enough to turn the switch off.

REMEMBER

Be sure to frequently check the float to ensure that it's clean and moves freely. Every fall, check it by filling the sump with water.

Sump pumps run on 120-volt power, which often fails in heavy rains. If your system has a battery backup, make sure the battery is in good condition by running the sump pump a second time with the house power off. (Replacing a battery is a lot less expensive than a flooded basement.)

TIP

The discharge line that travels up and out of the basement contains a *check valve*, which prevents discharge water from traveling back into the sump. This valve can occasionally become stuck shut. If, during your test, everything seems to be operational, but water remains in the sump, the check valve may need to be replaced. Also make sure the sump pump discharge is draining at least four feet from the house. Otherwise, that water will return right back to the pump — over and over again!

Freshening the air: Dealing with dehumidification

Reducing humidity in a basement (or crawlspace) requires a two-step approach. The first step is to reduce the overall volume of moisture to which foundation walls are exposed. If you've followed the advice earlier in this chapter, you can mark that to-do as done! The second step is to eliminate the minimal, remaining amounts of soil moisture that get into basement air via evaporation through basement walls and floors.

High humidity in a basement leads to condensation of water on the coolest surfaces, such as floors, lower masonry walls, air conditioning ducts, and cold-water pipes. This condensation combines with humidity to seriously damage furniture, finished surfaces, and stored belongings.

To keep moisture at bay, you should include humidity control in your overall basement remodeling plan.

Selecting a dehumidifier

You have several dehumidifier options to choose from for treating your basement space. You can add a whole-house dehumidifier to your current home system, or choose a unit that is stationed in the actual basement space. Basement-based dehumidifiers are available in a range of installation formats, from free-standing units in different sizes, to ceiling-suspended dehumidifiers, to in-the-wall units that fit inside or through wall studs.

Dehumidifiers also offer a range of capacities, based on the size of the space to be treated and its projected humidity level. When shopping for units designed for basements and crawlspaces, know the square footage of the space you need to dehumidify, and you'll find choices suited to your needs. Dehumidifiers can typically be matched to spaces ranging from 1,200 to 4,000 square feet, with water-removal capacities from 4 gallons to 19 gallons or more per day.

Also pay attention to how and where a unit is designed to dispose of collected water. Smaller dehumidifiers have a water reservoir that must be monitored and manually emptied, while more advanced models can be connected to a plumbing line, hub drain, or condensate pump or sump pit for automatic water removal.

Crawlspace vapor barriers

Excessive dampness in a crawlspace can condense, causing floor framing to become damp and covered with fungus, efflorescence, and rot. In addition to the mechanical dehumidification described previously, crawlspaces should be dehumidified through the installation of a vapor barrier, as well as foundation vents.

A crawlspace vapor barrier consists of one or more layers of sheet plastic (6 Mil polyethylene) laid on top of the soil in the crawlspace. (See Figure 4-8.)

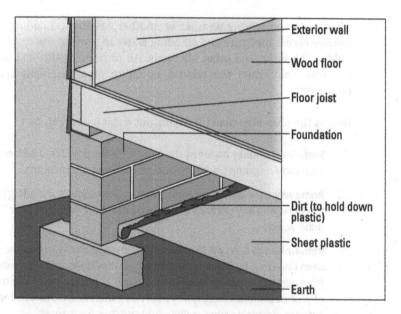

Exterior wall

Wood floor

Floor joist

Foundation

Dirt (to hold down plastic)

Sheet plastic

Earth

FIGURE 4-8: Installing a vapor barrier.

Overlap the plastic a minimum of 12 inches and seal the seams with duct tape. Cut around piers and along the inside edges of the foundation. In severe cases, you can run the plastic up the sides of piers and the foundation, and secure it with duct tape or anchor it with a line of soil at the perimeter.

In addition to the vapor barrier, most crawlspaces are constructed with foundation vents. These are the size of a typical concrete foundation block and have a sliding louver to allow them to open or close. Foundation vents allow moist, damp air inside the crawlspace to vent outside. In most four-season climates, these vents should be open spring, summer, and fall, and only be closed in the coldest months of winter. Fully closed and conditioned crawlspaces are preferable to vented crawlspaces in the warm, moist climate of the southeastern US.

TIP

For excessively damp crawlspaces, foundation vent fans can speed up dehumidi-fication. Once installed, they operate on a *humidistat* — a humidity-sensing switch that turns the fans on only when the humidity in the crawlspace is high.

What to do if your basement floods

Try as you might, the day may come when your basement actually floods. This chapter provides directions for a long-term, permanent fix for leaking basements and crawlspaces. However, if you are ankle-deep in water right now, it's impor-tant to dry out that space quickly and then tend to the long-term solutions.

After sustained stormy weather or another basement-flooding event, you must remove excess moisture and standing water to prevent the development of mold, mildew, bacteria, and other allergens. All of these health and structural threats can take hold when the relative humidity of a basement space rises above 60 percent.

Here is the four-step plan for drying out a wet basement, fast:

1. **Remove standing water** by the easiest means possible, which may include such tools as pumps, brooms, buckets, and wet-dry vacuums.

2. **Remove water-damaged items** from your basement, including rugs, furniture, and any portions of finished basement walls that have been underwater.

3. **Remember to turn off the electricity** in any part of the basement that has been impacted by flooding. Note that you may need to run an extension cord from upstairs to power cleanup tools, such as pumps. Also note that if any part of your basement's electrical system has gotten wet, it must be replaced. This includes electrical wiring, outlets, and switches for fixtures.

4. **Use a large-capacity, high-efficiency dehumidifier** to start drying out the basement space. It will speed up the process by lowering humidity, adding heat, and increasing air movement.

Once your basement has been dried out, you can proceed to repair and improve the space. These plans should include a long-term solution for controlling basement humidity, with installation of a humidification system as your next step.

Tackling Squeaks and Slopes in the Floors

Unless your home is built on a slab, the floor frame sits on top of the foundation. Despite all the strength that the floor frame provides, it's often plagued with a couple of common problems that I tackle here: squeaks and slopes! Floors that announce their presence with every step or those that aren't level are common. While many consumers would rightly believe that these issues are cause for alarm, the fact is that they are typical and rarely indicate a more serious structural problem.

Step-by-step tips to silence squeaking floors

No matter what kind of finish flooring you may have — carpet, vinyl, tile, or hardwood — unless your home is built on a concrete slab, underneath it's wood. And it's that wood that causes the squeaks — well, sort of. Usually, the squeak is a loose nail rubbing inside the hole it was originally driven into. Lumber that's used to build homes contains a certain degree of natural moisture, which makes the wood easy to cut and minimizes splitting when it's being nailed together. Unfortunately, as the wood dries, it shrinks — a natural process that can take years. When the wood shrinks enough, once tightly seated nails can loosen and rub when the wood flexes below the pitter-patter of foot traffic, creating the familiar irritating sound: a floor squeak.

The good news is that floor squeaks aren't as tough to fix as they are to listen to! They're not difficult or expensive to repair, and with a little guidance, you can avoid the frustrating part of the task: actually finding the cause of the squeak.

First up: Finding the squeak

The first step in repairing a floor squeak is to find the nail that's rubbing up against the wood floor — a task akin to finding a needle in a haystack. Here's a trick that I use to pinpoint a floor squeak so that I can make a repair: Use a short length of garden hose as a stethoscope. Hold one end of the hose to your ear and the other end on the floor while someone else walks across the floor to make it squeak. (See Figure 4-9.)

TIP

If you can listen to the floor from a basement or sub-area, the makeshift stethoscope yields more accurate results.

FIGURE 4-9:
Finding floor
squeaks.

Listen for squeaks.

Fixing the squeak

If the problem is a loose *subfloor* (the wood floor beneath the carpet, vinyl, hardwood, and so on), the repair can get sticky depending upon the type of finish flooring you have. However, if access below is available (that is, you can get to the subfloor through the basement or crawlspace), installing a wood shim shingle between the subfloor and the floor joist is a quick and easy means of preventing the subfloor from flexing, and it quiets the squeak. Just squirt some carpenter's glue on the thin end of the shingle and tap it in with a hammer. (See Figure 4-10.)

FIGURE 4-10:
Tapping in a
shingle with a
hammer.

Tap in shingle with hammer.

TIP

Most squeaks can be solved by driving an extra screw through the subfloor to the floor joists directly underneath the squeak. But when the floor is covered with wall-to-wall carpet, that can require taking the carpet up. Here's a shortcut: take a 12d finish nail (use a galvanized nail — it holds better) and drive it through the carpet into the subfloor and joist below. You'll find this leaves a divot in the carpet, which will no doubt have you (or your spouse) thinking you've just ruined the rug! Ah, but not so fast! Just grab the nap of the carpet above the divot and pull it up until the nail pulls through the carpet backing. Voilà, the divot will have disappeared right along with the squeak!

Another means of quieting a squeaking floor by preventing it from flexing is a nifty gadget called a Squeak-Ender. It consists of a metal plate and threaded-rod assembly that's screwed to the underside of the subfloor and a steel bracket. You slip the bracket beneath the joist and over the threaded rod; then you tighten a nut onto the rod to pull down the floor and close the gap. For more information on the Squeak-Ender, go to www.squeakender.com or call 586-978-3377.

If access below is not available, after you locate the culprit nail, the next step is to create a better connection. Don't use nails to make the repair — use screws. Just follow these steps:

1. **Locate the squeak using the method discussed in the preceding section.**

2. **Locate the nearest floor joist under the squeak.**

   The *floor joist* is the horizontal floor framing member that the wood subfloor is attached to. If the subfloor is exposed, this is easy — just look at the nails, which will line up over the floor joists. If not, you can locate the joist using a *stud finder*, an electronic tool used to locate wood studs to joists below walls or floors.

3. **Near the existing squeaking nail, drill a small pilot hole through the wood subfloor and into the floor joist.**

   Drilling a small pilot hole in the floor joist makes driving in the screw easier. You can leave the old nail in place, or, if it's loose, remove it using a nail puller or pry bar.

4. **Drive a construction screw into the pilot hole, through the subfloor, and so on. (See Figure 4-11.)**

   When working on a hardwood floor, *countersink* (recess) the screw head so that it can be concealed with hardwood putty. Use a putty knife to install hardwood putty. Touch up the floor finish with 400- to 600-grit wet/dry sandpaper.

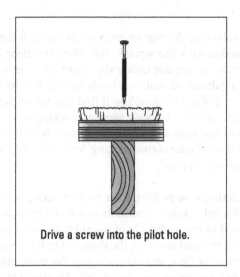

FIGURE 4-11:
Drive a screw in
the pilot hole.

Drive a screw into the pilot hole.

TIP

I recommend construction screws because they're easy to drive and they grip like crazy. You can purchase screws with a finish head (like a finish nail), which makes them a particularly good choice when working on a hardwood floor. You simply countersink them slightly and place putty over them. A construction screw's coarse threads and really sharp tip make it the perfect fastener for old, dry wood. The sharp tip gets through harder lumber more easily, and the coarse screw threads go in faster and hold better.

Still struggling with a squeaking floor? Major foundation settlement or an out-of-level floor could be the problem; see the following section for more information. Because this is a more expensive repair, you may want to consider the positive aspects of owning your own floor squeak as a dose of old-house charm.

Getting on the level with your floors

Have you ever walked across a room and felt like you were navigating a mini roller coaster? If so, it's probably time to consider leveling the floor. Out-of-level floors are not only a nuisance to walk over, but they can also become a real safety hazard. Plus, when floors settle, sag, or rot, they can take your walls, windows, and doors along with them for the ride — resulting in wall cracks, as well as windows and doors that shift, making them difficult to open or close.

The first step toward repairing a sagging floor is determining why it's out of level. Floors can fall out of level for lots of reasons, so step one would be to figure out why that's happened. Possible causes could include the following.

>> **Foundation settlement:** If your foundation drops, the floor structure above will drop with it.

>> **Sagging or cracked floor joists:** Clearly, if your floor joists are in sad shape, the floor itself is going to suffer.

>> **Rot:** This can prove especially damaging where a moisture problem is present.

>> **Insect damage:** The prime suspects here would be termites, carpenter ants, powder post beetles, or other wood-destroying insects.

>> **Excessive span:** Older homes may have beams that are undersized by today's standards. These longer floor joists are more likely to bend and crack.

There are a number of ways to address out-of-level floors — some simple and some not. Seriously flawed floor framing will require the services of a skilled contractor, as well as those of a licensed structural engineer. For this chapter, I'll focus on repairs that a majority of DIYers can handle.

WARNING

While the perfectionist in you may want to restore an out-of-level floor by jacking up the floors or beams from below, this can have some very negative consequences. It can take many, many years for a floor system to settle and become unlevel. Jacking it back up can stretch electrical wires, break plumbing pipes, and cause walls to crack. You're almost always better off stabilizing these unlevel areas so they don't move further.

REMEMBER

Most homes with floors not on the level probably didn't start out that way. Poorly compacted soil, excessively damp or dry soil, and shrinking support posts under the floor are a few of the most common causes of this condition. Homes constructed on a hillside, on soil that expands when wet, or in earthquake country fall into a totally different category. Although some of the fixes suggested in this section may indeed apply to these homes, chances are you'll need the services of a licensed soil engineer and structural engineer.

First things first: Stabilize the soil around your foundation

Before embarking on any floor-leveling project, I suggest that you start by stabilizing the moisture content of the soil nearest the foundation. Installing gutters and downspouts (and keeping them clean), installing downspout diverters (splash blocks), controlling landscape irrigation, and grading soil to shed water away from the foundation are all effective means of controlling excessive moisture. (See my drainage advice earlier in this chapter.) Managing the moisture around your house will help to stabilize settlement and prevent additional movement of both the foundation and the floor frame above.

Take your floor to new heights with a floor-leveling compound

While many floor-leveling projects involve structural work within a basement or crawlspace, the most straightforward solution for fixing an uneven floor often lies above. Enter floor-leveling compound — a self-leveling underlayment. With a consistency like pancake batter, floor-leveling compound flows and fills in uneven surfaces, providing a perfectly level surface for your new flooring. (See Figure 4-12.)

This versatile solution is ideal for several scenarios.

>> **Uneven subfloors:** If your subfloor resembles a topographical map more than a smooth surface, leveling compound is your go-to remedy.

>> **Preparing for new flooring:** Planning to install finished flooring like hardwood, laminate, or tile? Leveling compound takes center stage as the pre-game MVP, making sure your new flooring lays flat and flawless.

>> **Renovation rescues:** Whether you're revamping an old space or giving a room a facelift, leveling compound can provide an even playing field across rooms, eliminating transition-trip hazards.

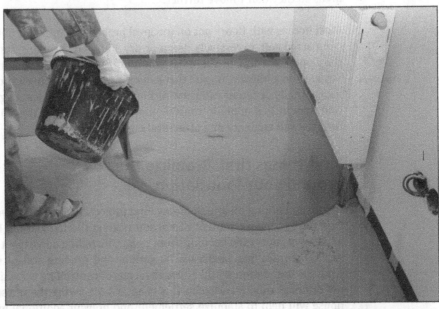

FIGURE 4-12:
Floor-leveling compound being poured across a floor.

Salamatik/Adobe Stock Photos

The best part? Using floor-leveling compound can be a DIY project. Here's a step-by-step guide on how to get it done:

1. **Prepare the subfloor.**

   Start by cleaning and sweeping the subfloor, removing any debris, dust, or remnants of the previous floor. The cleaner, the better!

2. **Appy a primer.**

   This is an essential step to make sure the leveling compound sticks solidly to the old floor. This not only enhances adhesion, but also helps the self-leveling compound to flow more easily.

3. **Mix the leveling compound.**

   Be sure to follow the manufacturer's instructions to the letter. You should also purchase enough compound for your project, plus an extra bag or two. Once the first batch is mixed and poured, you'll need to have the next batch ready to go until the entire floor is covered.

4. **Pour and spread the leveling compound.**

   Not a particularly complicated step — you just have to pour the mixed compound onto the subfloor and use a smoothing tool to spread it evenly until all nooks and crannies are filled.

5. **Let the leveling compound set.**

   Allow the compound some time to settle, level itself out, and harden. The curing time varies, with faster cures allowing for quicker installation of your new flooring. Beginners may prefer a slower cure for added time to ensure a precise job.

TIP

Determining the ideal height for your floor using leveling compound can be tricky. To help, starting at the lowest point, partially drive a screw into the old floor. Position one end of the level on the screw and the other on the highest point of the floor you are leveling. Adjust the screw's height until it reflects the desired compound height. Repeat across various spots and monitor the flow during pouring to ensure it reaches the top of the screws.

Shimming your way to a perfectly level floor

For carpenters, shims are indispensable tools with a multitude of applications. Similar to floor-leveling compound, these slim, tapered pieces of wood — also known as pearlings or surface shim boards — offer a simple solution for leveling any unevenness in the subfloor. (See Figure 4-13.) Here are some scenarios where shims truly shine.

» **Old house, new floors:** When renovating a charming yet slightly crooked older home, adding shims on top of the original flooring ensures a level playing field.

» **Subfloor challenges:** If your subfloor resembles a topography map, shims can provide a smooth surface for your new hardwood, vinyl plank, or laminate flooring.

» **DIY doable:** Shimming is a simple, cost-effective project that provides instant gratification as you witness your floors undergo a transformation from lumpy to flat.

FIGURE 4-13: Tapered shims installed on top of a sloped floor to level it.

Ready to shimmy your way to a level floor? Follow these straightforward steps:

1. **Identify low spots.**

   These will be where your shims get placed.

2. **Prepare the shims.**

   The most common shim material is a type of cedar shingle called *undercourse*. It's a thin, rough-sawn, tapered shingle that's easy to trim or stack up to achieve the desired thickness.

3. **Position the shims.**

   Strategically place the shims in the trouble zones, focusing on areas where your floor is lowest. Stretch a level from the shims to the high spots in the floor to determine the required thickness for a flat and level surface.

4. **Secure the shims in place by nailing them to the subfloor to prevent any movement.**

Once the shims are secured, you can install your finished flooring on top. If the shims are thick, you can add another level of subfloor over them.

TIP

When shimming a large section of flooring, it's often best to cut your own shims. For instance, I once had to raise a six-foot-deep section of flooring by a full inch. To do so, I cut six-foot strips of wood with thickness that tapered from one inch down to zero. I attached the shims to the old floor and added a layer of plywood on top for a clean, flat, and perfectly level floor!

Sistering: Your floor joist's new best friend

If your floor joists are showing signs of damage from beneath, sistering is the solution you need. This process involves attaching a new joist alongside the compromised one, effectively restoring the structural strength of your floor. It's like giving your floor joists a sibling that has their back, ensuring they stand strong together. (See Figure 4-14.)

Wondering if sistering is the remedy for your floor joists? Look out for these signs indicating it's time to bring in the family for help.

>> **Cracks and breaks:** Visible cracks or breaks in your floor joists are a clear signal for assistance. Sistering steps in to strengthen the weakened joists.

>> **Sagging floors:** If one or more floor joists have sagged, or if your floors feel weak or bouncy, sistering is the solution.

Unlike leveling a floor using shims or a floor-leveling compound, sistering requires working from beneath the floor in an unfinished basement or crawlspace.

WARNING

Seriously, working in a crawlspace is H-A-R-D! You'll be working on your hands and knees. It's dusty. It's dirty. You'll need a good dust mask to protect your lungs as well as safety glasses, which will repeatedly fog up at a frustrating rate. Don't do this project by yourself — convince a buddy to join you. Just be sure to tell them that they should prepare themselves for an exhausting adventure into the dungeon of your home sweet home.

FIGURE 4-14: Sistering a floor joist with a new joist can help restore strength to the damaged joist.

Here's a step-by-step guide on how to sister one or more floor joists:

1. **Identify the damaged floor joists, noting how many are sagging or damaged.**

2. **Choose a new joist of the same size and material as the damaged one.**

   It's important that the sister joist be of the same length, especially if the damaged joists are supported by the foundation.

3. **Clear the space around the damaged joist, ensuring it's clean and ready for the sistering process.**

   Be sure to temporarily remove any pipes or wiring running through the damaged joists as well.

REMEMBER

4. **Crown the sister joist.**

   All wood joists have a slight bow called the *crown*. When installing the new joist, place the crown (convex edge) up to minimize the risk of sagging. Draw an arrow on the joist pointing up to indicate the crown.

5. **Attach the new joist next to the damaged one, creating a doubly supportive pair. (See Figure 4-15.)**

   Use construction adhesive and screws or bolts to secure the sister joist to the damaged joist.

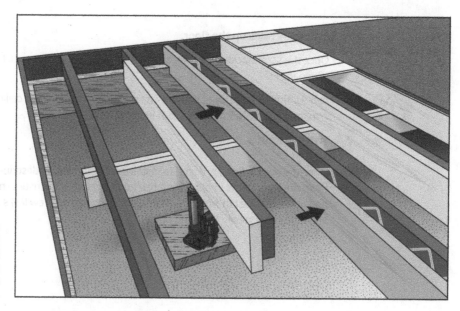

FIGURE 4-15:
Jacking up and sistering several floor joists can help level a section of floor.

Sistering a sagging set of floor joists using screw jacks

Sistering floor joists isn't just about repairing damage; it can also be a solution for leveling multiple joists to lift a sagging section of the floor. To execute this project effectively, follow these steps:

1. **Install a central beam.**

   This involves placing a beam (usually 4x4 or 4x6) at the midpoint perpendicular to the floor joists. Temporarily support the new beam with 2x4s at both ends.

2. **Set up your screw jacks.**

   You'll use the threaded shafts of the screw jacks (also called *jack screws*) to raise or lower the supported structure.

   REMEMBER

   Be sure to position a screw jack on solid wood or concrete blocks at each end of the new beam. You also need to insert (2) 2x4s or a 4x4 between the screw jack and the underside of the beam.

3. **Measure the sag.**

   I use a string stretched across the top side of the floor from end to end to gauge the existing sag. Repeat the measurement as you lift the floor to monitor progress.

4. Gradually raise up the floor.

Once the screw jacks are in place, turn them a little each day until the sag is eliminated.

WARNING

Avoid lifting too quickly to prevent stress cracks in the walls or ceilings above. Aim for a gradual lift of ¼ inch to ½ inch per day.

5. Sister the joists.

Once the floor is level, proceed to install the sister joists as described earlier. Keep the screw jacks in place for a few additional days to ensure the construction adhesive dries thoroughly. Afterward, remove the screw jacks and beam, and enjoy your newly flattened floor!

IN THIS CHAPTER

» **Stopping leaks before they begin**

» **Discovering the destructive side of icicles**

» **Getting into gutters**

» **Painting for more than appearance**

» **Caring for siding**

Chapter **5**

Roofing and Siding

Your entire home and its contents depend on the integrity of your roof and exterior walls in the same way that you depend on protective clothing to keep you dry in foul weather. Getting temporarily stuck in bad weather can make you slightly uncomfortable, but left unchecked, a roof leak — even a tiny one — can end up costing a fortune in damage to a home's interior and its precious contents. Damage to flooring, walls, ceilings, furniture, important papers, and more is no small matter. To avoid problems like these, you need to keep your roof and siding in good condition and repair. This chapter tells you how.

Understanding Your Roof: The Fifth Wall of Your Home

Most folks are pretty conscientious about maintaining the exterior walls of their homes. On just about any day during good weather, you can drive through a neighborhood and find the sides of at least one home under siege by painters. But rarely do you see anyone on the roof of a home unless the roof is being replaced. For some reason, people just don't pay as much attention to their roofs, which is a mistake.

The whole idea of maintenance is to ensure longevity, reduce costs, and improve value. This concept should apply to the roof in the same way it does to the walls.

In fact, I like to think of the roof as the fifth wall of the home — and it should be maintained with the same regularity as the walls that support it. With proper installation, care, and maintenance, a roof can outlast its warranty without leaking a drop or suffering any ugly damage.

Staying safe on the roof

WARNING

A pitched roof is an alien plane. No, not a spaceship from another planet. Rather, it's an unfamiliar surface to walk upon. And for the novice, an angled surface can be dangerous. Aside from the roof pitch, mineral granules separate from asphalt shingles as they age and act like ball bearings underfoot. Add in risks from slippery roof moss or algae and it's a wonder more people don't learn the hard way that they can't fly. To stay safe, follow this advice:

>> **If you aren't agile or athletic, or if you have a fear of heights (or falling), think about hiring someone to maintain your roof.** Your best bet would be a roofing contractor. They have the equipment, the know-how, and, best of all, the experience of working up high on an unlevel plane.

>> **If you do go up there, be sure to wear rubber-soled shoes.** These have the best grip.

>> **Wear a safety harness.** Safety harnesses have fabric straps that wrap around your legs, your waist, and the trunk of your body, and you connect them to a rope that's securely anchored to a tree trunk — or other fixed and secure object — located on the other side of the roof. These harnesses could prevent broken bones or even save your life. You can find them online, at construction-supply stores, or at a sports-supply or camping store that sells products for rock climbing and rappelling.

TIP

Be sure to adjust the slack in your safety line as you work your way up the roof. The less slack, the less sudden the stop!

>> **If you're cleaning your roof, applying a preservative, or doing some other similar task, never stand downhill of your work.** You can very easily slip on a wet surface. Always stand uphill of your work. (See Figure 5-1.)

TIP

>> **If you want to inspect your roof safely, grab binoculars, use a camera with a zoom lens, or even unleash a drone to get an up-close look at your roof without the dangers of climbing up.** From the comfort of the ground, scan your roof for loose, broken, or missing shingles or flashing. If your shingles are curling up or showing cracks, it might be time for a roof makeover. And if your roof is sporting a mossy or algae-covered look, it's time for a spa day — a good cleaning is in order! Whatever might be up there, there's no need to break a sweat or risk an emergency room visit to find out; just stand back, zoom in, and let the roof revelations unfold!

FIGURE 5-1:
When cleaning or applying a preservative, always stand uphill of your work.

Cleanliness is next to godliness

Streaking or discoloration can cause a perfectly good roof to look old, tired, and tattered. So, for appearance's sake, keep your roof clean. You can use the Universal Roof-Cleaning Formula featured in Chapter 20, which not only cleans off dirt but also gets rid of mildew, moss, and algae, all of which can cause extensive damage if left unattended.

If you prefer not to make your own, you can also use one of dozens of available commercial roof-cleaning solutions. Although many of them simply contain detergent and bleach like my recipe, others contain peroxide, fungicides, disinfectants, and other fancy fluids. Some are better at killing mold and mildew. Some are better at removing stains. Some are easier on your landscaping. To find out more about the options, visit your favorite home center or hardware store.

To clean your roof, you need these supplies:

>> Cleaning solution

>> Safety glasses

>> Pump garden sprayer

>> Stiff-bristle broom

>> Tall ladder (how tall depends on the height of your roof)

» Garden hose

» Safety harness

Choose a cool, humid, overcast day to make sure that the cleaner doesn't dry too fast on the roof, and then follow these steps:

1. **Pour your cleaning solution into the garden sprayer.**

TIP

Most commercial cleaning solutions are concentrated, requiring you to mix them with water and apply them using a garden sprayer. However, many of these solutions also come in a ready-to-use (RTU) container that easily connects to a garden hose. While RTU cleaners may be pricier, the upside is convenience. It is particularly advantageous if you can access the entire roof from the top of a ladder leaned against it, eliminating the need to walk on the roof.

2. **While standing on the roof, spray the cleaner on a strip about 3 feet high and 10 feet wide and let it sit for about 15 minutes.**

WARNING

Begin cleaning the lower portion of the roof, moving up as you clean each lower section. That way, you always stand on dry ground and reduce the chance of slipping. (Refer to Figure 5-1.)

3. **If the cleaner begins to dry out, spray on a bit more.**

4. **Use the broom to gently scrub the area as needed to get it clean.**

   Note: You don't want to scrub off the granules from your asphalt shingles or scrub your wood shingles loose.

5. **Rinse the cleaned area with fresh water.**

   Repeat the process until the roof is clean.

BEST ALL-NATURAL AND ALWAYS-FREE ROOF CLEANER EVER!

Roof cleaners are costly to purchase, and difficult and sometimes even dangerous to apply. But what if they were always free and went to work, day in and day out, keeping your roof clean as a whistle? Well, there exists such a magical roof scrubber! It's called "The Sun!" Yes, sunlight is the always-on and always most effective way to keep a roof clean. Most roofs that grow moss or algae do so because they are shaded. (See the left side of the following figure.) If the sun reaches the roof, it naturally kills the early formation of these roof growths. So, if your roof gets covered with moss or algae, trim your trees enough to let the sunshine through! You don't need to remove the trees, just thin out the branches to let the light do its work.

Besides maximizing the sunlight that gets to your roof, here's another almost no-cost way to keep the roof clean over the long haul. It's called "Rain!" Once you've completed your roof-cleaning project, just install a strip of copper flashing under the ridge of the roof. Make sure that at least 6 to 10 inches of copper stick out from under the top row of shingles. (See the right side of the figure.) When it rains, that copper will get wet, releasing a bit of metal that acts as a mildewcide, gently washing over the roof and killing the moss and mildew as it goes!

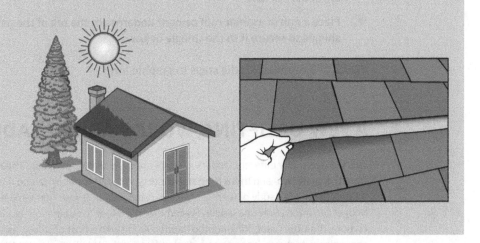

Replacing an asphalt shingle

Shingles made of asphalt fiberglass, sometimes called *composition shingles*, are by far the most popular roofing material. Asphalt (tar), reinforced with fiberglass matting and covered with mineral granules, makes for good-looking, long-lasting shingles that need very little maintenance. Composition shingles are more flexible and, therefore, somewhat more forgiving than wood shingles. (See the next section.)

From time to time, asphalt shingles will break or tear and need replacement. When that happens, here's how you'd replace a shingle (see Figure 5-2):

1. **Using a thin flat pry bar, carefully break the self-seal strip under the shingle(s) immediately above the one you want to remove.**

   This is more easily done when shingles are cool or cold.

2. **Slip a flat pry bar under the shingle you want to remove.**

3. **Wiggle the pry bar from side to side to loosen the shingle, and then remove each of the nails holding the damaged shingle in place.**

4. **Slip a new shingle in position to replace the one that you removed.**

5. **Nail the new shingle in place, using a flat pry bar as a hammer extension.**

   Using a flat pry bar as a hammer extension, you can drive the nail in from beneath an overlapping shingle. First, press the nail into the shingle by hand; then position the bottom of the flat pry bar so that the straight end rests atop the nail head; then strike the flat pry bar with a hammer. The offset below drives the nail home.

6. **Place a dab of asphalt roof cement underneath the tab of the new shingle to secure it to the shingle below.**

Figure 5-2 summarizes the steps in graphic form.

A FEW UPLIFTING WORDS ABOUT LADDERS

There are as many different ladders as there are tasks that require one. They range from the small two- and three-rung step-stool type to the common 6- and 8-foot folding models to the big daddy of them all, the extension ladder. If your home-maintenance budget can afford only one ladder, I recommend a 6-foot "combination" ladder, like my favorite, the Little Giant "King Kombo" ladder. Along with a host of safety, useability, and convenience features, it serves as a stepladder or unfolds to become an 11-foot straight ladder. This combination gives you the length you need when tackling most home-maintenance and repair projects, like changing light bulbs, painting rooms, or cleaning gutters. If your project involves a multistory roof, you need an extension ladder.

Whichever type of ladder you choose, be sure to check its *class rating*, which establishes the maximum amount of weight it's rated for. These include

- Type III (Light duty)200 pounds

- Type II (Medium duty)225 pounds

- Type IAA (Extra-heavy duty)375 pounds

- Type IA (Extra-heavy duty)300 pounds

- Type I (Heavy duty)250 pounds

  Source: American Ladder Institute

Don't try to save money by purchasing a cheap ladder. Cheap ladders fall apart in no time — usually with someone on them. When buying a ladder, look for secure connections, metal-supported steps, and superior hinges. As the ladder gets older, keep an eye out for loose connections, splits, cracks, and missing rivets.

Over 20,000 ladder injuries occur each year. Follow these tips to help you avoid any unplanned downward trips off your ladder:

- **Stabilize the ladder by adjusting the feet based on the surface you are working from.** Many ladders have dual-action feet that rotate, from a flat, slip-resistant foot for solid surfaces, to a spiked foot to dig securely into soft surfaces, like dirt, ice, gravel, or snow.

- **When setting up a ladder, place the bottom of the ladder away from the wall one-quarter of the ladder's length.** If you have an 8-foot ladder, place the bottom of the ladder 2 feet away from the wall. (See the following figure.)

- **When working on the roof, make sure that the ladder extends a minimum of 2 feet above the edge of the roof.** (Again, see the following figure.)

- **Never climb onto a roof from the gable end where the roof crosses the ladder rungs at an angle.** Instead, mount the roof from a horizontal side. The plane of the roof should be parallel to the ladder rungs at the point where you leave the ladder to mount the roof.

- **To maintain proper balance, keep your hips between the side rails when climbing the ladder or when reaching out.** Keep one hand on the ladder and the other free for work.

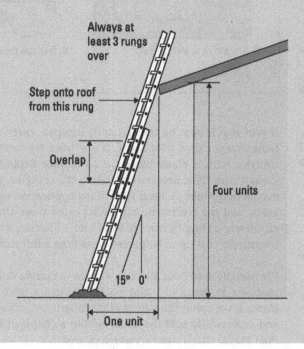

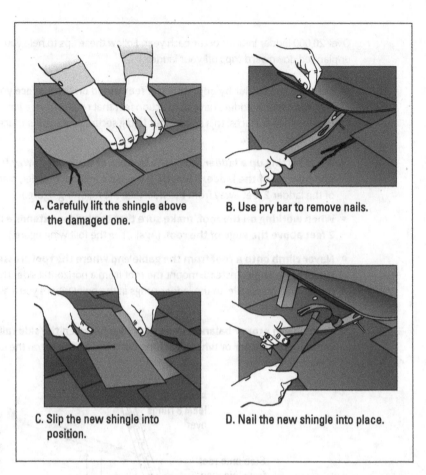

A. Carefully lift the shingle above the damaged one.

B. Use pry bar to remove nails.

C. Slip the new shingle into position.

D. Nail the new shingle into place.

FIGURE 5-2:
Replacing a composition shingle.

TIP

If your roof is nearing the end of its lifespan, there's an alternative to immediate replacement called Roof Maxx. It's a "roof rejuvenation" treatment that infuses shingles with a plant-based oil to replace depleted petrochemical oils in the asphalt core. This process revitalizes the shingles, restoring their flexibility and overall performance. Each Roof Maxx application extends your roof's life by five years, and the treatment can be repeated three times within a five-year cycle, effectively adding 15 years to your roof's lifespan. The best part is that Roof Maxx treatments cost up to 80 percent less than a full roof replacement.

I personally used Roof Maxx on a home in Florida that my mom needed to sell. The roof was 16 years old, and potential buyers were insisting on a replacement. Instead, we opted for a Roof Maxx treatment, obtained a new 5-year warranty, and successfully sold the house within a couple of months. To learn more about Roof Maxx, visit https://roofmaxx.com/.

Preserving a wood-shake or shingle roof

Wood-shake (hand split) or wood shingle (machine cut) roofs are popular for their natural beauty, especially in the western part of the United States. But they also have major limitations. Wood roofs are not fire resistant, a huge concern in areas prone to wildfires. Despite their significantly higher cost over asphalt shingles, they're really not all that durable (typically lasting 25 years or less) and need far more maintenance than virtually any other type of roof.

No matter how clean you keep your wood roof, it usually starts looking a little worn out after only a few years. Exposure to the sun causes most of the damage, drying out shingles, causing them to split and weaken. These wood roofs can lose virtually all their moisture (water and natural resins) in as few as five years, which can result in cupping, curling, splitting, and an almost certain early demise. However, if you really, really want to put yourself through the hard work, with proper care and maintenance, you could double or even triple the life of a wood-shake or shingle roof.

REMEMBER

Most preservative applications last three to five years, depending upon the climate. Keeping the roof clean and debris-free helps extend the lasting quality of the preservative and, therefore, the life of the roof.

TIP

For more information on wood-roof maintenance, download "Installation, Care, and Maintenance of Wood Shake and Shingle Roofs," a free guide published by the United States Department of Agriculture (USDA). Search for the USDA guide online or contact the Cedar Shake and Shingle Bureau at (604) 820-7700 or by visiting www.cedarbureau.org.

Preserving your roof begins with a thorough cleaning that completely exposes all the pores of the wood so that the preservative you apply later can penetrate deeply and completely into every pore. This super-cleaning also cuts through grime and makes your wood-shake or shingle roof look almost as good as new. Here are the steps:

1. **Pressure-wash your roof.**

    When using the pressure washer, hold the spray tip approximately 8 to 12 inches from the roof's surface while working backward from the lowest part of the roof up to the highest part. Be sure to use the gentlest setting for the least amount of force. Set too high, a pressure washer can easily destroy your shingles.

2. **(Optional) Follow the pressure washing with an application of a mold-killing mixture.**

    When green growth covers your wood roof, a pressure wash might not be sufficient. If that's the case, you should use a mold-killing solution (1 quart of bleach to 1 gallon of hot water) to eliminate any remaining growth that may reside deep within the pores of the wood. Place the mixture in a garden sprayer and thoroughly wet the entire roof. Keep it wet for at least 15 minutes and then rinse with fresh water.

3. **(Optional) Apply a preservative.**

Once the roof has thoroughly dried, consider applying a preservative. While optional, a preservative can help restore natural oils to the wood fibers, safeguard the roof from fungus and rot, and protect it from the harmful ultraviolet rays of the sun. You'll find both oil-based and water-based preservatives at the stores; I prefer the oil-based type because it penetrates deeper, combats weather stress better, and lasts longer.

To apply the preservative, just spray the oil onto the roof, being sure to work backward from the low end to the high end and be careful not to walk on an already-treated area, which could be very slippery. (Refer to Figure 5-1.) When the surface becomes shiny, stop spraying in that area and move on.

WHAT ABOUT OTHER TYPES OF ROOFS?

While asphalt roofs are undoubtedly the most common type of roof across the nation, there are several other durable, beautiful, and popular options to consider.

Synthetic: Made to match traditional slate, wood shingles, shake, or clay tile, synthetic roofing products offer all the beauty and durability at a lower cost.

Metal: While metal roofs have been around for well over 100 years, the newest metal roofs deliver beauty, energy efficiency, and storm resistance like never before. Available in an incredible array of colors and styles, today's metal roofing also feature coatings that reflect the heat of the sun, reducing cooling costs. If you'd like to learn more about metal roofs, you can find a number of helpful guides by visiting the Metal Roofing Alliance at www.metalroofing.com.

Slate tiles: Slate is a natural stone that can last anywhere from 50 to 100 years. Slate roofs are costly, but durable enough to withstand high winds and high temperatures. They're also fireproof, need little maintenance, and may even help to increase the value of your home.

Clay and concrete tiles: Tile roofs — clay tile as well as concrete tile — are terribly expensive, and their use is virtually limited to homes with Mediterranean architecture. But they seldom need repair, and a well-installed tile roof can last up to 75 years. If a tile roof is appropriate for your home, it's actually a good value when you spread the cost out over the life of the roof.

TIP

You know that nasty green stuff that grows on roofs? Most people would call that "mold"; worse, they may fear it's the "toxic mold" kind that can make people sick! Rest assured this is rarely true. That green stuff is more likely to be moss, algae, lichen, or mildew. And while it looks nasty, it won't damage asphalt shingles. Follow my tips earlier in this chapter to restore cleanliness to your roof!

REMEMBER

When selecting a new roof, consider how long you expect to own the home. Opting for a 50-year roof if you only expect to be there for 10 years isn't worth the extra cost. While a good roof enhances home value, it won't fully recoup its cost. So, at best, investing in an expensive, long-lasting roof mainly offers a slight competitive edge when selling compared to neighboring houses.

Exposing the naked truth about flashing

Flashing failures are the cause of the vast majority of roof leaks. No matter how well you take care of your roof, you'll still get leaks if you don't also take care of your flashing. Here's why: Roof flashing creates a watertight connection where the roof joins a wall, as when a first-story roof connects to a second-story wall. Roof flashing also creates watertight connections between the roofing and items that penetrate it, including plumbing pipes, furnace flues, skylights, and chimneys. Good, tight flashings around chimneys, vents, skylights, and wall-roof junctions are the key to preventing water infiltration — and damage to walls, ceilings, insulation, and electrical systems.

Here's a list of the most common types of flashing failures and how to make the repair.

>> **Chimney flashing:** The gap between a brick chimney and a roof is one where a lot of movement takes place. To seal this gap, a two-part flashing system should have been installed. (See Figure 5-3.) It consists of a base flashing that weaves in between the shingles and lays flat against the chimney. Also needed is a *counterflashing* — flashing that's notched into the chimney's mortar joints and folds flat overtop the base flashing. This two-piece system provides both the water repellency and flexibility needed to keep leaks from breaking through to your house.

Chimney flashing often leaks when the counterflashing gets loose and pulls away from the chimney. When this happens, too many of the lazy roofers that folks hire will smear black, gooey asphalt roof cement across the entire base of the chimney to "repair" the problem. This works for about as long as it takes your check to clear. If the chimney flashing leaks, it needs to be repaired the same way it was originally installed. If your roofer can't handle this, find another roofer.

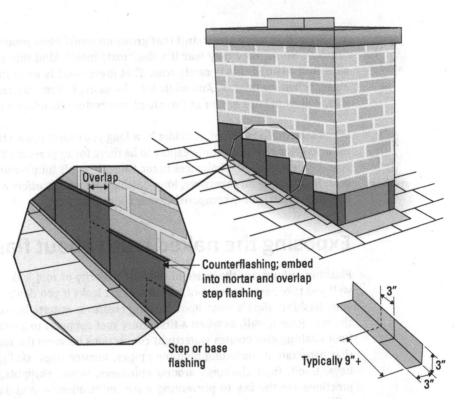

Overlap

Counterflashing; embed
into mortar and overlap
step flashing

Step or base
flashing

Typically 9"+

3"

3"

3"

FIGURE 5-3:
A two-part
chimney
flashing system.

» **Roof-to-wall flashing:** Similar to chimney flashing, roof-to-wall flashing is accomplished by installing a base flashing between the roof shingles and the wall. But in this case, the home's siding provides the counter flashing. Leaks in this area often happen when wind-driven rain forces water up under the siding and into the house. When that happens, the most permanent fix is to remove the siding and reflash the intersection, making sure to extend the flashing well up under the siding.

» **Plumbing vent flashing:** Look up at any roof, and you'll find a variety of plumbing pipes sticking out. These are plumbing vents and they utilize a type of flashing called a *plumbing vent boot*. This vent pipe flashing has a rubber gasket that fits over the vent pipe, as well as an integrated metal flashing that slips under the roof shingles. Over time, the rubber gaskets dry out, crack, and allow water to leak, usually to the bathroom below. When that happens, the boot needs to be replaced. This is also one of those repairs that roofers like to make by sealing around the pipe with roof cement, which is not an appropriate repair.

Stopping ice dams cold

Imagine a beautiful winter morning. You glance out your window and see lots of pretty icicles hanging from your roof and think, "Oh, how pretty!" After 20 years as a professional home inspector, I look at those same icicles and think, "Here come ice dams and roof leaks!"

When snow falls on a roof, it seals the roof, which becomes almost airtight. As the house warms to a nice toasty temperature, heated air escapes into the attic. As the attic gets warmer, it melts the snow on the roof, and water rushes downward toward the overhangs. The moment the liquefied snow hits the cold (uninsulated) overhang, it begins to freeze. The water that freezes *after* it rolls over the edge becomes icicles. Water that freezes *before* it rolls over the edge builds up to create a barrier known as an *ice dam*, which becomes larger and larger as runoff continues to freeze. Finally, the ice on the overhang widens to the point where it reaches the edge of the attic. At this point, the water remains liquid and the ice dam causes it to back up under the roof shingles and into the attic where it can leak into the home.

Ice buildup can also damage rain gutters, causing the need for costly repairs. By preventing ice buildup, you might be able to save your house from being flooded during a freeze and add a little life to your gutters as well.

To prevent an ice dam, you need to keep the underside of the roof in the attic cold. If the attic is cold, the snow on the roof won't melt, and ice dams won't form. Here's how to make it happen:

>> **Don't close off eave and roof vents during the winter.** Sealing the vents traps the warm air that can melt the snow on the roof.

>> **Fill all penetrations between the living space and the attic area with foam sealant.** You can buy expanding foam sealant in a spray can. Look for penetrations in the ceiling in the following places (many may be hidden beneath attic insulation):

- Plumbing vents
- Ventilation ducts
- Heat registers
- Electric wiring
- Ceiling light fixtures

Any hole that can allow heat from the home into the attic is a bad thing.

Don't seal around furnace flues. A flue that contains hot gases should not come into contact with combustibles such as wood or foam sealant.

WARNING

>> **Check your attic insulation.** Be sure that your attic insulation is fluffy and hasn't been packed down by any storage that was laid on top. Measure the insulation you have and add more if needed. The Department of Energy recommended level for most attics is to insulate to R-38 or about 10 to 14 inches, depending on insulation type. If you need more, lay new fiberglass batts perpendicular to and on top of the original insulation.

>> **Install ice and water shield.** The best long-term fix for ice dams is to install a material called "ice and water shield," a rubberized roof material that's installed under roof shingles at the eaves; it seals the gaps between shingles so any water backing up can't leak through to your house. Unfortunately, you must add the ice and water shield when the roof is first installed or when it's replaced. It's required by building codes in far northern climates, but is a smart addition anywhere it gets cold enough to snow.

TIP

Ice dam leaks can cause thousands of dollars of damage, in part because the repair requires removing shingles from your roof, installing ice and water shield, and replacing the shingles. But it's possible that the cost of this repair may be covered by your homeowner's insurance. Be sure to check with an agent or hire a public insurance adjuster to examine your roof and determine if there's a potential claim to be made.

Finding a roof leak

The first step in repairing a leak is finding its point of origin. Most leaks occur where plumbing vents, vents, or chimneys protrude through the roof, or where roofs and walls intersect. Examine these areas carefully, and the leak may reveal itself. If not, you can use a garden hose to try to nail the location down. The process requires two people — one on the roof and one in the attic (or living space below if no attic exists). You also need the following tools:

>> Ladder

>> Garden hose

>> Flashlight

Then follow these steps:

1. **Station your helper in the attic and tell them to holler at the first sign of water.**

    Where's the water coming from, you ask? From you, or, more precisely, from your garden hose, as explained in Step 2.

2. **Use the garden hose to run a modest amount of water over the roof at a point below the area where a leak is suspected. (See Figure 5-4.)**

Don't run the hose full-blast, don't use a spray nozzle, and don't force the water between the shingles. Doing so may force water into the home, creating the illusion that you've found a leak when, in fact, you did nothing more than temporarily create one.

Work from the lowest point of the roof (near the eaves or gutters) in an area of about 4 to 6 feet wide. Work your way up the roof a couple of feet at a time.

Before you use the hose, call your helper on a smart phone to establish communication.

3. **Have your helper in the attic let you know the moment water is visible, and mark the spot on the roof with chalk.**

Keep in mind that water has a bad habit of traveling a distance between the roof leak location and where it shows up inside your house, so the leak may not be directly over the leak stain!

FIGURE 5-4:
Water-testing a
pitched roof.

Getting Your Mind into the Gutter

Gutters do far more than keep rain from dousing you with loads of water on the way in or out of your house. Clogs from leaves, twigs, or the occasional tennis ball can lead to significant and costly home repairs. Gutters play a crucial role in managing water around your home, and failure to clean them can result in a whole host of unexpected problems, including

>> **Leaking basements and crawlspaces.** Clogged gutters are the primary cause of basement water problems. When gutters are blocked, water overflows from the roof and collects around the foundation, increasing the risk of basement leaks.

>> **Cracked foundations.** Excess water against the foundation due to clogged gutters can cause cracks in the foundation wall, especially in colder months when frozen water leads to *frost-heave* — which happens when the wet soil freezes and expands, pushing the foundation wall inward and causing it to crack.

>> **Rotten wood.** Water backing up from clogged gutters damages the wood fascia around the house. If not addressed promptly through gutter cleaning, the rot can worsen.

>> **Leaking roofs.** Clogged gutters in winter can result in ice dams, causing snow to accumulate and freeze. During thaws, water is blocked, leading to significant damage to walls and ceilings.

>> **Slippery surfaces.** Overflowing gutters deposit water on walks and driveways, creating a slipping hazard when it freezes. Regular gutter cleaning and extending spouts away from traffic areas can prevent this from happening.

>> **Cracked driveway.** Misdirected and clogged gutter spouts can cause driveways and sidewalks to sag and crack over time.

>> **Washed-out landscaping.** Excess water from clogged gutters can kill newly installed plants, grass, or trees and cause severe erosion, prematurely ending young plantings.

>> **Wood-destroying insects.** Bugs are attracted to moisture. Keeping gutters clear and the soil around the foundation dry can discourage insects from feasting on damp wood.

For these reasons and even more, it's important to keep your gutters clean and free-flowing.

Cleaning gutters and downspouts

If your gutters are due for a good cleaning, keep these tips in mind.

>> **Prioritize safety:** If you're not comfortable with heights or don't regularly use tall ladders, it's best to avoid cleaning the gutters yourself. Consider hiring a handyman for assistance. If you choose to do it yourself, be cautious of potential hazards like electric lines and bees' nests.

>> **Clean the gutters:** Using a ladder, work gloves, and a hose, start cleaning the gutters from one end to the other. Always work from the ladder, not the roof, to prevent falls. Tighten any loose gutter sections as you progress.

TIP

Most gutters are attached to the house using *gutter spikes*, long nails that pass through the gutters and into the wood fascia behind it. If the gutters are loose, replace the gutter spikes with *gutter screws* — long lag screws that can be tightened securely in place and will never loosen up.

>> **Spray out spouts:** When you reach the end of the gutter with the spout, use the hose to spray down the gutter spout to ensure it's clear. If the spout is clogged, it can lead to water backup and problems. Clearing clogged spouts may involve removing debris from both ends and flushing the rest with a hose. If this doesn't work, you might need to disassemble the spout for a thorough clearing. After clearing the spouts, make sure the discharge end extends at least 4 to 6 feet away from the house to prevent issues.

TIP

I haven't personally cleaned the gutters on my home in over 10 years. Before you think I'm neglecting an important task or found the world's most effective gutter guard, I haven't. The reason is simple: a decade ago, I upgraded my standard 5-inch gutters to 6-inch ones.

While the shift from 5-inch to 6-inch gutters may seem like a minor change, it's actually significant. The larger 6-inch gutters can handle approximately 50 percent more water than the standard 5-inch ones. What's even more crucial is the transformation in the downspouts, which grow from 2 inches by 3 inches to 3 inches by 4 inches. This substantial increase allows most leaves, pine needles, and other debris to pass through without causing blockages. As a result, I've been spared the chore of regularly cleaning my gutters.

Maintaining gutter-protection systems

The whole idea of gutter-protection systems is that you don't have to get up on a ladder and scoop the glop out of the gutters every fall. As a result, there are literally dozens of gutter covers on the market, all claiming to keep your feet firmly on the ground.

SOLAR PANELS: LET THE SUNSHINE THROUGH

Harnessing the power of the sun through solar panels is an increasingly smart and eco-friendly investment. To make your solar panels operate efficiently and thus generate the maximum power you're expecting, it's important to keep them clean and unobstructed.

- Dust, dirt, and debris can accumulate on the surface of your solar panels, which slows sunlight absorption. Clean the panels regularly with a soft brush or sponge and a mild detergent. Avoid abrasive materials to prevent scratching.

- Overhanging branches or foliage can cast shadows on your solar panels and reduce their efficiency. Trim trees to ensure maximum exposure to sunlight.

- Birds, insects, and rodents may find the space beneath your solar panels appealing for nesting. Check for signs of pests and take appropriate measures like adding mesh around the panel to deter them without causing harm to the animals.

Keep in mind that working on a roof is difficult and dangerous work. Think carefully before taking on this project yourself!

In my experience, the most effective gutter guards are either flat mesh guards with numerous tiny holes, allowing water to flow through while keeping leaves out, or *micro-mesh* — a finely woven stainless-steel mesh that prevents even the smallest pine needles from entering your gutters. While these guards perform well, it's important not to be misled into thinking you'll never have to take any further action. Eventually, all gutter covers need to be removed, and debris must be scooped out.

WARNING

Gutter guard companies are known for aggressive sales tactics and exorbitant prices. A nationwide survey uncovered instances where consumers were charged anywhere from $1.16 to $90 per foot for comparable products. Don't become a victim. Instead of dealing with these high-pressure salespeople, consider purchasing micro-mesh or perforated gutter guards directly from home centers or big box stores such as Costco; then hire a handyman to handle the installation.

Siding: A Raincoat to Keep You Dry

Just like a good jacket, siding serves as the outer layer of your house, protecting it from the rigors of nature and the force of the elements. But even the best of jackets can develop a tear, and the same can happen to siding. Wind can tear away siding sections, which can lead to water penetration, which can, in turn, lead to rot, mold, and an invasion of wood-destroying insects intent on making a meal of your house. Weather can range from intense sunshine to sub-zero temperatures, with all wreaking havoc on siding surfaces. While all siding is subject to wear and tear, some types need more maintenance than others to stay secure and protective of your humble abode.

Vinyl siding

Vinyl siding stands out as one of the most popular choices for home exteriors, due to its aesthetics, durability, and affordability. Homeowners appreciate its long-term protection and minimal maintenance requirements. However, despite its resilience, continuous exposure to the elements necessitates occasional attention. Here are common maintenance tasks associated with vinyl siding.

>> **Repairing loose pieces:** High winds can occasionally dislodge sections of vinyl siding. Repairing this issue is often straightforward, involving the simple snapping back into place of the loosened pieces.

>> **Dealing with wavy or buckled siding:** If your vinyl siding appears wavy, particularly on the south or west sides, improper installation may be the cause. Vinyl siding is designed to be installed loosely to accommodate its high expansion and contraction rate. Correct installation involves allowing the siding to slide back and forth. If the siding is nailed too tightly, especially on warmer sides of the house, it may buckle. The only remedy for this is to remove and reinstall the siding properly. Fortunately, while it may affect the appearance, wavy siding typically does not lead to leaks.

>> **Painting vinyl siding:** Although vinyl siding does not require painting, advancements in paint coatings allow for this option. High-quality acrylic latex paints adhere well to vinyl. When choosing colors, consider that darker shades absorb more heat and may contribute to warping in the summer. Brands like Sherwin-Williams offer VinylSafe® Paint Color lines, with colors proven to work well on vinyl. Adhering to manufacturer guidelines, especially regarding the need for a primer, is crucial for successful paint application.

>> **Cleaning dirty siding:** It's pretty amazing how much dirt floats around in the air, with much of that landing on your siding. Regular pressure washing, ideally once or twice a year, is a wise maintenance practice. However, given vinyl's soft nature, it is essential to use gentle pressure-washer tips designed for tasks like washing cars or cleaning woodwork. Choosing the wrong tip can lead to damage, potentially turning a cleaning task into a siding replacement project.

Because vinyl siding is so prone to warping from heat, extra caution should be taken to keep grills or firepits well away from the siding. If not, it leaves a very distinct "halo" warp pattern in the vinyl, which would need to be replaced.

Stucco surface 'siding'

Stucco is a super-durable surface for your exterior walls. It's a masonry mixture made of Portland cement, sand, lime, and water. It also rivals vinyl siding in popularity, especially in the western United States. Stucco doesn't rot, and compared to other types of siding, it's relatively easy to maintain. It's very porous and holds on to paint better than most other kinds of siding. Also, it's one of the easiest surfaces to prepare and paint. So, if you have stucco, count your blessings.

Caring for cracks

The most challenging stucco maintenance is crack repair. Stucco's tough but brittle surface sometimes can be a drawback. When the house shifts, rigid things crack.

You can turn your home into an interstate road map of ugly, obvious crack repairs if you aren't careful. When it comes to stucco crack repair, less is more. Don't try to patch every crack. Hairline cracks and those that you can't get your fingernail into should not be patched; in fact, paint usually will fill those cracks. Wider cracks (those up to ¼ inch wide) should be filled with a high-quality, exterior-grade, paintable silicone caulk. Have a damp sponge handy to wipe away any excess caulk that escapes.

Just follow these simple steps:

1. **Clean all loose debris from the crack.**

   The V end of an old-fashioned can opener and a vacuum cleaner work wonders here.

2. **Use a paintable silicone caulk — and your finger — to make an invisible repair.**

   Don't use a putty knife, because it prevents you from matching the existing texture. And don't use just any caulk; use the 50-year kind, which really does hold better and longer than the other types.

3. **With a damp sponge, wipe off the excess caulking in all directions.**

4. While the caulk is still wet, place fine texturing sand into the palm of your hand and, holding your hand in front of the caulking, blow across the sand to scatter it onto the surface of the damp caulk.

The sand makes the patch less obvious and prevents the road-map effect by helping the caulk blend into the surrounding finish.

TIP

I've always found that my finger makes a pretty good trowel when I'm trying to press acrylic latex caulk into a crack. But try that with silicone caulk, and you'll find your finger's pretty darn useless as the caulk sticks to it. The solution is to dip your trowel-finger in dish soap before smoothing the caulk. It works like a charm!

Taking a chunk out of gouges

You can repair wider cracks and gouges with a stucco patching compound. Follow mixing instructions carefully because the amount of water you use can change the properties of the compound. If the properties of the compound change, it may not hold as well.

Follow these steps:

1. Clean all loose debris from the crack or gouge.

2. Use a latex patching product and a putty knife or trowel to fill the area.

3. Apply a second coat to match the surface texture.

Thin the patching compound to a pancake-batter consistency. Dip the end of a paintbrush into the mixture. Holding your hand between the wall and the paintbrush, slap the handle of the brush against your hand. The patching compound splatters onto the surface, matching the texture of the stucco. If the texture is flat, wait for the splattering to become slightly firm and then wipe it to the desired flatness with a putty knife or a trowel.

Painting stucco

To paint stucco, use a thick-roller for small jobs; for larger jobs, use an airless sprayer. A brush is not recommended for painting stucco, but you can use one to add texture: After you spray the paint onto the surface, use a deep-nap roller (¾ inch to 1 inch) to work the paint into the surface and to achieve a uniform texture.

Although one coat may do the trick, stucco usually will require two coats, due to its high level of absorption and to conceal cracks and other repairs.

Wood siding

Wood siding includes both pine and cedar, and you'll find it used as shingles, clapboard, panels, or trim. While wood siding is the oldest and most traditional siding, it does require significant regular maintenance.

Managing moisture is key. When wood's moisture content reaches 20 percent to 30 percent, fungi deep within its fibers begin to grow and flourish, causing dreaded wood rot. To prevent wood rot, wood siding and trim needs to be regularly maintained with an application of exterior stain or paint. These materials act as a barrier, preventing water from coming into direct contact with the wood.

Which finish you choose is more than an aesthetic choice. Durability and ease of application are also important factors. Let's dive into to some of the differences:

>> **Exterior wood stain** provides UV resistance and prevents moisture absorption into the siding. It contains pigments mixed into the finish, and there are three transparency levels to consider: clear, semi-transparent, and solid color. Clear is entirely transparent, adding no color to the siding. Semi-transparent includes enough pigment for color variations within the siding. Solid color has the most pigment, offering superior protection, which makes it my preferred choice for exterior wood stain. It's important not to confuse solid-color stain with a painted surface; the beauty of the wood grain still shines through. Unlike paint, as stain fades over time, it does not crack and peel.

>> **Paint** penetrates and protects similarly to stain but coats the wood surface with a thin, durable, waterproof layer. While paint lasts longer, it is more challenging to apply and is prone to issues like chipping, splitting, and blistering.

TIP

As the saying goes, you get what you pay for. Given that 75 percent of the painting (or staining) process is preparation, using anything other than the best paint means you'll likely need to repaint sooner. Consider this an investment with a cost-per-year perspective. Although the labor for preparation and painting remains constant, the longer the finish lasts, the lower the cost per year. Lower-quality paint may last 3 to 5 years, while a top-quality product can last for 10 years or more.

Preparing painted surfaces

To prepare wooden surfaces for repainting, follow these steps:

1. **Completely remove all old loose paint and sand the spots where a painted surface meets a bare spot.**

If your home was built before 1978, it may have been painted with lead paint, exposure to which can be harmful to children. Sanding, scraping, or otherwise striping lead paint is a job that should be left to professionals. Step one is to test the paint to determine what you have. If it is lead-based, it's time to call in a pro.

A new coat of paint won't stick any better than the old paint below it; that's why removing all loose paint is so important, and tapering or feathering these transition points makes them less visible and guarantees a nicer-looking finished product.

2. **Prime all bare spots with a high-grade primer.**

   Tinting a standard white primer a shade or two lighter than the finish coat can improve coverage. For example, a light-brown finish coat covers a beige primer more effectively than it covers a white primer.

3. **Caulk all joints, as well as the seams around windows and doors, with a high-grade, 50-year, paintable silicone or polyurethane product.**

   Doing so prevents water from getting behind the wood siding.

Now you're ready to paint.

Fiber cement siding

In my view, fiber cement siding stands out as the most resilient of all siding options. Popularized by the JamesHardie™ company, this siding closely mimics the appearance of wood clapboard or shingle siding but is composed of cement, sand, and cellulose fibers. The combination of these materials results in an exceptional surface that not only enhances the aesthetic appeal of homes but also provides outstanding protection. This siding is available as a plank, shingle, or vertical panel. Fiber cement siding needs very little maintenance. An occasional gentle power washing to strip away dirt is all that's required.

When I built a detached two-car garage next to my own historic 1886 home, I wanted a siding that would match the traditional cedar shingles we had on the house. I chose a composite JamesHardie™ product called Hardie® Shingle. It came prefinished and looks as good today as the day it was first installed — over 20 years ago!

Chapter **6**

Windows, Exterior Doors, and Insulation

Most home-maintenance projects save you money over time, but only a few produce an immediate and measurable return. Maintaining your home's energy envelope is one such project. The floors, walls, ceilings, doors, and windows of your home combine to make up its *energy envelope*. When the energy envelope is properly maintained, not only does your personal comfort level reap the benefits as you are better protected from the elements, but it also leads to a noticeable reduction in heating and cooling costs.

Improving your home's insulation, windows, and doors is crucial for reducing energy costs and enhancing comfort. However, determining which enhancement offers the best return on investment isn't always straightforward. Complicating matters, many contractors in this field tend to exaggerate the energy savings resulting from their work.

For example, during my early days as a syndicated home improvement radio host, a station carrying our show asked me to voice a commercial promoting new windows for an advertiser. While I'm generally willing to do so, I always insist that the script accurately represents a product's features and benefits. Shortly after, I received a script claiming that homeowners would save "50 percent on their energy bills" by installing these windows! I pointed out to the station that such savings might be true if you had no windows to begin with. I made it clear that if they wanted me to proceed, a thorough rewrite and a sincere consideration of the importance of truth in advertising were necessary.

If this sounds frustrating, that's because it is. However, you don't have to guess or take the word of profit-motivated contractors to find out which energy-saving improvements pay off. A home energy audit can help you make smart decisions, and you can even do it yourself! (Check out the sidebar, "Home Energy Audits: First Step to Comfort and Savings," later in this chapter.)

Saving Energy with Insulation

If your home is like most, your attic and exterior walls are insulated. If you're really lucky, you also have insulated floors. But if your home is at least 20 years old, your insulation is probably due for some updates to maintain its energy efficiency. How will you know? Well, if you're uncomfortable, that's a clue. The good news is that insulation is pretty to maintain, as the following sections explain.

TIP

A couple of years ago, I upgraded my outdated and highly inefficient gas boiler to a high-efficiency tankless "combi" boiler that handles both heating and hot water. The original boiler, typical of those over 30 years old, was constructed from cast iron and got pretty hot during operation. It was situated in my basement, which was connected to a spacious crawl space.

Following the installation of the new boiler, I was puzzled as to why my first floor remained uncomfortably cold. Then it dawned on me: The old boiler was so inefficient that it was unintentionally heating the entire underside of my *uninsulated* first floor from the basement! Once I took on the project of insulating the crawl space, the first floor became comfortably warm, and the gas bills plummeted to a fraction of what I had previously paid.

Demystifying insulation: Types and materials

The first step toward improving your current insulation is to take note of the type of insulation your home has, as well as the specific insulation material.

Insulation types

Insulation comes in many shapes and sizes, covering a variety of applications. Here's an overview of the most common types and uses:

>> **Batt insulation:** Insulating fibers are woven together to create a continuous blanket of material — a "batt." Batt insulation is available in 16- and 24-inch-wide rolls (or 4-foot strips) to fit standard spacing between ceiling and wall framing members. It is also either *faced* (with a thin vapor barrier attached to one side) or *unfaced* (with just a raw batt).

TIP

When installing batt insulation, always place the side with the backing toward the heated side of your home. For example, with ceilings, the backing faces down, and with floors, the backing faces up. If you're adding additional insulation overtop existing insulation, use unfaced insulation to avoid trapping moisture between the old and new layers.

>> **Loose-fill insulation:** This kind of insulation is made out of small, individual chunks of fibers. It's also known as *blown insulation* because it's installed with a *blower*, a giant vacuum cleaner that works in reverse. Loose fill is useful in spaces that are difficult to get to, like an attic constructed with trusses or minimal head room.

>> **Rigid foam-board insulation:** Rigid insulation is produced in 4-foot by 8-foot sheets and typically installed over walls, floors, or roofs as an additional layer of insulation. These boards are formed from a variety of insulating materials including polyurethane, polyisocyanurate (also called *polyiso*), and extruded polystyrene. Some include a reflective foil facing and all are available in varying thicknesses and *R-values* — the measure of an insulation's resistance to heat transfer).

>> **Radiant barrier insulation:** A popular option for homes in southern states, radiant barrier insulation uses a material that reflects radiant heat. It's typically installed in attics to minimize the absorption of radiant heat and, in turn, to reduce summer heat gain in order to lower your cooling expenses. According to the Department of Energy, certain studies indicate that the use of radiant barriers can lead to a 5 to 10 percent reduction in cooling costs in warm, sunny climates. However, it is generally more economical to enhance batt or blown-in insulation, rather than adding a radiant barrier.

>> **Duct insulation:** Used to surround HVAC ducts, this insulation is soft and pliable. It's 1 inch thick, comes in 1-foot-wide rolls, and is specifically made to be corkscrew-wrapped around ducting.

>> **Pipe insulation:** Preformed, tubular foam or fiberglass pipe insulation is often used to insulate water or heating pipes. This material is available in a variety of diameters to match standard pipe sizes. It's typically sold in 3- to 6-foot lengths and is easy to cut with scissors or a razor knife. Each section of insulation is split lengthwise to ensure quick installation.

Insulation materials

Many of the insulation types noted here are available in a variety of materials. Here's an overview of the most common ones.

>> **Fiberglass insulation:** This is the most popular and widely available type of insulation. It's an effective insulator, and you can buy it as either batts or loose fill. It's relatively inexpensive, and the batts are very easy to install. It's nonflammable and resists damage from water.

TIP

Traditional fiberglass insulation can irritate your skin and lungs, so it's important to take precautions while handling it, like wearing a dust mask, protective clothing, safety glasses, and a hat. However, Owens Corning recently developed a new type of fiberglass insulation called PINK Next Gen, which has eliminated virtually all of the unpleasant aspects of working with traditional fiberglass. Owens Corning PINK Next Gen™ Fiberglas™ insulation is made with advanced fiber technology, resulting in a soft texture that resists shedding and feels much like cotton.

>> **Stone wool insulation:** Commonly known as mineral wool, ROCKWOOL®, or Thermafiber®, stone wool insulation is created by spinning super-heated molten rock and minerals with steel slag to create a cotton-candy-like wool product. The result is a highly effective insulator that also absorbs sound and is both moisture and fire resistant.

>> **Spray-foam insulation:** This is perhaps the most effective insulation available. Made from a two-part polyurethane and mixed on-site by the applicator, not only is spray foam an efficient insulator, but the expanding foam also seals virtually every gap, crack, or crevice, thus eliminating drafts and wasted energy. While spray foam is a great choice for new homes, it's also an effective insulator for existing homes, with the only limitation being that it can only be installed into an open wall, floor, or roof cavity.

>> **Cellulose insulation:** This is an organic, loose-fill material made from recycled paper that has been chemically treated to resist moisture, fire and pests. Frequently installed as a blown insulation for existing older home walls, cellulose insulation often settles inside the walls, leaving large sections of the wall uninsulated.

TIP

If you have cellulose insulation in your walls or ceilings, it's likely to have settled, reducing the insulation value substantially since it was first installed. The degree of any such settlement can be determined by an infrared scan, a technique commonly used by energy auditors that can identify cold (uninsulated) versus warm (insulated) areas of a wall. When loose-fill insulation compacts in walls, it should be vacuumed out so that fresh insulation can be added.

WARNING

Some insulation is manufactured with formaldehyde. When buying insulation, check to ensure that the insulation you choose does *not* contain this nasty chemical.

HOME ENERGY AUDITS: FIRST STEP TO COMFORT AND SAVINGS

A home energy audit is the best first step to identify improvements that bring genuine energy savings and comfort. Available at no cost from many utility companies and for a fee from trained, experienced technicians, home energy audits can identify the locations and severity of energy losses within your home, recommend specific improvements, and even calculate how long it would take to recoup improvement expenses through lower energy bills.

Properly equipped and well trained, professional home energy auditors use tools like blower doors, duct blasters, and infrared thermographs to take the guesswork out of identifying places where your home is losing energy. Whether you are considering replacing windows or doors, upgrading heating systems, or improving insulation, a professional home energy audit provides insights and recommendations that you'll need to make an informed decision.

While a do-it-yourself (DIY) energy assessment may not be as thorough as a professional audit, it helps narrow down areas for improvement. The U.S. Department of Energy has an Energy Savers website at www.energysavers.gov that offers a comprehensive checklist to aid homeowners in their energy assessments, covering aspects like

- Identifying and sealing air leaks
- Reviewing ventilation
- Checking insulation levels
- Inspecting heating and cooling systems
- Optimizing lighting
- Evaluating appliances and electronics
- Planning for energy-saving improvements

A DIY energy audit can work for you if you only want to focus on the essential areas, but opting for a professional assessment is a wise move if you think you need a thorough energy analysis before committing to any major home improvements.

Understanding R-values

Insulation *R-values* are a measure of an insulation's resistance to heat transfer. The higher the R number, the better the insulation value. Recommended R-values vary widely between climate zones, with more northern states requiring higher

R-Values than southern states. They also vary between walls, floors, and ceilings. For example, an R-value of 11 (R-11) may be recommended for your floor, your walls may need R-13, and your attic may need R-38.

Over the years, insulation requirements in homes have changed. R-19 was once sufficient for use in attics, while today, R-38 is recommended for most climates. In extreme climates, R-60 may be necessary.

The U.S. Department of Energy's Energy Star website (at www.energystar.gov) is an excellent resource to find out what level of insulation is recommended for your part of the country.

Finding out where to add insulation around your house

My two-story home was built in 1886, but it has a "newer" one-story kitchen addition — that part was built in 1901! Because the addition was more exposed than the rest of the house, it was always 10 to 15 degrees colder in the winter and warmer in the summer. Several years ago, we were ready for a roof replacement, and I knew that would be the time to solve my uncomfortable kitchen problem by adding spray foam insulation.

Working together like a well-rehearsed ballet, my roofers removed the old roof and sheathing, and my spray foam applicators worked right behind them applying the insulation to the open ceiling cavities, before the roofers returned to install the new roofing. The next day, I walked into a kitchen that, for the first time in over 100 years, was the same temperate as the rest of the house! _That's_ the power of insulation.

Oh where, oh where does my energy go? Insulating attics, walls, and floors!

When it's done well, nothing keeps on working — for free — like insulation. In this section, I walk you through all the parts of your home that should be insulated and tell you how to fill in the gaps.

WHERE TO START: THE ATTIC

If your home just doesn't seem to stay warm, the attic is the first place you should look. As we all learned in grade school, heat rises. In a house, that means most heat is lost through the ceiling, and most homes simply don't have enough insulation.

How much insulation do you actually need? Insulation levels vary based on climate. To find out how much you need in your part of the country, open a browser and type **energy star how much insulation do I need?** This will return specific sections of the U.S. Department of Energy's Energy Star website (www.energy star.gov), where you can look up the recommendation for your area.

Replenishing sagging or settled insulation or just adding more is a simple DIY project:

1. **Grab a ruler or tape measure and head up to your attic.**

2. **Measure the depth of the insulation you have now and compare that to the recommended amount listed by Energy Star to figure out how much additional insulation you'll need.**

3. **Most homes have fiberglass insulation, so if that's what you find in your attic, purchase unfaced fiberglass batt insulation and lay it perpendicular to existing insulation and completely cover the original layer.**

TIP

Keep in mind that insulation only works when it's fluffy. If you plan to use your attic for storage, don't pile things on top of the insulation. Instead, select a dedicated area for storage near the attic hatch and only use as much insulation there as will fit below the attic floor.

And speaking of the attic hatch, remember that heat rises! Make sure you also add weatherstripping around the hatch and insulate the back of it to prevent energy loss in that area.

4. **Enjoy your newly insulated, energy efficient, and comfortable home!**

WARNING

When adding insulation to an attic floor, be sure to keep it clear of recessed light fixtures. Unless they are specifically rated IC (for *insulation contact*), light fixtures covered with insulation can overheat and result in a fire.

Also, don't block your attic vents. Good attic ventilation is essential to reduce heat load in the summer and moisture buildup in the winter, which renders insulation far less effective and can lead to mold and mildew growing on the underside of your roof.

THE EXTERIOR WALLS

Adding insulation to an existing exterior wall is much more difficult than adding it to an attic (see the preceding section) because in a wall, the insulation is hidden between the interior and exterior wallcoverings. Opening up walls to insulate the wall cavity just isn't cost effective. It's cheaper and easier to create small penetrations in the wall so that the insulation can be blown in. For that reason, blown insulation is usually the preferred choice when you have to re-insulate a completed wall, and is a job best left to a pro.

As I just noted, if you already have blown insulation in your exterior walls and are still uncomfortable, it's worth having an infrared scan done of your home's exterior walls to identify areas where the insulation may have settled.

TIP

Gaps, cracks, and crevices around windows and doors can lead to as much (if not more) heat loss as an exterior wall. These tiny spaces are common entry points for outside air and can allow for big energy loss, letting in cold air in winter and hot air during summer. Caulking and weatherstripping can play an important role in preventing these drafts, ultimately reducing heat loss and improving your comfort. To find drafts, here's a trick-of-the-trade: Run the back of your hand along the perimeter of the windows or door. The backs of our hands are much more temperature sensitive than our palms. If drafts are sneaking in, they'll be easy to find, and you'll know where to focus your efforts to seal these spaces.

THE FLOOR

If you hate cold floors and want to keep your tootsies toasty, floor insulation is your friend. Aside from improving your comfort, floor insulation substantially reduces the loss of heat and also helps to eliminate mildew- and rot-causing condensation. If you have hardwood floors, you should be especially interested in maintaining your floor insulation because lack of floor insulation can cause planks of hardwood flooring to twist, buckle, and curl.

If your home is built on a crawl space or unfinished basement, periodically check the condition of the floor insulation to ensure that it's properly positioned. Here, sagging is the biggest problem.

Floor insulation is normally held in place with netting or bailing wire attached from one joist-bottom to another. If the insulation netting sags, you need to reattach it or replace it:

>> **To reattach insulation netting,** you can use nails or staples. Nails hold better but are hard to drive in tight spots. Staples are easier to install, but you may need to buy a *hammer tacker* — a construction-grade staple gun that you can find at your local hardware store or home center. If the vapor barrier has become brittle and tears, you can staple or nail directly through the insulation.

>> **To replace insulation netting,** wire insulation supports (also called *lightning rods* due to their speedy installation) are a handy alternative to netting or bailing wire. These lightweight, flexible steel rods hold the insulation in place through spring tension. Just place one end of the rod against the side of a floor joist and bend it slightly so that the other end is forced into place against the face of the opposite joist. (See Figure 6-1.) Use one hand to hold up the insulation and the other hand to whip the lightning rod into place.

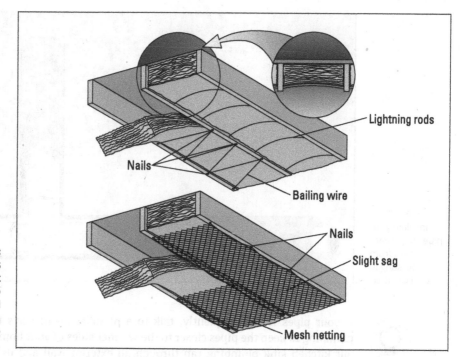

FIGURE 6-1:
Lightning rods
are a great
alternative to
traditional
insulation netting,
but both do
the job.

Lightning rods

Nails

Bailing wire

Nails

Slight sag

Mesh netting

Insulating water pipes

Insulating accessible water pipes in unheated spaces like crawl spaces and attics (see Figure 6-2) saves energy and prevents pipes from freezing and breaking during very cold weather. It's also cheap insurance. A burst pipe can spew water for hours or days until it's discovered. I once was asked to inspect a vacant home just a day before it was scheduled to be sold to a new buyer. When I opened the door to this bi-level, I found the lower level had been converted to a swimming pool thanks to a water pipe that froze and broke days earlier!

Adding pipe insulation is a simple DIY project. Just slip the foam insulation tubes around the pipe and use electrical tape to hold them in place. A serrated knife is a very handy tool for cutting foam insulation to the right length. When you come to a corner, make a 45-degree miter joint so that the insulation covers all sides of the pipe.

WARNING

Heat tape is a heating appliance that is used to prevent water pipes from freezing during periods of very cold weather, and also to thaw them. If you've installed heat tape, don't insulate over the heat tape. Doing so can cause the tape to overheat and cause a fire. It's also important to note that heat tape must never be left "on" all the time. It should only be used temporarily.

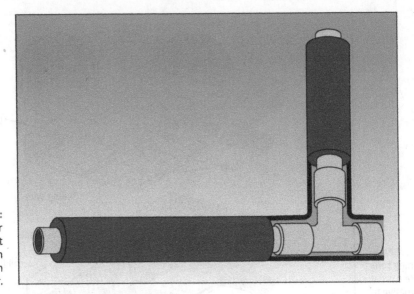

FIGURE 6-2:
Insulate your
pipes to prevent
them from
bursting in
cold weather.

TIP

If your pipes freeze frequently, talk to a plumber about ways to re-route the plumbing to keep the pipes closer to the warmer sides of your home. For example, our kitchen sink plumbing ran through an exterior wall and used to freeze up more than I liked. To solve the problem, I replaced the pipes with PEX (flexible, plastic supply pipe), which I ran from the basement into the bottom of the sink cabinet, where the warmth of the house successfully kept it from freezing ever again.

Insulating HVAC ducts

As with other kinds of insulation, the material that surrounds your heat ducts reduces energy costs while improving the effectiveness of your central heating and cooling system. It also helps prevent unwanted condensation in attics and crawl spaces, thereby reducing the chance for mold, mildew, and the foul odors associated with them.

REATTACHING AND ADJUSTING INSULATION

Insulation is either wrapped around and around the duct in a corkscrew fashion (see Figure 6-3) for metal ducting or built into flexible ducts. Air currents, rodents, house movement, and vibration in the heating system can cause the insulation to loosen and fall away from the ducting. For metal ducts, reattaching or adjusting the insulation to cover the ducting is a good thing. While you're there, add an extra layer — it couldn't hurt.

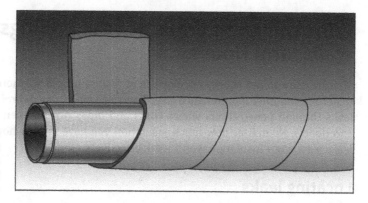

FIGURE 6-3:
Heat-duct
insulation keeps
your energy
costs low.

With *flex ducts* (short for flexible ductwork), a thin layer of plastic acts as a vapor barrier, surrounding modern insulated ducts and preventing moisture from attacking the insulation and the ducting. If the thin plastic vapor barrier becomes damaged, you can use plastic sheeting (of any kind) and metal duct tape to fix the barrier.

TIP

Surprisingly, most so-called duct tape is actually not recommended for ducts! Most duct tape adhesive dries out and the tape falls off the ducts, resulting in air leaks that waste energy. Instead, look for UL 181 tape. This shiny, sturdy duct tape has a heat-resistant adhesive and won't easily separate from the metal duct seams that it's sealing.

PERFORMING A DUCT LEAK TEST

Leaking HVAC ducts, caused by loose duct tape, disconnected ducts, or simply a poor installation, can substantially increase your energy bill. Therefore, checking for duct leaks can pay off big time. However, because most ducting is covered with insulation, leaks can be hard to find.

Here are a few signs that may indicate a leak:

» Ducting that is crushed or badly bent

» Insulation that has darkened

» An area around the ducting that is warmer than normal in the winter or cooler than normal in the summer

A duct leak test, performed by an energy auditor, can determine the extent of this problem. To perform a duct leak test, the energy auditor will cap off all supply registers and pressurize the duct system. If pressure loss occurs, a contractor can use a specialized non-staining smoke to find and repair the leak.

Controlling air leaks in your ceilings, walls, and floors

There's more to the energy envelope than maintaining insulation. You also need to perform another maintenance step, known as *infiltration control* (controlling air leaks through penetrations where wires and pipes run between ceilings, walls, and floors). No matter how much insulation you have in your home, if major air leaks exist, your insulation won't work effectively.

Locating leaks

Unwanted air can leak into your home from all sorts of places: weather stripping; door and window frames; attic and sub-area plumbing and electrical penetrations; heat registers; and, yes, even electrical switches and receptacles. Infiltration also occurs where pipes and wires in walls penetrate into the attic or sub-area.

Here are some tips for finding leaks in different areas of your home.

>> **In an attic or crawl space:** Finding a penetration in an attic or crawl space isn't terribly difficult when it comes to plumbing pipes, flues and ventilation, and heating ducts. Just check the point where a pipe or duct runs through the ceiling or floor and look for gaps.

>> **Around wiring:** Finding penetrations around wiring — especially in an insulated area — is a challenge. Short of removing the insulation, you can't see where penetrations exist because the wiring normally doesn't stick up beyond the insulation like a pipe or a flue does. Therefore, you have to search through insulation until you find a point where a wire travels down through the top of a wall.

>> **In walls, ceilings, and floors:** The amount of infiltration from walls, ceilings, and floors is simply amazing. Fortunately, you can easily locate these leaks in the myriad of places that they occur: around light switches, electric receptacles, drain and water pipes, heat registers, thermostats, wall and ceiling light fixtures, smoke and carbon monoxide detectors, floor receptacles, doorbell chimes, doors, and windows. To find leaks, pick up a handy tool called a *Smoke Pencil* (www.smokepencil.com). The smoke pencil emits a non-toxic fog in small puffs. Use it to pinpoint leaks around windows, doors, pipes, wires, or other areas where leaks are suspected.

>> **Around windows and doors:** When it comes to leaks, doors and windows are major culprits. Even the slightest seasonal house shift can cause a previously

well-maintained and properly adjusted door or window to leak like a sieve. Check the weatherstripping on doors and windows twice each year: once during mid-spring and again during mid-winter to avoid energy loss. Here's an easy way to check for air leaks at the bottom of a door: At night, and from the outside of the door, point a flashlight toward the bottom of the door. If light can be seen from inside, an adjustment is needed.

Stopping infiltration

In the past, we used to address drafts by filling small cracks (no wider than ¼ inch) with caulking. For larger gaps, we would use insulation or steel wool, and for the biggest holes, we used tin plates or wood covers.

Nowadays, a more convenient solution is available: expanding polyurethane spray foam in a can. Gone are the days of laboriously installing tin plates or replacing fallen insulation or steel wool. With this innovation, you simply spray a bit of expanding foam into the gap, and it promptly expands to permanently seal the hole. (See Figure 6-4.) It's like home maintenance in a can — an ingenious invention!

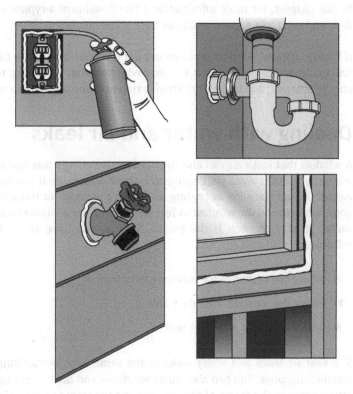

FIGURE 6-4: Stopping air infiltration with spray foam.

Where polyurethane spray is now best for large gaps, then and now, caulking is still best for narrow cracks. The kind of caulking to use depends on the area being caulked. Glass, metal, wood, plastic, and other surfaces respond differently to caulk. Caulk made for exterior surfaces has more UV resistance, while caulks made for a kitchen or bath provide more mildew resistance. Read the manufacturer's label carefully before making your purchase.

Another easy infiltration-control method is installing precut gaskets behind the cover plates of electrical switches and outlets. The gasket material consists of a thin foam and effectively stops drafts that manage to get into exterior walls.

Looking at Windows: See the Light, Feel the Cold

As beautiful as they are, most windows aren't as energy efficient as an insulated wall. Unfortunately, you can't see through a wall. The R-value (insulation value) of a typical wall is about R-13. (See the section, "Understanding R-values," earlier in this chapter, for more information.) The R-value of a typical window is about R-2, and even triple-pane windows have a low insulation value.

If highly efficient window replacement isn't in your immediate future, here are a few maintenance suggestions for your windows that will make them a bit more energy efficient, add longevity to their existence, and make them easier to operate.

Dealing with water and air leaks

A window that leaks air can also mean excessive energy loss and cost. Summer or winter, you don't want your house to leak air, especially if you spend your hard-earned dollars warming or cooling it. To test a window for leaks, wave the back of your hand around the window to feel for leaks or use a Smoke Pencil, as described earlier in this chapter. If the smoke flickers, you have an air leak. Check the following:

>> Where one section of the window meets another

>> Where the windows meet the frame

>> Where the frame meets the wall

You seal air leaks and water leaks in the same way: by caulking and replacing weatherstripping. You can also inject window- and door-rated spray foam insulation between the frame of the window and the frame of the house.

Caulking

Water leaks at a window often result from a breakdown in the connection between the window frame and the wall. To prevent leaks, caulk the window where it meets the exterior siding. (See Figure 6-5.) If the window is surrounded by wood trim, use a high-grade silicone caulk to seal all gaps between the trim and the siding (and the trim and the window).

TIP

Take special care to seal the top side of the top piece of trim. Puddling water at this location causes many window leaks.

FIGURE 6-5:
Caulking an outside window.

Expanding spray foam

If you're willing to remove either your exterior or interior window trim, you can do a much better job of sealing window and door leaks — permanently! — than you can with just caulk. Using expanding foam not only prevents air infiltration, but it also makes the treated area watertight.

TIP

Polyurethane spray foam comes in two different formulations. Standard spray foam expands rapidly and dries hard. On the other hand, foam intended for use around windows and doors expands slowly and dries to a soft, cushy consistency. Choosing the right product is important. If you were to use standard spray foam around a window or door, the strong expansion could cause the jambs to move inward, preventing proper opening.

Here's how to insulate around your windows and doors using spray foam:

1. Use a pry bar and a hammer to remove the window trim (either inside or outside — not both).

2. **Fill the void with expanding window- and door-rated spray foam in a can.**

   Don't worry about overfilling. Let it bulge out of the wall. What you don't want to do is touch the foam while it's wet; you'll make a huge, hard-to-clean-up mess.

3. **After the foam dries (it'll take several hours), use a razor knife to cut off the excess.**

4. **Replace the trim in the reverse order in which you removed it and touch up the paint as necessary.**

Weatherstripping

Leaks also occur when weatherstripping wears out. You may have to remove the operable portion of the window to find the weatherstripping:

>> **For sliding windows,** open them halfway and lift the window out of the bottom track. Then pull the window out of the opening, bottom first.

>> **For single-hung windows (windows with one sliding sash),** usually you just release a lever on the side track(s) of the window frame. Contact the manufacturer for specific instructions.

>> **For older double-hung windows (windows with two sliding sashes),** weatherstrip the areas where the window seals against the bottom windowsill.

After you remove the operable portion of the window, it becomes pretty obvious where the weatherstripping is and how it has to be replaced. Most home centers offer replacement weatherstripping in peel-and-stick rolls. If you aren't sure about what to do, take the section that you removed to the store with you or photograph the area that needs attention. A picture is definitely worth a thousand words!

You may need an adhesive solvent to unstick old weatherstripping. Adhesive solvent is available in spray cans for easy application.

WARNING

Adhesive solvent can be pretty caustic stuff. Read the can to be sure that it won't damage your window frame.

TIP

If you have metal or vinyl frame windows, or even storm windows, check the drain holes at the outside edge of the bottom portion of the window frame. During rain, water can fill the bottom track, leak to the inside of the home, and literally flood the area surrounding the window. Drain or weep holes allow water to escape from the frame, preventing flooding. You can use a piece of wire or a small screwdriver blade to ensure that the holes are clear.

Preventing condensation

If you have windows that seem to drip-drip-drip inside your home even when it's not raining, you've got a condensation problem. Window condensation is most prevalent in cold weather; warm, moist air inside your house hits the cold glass of a window and, as the warm air chills, it releases moisture that drips down to the windowsill and walls below, creating quite a mess!

There are a number of ways to reduce or eliminate condensation:

>> **Sealing air leaks around windows** (see the section, "Dealing with water and air leaks," earlier in this chapter).

>> **Adding cellular window shades or heavy curtains to the windows.** These will reduce the volume of warm air reaching the windows and slow the drips.

>> **Using storm windows.** The extra layer of glass they provide will allow the inside windowpane to remain warmer, reducing the risk of condensation.

>> **Replacing single-pane windows with double-pane "insulated" glass,** which prevents the inside of the glass from getting cold and allowing condensation to form.

TIP

If you have double-pane insulated windows and see fogging between the two sheets of glass, the insulating seal between the insulated glass panes has failed. While this is not repairable and renders your windows somewhat less efficient, it's mostly a cosmetic issue. Replacing the insulated glass is possible but is costly and not usually recommended.

Maintaining storm windows

Storm windows are necessary when you have old, single-pane windows. A *storm window* is nothing more than a second window that improves weather resistance and reduces drafts that too easily find their way past wooden window frames. Storm windows have multiple tracks that include

>> A fixed upper glass pane

>> An operable lower glass pane

>> A screen

In practice, the operable glass pane should be lowered in fall/winter and raised in spring/summer, when the screen is also lowered to provide insect-free fresh air.

TIP

If you have central air conditioning, you might consider keeping the storm windows down during the summer. Those same chilly cold-weather drafts that lead to increased heating costs are replaced by warm drafts in the summer. While not nearly as noticeable, these warm air leaks drive up cooling needs and contribute to higher air conditioning bills.

Storm windows are a holdover from years past when window efficiency didn't exist. If you have them, they're worth maintaining until you decide to upgrade your old wooden windows to modern, energy-efficient ones.

Storm window maintenance is pretty simple:

>> **Check the weep holes.** These are small holes drilled into the windows just above the sill to provide for rainwater drainage and must remain open.

>> **Replace cracked panes.** Leave this task to a pro.

>> **Clean the panes every time you take the windows down or put them back up.** Use standard glass-cleaning methods.

>> **Wipe the frames with lacquer thinner.** Lacquer thinner cleans off the weird aluminum corrosion and shines up the frames.

>> **Periodically (at least once a year), caulk the area between where the frames meet the walls and the sills.** Be sure not to block the weep holes!

Maintaining screens

Window screens are a simple but important component for your home's fresh air ventilation system. Newer, more energy-efficient homes don't allow for the passive exchange of air through cracks, gaps, and penetrations as older homes did. This condition allows for stale air to be trapped within the home. Add in people and pets, cooking, bathing, allergens, along with the fumes coming off furniture, building materials, cleaning products and more, and you'll be dying to throw open the windows to let in some fresh air — which is where screens come in.

Cleaning screens

In order to get a good exchange of air, you have to keep your screens clean. Grit and grime can also hasten deterioration, thereby diminishing the life of a window screen. As if that weren't enough, dirty screens also prevent light from making its way into your home. Finally, a gust of wind can blow dust from a screen straight into your home, aggravating allergies and increasing housekeeping chores.

To clean your screens, remove them from their frames and lay them flat on a smooth, cloth-covered surface, such as an old sheet on a picnic table. Scrub them gently with a soft nylon brush, rinse with a hose, and shake off excess water. It's smart to wash your screens once in the spring and again in the fall. You can also remove the screens and store them for the winter. Doing so will reduce their exposure to the sun and make them last longer.

TIP

Never use a pressure washer to clean window screens. Screen material is delicate, and using a pressure washer will tear a hole right through it.

Patching a screen

Screen patch kits are available at hardware stores and home centers. They're inexpensive and easy to use. (The process takes less than a minute.) You can also use any of the following methods to repair small holes in window screens, depending upon the type of screen material:

» **Apply a small amount of clear nail polish to a small hole or tear in a vinyl or fiberglass screen.** The polish acts as an adhesive, sealing the damaged area.

» **Mend small tears in metal or fiberglass screens with a dab of clear silicone adhesive.** If necessary, dab it on in successive layers until the tear is completely filled.

» **Darn small holes in metal screening.** Simply unravel a strand or two from a piece of scrap screening and sew the hole shut, weaving the strands through the screen fabric with a needle. (See Figure 6-6.)

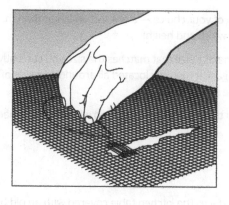 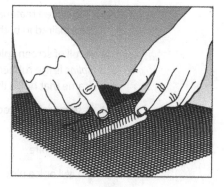

FIGURE 6-6:
Left, sewing a screen; right, patching a hole in a screen.

Large holes in metal screen material take a little more effort. Follow these steps:

1. **Neatly trim the damaged area to a ravel-free square or rectangle using tin snips (metal shears).**

2. **Cut a piece of patch screen material that measures about 1 inch larger (in both directions) than the damaged area.**

3. **Unravel a couple of strands of material around the entire perimeter of the patch; then bend the unraveled ends at each side of the patch at 90 degrees.**

4. **Place the patch over the damaged area and carefully thread the bent wires through the screen fabric (refer to Figure 6-6); then bend the wires flat again to hold the patch in place.**

For large holes in fiberglass screening, simply cut a patch of similar material and affix it to the good material using transparent silicone glue.

Replacing a screen

Whether it's a window or a door, rescreening is easy. Screen material is available in metal and fiberglass. It's also helpful to know that fiberglass screens are available in various thickness. For my home, I always opt for *pet resistant* screening, not because I have pets but because it's a much heavier and more durable screen material.

Rescreening with metal is slightly more difficult than with fiberglass (metal is not as flexible as fiberglass), but metal seems to stretch tighter, and it does last longer. In either case, you'll need the following tools and materials:

>> The screen material of your choice — a few inches larger than the screen to be repaired in both width and height.

>> A roll of screen spline of a size that matches the size you currently have. (The *spline* is the rubber gasket material located all around one side of the screen's frame that holds the screen in place.)

>> A *spline roller* (a tool that is composed of a grip with a rolling wheel at each end).

>> A razor knife.

>> An awl or ice pick.

>> A large, flat work surface. The kitchen table covered with an old blanket or a piece of cardboard works well.

Replacement is pretty easy. Lay the screen, spline side up, on the work surface and then follow these steps:

1. **Poke the awl into the old rubber spline and pull it out of its recess.**

   When enough of the spline has been removed, you can pretty much do the rest by grabbing and pulling.

2. **Remove and discard the old screen.**

3. **Lay the replacement screen centered over the frame.**

4. **At one corner, use your fingers to press the spline material into the spline groove in the frame.**

5. **When an inch or two of the spline is started, use the spline roller to steadily push the spline into its groove around the entire frame. (See Figure 6-7.)**

   Keep the edge of the screen aligned with the frame and do one side first, and then the opposite side. Then do the top and finish with the bottom. Make sure to keep the screen taut. A helper may be in order here.

6. **With the spline in place, cut the end and use the razor knife to remove the excess screen material.**

   Place the razor knife in the outside edge of the spline groove, pointing the tip away from the spline. Gently wipe the razor knife along the groove. It will easily cut away the excess.

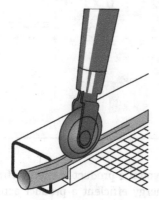

FIGURE 6-7:
Using a spline roller tool.

Buying new windows

If your windows are old and drafty, simply repairing or maintaining them offers a minimal return on your effort. But buying new windows is expensive, and it's often really hard to sort through the many brands and competing claims of energy efficiency they tout.

Here's a simple strategy for window shopping that will help flush out the best possible options for your home:

>> **Look for ENERGY STAR certification.** Administered by the U.S. Environmental Protection Agency (EPA), ENERGY STAR is a voluntary program that establishes minimum energy efficiency standards for various products, including windows. Products meeting these criteria have the option to display the ENERGY STAR logo.

>> **Look for the NFRC label.** The National Fenestration Rating Council (NFRC) is an independent non-profit certification organization and establishes objective ratings for window energy performance across various categories. The NFRC label includes ratings for U-Factor, Solar Heat Gain Coefficient, Visible Transmittance, and Air Leakage. (See Figure 6-8.)

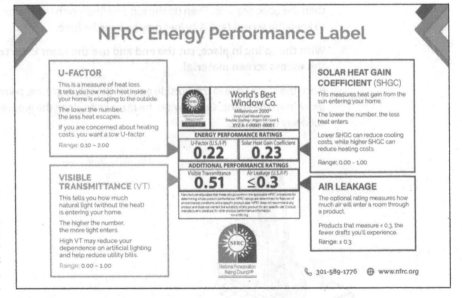

FIGURE 6-8:
The NFRC label provides energy performance ratings in multiple categories to help you compare energy-efficient windows, doors, and skylights.

While the ENERGY STAR label tells you if a product is energy efficient, the NFRC label helps you understand *how* energy efficient a product actually is. Ratings listed on the NFRC labels are a useful tool to compare energy performance for windows (as well as doors and skylights). By using both of these certification standards to identify and compare windows, you'll be able to make an informed choice based on independently verifiable energy saving standards. Learn more at the NFRC website at efficientwindows.org.

TIP

Replacing windows is a costly remodeling project, but there's no need to replace all your windows at once. By replacing windows on one side of your home every year or two, you can spread out the costs. Start with the side that offers the greatest energy savings. If you live in a cold climate and want to reduce heating expenses, start with the north side of your house, then replace east, west, and south sides in subsequent years. For southern climates, reduce cooling costs by replacing south-facing windows first, followed by west, then east and north.

Looking at window installation styles

If you are replacing windows in your home, there are two styles of windows to consider.

>> **Replacement windows:** These windows are custom made to fit inside the jambs of the old window and don't require removal of the exterior window trim. Replacement windows install quickly and easily, with little disturbance of the interior or exterior walls.

>> **New construction windows:** Designed to install into a wall before the exterior siding is added, these include a flange that is nailed to the exterior wall, and then covered with siding and exterior trim. On the inside, window trim and a new sill also need to be added.

TIP

I recommend using replacement windows. You'll achieve a dramatic increase in energy efficiency, with a relatively quick and painless installation.

Getting In and Out: Maintaining Exterior Doors

Doors work hard opening and closing thousands of times a year. Wear and tear, seasonal shifts, and exposure to the elements all add up. That's why exterior doors need a steady stream of maintenance to remain functional and energy efficient.

TIP

If you get tired of the often-backbreaking maintenance that you have to perform to keep your wood front door looking presentable, consider replacing it with a fiberglass door. Today's fiberglass doors feature wood grain patterns and colors identical to the real thing. But, unlike wood, they are five times more energy efficient and some have multi-point locks that are far more secure.

Fixing leaks between the threshold and door bottom

If you notice moisture on the entry floor, it may be due to a leak between the threshold and the bottom of the door. The threshold is the platform, usually made of wood or metal, at the base of the doorway that typically tilts outward to shed water. Most exterior doors have a metal door bottom, or shoe, with a rubber gasket to prevent air and water infiltration. The door shoe is adjustable, allowing for changes in the house structure.

Despite the effectiveness of the door shoe and threshold in preventing leaks, another issue may arise: the threshold itself may leak. During installation, exterior door thresholds are usually sealed with a thick layer of caulk. Occasionally, this caulk may shrink over time, leading to leaks.

To prevent future leaks, you should remove the threshold screws and apply caulking between the threshold and the floor. It's important to warm the caulking first to ensure it flows easily, and a hairdryer can be useful for this purpose. Stop the caulking process when you see the caulking oozing out of the edges.

Stopping air leaks with weatherstripping and sealant

Air leaks in doorframes are a common issue, but you can easily address them by applying foam sealant between the door frame and the house frame. To do this, carefully remove the wood trim covering the joint, using a flat pry bar to avoid damage. Once the trim is off, use expanding spray foam to fill the gap. Don't worry if the foam expands beyond the surface; after it dries in a few hours, you can trim the excess with a knife. After trimming, reinstall the trim and touch up the paint as needed.

WARNING

Make sure to use expanding foam sealant specifically designed for windows and doors. Using standard foam sealant can lead to aggressive expansion, potentially forcing the door jambs inward and sealing the door shut. Window and door sealant remains spongy, providing effective sealing without affecting the door's functionality.

Additionally, check for leaks between the door and the doorframe. Inspect the weatherstripping to ensure it's in good condition and fits tightly when the door is closed. If the existing weatherstripping is worn out, replace it.

Here's how to install new weatherstripping:

1. **While standing outside the door, with the door in the closed position, gently press the rubber portion of the new weatherstripping against the door and the metal strip against the frame — both at the same time.**

2. **While holding the weatherstripping in place, attach the metal section to the frame of the door with the nails or screws provided.**

3. **Weatherstripping features oblong holes that allow fasteners to be placed loosely in the center, enabling the weatherstripping to slide back and forth during installation.** Once the weatherstripping is correctly positioned, the fasteners can be tightened to secure it in place. This design also provides an opportunity to adjust the weatherstripping later on, accommodating any shifts in the door due to house movement.

Caring for and painting wood

Wood and water don't mix. For that reason, exterior doors must be protected (painted or varnished) on a regular basis. Whether painting or applying polyurethane, follow the same process:

1. **Clean the door with TSP.**

   Trisodium phosphate (commonly known as TSP) not only cleans but also etches the finish, creating a surface that the new finish will readily bond to.

2. **Lightly sand imperfections and clean the entire door using a clean, lint-free rag and some paint thinner.**

   You can also use a *tack cloth* (a cloth with a sticky substance that readily collects dust). Tack cloths are great for pre-paint cleaning.

3. **Prime bare spots on painted doors and follow with your chosen finish coat as soon as the primed areas are dry.**

   And don't forget to paint all four edges of the door — top, bottom, hinge side, and strike side. The paint will thoroughly seal the door and prevent it from swelling. (You don't want swelling, unless you really enjoy your door rubbing or sticking.)

TIP

I find it worthwhile to remove the door from the hinges and set it on sawhorses for prep and painting. Just time your work so that after the first coat dries, you still have time to flip the door over and paint the back before you have to reinstall the door for the night.

Finding solutions for sliding glass doors

Have you ever tried to open a sliding glass door and felt resistance, as if the door was pulling back? Unlike traditional exterior doors that swing on hinges, sliding glass doors operate on rollers — small wheels typically made of neoprene or metal. However, these wheels can wear out over time due to regular use. Considering that the wheels on the bottom of a sliding glass door move within a threshold often filled with dirt and sand, it's remarkable that they last more than a year or two.

If you have sliding glass doors, you can ensure their longevity and effortless operation by providing them with some tender care. Regular cleaning and lubrication, along with adjustment or replacement of the rollers as needed, can turn your efforts into a door that opens and closes smoothly. The following sections provide detailed explanations on how to achieve this.

Keeping sliding doors clean and lubricated

Always keep the bottom track of the door clean and free of dirt and sand. In addition, regularly spray the track and the wheels with a waterless silicone spray. The absence of water in the spray reduces the chance for rusty wheels, and the silicone is a colorless lubricant that won't stain or attract dust.

Adjusting (or replacing) the rollers

Just like other doors in the home, a sliding glass door can be knocked out of whack when the house shifts. Adjusting the wheels at the bottom of the door can compensate for this problem. Raising or lowering opposing wheels (located at the underside of each end of the door) can straighten a crooked door, allowing it to close parallel to the doorframe. Raising both wheels evenly can prevent the bottom of the door from rubbing on the track as the wheels wear out and become smaller.

For wheels that are adjustable, simply turn the adjacent screw. In most cases, you'll find a hole at each end of the bottom track of the sliding door through which a screwdriver can be inserted. Use a pry bar to slightly lift the door to take pressure off the wheel while you turn the adjustment screw. If the door is lowered when you wanted to raise it, simply raise the door and turn the screw in the other direction.

Rollers that are completely worn out (or those that can't be adjusted) can be replaced. Open the door about halfway, raise it 1 inch by forcing it into the top track, and, at the same time, pull out on the bottom to remove the door. With the door out of the opening, lay it on sawhorses, snap out the old rollers, and pop in a pair of new ones.

3

Key Systems — Plumbing and HVAC (Heating, Ventilation, and Air Conditioning)

Chapter 7

Plumbing, Part I: Pipes, Water Heaters, Water Softeners, and More

This chapter is devoted to the water delivery system — the water pipes, if you will. They're the thin pipes that run through the walls, basement, crawl-space, carrying water in and out. In contrast, drain, waste, and vent pipes are larger-diameter pipes and are not *pressurized* (filled with water under pressure); you can find out about them in Chapter 9. For the most part, water pipes are hidden in walls, attics, crawl spaces, basements, and below cabinets, and they require little or no maintenance — that is, until they spring a leak or become so clogged that they deliver little more than a trickle. In this chapter, you'll find out how to deal with both of these issues, along with a few other challenges that may pop up from time to time. I'll also tell you about getting the most out of your water heater and water softener.

REMEMBER Don't confuse gas lines with water lines, as they sometimes resemble each other. In older homes, gas lines are often made of the same material as water lines, but gas lines travel from the gas main to fuel-burning appliances such as a water heater, range, furnace, or gas-powered dryer.

Essential Plumbing Preparedness! Turning Off Your Main Water Valve

The first thing to know about your home's plumbing system is how to turn it off if it springs a leak. The best place to start is by finding and labeling your main water valve. This key plumbing system component is what you'd use to stop thousands of gallons of water from flooding your home should a serious leak happen.

Most homes have at least two main water valve locations. The first is typically located in a precast concrete or steel vault in the front yard near the curb or sidewalk in front of your home. It may require a special wrench to open and operate, which is why this "street valve" is really only designed for use by a local water utility company or plumber.

The more common main water shut-off valve will be located inside your home — typically in a basement, crawl space, or closet on the street-facing side of your home. Depending on the valve type, it is operated by a lever or handle that is rotated to the right to stop the flow of water and to the left to get the water flowing once again. (To recall the correct way to shut off a valve, just remember this simple saying: "righty-tighty, lefty-loosey.")

In addition to identifying the main water valve's location, it's essential to locate other shut-off valves within your home's water system. Here are some key valves to be aware of.

>> **Hose bib valve:** This controls water flow to your exterior hose spigots. It should be turned off in winter to prevent the hose pipe from freezing and bursting.

>> **Water heater valve:** Positioned on top of the water heater, this valve allows cold water to enter the heater, where it's warmed and distributed throughout the house. In case of a water heater leak, this valve can halt water flow into the house, minimizing potential damage.

>> **Ice-maker valve:** Typically found inside the kitchen sink cabinet or wall behind the refrigerator, this valve regulates the water line supplying the ice maker and should be labeled for quick access. Despite it being a small pipe, a leak in this line can cause significant damage.

>> **Washing machine valves:** The rubber supply hoses feeding washing machines are prone to breaking and causing water damage. Locate and label the washer supply valves to shut off water when needed. Consider replacing rubber hoses with more durable braided steel hoses to reduce the risk of leaks. Also consider replacing traditional valves with a single lever valve, which makes it easy to turn both hot and cold water off between uses, eliminating any possibility of a hose leak.

TIP To prevent the water valves from becoming difficult to operate, periodically turn them on and off. Don't leave valves tight open. Instead, turn them slightly toward closed so they don't get stuck.

Replacing a Damaged Section of Pipe

If you've ever had a faucet that went drip-drip-drip, or a pipe that burst wide open, you know that whether the leak is small or full blast, all water pipe leaks have the potential to deliver a lot of heartache to your humble abode. Minor leaks often lead to mold buildup, and major leaks can cause rotted lumber, swollen drywall, and lots of damage to your home's contents. The good news is that you generally won't need to tear up walls and rip out vast amounts of plumbing pipes. You can save the day (and lots of time and money) by replacing a damaged section of pipe.

Why water pipes leak

Most household water supply lines are made from copper and develop leaks due to the following:

>> **Freeze damage.** Pipes in exterior walls or unheated areas like crawl spaces or basements can freeze, expand, and burst open, letting a torrent of water pour out until the leak is found and the water is shut off (see the section, "Protecting pipes in frigid weather"). This is another good reason to locate and label your main water valve, as explained earlier in this chapter!

I once was called to inspect a home that was about to be sold to my out-of-town client that same day. The realtor met me at the home to open it for inspection and joined me in absolute shock when we stepped into the bi-level home to find four feet of water in the lower level! A pipe had burst, and with no one home to notice the leak, it just ran and ran and ran until we arrived. What a mess!

>> **Leaking valves.** Water valves are very reliable, but old ones can wear out and become leaky and difficult to turn off.

>> **Broken solder joints.** Copper pipes are assembled using copper-tin (lead-free) solder. Joints that are not perfectly made can loosen and break open, causing leaks.

>> **Pinhole leaks.** In areas where the water supply is acidic, small, pinhole-sized leaks can develop in copper pipes. This problem won't go away but can be minimized by reducing water pressure in the lines and adding a water neutralizing system to reduce the water's acidity to a neutral state (around a pH of 7). Note this differs from a water softener which removes hard minerals out of the water to prevent scale buildup.

How to repair leaks in copper pipes

There are two ways to repair leaks in copper pipes, which I'll call *easy* and *really hard!* The hard way is to remove and replace the damaged section of copper pipe by soldering in more copper pipe.

WARNING

This method takes considerable skill and involves the use of a fire-breathing torch to heat the pipes and solder, usually in a very confined area surrounded by very flammable wood framing. Needless to say, it's a potentially dangerous tool in the hands of any professional, and even more so for a less experienced DIY plumber.

The easy method is to cut out the damaged copper pipe and replace it with PEX. Short for *cross-linked polyethylene*, PEX is a durable, flexible water supply pipe that is easy to work with thanks to its solder-free push-fit connectors. Today, PEX is rapidly replacing copper pipe as the water pipe of choice for pipe and valve repairs to both copper and steel pipes, as well as the only pipe used in newly built homes.

Given the comparative convenience, safety, and ease of repairing a copper pipe with PEX, I'll walk you through this method in detail.

How to repair a copper pipe with PEX

To remove and replace a piece of copper pipe using PEX tubing, you'll need these supplies:

>> A measuring tape

>> A thin-point Sharpie marker

>> A copper-pipe tubing cutter

>> Fine sandpaper or emery paper (400 grit or finer)

>> Push-fit fittings (also known as push-to-connect or SharkBite® connectors)

>> A short length of PEX tubing (sized to match the length and diameter of the damaged copper pipe)

To replace the damaged piece of pipe, follow these steps:

1. **Turn off the main water shut-off valve; then open a faucet at the lowest point in your home (either the ground floor or, if you have one, the basement) to allow the line to empty.**

2. **Use the measuring tape to determine the length of pipe needed, and use the Sharpie marker to transfer the measurement to the pipe.**

   When figuring the overall length of the PEX replacement tubing, make sure to take into account the length of each end necessary to slide into push-fit fittings.

3. **Place the blade of the tube cutter over the mark on the pipe and gently clamp down on the pipe by turning the grip clockwise while rotating the cutter around the entire circumference of the pipe.**

   The pipe cut must be clean and straight to properly seal to the PEX push-fit fittings. The cutter should move freely. Applying too much pressure too fast will bend the end of the pipe and damage the cutting blade. A bent end can result in a leak.

4. **Use the deburring blade located at the end of the tube cutter or a small file to remove any burrs at the cut end.**

   This step is also key to assuring a watertight seal with the PEX fittings.

5. **Polish the outside of the ends to be connected to the PEX by sanding with 400-grit emery paper until it has a clean finish.**

   This polishing cleans the material and provides the necessary seal for a solid connection.

6. **Measure and cut the PEX tubing to the length needed to replace the damaged section of pipe you've removed.**

   When determining the length of pipe needed, refer to the instructions for the push-fit fittings to determine how much of each end of the PEX gets inserted into the connector on both sides.

7. **Insert the push-fit fittings onto the PEX tubing.**

   Be sure the fittings are fully seated on both ends. Then, assemble the PEX tubing and fittings onto the copper pipe. Once again, make sure the fittings are fully seated. **Note:** You may need to loosen the adjacent copper pipes where they attach to the house framing and/or bend the PEX tubing to fit in between the cut ends of the copper. One big advantage of PEX is that it bends easily and has a "memory," meaning that no matter how much it is bent or stretched, it will shrink back to its normal size in a matter of minutes!

8. **Slowly turn the water back on and check for leaks.**

While I've covered the basics of replacing a section of damaged copper pipe with PEX here, you should know that this same procedure works for galvanized pipe. Plus, PEX tubing and fittings are available for a wide range of applications, like valves for toilets, sinks, ice makers, hose bibs, and various water lines (including main water valves). These valves are durable and never get stuck or develop leaks like traditional copper valves.

Protecting Pipes in Frigid Weather

When the mercury drops, your water pipes become increasingly vulnerable and may freeze and burst. When water freezes, it expands, and the force of that expansion can split a copper pipe wide open. A burst water line can cause tens of thousands of dollars in damage and forever destroy personal possessions in the path of the raging water. The good news is that you can take steps to help prevent a burst pipe and the chaos that it causes.

Using an ounce of prevention

TIP

If you've ever experienced a frozen water line that did not burst wide open, consider yourself lucky! Before that luck wears out, it's smart to take a few steps to prevent your pipes from freezing and keep water running all winter long:

>> **Turn on your faucets just a little.** A faucet left dripping at the fixture farthest from the main water inlet allows just enough warm water movement within the pipes to reduce the chance of a freeze.

>> **Insulate your above-ground pipes.** Pipes in unfinished spaces are most susceptible to freezing. Insulating these pipes prevents them from freezing during most mild-to-medium chills — even when faucets are off. Be sure to focus on insulating pipes in the crawl space, basement, attic, and any pipes that are located along exterior walls, such as a main water line and shut-off valve.

>> **Open your cabinets.** If the pipes that supply water to your kitchen or bathroom sink faucets are prone to freezing, leave the cabinet doors open at night. The open doors allow warm air to circulate in the cabinet and warm the cold pipes.

>> **Install electric pipe heating cable.** If you're in an area where temperatures frequently drop below freezing, think about purchasing pipe heating cable, commonly known as *heat tape*. Heat tape is an electric appliance that is attached to copper pipe. When temperatures drop, a thermostat activates the heat tape and keeps the pipe warm to prevent it from freezing. Heat tape is also useful for thawing out a pipe that's frozen.

WARNING

Heat tape must be used cautiously, and strictly according to the manufacturer's instructions. Throughout my 20 years as a professional home inspector, I frequently observed heat tape being misused more often than being used correctly. It wasn't unusual for me to find heat tape that got so hot, it singed wood framing or insulation! To prevent a fire, never overlap one section of heat tape on top of another and never add insulation to a pipe where heat tape is being used. Doing so can cause the heat tape to overheat and lead to a fire. Lastly, heat tape is not designed to be plugged in all the time.

If the same pipes in your home freeze over and over again, you are better off replacing that section of copper pipe with PEX, which can be rerouted through warmer areas of the home instead.

I did this exact project in my home some years back. The water supply for our kitchen sink ran through the exterior wall and frequently froze in cold weather. To fix the problem, I disconnected the copper pipe, inserted a section of PEX tubing, and ran it inside the kitchen cabinet, where it never froze again!

Applying quick fixes for burst pipes

Being prepared to defend your home's plumbing system against a sudden burst pipe can save you thousands of dollars in damage. Think of these quick, easy fixes as plumbing first aid — they slow or stop a leak long enough to give you time to enlist the services of a qualified plumber during business hours.

Turning off the water valve

The first step to quell any water pipe leak is to turn off the valve supplying water to the leaking section of pipe. You'll find a list of the most important valves to find and label earlier in this chapter. Knowing where these valves are located in advance of an emergency will enable you to find them quickly and prevent more serious water damage.

Stopping pinhole leaks

TIP

To temporarily stop a pinhole leak, you'll need to apply pressure to the hole. The solution? Pick up a roll of pipe leak tape and wrap it around the pipe. Pipe leak tape is available from a variety of manufacturers and designed to make quick repairs of minor leaks. While not a permanent solution, it solves the problem long enough to prevent damage while you consider your options for a more permanent repair.

Using a sleeve clamp for larger leaks

A sleeve clamp stops everything from pinhole leaks to larger leaks. A sleeve clamp consists of two semicircular pieces of metal and some gasket material. When put together, the clamp completely surrounds the pipe — hence, the name *sleeve*.

REMEMBER

The clamp is about 3 inches long, but you have to buy one to fit your specific pipe size — a sleeve clamp made to repair ½-inch pipe is smaller than one needed to repair ¾-inch pipe. I've even used sleeve clamps to repair rusted-out sections of 2-inch galvanized steam pipes!

Other than the sleeve clamp, you only need a screwdriver or an adjustable wrench to tighten the clamp. Here's how it works (see Figure 7-1):

1. **Wrap the damaged section of pipe with the gasket material provided.**

2. **Surround the gasket-wrapped pipe with the two semicircular clamps.**

3. **Tighten the screws that connect the two halves of the sleeve clamp.**

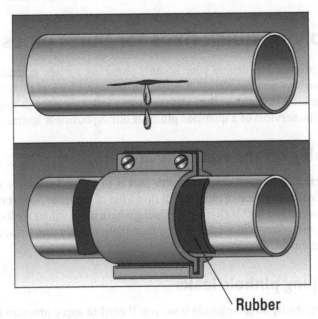

FIGURE 7-1:
Using a sleeve
clamp.

Rubber

TIP

Today, smart home technology has extended to your plumbing system in the way of a "smart" main water valve. These smart valves serve to both monitor the flow of water into your home and instantly shut off the water should an "unusual" flow be detected, like when a busted pipe starts flooding your first floor! They're also Wi-Fi enabled and can alert you if the valve is triggered so you can get back home ASAP and take care of whatever caused the leak.

Quieting Noisy Water Pipes

Imagine a fast-moving stream of water traveling down a narrow pipe. Suddenly and unexpectedly, the water finds a closed valve in place of what, moments earlier, was an escape point. All of a sudden, the water has nowhere to go. As it comes to an abrupt stop, a loud thud results, and it can be heard reverberating through-out the entire house. This banging sound is known as a *water hammer*. Water is heavy, weighing in at 8 pounds per gallon, and the hammering action that creates the horrible racket when all that water comes to a screeching halt is actually capable of damaging joints and connections in the pipe.

Combating water hammer

There are three common ways to stop water hammer from happening.

Tightening loose pipe-mounting straps

Sometimes water hammer can occur when pipe-mounting straps, hangers, or clamps are loose. As water is turned on and off, a pipe strap that is not well connected to the wood framing members will allow the pipe to shake and rattle. Check all accessible pipes to make sure they're securely attached, and add any additional straps as needed.

WARNING

Never use galvanized plumber's tape or galvanized straps on copper pipe. When different metals contact one another, corrosive electrolysis can occur. (The electrolysis causes the galvanized steel to corrode, not the copper. In this example the copper pipe will not corrode and leak — the tape or strap will.)

Installing water hammer arrestors

Water hammer arrestors are the shock absorbers of a modern plumbing system. Installed at the end of a plumbing line, they use a special valve to absorb the force of water coming to a sudden stop. If your home doesn't have water hammer arrestors installed, they can easily be added by a plumber.

Replenishing air chambers

An *air chamber* is a vertical pipe located in the wall cavity at the point near a faucet or valve where the water-supply pipe exits the wall. Air chambers act as cushions to prevent water from slamming against the piping. Because air compresses, it absorbs the shock of the fast-moving water before it has a chance to slam against the end of the pipe.

Many older household plumbing systems have air chambers built into them at critical locations — like the clothes washer and dishwasher — where electric shut-off valves close rapidly. In some homes, air chambers exist at every location where water is turned on and off — even the toilet.

To eliminate water hammer, you need to replenish all the air chambers with air. You can't inspect the air chambers, so this procedure is a must whenever you notice a faint noise in the pipe. Here's how you replenish the air chambers:

1. **Shut off your home's main water supply valve.**

2. **Open the highest faucet inside your house.**

3. **Find the lowest faucet on the property — it's usually on the first floor somewhere outside or in the basement — and turn it on to completely drain all water from the pipes.**

   As the water drains from the pipes, air automatically replaces it.

4. **The moment the water is completely drained from the piping, turn off the lowest faucet and reopen the main valve.**

   Air pushes out of the water lines, sputtering as it exits the faucets inside. However, air remains in the air chambers, eliminating water hammer.

Adjusting excessively-high water pressure

Another reason for banging pipes is excessively-high water pressure. You can adjust water pressure with a water-pressure regulator or pressure-reducing valve. Most modern homes have a regulator mounted at the location where the main water supply enters the home.

TIP

If you don't have a regulator and the water pressure exceeds 75 psi, consider having one installed. A professionally installed pressure regulator can cost several hundred dollars, but it's a good investment in the long run. (Only do-it-yourselfers with some serious plumbing skills should try to install a pressure regulator themselves.)

REMEMBER

Not only is high water pressure wasteful, but it can also damage dishwashers, ice makers, washing machines, and other water-supplied automatic appliances. In fact, many appliance warranties are voided when water pressure exceeds 100 pounds per square inch (psi). Testing water pressure is important regardless of whether you have a pressure regulator.

You can test the water pressure yourself using a water-pressure gauge designed to screw onto a hose bib; in most communities, the local water company will conduct the test at no charge. Normal water pressure runs between 30 and 60 psi for well systems and up to 75 psi for public water systems. If you already have a regulator, (usually preset at 75psi), you can use a screwdriver and wrench to adjust pressure to your preference — lower pressure is better as long as you are satisfied with performance. (See Figure 7-2.)

FIGURE 7-2:
Adjusting the
water pressure.

TIP

By the way, if you have low water pressure, consider adding a booster pump with a pressure tank. The pump will increase the flow of water into your house, and the pressure tank will assure a smooth and steady increase in water supply.

Some Like It Hot: Checking Out Your Water Heater

Thanks to the water heater, it's been a while since most people in our modern civilized society heated water for daily use over an open flame. Instead, the dilemma facing most folks is one of short showers and high utility bills. If this situation sounds familiar, it's time to take action! A bit of preventive maintenance on the water heater can provide hot water longer, result in energy savings, and even extend the life of the water heater.

Maintaining your water heater

A gas-fired water heater, shown in Figure 7-3, has three basic parts: the enclosure, the water tank assembly, and the burner and control assembly. The enclosure holds everything together and protects the tank and other fragile parts from damage. The water tank stores water that arrives cold and leaves heated. The burner and control assembly are responsible for heating the water, discharging combustion gases, and adjusting the temperature.

An electric water heater varies slightly. It has an enclosure and a tank, but instead of a burner, it contains one or two electric elements that heat the water. Consequently, there is no need for a flue to exhaust combustion gases. Aside from these differences, gas and electric water heaters function essentially the same and require essentially the same tender loving care.

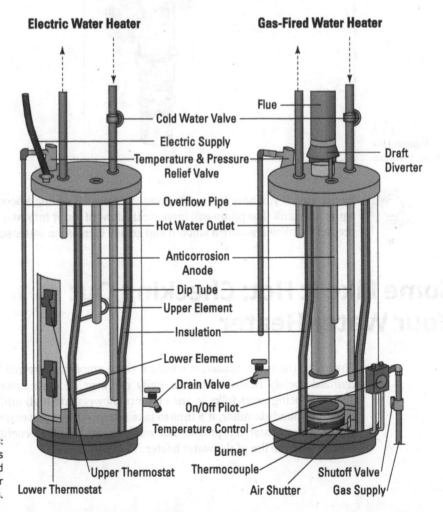

FIGURE 7-3:
The major parts of gas-fired and electric water heaters.

Insulating for improved efficiency

An insulation blanket can make some water heaters more energy efficient. If your water heater is located in unconditioned space (a garage, basement, or attic where central air or heat doesn't necessarily reach) or you don't want added heat, install a heavy blanket — R-11 or better. The higher the R-value, the thicker the blanket and the more insulating horsepower.

REMEMBER

For gas-fired water heaters, never insulate above the top of the tank or across the burner compartment. For electric water heaters, leave access to the panels covering the top and bottom heating thermostats and elements in case they ever need to be adjusted or replaced.

Keeping your water heater clear of sludge

If the bottom of your water heater fills with sludge, the heater won't operate at peak performance. Aside from being a breeding ground for bacteria, sediment at the base of a tank significantly diminishes the efficiency of a gas water heater and can cause it to rumble like a freight train. Sediment buildup also causes the water at the base of the tank to super-heat and turn to steam, resulting in mini explosions that blast small amounts of sediment off the bottom of the tank.

To clean the sediment out of a water heater, follow these steps:

1. **Turn off the power or gas controller for the water heater and close the cold-water inlet valve at the top of the water heater.**

2. **Unscrew the cold-water supply line at the top of the water heater and remove the nipple screwed into the cold-water port.**

3. **Pour a citric-acid-based cleaner into the open hole and wait about eight hours for the acid to dissolve the minerals at the bottom of the tank.**

TIP

One citric-acid-based cleaning product I recommend is called Mag-Erad, which is available in stores and online at Menards. If you have trouble finding it, call the Mag-Erad manufacturer, Tri-Brothers Chemical Corporation, at 847-564-2320.

4. **After the cleaning agent has had time to work, flush the tank.**

Connect a garden hose to the drain valve located at the bottom of the water heater and run the hose out into your yard. Open the drain valve, reconnect the cold-water supply line, and then turn on the cold-water supply to the water heater. The cloudy water and sediment that comes out of the end of the hose will amaze you.

5. **When the water runs clear, close the drain valve, and remove the hose.**

6. **Bleed air from the system by turning on the hot-water faucet farthest from the water heater; when water runs from this faucet, turn it off and repeat this process at other faucets throughout the house.**

7. **Turn the power or gas controller to the water heater back on.**

Hopefully, you'll now be in hot water!

Avoiding rust

Most water-heater tanks are made of glass-lined steel. If water gets through imperfections in the glass, then you can count on rust and eventually a leak. But because the tank has no inspection ports, it's hard to tell when it's dirty or beginning to rust. Actually, tank rust usually isn't discovered until after a leak occurs — and then it's too late. You're not totally without recourse, though.

A special rod called a *sacrificial anode* is built into the water-heater tank assembly to prevent rust. Usually made of magnesium or aluminum, this long metal rod is mounted through the top of the water heater and runs through the tank's interior. As long as the rod is in good condition, deterioration of the tank is drastically reduced.

Unfortunately, you can't determine the condition of the anode by just looking at your water heater. You have to turn off the power and the water to the water heater and remove the anode with a wrench. Check the anode for deterioration about once a year; this will give you an idea of how long the anode will last. If more than half of the rod is deteriorated, it's time for a replacement.

When you replace the sacrificial anode, a $25 to $50 item, it takes about 30 minutes to install a new one. Sacrificial anodes are typically available through a plumbing-supply company. Because anodes come in all shapes and sizes, be prepared to give them the make and model of your water heater so that you get the right one. You can find this information on a label located on the water-heater housing.

To replace the sacrificial anode, follow these steps:

1. **Turn off the power to the water heater and close both cold and hot-water inlet valve at the top of the water heater.**

   If there is no hot water valve (usually the case) the hot water pipes must be drained down to below the top of the tank to prevent water flooding from the tank when the anode rod is removed.

2. **Unscrew the hex bolt holding the sacrificial anode in place and remove the rod — or what remains of it.**

   A sacrificial anode is about 3 to 5 feet long, about ¾ inch in diameter, and has a hex bolt welded onto one end. The hex bolt screws into the top of the tank, holding the rod in place inside the tank, and, when tightened down, the nut also makes a watertight seal at the same time.

   If you find that the sacrificial anode has been consumed by more than half its length, replace it.

TIP

   The clearance between the top of the tank and the ceiling above it must equal or exceed the length of the anode rod. Otherwise, the tank must be completely drained and detached from water pipes and the gas pipe to replace the rod — a lengthy job.

3. **Install the new anode.**

   Insert the new anode in the reverse order that the previous one was removed. Be sure to use Teflon tape on the threaded fitting to prevent a leak.

4. **Turn the water and power to the water heater back on.**

TIP

Most factory-installed anodes are magnesium, which can produce a sulfite-reducing bacteria that makes your water smell like rotten eggs. (Peewww!) Using a replacement anode made of zinc or aluminum will prevent this problem.

Controlling temperature when things get too hot

Water temperature is another important factor in controlling energy costs and extending a water heater's life span. The U.S. Department of Energy recommends that consumers set water heater thermostats to 120 degrees, warm enough to slow down any mineral buildup and corrosion while also reducing scalding. On a gas-fired water heater, you can adjust the temperature by turning the dial located on the front of the gas controller. On an electric model, the thermostat is located behind an access panel adjacent to a heating element.

WARNING

Don't set the temperature below 120 degrees. A temperature setting less than that could allow harmful bacteria to propagate within the tank.

Testing the temperature and pressure relief valve

The temperature and pressure relief (TPR) valve opens to release pressure buildup in the water heater when the temperature or the pressure get dangerously high, preventing a possible explosion.

A buildup of mineral salt, rust, and corrosion can cause a TPR valve to freeze up and become nonoperational. To test the valve to ensure that it's working properly, first make sure a drainpipe has been installed to the discharge side of the TPR valve. Then, simply raise and lower the test lever several times so it lifts the brass stem that it's fastened to. (See Figure 7-4.) Hot water should rush out of the end of the drainpipe. If no water flows through the pipe or you get just a trickle, replace the valve.

Some water-heater experts recommend testing every six months. More frequent testing can reduce the chance of a leak caused by mineral and corrosion buildup. However, if a leak results immediately after a test, simply operate the test lever several times to free lodged debris that may be preventing the valve from seating properly. If the valve is doing its job and hot water is still dripping or spewing out of the TPR drain valve, contact your plumber or HVAC service company for further evaluation of the problem.

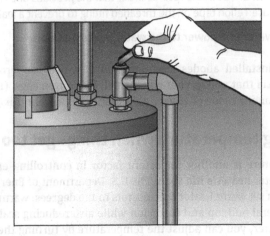

FIGURE 7-4: Testing the temperature and pressure relief valve.

Here are other things to pay attention to:

>> **The pipe leaving the relief valve should be the same diameter as the exhaust port of the valve — usually ¾ inch.** Moreover, the pipe should be made of a material that is not adversely affected by heat, such as copper. If the pipe is undersized or not heat-resistant, replace it with copper or have a plumber do it for you.

>> **The TPR drainpipe should terminate a few inches off the floor next to the water heater.** This way, any leakage indicating an excessive pressure in the water heater will be readily apparent.

Preventing "Shower Shock!" Dealing with sudden blasts of cold water

If you've ever stepped into your shower, adjusted the perfect hot/cold water mix, and then suddenly found the water temperature changed to very hot or very cold, you've officially experienced "Shower Shock!" This rude awakening results from an imbalance in the hot/cold mix you originally set. This can occur when someone flushes a toilet, runs the dishwasher, starts doing dishes, or anything else that demands a share of the hot or cold water running through your plumbing system. When that happens, that perfect hot/cold mix you'd set goes right out the window.

The solution is to install a *pressure balanced valve*. This would replace your current shower/tub valve and has the ability to maintain the hot/cold mix you set, regardless of whether water is demanded somewhere else in the house. While the pressure of water through the valve may temporarily change, the mix of hot/cold blend remains the same.

Installing a pressure balanced valve is a job for a plumber, but well worth the investment to stop shower shock once and for all!

Tightening the cold-water shut-off valve

If you discover rust at the top of your water heater, it may be due to a leaking pipe fitting or a leak at the cold-water shut-off valve. If all the fittings are in good shape, and the valve is the culprit, try to stop the leak by using a wrench to tighten the packing nut.

Securing your water heater to a wall

A water heater thrown over during an earthquake or other disaster can cause both broken gas lines and broken water lines. You can prevent such a scenario if you strap the water heater securely to an adjacent wall.

Metal straps around the belly of the heater can be screwed to the housing and then anchored to wall framing. You can also install a special anchor that attaches to the water pipes at the top and to wall framing. In either case, your best bet is to check with your local building department for recommendations and a diagram on how best to anchor your water heater.

SPEEDING UP HOT WATER TO YOUR FAUCETS

On my nationally syndicated home improvement show and podcast *The Money Pit Home Improvement Show*, I often hear from listeners frustrated by the time it takes for their shower water to get hot, as well as the water wasted waiting for that to happen. The reason has nothing to with the type or size of your water heater, but everything to do with the distance between your water heater and your shower.

Water heaters maintain the temperature of water **inside** the tank. Once you turn on the faucet, that hot water has to travel the length of pipe from the water heater to your bathroom, which can take a frustratingly long time. Here are couple ways to speed things up:

- **Run hot water from both the shower and sink when you first step in the bathroom.** Once the warm water arrives, shut off the sink faucets and adjust the hot/cold mix at the shower. This will shorten the wait time and waste a bit less water.

- **Install a hot water recirculation system.** In this system, a pump is used to create a loop from the water heater to the faucet farthest from the water heater, and back again. By keeping hot water circulating, there's little wait for hot water when you need it, as well as no wasted water. The only downside is that energy costs can go up as the water heater runs longer to keep up with demand. This cost, however, can be reduced if the pump is set to work on a timer that limits operation, for example, to just the morning shower time.

Maintaining your gas water heater

The controller, burner, thermocouple, and venting system are components that are fundamental to the safe and efficient operation of a gas water heater. Keeping them clean and in good working order will keep you safe and help manage utility costs.

The controller: The brains of the operation

The *controller* is the device you use on a gas water heater to light the pilot and turn the unit off and on. It's also used to adjust the temperature setting. The controller is usually pretty reliable and doesn't require much maintenance other than an occasional dusting. However, if you have too little hot water, water that is not hot enough, or water that is excessively hot, it may be time to replace the controller. This is a job best left to a pro.

The burner: Just an old flame

On a gas water heater, the burner assembly is located at the bottom of the unit below the tank. (Refer to Figure 7-3.) When the water temperature in the tank drops below the desired temperature, a thermostat activates the burner. The same process occurs with an electric water heater, but instead of a burner, electric heating elements are activated.

Periodically inspect the burner to make sure that it's burning safely and efficiently. A dirty burner chamber can cause a fire and can make the burner less efficient. (If your burner is operating at peak efficiency, you'll see a blue flame. If the flame is orange, adjust the shutter until it turns blue.)

To clean the burner, first turn off the gas shut-off valve (located on the gas supply to the water heater), remove the access panel, and vacuum the burner and chamber. Use a stiff wire and a wire brush to clear clogged burner ports and remove rust. If you aren't successful in getting a blue flame, call in a service rep from your utility company or a plumber or heating specialist.

The thermocouple

If you have a gas water heater with a pilot light that won't stay lit, it's probably due to one of two things:

WARNING

>> **There is a blockage in the tiny tube that supplies gas to the pilot.** If the tube is blocked, you can clear it by inserting a thin piece of wire or blowing air through it.

Make sure that the gas controller is in the off position before attempting this repair.

>> **The thermocouple has failed.** The *thermocouple* is a thermoelectric device that shuts off the gas if the pilot light goes out. In simple terms, it's a short piece of tubing that runs from the gas controller to the pilot. The pilot end of the thermocouple and the pilot are held side by side in a bracket that's anchored to the burner. If your pilot light won't stay lit, the thermocouple probably needs to be replaced. A new one costs about $20 and is easy to install.

If the thermocouple has failed, follow these steps:

1. **Turn off the gas supply.**

2. **Remove the whole burner and thermocouple assembly.**

   Unfasten the three nuts that hold the thermocouple and the two gas tubes to the valve. The burner typically sits loosely — or under clips — in the burning chamber and just slides out.

3. **Detach the thermocouple from the burner.**

The thermocouple is usually attached to the pilot gas supply tube with one or more clips that snap into place. The end of the thermocouple is inserted into the pilot assembly and can simply be pulled out.

4. **Take the detached thermocouple with you to the home center or hardware store and buy a new one.**

5. **Install the new one the same way that you removed the old one.**

Attach the end of the new thermocouple into the pilot assembly and reattach the thermocouple to the pilot gas supply using the clips previously removed. Reinstall the burner and, using a small open-end or adjustable wrench, reconnect the thermocouple lead, the gas tube to the main burner, and the pilot gas tube to the valve.

6. **Turn the gas back on and follow the lighting instructions on the water heater.**

7. **Check for gas leaks by applying soapy water to joints and looking for bubbles while the main burner is firing.**

The venting system

The venting system of a gas water heater consists of a flue that runs up the center of the water heater from the burners, out the top of the water heater, and through the rooftop to vent deadly gases created by combustion. At least twice each year, inspect the venting system to ensure that it's properly aligned at the top of the water heater and that the connections are secure.

TIP

Here's a quick test you can use to see if your gas water heater is venting properly: With the water heater running, hold a match near the *draft diverter* (the opening at the top of the water heater where the vent pipe connects to the unit). If the flame on the match leans in toward the vent pipe, your draft is good.

WARNING

If the flame leans back toward the room, or worse yet, if it blows out the flame, your unit may be back-drafting, a potentially dangerous situation. If this happens, immediately turn off the unit and call the gas company for assistance. Chances are, your vent pipe or chimney is blocked somewhere, and your house may be filling with deadly combustion gases.

Maintaining your electric water heater

Electric water heaters have no burners to clean, no thermocouples to replace, and no venting systems to be concerned with. However, an electric water heater is not without its own set of maintenance tasks.

Cleaning your water heater's electric elements

An electric water heater contains one or two heating elements similar to what you might find in your electric oven, except that they're short and narrow. These electric elements can become laden with lime and mineral deposits that reduce their effectiveness or cause them to overheat and short out.

To clean your electric elements, follow these steps:

1. **Turn off the power to the water heater.**

2. **Drain the tank by turning off the cold-water valve at the top of the water heater, attaching a garden hose to the drain valve at the base of the water heater, and opening the drain valve.**

   To facilitate draining, open a hot-water faucet somewhere in the home. This lets air into the pipes and speeds the draining of the water heater.

TIP

3. **After the water heater empties, use a screwdriver to remove the access panels to the elements.**

   Depending upon the number of elements, one or more access panels will have to be removed. You may need to move a piece of insulation to expose the element.

4. **Using your screwdriver, remove the elements and detach any electrical wires that power them.**

   Elements are generally attached with a series of bolts or they have a threaded base that screws directly into the tank. Take a photo of the wiring of the elements so you can remember exactly how to reinstall wires after the elements are cleaned.

5. **Clean or replace the element.**

   To clean the removed element, use a solution of vinegar and water or sodium carbonate and water (2 tablespoons of vinegar or 2 tablespoons of sodium carbonate in 1 quart of hot water) and a scouring pad.

   If an element has begun to corrode, replace it with a new one. Many different element types and styles are widely available; simply take the old one to the hardware store and find a match. Cooler-than-normal water, sporadic hot water, and a short supply of hot water are all telltale signs of a corroded element.

6. **Reconnect the wires and refill the water heater.**

   To refill the water heater, close the drain valve and turn the cold-water supply valve on, making sure that the hot-water faucet farthest from the water heater is left open to express all the air from the system.

7. **Check for leaks around the elements.**

8. **After you're sure that there are no leaks, replace the insulation and access panels and turn on the power.**

Hard water and an electric water heater are a disastrous combination. You will forever be cleaning and replacing electric elements. If you're plagued with hard water, consider installing a water softener.

TIP

Fixing a defective thermostat or tripped limit switch

If you still have a problem getting hot water out of your electric heater, it may be due to a defective thermostat or a tripped or defective high-temperature limit switch. The limit switch cuts off power to the element when the water temperature exceeds a certain limit — usually 190 degrees. You can reset a tripped high-temperature limit switch with the push of a button behind the access panel.

If the switch continues to trip, it may be due to either a defective limit switch or element. In either case, one or both need to be replaced. To replace a thermostat, follow these steps:

1. **Turn off the water and power to the water heater and remove the access panel and insulation.**

2. **Use a screwdriver to remove the wires from the thermostat.**

3. **Loosen the bracket bolts that hold the thermostat in place and slide the thermostat out.**

As always, take the old thermostat with you to your local hardware store when trying to find a match.

REMEMBER

4. **Slide the new thermostat into place, tighten down the bolts, reconnect the wires, and press the Reset button.**

5. **Reinstall the insulation and access panel; then turn on the water and power.**

Caring for your tankless water heater

Tankless water heaters are quickly becoming the most popular water heater for many reasons. Beyond the fact that they're more energy efficient and deliver an almost endless supply of hot water on-demand, they don't have the cleaning and maintenance woes associated with traditional tank-style units. However, a few tasks will ensure that your tankless water heater has a long, prosperous, and energy-efficient life:

>> **Keep control compartments, burners, and circulating air passageways of the appliance clean.** First, turn off and disconnect electrical power and allow the unit to cool. Then remove and clean the water inlet filter. Using pressurized air, clean dust from the main burner, heat exchanger, and fan blades. Finish by using a soft, dry cloth to wipe the cabinet.

>> **Inspect the vent system for blockages or damage at least once a year.**

>> **Flush the heat exchanger to get rid of lime and scale buildup.** Consult the owner's manual for specific instructions on how to flush the heat exchanger.

>> **Visually inspect the flame.** The burner must flame evenly over the entire surface when operating correctly. The burner must burn with a clear, blue, stable flame. Consult a pro to clean and adjust the burner for an irregular flame.

TIP

Beyond the benefits of an unending supply of hot water, larger tankless heaters known as "combi" units can replace traditional boilers for homes heated with hot water. These combination units are dramatically smaller and far more efficient than hot water boilers. They're also frequently eligible for state and federal rebates or tax credits that reduce the cost of installing one even further.

Softening Your Water

If the area you live in has water that is filled with mineral deposits, you have hard water. (If you're unsure, an inexpensive home testing kit can be found at most major home centers.) With the exception of adding salt to the brine tank on a regular basis, a water-softening system is reasonably maintenance-free. Every now and then, the brine solution becomes clogged at the base of the brine tank, which prevents the solution from being siphoned into the resin tank. You know that this is the case if your brine tank is full of salt, yet your water doesn't have that "slick" feel of softened water.

You can correct this problem by removing all the salt from the brine tank and flushing the bottom of the tank with a garden hose and water. Before replacing the salt in the brine tank, manually cycle the unit to ensure that it's operating properly. Individual units will have either a lever or a button that, when pressed, manually cycles the system. Check your owner's manual to determine where the manual cycle button is on your water softener.

Wishing Your Well Is Working Well

If you don't get your water from a municipal water source, it probably comes from a private well. Water is pumped from the source with a submersible pump that's usually about 10 feet from the bottom of the well to a pressure tank in or near the house. The tank, in turn, feeds the water-supply lines. In a standard pressure tank, incoming water forces air into the upper third of the tank, where it forms a spring-like cushion. When the air pressure reaches a preset level — usually between 50 and 60 psi — the spring action of the compressed air triggers a pressure switch, which shuts off the pump. As water is drawn from the tank, pressure diminishes. When it reaches a preset level — 30 to 40 psi — the switch turns the pump on again.

When the pressure tank loses too much air pressure, it can become "waterlogged," which causes the pump to switch on and off frequently. You can solve this problem by doing the following:

1. **Turn off the power to the pump; then attach a garden hose to the drain valve at the bottom of the tank and open the valve and leave it open until there's no more pressure in the tank.**

2. **Open a faucet in the house to drain all the water out of the tank.**

3. **When the tank is empty, turn off the faucet, close the drain valve on the tank, remove the hose, and turn the pump back on.**

A leaking tank is another common problem. If a leak develops, it usually appears first as an oozing, rusty blemish. Although tank plugs are available, they're only a temporary measure. The tank should be replaced as soon as possible.

Occasionally, the pump may stop working. If this is the case, first check for a tripped circuit breaker. A loose wire may also be the source of the problem. If all these check out, your best bet is to call in a well service technician.

Chapter **8**

Plumbing, Part II: Fixtures

You may be able to live with peeling paint, a squeaking floor, or doors that won't shut properly. But when it comes to your toilet and the woes that it encounters — not flushing properly, overflowing, or looking like a full-blown science experiment — that's where you draw the line! Fear not! Armed with this chapter, a closet auger, a pumice stick, vinegar, turpentine, a wax ring, and other assorted paraphernalia, you'll not only tame your toilet, but you'll also transform your tub, shape up your shower, do away with dirty grout, and make your faucets sparkle!

Maintaining Fixture Surfaces: Stainless Steel, Cast Iron, Fiberglass, and More

Sinks, tubs, toilets, and shower pans are some of the hardest-working parts of any house. It's no fun when these fixtures become tattered. In many situations, cleaning is all it takes to make a worn-out fixture look brand spanking new!

Stainless-steel fixtures

Porcelain and the more durable vitreous china fixtures are common in bathrooms. But when it comes to kitchen sinks, one made of high-quality stainless steel wins hands down. Stainless-steel sinks are light and easy to install, they don't chip, and they're easy to keep clean.

To clean a stainless-steel surface, use one of the following:

>> One drop of liquid dish soap in 1 quart of hot water

>> Baking soda mixed with water until it forms a paste

>> One part vinegar to one part water

Clean and then dry with a soft cloth. For tougher cleaning tasks, look for a commercial stainless-steel cleaning product that contains oxalic acid. Regardless of the cleaner, a nylon scrubbing pad will help.

REMEMBER

When caring for stainless steel, follow these two simple rules:

>> **Never use steel wool.** Steel-wool fibers can lodge in the surface of the stainless steel and eventually rust, giving the appearance that the *stainless steel* is rusting. What a mess!

>> **Don't use abrasive cleaners.** They can scratch the surface over time.

TIP

If you'd like to make your stainless-steel sink look newer, consider investing in a stainless-steel scratch eraser kit. Kits retail for about $50; they can be found at home centers, hardware stores, appliance retailers, or online, and include a series of polishing products to help buff out scratches and restore stainless-steel surfaces.

Porcelain-on-steel and porcelain-on-cast-iron fixtures

Porcelain on steel and porcelain on cast iron are both used primarily for kitchen sinks, laundry sinks, and bathtubs. Although cast iron is a stronger base, making porcelain fixtures generally more durable, porcelain does chip, and the finish is every bit as easy to scratch as vitreous china.

When porcelain is new, its surface gleams and glistens, but over time, it can lose its luster, especially if you use abrasives for cleaning. Plus, if you drop a heavy object onto a porcelain fixture, you may not shatter it, but you may chip the enamel. Here are the options for restoring a porcelain surface:

>> **Repair chips.** A chip can be professionally repaired for about $75 to $125. Chip touch-up kits are available at your local home center or hardware store, but I think they're useless — they don't last, and the finished result usually looks terrible.

>> **Reglaze.** Porcelain and ceramic sinks, tubs, and other bathroom fixtures that are badly scratched, are chipped, and have lost their luster can be *reglazed* (refinished) by a professional porcelain refinisher. The process is expensive, time consuming and frankly, unless the fixture can be removed from the house for the reglazing process, somewhat dangerous given the caustic products required.

Reglazing is very expensive. In fact, reglazing a porcelain fixture isn't worth the cost or effort unless it's a valuable antique or a family heirloom, because replacing the fixture is far less expensive.

>> **Refinish.** Refinishing — applying a paint-like coating — is a far less expensive alternative to reglazing and can produce finishes with varying degrees of durability.

TIP

For many years, I hesitated to recommend refinishing products because they just didn't last. That all changed when I discovered a product called ECKOPEL 2K. Using this durable, odor-free, two-part epoxy refinishing kit, I was able to restore the surface of a beautiful antique tub in just a weekend. The directions for using ECKOPEL 2K are very specific, especially as it applies to the prep and epoxy mixing process. I recommend you watch the application videos offered by the manufacturer before beginning. You can find out more at www.refinishedbath solutions.com.

Fiberglass fixtures

Fiberglass fixtures are popular because they're competitively priced. Fiberglass has been around for a long time and is used most commonly in tubs and shower pans. Fiberglass fixtures aren't as durable as other types of fixtures and must be treated with care. However, given such care, they'll last as long as any other.

A stained fiberglass tub or shower pan is a breeze to clean. Simply wet the entire surface to be cleaned with water, sprinkle on a thin layer of automatic dishwashing powder, and let it sit for about an hour. Keep the surface wet by spraying it with clear water. After an hour, use a nylon bristle brush to scrub away stains. Finish up by rinsing the entire area with fresh water.

TIP

For severely stained tub or shower floors, plug the drain and fill the tub or shower pan with about an inch of water. Sprinkle the automatic dishwashing powder over the entire surface and allow it to sit overnight. Use the nylon brush to scrub away stains and thoroughly rinse with fresh water. You'll be amazed by its like-new appearance!

Composite fixtures

Although fiberglass is a resin painted onto a backing, composite fixtures are great, thick hulks of plastic that are also known as *solid surface* material. What you see on the surface goes all the way through to the other side of the fixture. Composite fixtures are long lasting and far more durable than fiberglass.

Ordinary spills on composite surfaces require only a damp cloth for cleanup. If a composite sink ever becomes really grungy, try filling the sink with a solution of bleach and water. The bleach works very well and will bring back the sink's original color.

Most composite fixture manufacturers have product cleaning, repair, and maintenance kits or recommend specific cleaning products. Check with the manufacturer or contact the dealer who installed the fixture.

TIP

Because the finished look of a composite fixture goes all the way through, light sanding can remove burns, stains, or minor scratches. Polish the sanded area with fine 400- to 600-grit wet-dry sandpaper lubricated with turpentine to restore the surface to its original beauty. Wipe up the excess turpentine with a paper towel and finish the job by cleaning with a mild detergent and a fresh-water rinse.

Vitreous china fixtures

Vitreous china — a smooth form of baked clay with a shiny or glassy look — is used primarily for bathroom sinks, toilets, and bidets. Although it's strong, it can be chipped or broken if hit with a hard object, such as a tool. The bottom line: Be careful around vitreous china, especially during repairs and maintenance.

Vitreous china is also easily scratched, so for most cleaning, leave your scouring powder and abrasive pads in the cupboard. *Note:* A variety of commercial products claim to clean vitreous china without causing damage, but proceed with caution. Abrasive cleaners slowly wear down it's brilliant surface, although the process can take years. Make sure that the cleaner you select states that it is nonabrasive.

TIP

For lime deposits, CLR is an effective cleaner. Apply the cleaner and scrub the surface gently using a Scotch-Brite non-abrasive pad. CLR works well to remove the trifecta of bathroom stains: calcium, lime, and rust. (Any guesses why it's called CLR?)

Remove tea or coffee stains with a solution of 2 tablespoons chlorine bleach per 1 quart of water. Soak for just a minute or two; then rinse promptly.

SHOPPING FOR RECYCLED OR VINTAGE FIXTURES

When it's time to replace fixtures, either because you're ready for a change or because the old ones are beyond repair, before you run out to buy new, think about buying used. Using recycled fixtures can have several benefits: Beyond achieving the desired look (usually something vintage or retro), recycled fixtures are usually less expensive than new ones. Plus, using recycled fixtures is very "green" and environmentally friendly — it reduces what goes into landfills and, in the big picture, saves on the manufacture and shipping of new products.

Salvage and recycling centers sell used and surplus building materials at a fraction of normal prices. Although plumbing fixtures are among the most popular product categories, doors, windows, lumber, siding, trim, roofing, finish hardware, cabinetry, counters, flooring, lighting, radiators, and just about anything you can think of can also be found.

An entire network of salvage and recycling centers and retail outlets has sprung up across the land. An excellent resource for recycled fixtures is the Building Materials Reuse Association (www.bmra.org), which has several hundred affiliate members throughout the United States. Another option is Habitat for Humanity's ReStores, where you'll find a wide range of upcycled building materials, furniture, and more (www.habitat.org/restores).

WARNING

Never mix bleach with a solution containing ammonia. The combination can release a poisonous gas.

Cleaning Your Faucet Works

When a faucet becomes dull, it makes an otherwise bright and shiny decorating accessory look tattered and worn. It isn't worn out — it's just dirty. The bad news is that dirt that has built up for a long period of time can be difficult to remove. The good news is that you can remove it without damaging the faucet if you know a few tricks.

Cleaning a faucet is a two-part operation:

>> Cleaning the aerator

>> Cleaning and polishing the exterior finish

Cleaning the aerator

The aerator, a thimble-size accessory consisting of a very small disk filled with tiny holes, screws into the end of a faucet spout. It mixes the water with air and controls the amount of flow. When the aerator is operating normally, the water comes out of the spout in a smooth, gentle, even flow. If the water flow from your faucet is slow, if the water sprays out in random streams, or if a once-smooth flow has become sporadic and now sputters, then you probably have a clogged aerator.

Cleaning the aerator is really easy. Here's all you have to do:

1. **Unscrew the aerator from the spout by turning it counterclockwise.**

2. **Disassemble the aerator parts.**

   The parts simply sit one atop another inside the aerator housing.

   REMEMBER

   As you disassemble the aerator, note exactly how the parts are assembled. If you make a mistake during reassembly, the aerator won't work. I like to stack the parts side-by-side in the order they came apart so I know exactly how to reassemble them correctly.

3. **Use an old toothbrush and a toothpick and some vinegar to clean each part.**

   If you can't remove lime-deposit buildup easily, soak the parts in straight vinegar overnight. Then scrub them clean.

4. **Reassemble and reinstall the aerator.**

   TIP

   Be sure to align the threads correctly to avoid stripping them, which could cause a nasty spray leak every time you turn on the faucet.

Cleaning and polishing the outside of a faucet

To keep a faucet clean, regularly wipe it down with a damp cloth followed by a clean, dry towel. Built-up debris is a bit more difficult — especially when it's a thick layer of lime deposits. Several different cleaners are available that remove hard-water stains and other mineral-deposit buildup.

>> **Pure sodium carbonate:** Pure sodium carbonate (also known as *washing soda* or *soda ash*) is nothing more than laundry detergent. No fillers, no anti-bubbling agents, no odor eaters, nothing except pure cleaning power.

It's available at swimming-pool supply stores. To use pure sodium carbonate, mix ½ cup sodium carbonate with a few drops of warm water. Then, using a soft, clean cloth, rub the paste onto the faucet surface, and keep rubbing until it shines. To finish, rinse with fresh water and towel-dry.

>> **White vinegar and baking soda:** To use this foamy cleaner, mix equal parts of baking soda and white vinegar, wipe the concoction onto the surface of the faucet with a clean, soft cloth and rub until the surface is clean and shiny. Then rinse with clear water and towel-dry.

TIP

>> **Calgon:** Calgon is a common household product that acts as a really neat faucet-cleaning agent. To clean your faucets with Calgon, mix 1 teaspoon of Calgon into 1 gallon of hot water. Soak a rag in the concoction and very gently wring it out; then place the soaked rag onto the faucet, pressing the rag against all parts of the faucet, and cover it with plastic wrap (the kind you use with leftovers in the kitchen) so that it doesn't dry out. Come back in one hour, remove the rag, and use it to briskly wipe away the mineral buildup. Finally, rinse the Calgon away with fresh water and pat dry with a soft, clean cloth. *Note:* For long-time buildup, you may have to soak the rag in the solution and place it back onto the faucet several times.

>> **Plain vinegar:** Plain vinegar is great for removing a major mineral-salt buildup. You use it the same way you use the Calgon solution: With a vinegar-soaked rag, wipe down all the faucet areas; leave the rag on the faucet for an hour covered with plastic wrap; then wipe it down again, rinse, and towel-dry.

WARNING

Don't use abrasive cleaners on a faucet. Liquid cleaners work best without damaging the finish. Be sure to test a cleaner on an out-of-the-way spot to ensure that it doesn't remove or damage the finish.

Removing copper residue

If your plumbing pipes are made of copper, or if the faucet entrails are made of copper, chances are that a dark-green cast will appear at the faucet spout. The patina color indicates oxidation of copper. If left unattended, this condition will destroy the finish on a polished brass faucet in no time.

If you see green at the tip of your faucet, reach for a metal cleaner such as Brasso or Flitz. Both products are used in the same way: Pour a small amount of the cleaner on a soft, dry cloth and rub the cleaner onto the corroded area and keep rubbing until the ultra-fine polishing compound eats away at the bad finish. Let the remaining compound form a white haze and use another soft, clean cloth to wipe away the last remnants of the polish.

Toilet Training 101

What follows is a bit of toiletology that I hope will bring you and your family even closer to your bathroom and, specifically, your toilet.

REMEMBER

When you clean or repair your toilet, you often need to empty the water out of the *tank* (the reservoir that holds the water that enters the bowl when the toilet is flushed) and/or the bowl. Here's how to perform these very basic tasks.

>> **To empty the tank:** Turn off the water to the tank (at the shut-off valve) and flush the toilet. With the wall valve off, the tank will not refill. (The shut-off valve is the knob located below and behind the toilet.)

>> **To empty the bowl:** Turn off the water to the tank, flush the toilet (see the preceding bullet), and then fill a large container with 1 gallon of water and pour the water into the toilet bowl. This will force a final flush, draining most of the water that remains in the bowl. You can remove any water that remains with a small cup and/or a sponge.

Until you turn the water on and flush the toilet, the bowl and tank will remain empty.

Toilet running? Here's how to catch it!

Toilets are one of the most used and most durable fixtures in any household. They have only two "moving" parts: the *fill valve*, which — as the name implies — fills the toilet after each flush; and the *flush valve*, which releases water from the toilet tank to flush away something you hope to never see again!

While both valves are durable, they do wear out and need to be replaced every two to three years. When the fill valve begins to wear out, it tends to squeal a lot as water runs through it, which is mostly an annoyance. But when the flush valve fails, the toilet will run and can waste hundreds of gallons of water.

Fortunately, replacing both the fill and flush valves is an inexpensive, fairly simple plumbing project that most DIYers can probably handle without needing a plumber.

Testing the flush valve is pretty easy. Just open the lid of the toilet tank and add a few drops of food coloring. Then wait a half hour and check the toilet bowl. If any of that food coloring leaked into the toilet, you've got yourself a leaky flush valve that's ready to be replaced.

TIP

If either the fill or flush valve needs to be replaced, I recommend you replace both. Given that you'll need to drain the toilet in either case, it just makes sense to spend the few extra buck to do this.

Rather than walk you through all the steps to take apart and replace these valves, I'm going to point you to a super-helpful resource. Fluidmaster is the leading manufacturer of toilet valves and maintains a website chock full of videos and tutorials that walk you through every step of this project. You'll find everything you need at www.fluidmaster.com.

WARNING

Toilet shut-off valves have a bad habit of being difficult to operate. If you've tried to turn off the valve only to find it stuck, don't use a wrench or pliers to move it. Anything more than hand-pressure risks breaking the valve handle. Instead, turn the water off at the main valve to your house for the duration of the repair, and arrange to have the toilet valve replaced by a plumber in the near future.

TIP

If you do need a plumber, or really any other tradesperson, for a small repair like a stuck toilet shut-off valve, take the time to check all the other valves, fixtures, and faucets in your house for any needed repairs. Grouping small jobs together for a tradesperson to tackle is much less expensive than needing the repairs done individually — or worse, in an emergency!

Cleaning the toilet

Toilets that aren't cleaned regularly can become a mess, and toilet-bowl cleaners don't always do the job. The strong ones can be dangerous to work with, and the others aren't always strong enough to get things really clean.

Because bacteria love to live in toilets, pour 1 cup of bleach into the tank and mix it into the water. Let it set for a few minutes; then flush the toilet a few times. You've just sanitized your toilet.

WARNING

Bleach is great for killing bacteria, but it can also kill the rubber flush valve, or *flapper*, in your toilet. Some toilet bowl cleaners that are designed to be placed in your toilet tank and give the water in your bowl that ocean blue color contain chlorine, which, with prolonged exposure, can prematurely deteriorate the flapper and result in a leaking toilet. That's why the occasional shot of chlorine bleach followed by a full flush is a better option.

Asides from the wear and tear on your toilet, bleach can also have an adverse effect on a home's septic systems by disrupting bacteria that work to break down solid waste.

Cleaning the siphon jets

The siphon jets are the small openings under the rim of the bowl that help rinse the bowl and assist with the flush. If these jets become clogged, your toilet won't flush properly. If, when you flush the toilet, the water comes straight down rather than swirls, the holes are probably plugged. Discolored vertical lines in the bowl are another telltale sign that the holes need cleaning.

Inspect the rim openings with a pocket mirror (or an old cosmetic mirror). If they're clogged with mineral deposits, first empty the tank and the bowl and then carefully use a metal clothes hanger as a "pipe cleaner" to ream out the holes at the rim. (See Figure 8-1.) If the scale that exists is too hard to remove, try this trick to soften things up:

1. **Use a towel to completely dry the underside of the rim.**

2. **Apply a layer of duct tape to the underside of the rim to seal all of the holes.**

   If it doesn't stick, the rim is wet.

3. **Fill the tank with 1 gallon of pure vinegar (any kind).**

4. **Flush the toilet.**

   The vinegar travels from the tank into the rim of the toilet. Let it sit there for as long as possible — 24 hours is ideal.

5. **Remove the tape, scrub away the softened scale and flush the toilet yet again.**

   This solution should work beautifully.

FIGURE 8-1:
Clearing clogged siphon jets.

Siphon jets

Removing a ring around the bowl

If a white or brown ring forms in the bowl, pour a half-cup of borax into the bowl, followed by 2 cups of white vinegar. Use a toilet brush to swish the mixture around and scrub the bowl. Let the mixture sit for a half hour, then just flush the toilet and wipe away the softened buildup. If all goes well, you'll be looking at a sparkling clean toilet.

TIP

If your toilet is badly stained and the borax/vinegar approach doesn't do the trick, you may need to use CLR, a stronger cleaner.

Unclogging toilets

Over the years, toilets have evolved to use less and less water. What once used 5 gallons to flush, now uses as little as 1.28 gallons. While the water savings are terrific, the more efficient toilets often clog more than their wasteful ancestors. When that happens, you'll need a toilet plunger to clear the clog.

There are two types of toilet plungers worth considering.

>> **Flange plunger:** This type of plunger has a rubber flap along the bottom that helps form a good seal with the bowl and focuses the force of the plunger deep into the bowl where it's needed most.

>> **Accordion plunger:** This is shaped similarly to a flange plunger except that it's constructed of a flexible plastic, with an accordion-like shape and narrow base that supplies more force into the bowl.

REMEMBER

Although there is a third type of plunger — a so-called *drain plunger*, see Figure 8-2 — it's really designed for clearing sink drains. This type has no flap and will not work well on a toilet.

TIP

To use a toilet plunger, insert it into the toilet and tilt it toward you to improve the seal on the bowl. Then both push and pull the plunger in and out to free up the clog. Next, flush the toilet *once* to make sure you've been successful.

WARNING

If you flush a clogged toilet multiple times, you'll cause an overflow!

If your plunger hasn't fixed the issue yet, it's time to turn to a *closet auger*, also known as a *closet snake*. (See Figure 8-3.) You might find it odd to hear "closet" in the context of toilets, but historically, toilets were referred to as "water closets" and are still called a "WC" in Europe.

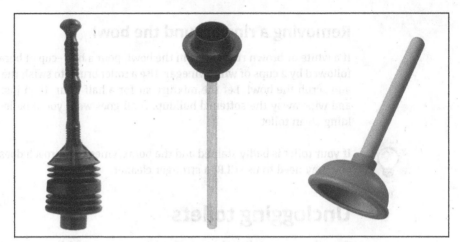

FIGURE 8-2:
An accordion
plunger, a flange
plunger, and a
drain plunger.

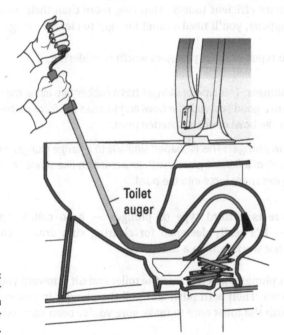

Toilet
auger

FIGURE 8-3:
A closet auger
(also called a
"closet snake" or
"toilet snake").

To use a closet snake, follow these steps:

1. **Pull the handle of the closet auger all the way out of the hollow tube so that the hooked end is up against the end of the tube and none of the cable is released.**

2. **Insert the auger end of the snake into the throat of the toilet.**

   Make sure that the vinyl sleeve is up against the porcelain to prevent damage.

3. Turn the crank slowly while, at the same time, pushing the rod and snake into the toilet trap and down into the sewer line; continue to turn the crank when retracting the snake.

If the snake doesn't work (or you aren't interested in getting this up close and personal with your toilet), call the plumber.

Preventing a sweaty tank

A toilet tank sweats when the cold water inside chills the tank in a warm bathroom. The sweat is actually condensation. The condensation can become so profuse that it can result in puddles on the floor that can damage floor covering, trim, and other finishes. One way to reduce sweating is to make sure that the water entering the tank isn't cold, by having a plumber add a mixing valve at the tank inlet to introduce warm water into the tank. Unfortunately, this fix is relatively expensive.

TIP

A far less expensive solution is one you can do yourself: Pick up a toilet tank liner. Made of waterproof, insulating foam sheets, the liner materials can be trimmed to size with scissors and fitted inside the toilet tank. By insulating the cold water from the toilet tank, you help ensure that the tank remains warmer and is far less likely to develop condensation. You'll find liner kits at home centers, hardware stores, or online at Amazon.com. Liners may be self-sticking, but if not, you can glue the liner in place with silicone cement. Just remember to let the adhesive dry for at least 24 hours before filling the tank. (See Figure 8-4.)

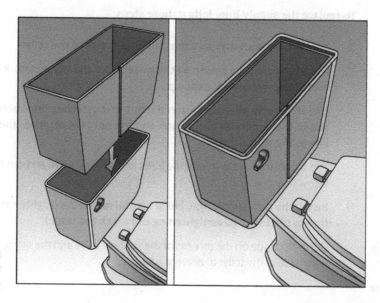

FIGURE 8-4:
Lining the inside of your tank.

Looking for leaks in and around the toilet

Some leaks occur outside the toilet. If the floor is wet around the toilet, you obviously have a leak (or a sweating toilet, as explained in the preceding section). The trick is finding where the leak is coming from (there are several places to look) so that you can take the proper steps to solve the problem.

The shut-off valve at the wall

Use a towel to dry the floor around the toilet; then lay a piece of toilet paper on the floor beneath the valve and wait for about 15 minutes. If the toilet paper is wet, the shut-off valve (or the supply tube connected to it) leaks. Try tightening the valve fittings. If that doesn't work, you need to replace the valve and/or supply line. Replacing this valve is tricky for DIYers. It's in a tight spot behind the toilet and is best tackled by a plumber.

Where the supply tube connects

Use a small clump of toilet paper to wipe the bottom of the tank where the *supply tube* (the thin, flexible tube that carries water from the shut-off valve to the toilet tank) connects. If it's wet, the leak is there. Tighten the nut and the supply line at that location. If that doesn't work, replace the supply line.

TIP

When choosing a new supply line, get a braided stainless-steel one instead of the vinyl hoses, which are not nearly as durable. A few extra dollars can prevent a flood that could save thousands of dollars and lots of heartache.

To replace the supply line, follow these steps:

1. **Turn off the shut-off valve that supplies water to the toilet.**

2. **Flush the toilet to remove all the water from the toilet tank. Remove any remaining water with a sponge.**

3. **Use adjustable pliers to loosen the nut that attaches the water supply line to the underside of the tank and the nut that attaches the supply line to the shut-off valve.**

   The supply line is now free of the toilet and shut-off valve and can be replaced with a new one.

4. **Install the new supply line, being careful not to over-tighten the connection to the toilet. (Overtightening can crack the tank.)**

   REMEMBER

   Use Teflon tape on the threads of the shut-off valve and the fitting at the underside of the toilet to prevent a leak.

5. Turn the toilet shut-off valve back open and use the toilet paper trick-of-the-trade mentioned earlier to check for leaks.

The area where the tank connects to the bowl

Two bolts hold the tank to the bowl. If either of them leaks, try tightening the bolts slightly. Don't over-tighten — you can crack the toilet. If tightening the bolts doesn't stop the leak, replace the rubber gasket that is on either bolt within the tank as well as the gasket between the tank and the bowl: Empty the tank, remove the bolts, replace the gaskets, and reinstall the bolts.

The toilet's exterior surface

Check the entire exterior surface of the toilet for hairline cracks. If you find any, the toilet needs to be replaced. Replacing a toilet may not be one of the most exciting ways to spend a Saturday, but then, that's the nice part about this particular project; you should be able to perform this little task and still have time to enjoy your afternoon.

Gather the following tools:

>> An open-ended wrench (¼ inch or ⅜ inch)

>> An adjustable wrench

>> A pair of adjustable pliers

>> A flathead screwdriver

>> A hacksaw

Then follow these steps to replace the toilet:

1. Turn off the shut-off valve to the toilet. (See Figure 8-5.)

   Turn the valve that is located below and behind the toilet clockwise until it stops.

2. Disconnect the water-supply line.

   Flush the toilet and remove any water that may remain in the tank or bowl with a small cup and a sponge. After all the water has been removed, disconnect the water-supply line at the base of the tank; use adjustable pliers to turn the nut in a counterclockwise direction.

3. **Unfasten the toilet from the floor. (See Figure 8-6.)**

Most residential toilets are anchored to the floor with a couple of fasteners called *closet bolts,* which are concealed by plastic caps. Pry the caps off by wedging a flathead screwdriver between the bottom lip of the cap and the porcelain. Remove the nuts that remain with an open-ended wrench, turning counterclockwise.

4. **Remove the toilet and as much of the (rather icky) wax ring beneath it as you can. (See Figure 8-7.)**

TIP

I suggest that you have one other person help you lift the toilet and carry it out because it's as awkward as it is heavy.

Grasp the toilet by the rim and the underside of the tank and lift it directly upward. Don't be alarmed by the gooey mess on the floor where the toilet once sat. It's some of the wax ring, which forms a seal between the toilet and the toilet flange that's connected to the sewer. Use a putty knife to remove the wax that remains; doing so improves the odds of a new, leakproof seal.

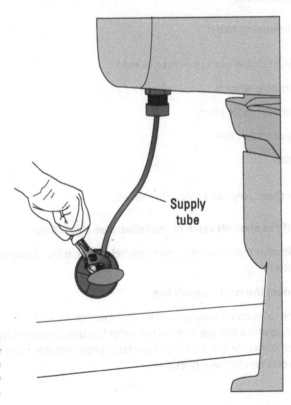

Supply tube

FIGURE 8-5:
Avoid a flood by turning off the water supply to the toilet.

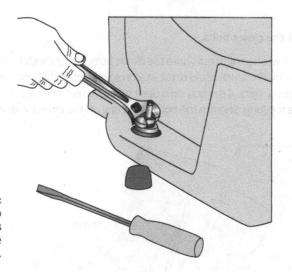

FIGURE 8-6:
Use a wrench to loosen the nuts that anchor the toilet to the floor.

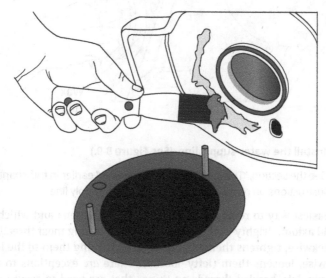

FIGURE 8-7:
The ring acts as a seal between the toilet and the flange. When reinstalling a toilet, make sure to remove as much of the old wax ring as possible for a good seal.

5. **Install the new toilet.**

With the toilet lying on its side, install the new wax ring (sold separately) by placing it wax side up against the underside of the toilet. (See Figure 8-8.) The wax ring will be slightly larger than the hole at the base of the toilet. Install new closet bolts (typically provided with the toilet) in the slots on the closet flange in an upright position, just as you found the old ones. Next, with the help of a friend, stand the toilet up and, without allowing the bottom to touch the floor, align the holes in the base of the toilet with the closet bolts, and then gently lower the toilet until it completely seats.

6. Connect the closet bolts.

Install the washers and nuts onto the closet bolts, being careful not to tighten them too much, which could result in a broken toilet. Ugh! Then place the bolt caps over the nuts. If the bolt caps don't properly seat, chances are that the bolts are too long. Shorten the bolts by cutting off the excess with a hacksaw.

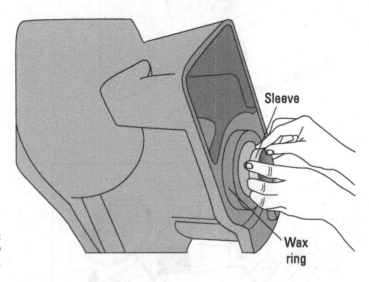

Sleeve

Wax ring

FIGURE 8-8:
Attach a new
wax ring.

7. Install the water-supply line. (See Figure 8-9.)

See the section, "The shut-off valve at the wall," earlier in this chapter, for instructions on removing and reconnecting a supply line.

TIP

The easiest way to remember which direction tightens and which one loosens is the old axiom, "righty-tighty, lefty-loosey." Turning most threaded things right, or clockwise, tightens them (righty-tighty); turning them to the left, or counter-clockwise, loosens them (lefty-loosey). There *are* exceptions to this rule — for example, left-handed threads on things that are used to secure things that also turn clockwise (like the blade on a table saw). So, if you run into a nut that just won't give, before muscling it any more, try switching direction.

Between the base of the toilet and the floor

The area between the tank and the floor is one that's prone to leakage. First, check the floor around the bowl by gently pressing down with your foot. If you detect any softness in this area, you may have a slow leak coming from the wax seal, which is located between the bowl and the floor. In that case, I'd remove the toilet (see the preceding section) and replace the wax seal and reinstall as described previously.

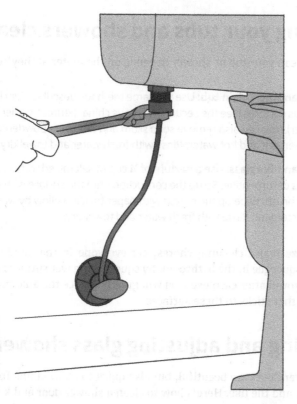

FIGURE 8-9:
Use a wrench to connect the water-supply line to the toilet fill valve.

Next, check the looseness of the bowl by grabbing both sides and gently twisting it from side-to-side to see if the toilet is loose. If the toilet moves, try tightening the bolt slightly. Don't over-tighten — you can crack the toilet.

TIP

Even if the floor is dry, if you have access to the area beneath the toilet (like in the basement or crawlspace), occasionally check to see if the toilet has developed a hidden leak. Look for damp wood or evidence of dripping water. If you find this telltale evidence, replace the wax ring.

Maintaining Tubs and Showers

Most people make at least one trip a day to the tub or shower. I don't know anyone who wants to perform a morning scrub-down in a mildew-lined fixture with a dangerously slippery floor. The following tub and shower tips show you how to easily maintain these fixtures.

Keeping your tubs and showers clean

How you clean your tub or shower depends on the material they're made of.

>> **To clean a porcelain tub:** Use the same methods described for cleaning vitreous surfaces (see the section, "Vitreous china fixtures," earlier in this chapter). You can also remove soap scum and dirt using powdered dishwashing detergent and hot water. Rinse with fresh water and towel-dry.

>> **To clean fiberglass:** Use a mixture of ¼ cup of salt mixed with 2 to 3 tablespoons of turpentine. Scrub the concoction onto the surface with a nylon bristle brush. Wipe up the excess with paper towels. Follow by washing with a mild detergent. Rinse with fresh water and towel-dry.

TIP

To minimize major cleaning chores, get everyone in the family to pitch in by keeping a squeegee in the bathroom. By squeegeeing wet surfaces or wiping them dry with a towel after each use, you will greatly reduce the amount of mildew and soap scum that sticks to these surfaces.

Cleaning and adjusting glass shower doors

Glass shower doors are beautiful, but also quick to show stains from hard water, soap scum, and the like. Here's how to clean a shower door and keep it that way.

Cleaning glass shower doors

When it comes to keeping your bath clean, there's no shortage of off-the-shelf products that can do the job. But if you want to save a few bucks, readily available household products can do the same. Here are a couple options for shower doors.

>> **Distilled white vinegar:** Vinegar breaks down hard-water stains. Warm ½ cup of vinegar in a microwave, then pour into a spray bottle. Apply to the shower doors and let it sit on the surface for a few minutes. Then wipe the doors down with a sponge or soft bristle brush, and rinse. For tougher stains, add a few drops of dish detergent to the mix.

>> **Lemon juice:** While not as effective as vinegar, lemon juice can also help cut stains on shower doors. And it smells a lot better as well! Add ¼ cup of lemon juice to 1 cup of water in a spray bottle. Again, spray the doors, let it sit for a few minutes, and then wipe it down with a soft sponge or even a microfiber cloth. No need to rinse, and it'll keep your bathroom smelling great!

Cleaning shower door tracks

Shower door tracks act as gutters, collecting water that runs down the shower doors and drains back to the shower pan. With all that water, tracks get pretty grungy from hard-water deposits and soap scum. Here's a quick tip to clean them:

1. **Dry out the tracks completely.**

2. **Place duct tape on the back side of the door tracks, being sure to cover the drain holes.**

3. **Pour white vinegar into the tracks until it completely covers the tracks and let sit for 24 hours.**

   The vinegar will soften any of the deposits and make them easier to clean.

4. **Rinse with clean water and wipe away any remaining deposits.**

Adjusting shower door tracks

If the doors get out of alignment, or the rollers come off the track, you can usually reset the doors by lifting them in the frame and resetting the rollers in the channel.

When the doors drag, or they don't stay in the bottom channel, you need to adjust the rollers. Follow these steps:

1. **Lift the outer door until the rollers clear the top track; then pull the bottom of the door out and away from the bottom channel and set it aside.**

   Do the same with the inner door.

2. **Clean debris from the bottom track and clean the door frames using my Easy All-Surface Mildew Remover. (See Chapter 20.)**

3. **Loosen the screws that hold the rollers to the door frame and adjust them to raise or lower the door as needed.**

   If the screws are rusted, replace them with zinc-coated or stainless-steel screws.

4. **Spray a dry silicone lubricant lightly on the rollers to keep them operating smoothly.**

Keeping Your Tile Terrific

Ceramic tile walls, floors, and countertops offer a trade-off: They last forever, but they require a lot more maintenance than most other materials. The tile itself is tough — it's the grout you have to worry about. Grout is a pretty durable material for sealing the spaces between tiles. But while it looks clean and bright when it's first put in, it climbs the "gross scale" pretty quickly thereafter.

Sealing out grout grunge

Grout sealer goes a long way toward preventing stains and keeping your beautiful new tile looking good. The trick is, you have to wait at least 72 hours for the grout to *cure* (dry) before you can seal it.

Your local home center probably has several different brands of grout-and-tile sealer with handy sponge-tip applicators. A silicone-based sealer is best.

Sealing grout can take several hours to do, depending upon the amount of tile that you have, so plan not to be in a big hurry. Follow each grout line with the sealer applicator, making sure you're getting the sealer down into the lines. (Follow the manufacturer's directions for application.) Apply a second coat 24 hours later and a third coat 24 hours after that. Big fun — but totally necessary.

Cleaning grubby grout

To clean your grout, you need a bottle of vinegar, water, and a *grout brush*, a stiff, narrow brush that looks a lot like an oversized toothbrush. Then follow these steps:

1. **In a big jar, make a solution of one part water, one part vinegar.**

2. **Dip the brush in the solution and start scrubbing the grout.**

   Yes, cleaning grout takes a while. And yes, it's tedious. The vinegar, a weak acid, helps remove hard-water deposits and other hard-to-remove chemical stains.

3. **Remove the sour-smelling solution by wiping the tile thoroughly with a damp sponge.**

If vinegar treatment doesn't do the trick, grab a bottle of hydrogen peroxide (the stuff for disinfecting cuts) and pour a generous amount all over the grout. The peroxide whitens the grout and helps dislodge stains caused by foods. Let it sit for about 15 minutes, and then scrub like crazy using a nylon scrub brush. After scrubbing, wipe down the surface with a damp sponge.

If neither vinegar nor hydrogen peroxide gets the grout nice and white, you have to scrub using a weak bleach solution — 2 tablespoons of bleach per quart of water. Open the windows, turn on the vent hood, and bring a box fan up from the basement. Wear old clothes, eye protection, and gloves. Scrub carefully, rinse thoroughly, and then rinse again.

When you're working with bleach, more is *not* better. If you use more than the recommended amount of bleach, you'll give yourself one heck of a headache and a wheezy cough. Ask any doctor: Breathing chlorine fumes is not good. And, as always, never mix other chemicals or household cleaners with bleach.

If your grout is still grubby after this all-out chemical assault, the only solution is to apply a grout stain (see the next section) or replace the grout (see the section, "Replacing grout," later in the chapter).

Staining grubby grout

The kinds of stains you'd use to cover up grout grubbiness are essentially paint. You can find them online or at any decent home center or tile store.

Before you apply the stain, you have to get the grout really, really, *really* clean: Clean the grout (see the preceding section), rinse it thoroughly, and allow the grout to dry overnight. Then apply the grout stain according to the manufacturer's instructions *exactly* — this is no time for creativity.

Although grout stain is a time- and energy-saving alternative to grout replacement, it doesn't last forever — you have to re-stain every year or two.

Replacing grout

Cracked, deteriorating grout can allow water underneath the tile, where wood rot can occur. Replacing grout will make your counters look better and last longer. How often can you kill two birds with one stone?

There are two different kinds of grout: cement-based and epoxy-based. For a number of very good reasons (cost and ease of use, primarily), you want to use cement-based grout. For thin (⅛-inch) joints between tiles, use plain, unsanded grout. For wide (¼-inch) joints, use sanded grout.

Grout comes in a rainbow of colors, and your choice has a big effect on the appearance of the finished countertop. Choose the color you want but know that dark-colored grout hides dirt and stains better — and is easier to clean — than light-colored or white grout.

Removing the old grout and debris

Before you can do any actual grout application, you have to "saw" out old, bad grout from the joints between the tiles. You can use a grout saw to remove the old grout (as shown in Figure 8-10), but for a speedier approach, use an oscillating power tool with a grout blade.

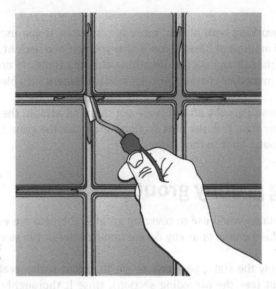

FIGURE 8-10:
Using a grout saw
to remove grout.

WARNING

If you use a grout saw or oscillating power tool, work slowly and carefully. Just aim to get out the loose stuff — if you get too aggressive, and the tool slips out of the joints, you'll gouge the tiles. (The same goes for doing the job with a Dremel tool, if you decide to go that route.) Stay focused and don't apply too much pressure. Also, be sure to wear eye protection.

When you've got all the loose grout out, vacuum the surface and wipe with a damp sponge to get up every bit of dust and debris.

Re-grouting your tile

With the grout and dust gone, it's time to get grouting! You need the following:

» Grout (powdered or premixed)

» Rubber float or squeegee

» Big sponge

» Popsicle stick

» Toothbrush

» Rags or cheesecloth

» Vinegar

» Bucket

» Rubber gloves (grout is caustic before it dries)

To re-grout, follow these steps:

1. **If you bought powdered grout, mix it with cold water, according to the manufacturer's directions.**

   Make only as much as you think you can use in 30 minutes, which is not a lot — typically less than a small pail. Be sure to use cold water; warm water can cause some colors to mottle when they dry.

2. **While wearing rubber gloves, apply the grout to the surface of the tiles diagonally, using the rubber float or squeegee held at a 45-degree angle to the surface of the tiles.**

   Work in a 3-foot-square area. Spread the grout liberally and force it into the joints. Use the Popsicle stick for corners and small, tough-to-reach spots. Remove excess grout with the rubber float and/or a damp sponge as you go.

3. **Let the grout set for 20 minutes or however long the manufacturer suggests.**

4. **Wipe the entire surface with a damp sponge and keep wiping until all the grout lines are even and the joints are smooth.**

   Rinse the sponge frequently.

5. **Let the grout dry for another 20 minutes.**

6. **Polish the tiles with a rag or cheesecloth.**

   Use an old toothbrush to get into the corners and hard-to-reach areas.

7. **Mix fresh grout and move on to another area, repeating Steps 2 through 6 until the entire tiled surface is grouted.**

8. **When all the freshly grouted areas are dry, remove any *grout haze* (residue left on the tiles by the grout) with a soft rag and a 10 percent solution of vinegar and water.**

   You may have to wipe off the haze several times before the tile surface is completely clean.

9. **Caulk where the tile forms 90-degree corners with the tub or shower pan or, in the case of a countertop, the backsplash.**

10. **Seal all the joints with grout sealer (see the section, "Sealing out grout grunge," earlier in this chapter).**

Replacing a broken tile

Got a loose tile? Dropped the big soup pot and cracked one? Worried about how it looks or that you might accidentally cut yourself on the sharp edge? It's time for replacement!

If you're lucky enough to have a leftover tile stashed in your workbench, you're ready to go. But if you don't, you have options:

>> Transplant a tile from a less visible place, such as under an appliance.

>> Bring the broken pieces to a well-stocked tile store, where you might be able to find a new one that's a close substitute.

>> Have tiles made to order. Custom tile makers can recreate the tile, using shards of the old tile to match the color.

TIP

If you can't find an acceptable match, consider replacing several tiles. You can randomly add tiles in a contrasting color or use *decos* (decorator tiles with pictures) as accents.

With your replacement tile in hand, grab the tools you need:

>> Grout saw, Dremel, or oscillating tool

>> Glass cutter

>> Hammer and a cold chisel (the kind that isn't for use on wood)

>> Power drill with a ¼-inch masonry bit

>> *Mastic* (tile adhesive)

>> Putty knife

>> Block of wood bigger than the tile

>> Masking tape

>> Eye protection

Follow these steps to replace the broken tile (and take note of how often I use the word *carefully*):

1. **Carefully remove the grout from the joints around the damaged tile using a grout saw, a Dremel, or an oscillating tool.**

2. **Use a drill to carefully bore a hole in the center of the tile and then use a glass cutter to carefully scribe an X in the tile (corner to corner).**

   Drilling a hole in the center and crosscutting the surface helps to relieve pressure when you begin to remove the tile with a hammer and chisel. Relieving pressure helps prevent damage to surrounding tiles.

3. **Use a hammer and chisel to carefully remove the tile, then clean out the area behind it.**

   Carefully remove all adhesive and grout. Try not to pry underneath adjacent tiles — you could loosen them.

4. **Test-fit the replacement tile to make sure it sits well with the other tiles.**

   You want it to be slightly recessed to leave room for adhesive.

5. **Carefully spread mastic on the back of the tile with a putty knife.**

   Keep the mastic ¼ to ½ inch from the edges for squishing room.

6. **Carefully place the tile in position and then wiggle it a little to ensure good contact between the tile, the adhesive, and the base.**

7. **Place the block of wood over the tile and give it a couple of gentle taps to make extra-sure the tile is flush with its neighbors and to make super-sure that the adhesive is stuck to everything.**

8. **Tape the wood over the repair to protect the repair.**

9. **Wait at least 24 hours and then apply grout. (See the section, "Re-grouting your tile," earlier in this chapter.)**

Re-caulking tubs and showers

If you have tile shower walls, there is a very good possibility that a leak could develop between the tile and the tub. As the house moves (a natural process that occurs in every home), a hairline crack can occur that allows water to get into the joint. Once water gets in, there is no telling how much damage can be done. That's why it's important to annually caulk the connection between your shower walls and the tub or shower pan.

Here's another good reason to re-caulk. If you've tried to remove the black mildew stains from caulk, you know it's sometimes hopeless. That's because the stains are often behind the caulk — between the caulk and the wall. The answer, of course, is to remove the caulk, kill the mildew, and then replace the caulk.

Removing old caulk

Removing what exists and then caulking from scratch are the way to go. Fortunately, removing the caulk isn't as hard as it may seem, thanks to a product called a caulk remover.

To remove caulk, simply apply a caulk remover and allow it to sit until the caulk has softened (it may take a few hours). Then remove the softened caulk with a plastic putty knife. Finish up by cleaning the joint with paint thinner and wiping the area dry with a clean rag.

Getting rid of mildew

After you've removed the old caulk, you can get rid of mildew by cleaning the joint with my Easy All-Surface Mildew Remover. (See Chapter 20.) Just spray the mixture onto the mildewed area and let it sit until the black mildew turns white. Rinse with fresh water; then use a hair dryer to thoroughly dry the area. The joint can now be re-caulked.

Although my Easy Mildew Remover mixture is relatively mild, don't forget to wear gloves and eye protection and make sure the area is well ventilated.

Improve the odds of preventing mildew from returning by wiping down the joint with denatured alcohol just before applying the new caulk.

Applying new caulk

For a professional-looking job, follow these steps:

1. **Apply blue painter's masking tape to the tub, ⅛ inch from the joint; then apply another strip of tape along the wall, ⅛ inch from the joint.**

   Now the caulking will go between the two pieces of tape, making straight, smooth lines.

2. **Fill the tub with water.** This pulls the tub downward, much like it would if you were in it taking a bath.

3. **Apply tub and tile caulk into the joint and smooth it with your finger, an old teaspoon, or a caulking spreader.**

   Note: This technique only works if you are using latex caulk. For silicone caulk, first dip your finger or other caulk-smoothing tool in dish soap to prevent it from sticking.

4. **Immediately remove the tape.**

   Pull it out and away from the freshly caulked joint. Be careful not to touch the caulk.

5. **Let the caulk dry overnight.**

   Caulk can take varying amounts of time to dry, depending upon the type being used and the temperature and humidity in your home. In general, your best bet is to allow the caulk to dry overnight before getting it wet.

6. **Let the water out of the tub.**

   By doing so, the tub will move "up" and compress the caulk, making it less likely to work loose when you step back in for your bath or shower!

You simply won't believe how beautiful your job looks and how long it lasts!

IN THIS CHAPTER

» **Getting to know your sewer system**

» **Keeping your sewer or septic system running clog-free**

» **Eliminating the most common clogs**

Chapter **9**

Plumbing, Part III: Sewer and Septic Systems

"Sanitation" is the collective term for those house systems that we use to send elsewhere what we hope to never see again — making it one of the most important systems in your home. A cracked windowpane, backed-up gutter, or broken fence board can wait until you have time to make the necessary repair. However, when it comes to your sewer or septic system, few things can put a cramp in your style quicker than a backed-up toilet, a sink that won't drain, or a tub that overflows! In this chapter, I'll tackle those challenges and more to keep things flowing in the right direction!

Uncovering Sewer-System Basics

Every plumbing fixture in your home is joined by the same drainpipe — that means the kitchen sink, the dishwasher, the washing machine, the toilets, and so on. The waste from each of these fixtures exits the house through this one drain-pipe. A problem caused by one fixture can easily become a problem for all the other fixtures.

Your common, everyday household sanitary sewer system consists of three basic elements. (See Figure 9-1.)

>> **The waste lines and drainpipe:** These carry solid and liquid sewage from each of the fixtures in your home down through the walls and under the floor, and then outside the home to either a public sewer system beneath the street or a septic tank somewhere below ground on your property. A clog in any of these pipes stops waste from reaching its destination away from your home — and it can back up into your home.

>> **The vent pipes:** These pipes travel from each plumbing fixture (or group of plumbing fixtures), upward (inside walls) and out through the roof. The vents allow air into the sewer lines so that they drain freely. A clogged vent pipe can lead to a host of problems and prevent good drainage of waste.

>> **The p-traps:** You have one of these traps in every fixture: sink, toilet, washing machine, you name it. If the fixture drains into the sewer system, the water or waste first travels through a p-trap. The trap allows water and waste to enter the sewer system while at the same time preventing sewer gases from backing up into your home. A clogged p-trap can inhibit the flow of waste from the home and can allow stinky gases to back up into the home through the fixtures.

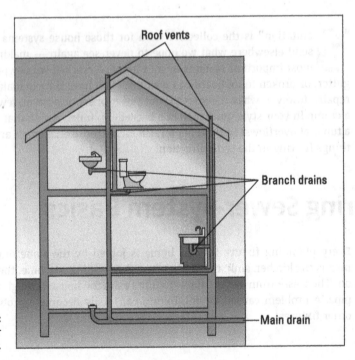

FIGURE 9-1:
Your sewer system.

Keeping Your System Clog-Free

When it comes to your home's drain and sewer system, the old saying, "An ounce of prevention is worth a pound of cure," applies perfectly. Trapping hair and soap scum in the tub or shower, using a lint filter in the clothes washer, and being careful about what you throw into the kitchen sink — including the garbage disposal — can prevent minor clogs that can cause major headaches and repairs. Following these few basic maintenance guidelines can keep your system in tip-top shape.

Being careful what you put down the drain

One of the absolute best ways to prevent slow or clogged drains is to be careful about what you put into them. Clever, eh?

TIP

Cooking grease, coffee grounds, hair, and soap scum are four of a drain's biggest enemies. Do whatever you can to avoid introducing any of these items into a drain. Here's how:

>> Let cooking grease cool and solidify, then wipe it out of the pan with a paper towel and dispose of it in the trash.

>> Throw coffee grounds away in the garbage or add them to your mulch or compost pile.

>> Use a screen or drain-grate to cover the drain's opening and minimize problems with hair and soap scum. Stop by your local plumbing-supply store to peruse the choices that are appropriate for your particular fixture. Take along a picture of the drain system to better explain your needs. Most filters and screens can be simply laid in place.

Doing preventive pipe cleaning

TIP

Regular cleaning has its merits. To keep drains in your home running freely — and absent of odor — try these methods:

>> Run hot water through the sink after each use. Hot water keeps oils in food products running down the drain, rather than building up on the interior surface of pipes, which can make drains sluggish and lead to clogs.

>> Throw a handful of baking soda into the drain and follow it with hot water. Baking soda is a terrific cleaning agent, and it's also great for absorbing

foul odors and leaving your drainpipes smelling like a rose. Okay, maybe not like a rose, but a lot better than they otherwise would.

>> **Pour 1 cup of vinegar down the drain and let it sit for 30 minutes; then chase it down with very hot water.** Vinegar is a wonder cleaner (as Chapter 20 explains). It contains acetic acid, which acts as an excellent organic solvent in removing organic buildup of crud in pipes.

Baking soda and vinegar are safe and effective cleaners for your household drains, but more importantly they are 100 percent safe for your septic tank and drain field. Bleach and ammonia-based cleaners can be harmful to the good bacteria in your septic tank.

If clogging is a regular problem at your place, try this solution out for size. It works on drains in sinks, showers, and tubs. You need ½ cup each of baking soda, salt, and vinegar and a couple quarts of boiling water. Do the following:

1. **Pour the salt and the baking soda into the drain.**

2. **Add the vinegar and let the concoction foam for about a minute.**

3. **Chase with at least 2 quarts of boiling water.**

For additional tips on cleaning your sink, toilet, tub, and shower, turn to Chapter 8.

For sinks with garbage disposals, you can also try this trick:

1. **Fill an ice-cube tray half-full with vinegar and top it off with clear water.**
   Vinegar alone won't freeze well. Be sure to mark the tray clearly — you wouldn't want an unsuspecting family member to end up with a mouthful of vinegar. Can you imagine how that martini would taste?

2. **Let your freezer do its thing.**

3. **Turn the disposal on and then throw in that new set of vinegar ice cubes.**
   Vinegar is a mild acid that cleans the disposal and the drain, while the ice literally chills and scrapes grease off its walls. (See Figure 9-2.) If you don't like the smell of vinegar, you can chase the cubes with one sliced lemon. Your disposal and your kitchen will smell great!

If you don't want to go the DIY route, there are a host of garbage disposal cleaner products available. I like those by Glisten. (Check out https://summitbrands.com/product-category/glisten/.) Just drop a packet in, run the water, and then watch the magic foaming action take place as it cleans and deodorizes your disposal!

A word about commercial drain cleaners

Commercial drain cleaners can seem like a simple enough way to clear a sluggish drain, but I don't recommend them. Lye is the active ingredient in most popular store-bought drain cleaners. While it dissolves soap scum and hair in a heartbeat, splashing it on your skin — or worse, in your eyes — can cause significant injury. Instead, I recommend using a drain plunger or mechanical snake to clear a clogged drain. If that doesn't do the trick, it's time to turn to a drain cleaning pro to get the job done.

Dealing with drains that stink

Smelly drains can happen due to a couple of reasons. First is biogas, which happens when bacteria in a sink or tub drain breaks down organic matter (like soap scum, hair, and so on) and releases a very nasty rotten-egg smell. The solution is to clean the drains using bleach.

>> Fill up a spray bottle with a 50/50 mix of bleach and water.

>> Spray the bleach in and around the drain, as well as the overflow channel (in a sink). Then pour a little full-strength bleach down the drain.

>> Let the bleach sit for 15 to 30 minutes, and then rinse the drain thoroughly.

The second reason drains develop odors is what's called a "dry trap." P-traps need to be filled with water to seal out sewage gas. If your home has been vacant, or you have bathrooms that are not used very often, the water in those traps will evaporate and allow smelly sewage gas to flow right into your house.

The solution is simple: Just run water in sinks or tubs or flush the toilet occasionally to restore the seal and keep those seldom-used fixtures from stinking up your house! And don't forget to pour a cup or two of water into floor drains as well.

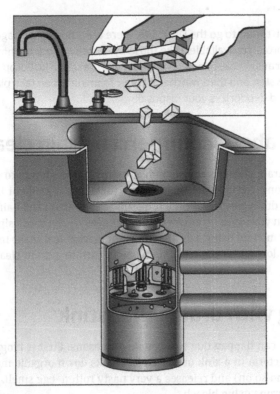

FIGURE 9-2:
Cleaning your
disposal with ice
and vinegar.

Unclogging the Waste Lines

The clean-out system to your sewer provides access to the waste lines for easy cleaning, which can save you hundreds of dollars in plumber's bills. A *clean-out* is a port with a removable plug that provides access to the inside of the sewer line.

So where are your clean-outs? The National Plumbing Code requires clean-outs to be placed in your waste lines at least every 100 linear feet of horizontal travel. Clean-outs must be even closer together when the total angle of all bends in the horizontal sections of line exceed 135 degrees.

TIP

The tell-tale sign of a clean-out is its plug. It's a flat, threaded disk fitted with a hexagonal or square protrusion at its center, which allows it to be easily removed (or replaced) with a wrench.

Clean-outs can be found under sinks, sticking out of exterior walls, and randomly in the area beneath the floor — but not buried below the soil. When you know where all your clean-outs are, you can use that knowledge to keep your sewer system clean on your own. And you can give your plumber a rest — at home, not in Tahiti with your money!

To clear a clog through the clean-outs, follow these steps:

1. **Using a wrench, remove the clean-out plug.**

   Keep a bucket handy as some stinky water may flow out when you remove the plug.

TIP

2. **Use a plumber's auger, or *snake*, to clear a clog at the first sign of a drainage problem. (See Figure 9-3.)**

   Most good do-it-yourselfers own a small version of a plumber's auger. Not only is a small auger inexpensive, but it's easy to store as well. (See Chapter 8 for information about snakes that are made especially for clearing toilet clogs.)

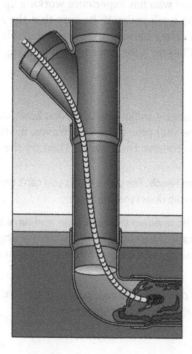

FIGURE 9-3:
Using a plumber's auger or snake to clear a line.

Keeping Vents Free from Debris

When a sink isn't draining properly, and the waste line isn't clogged, you may need to take a look upward to find the culprit — up toward the vent system. (You know, the plastic or copper plumbing pipes that stick up out of your roof.) When a vent becomes clogged, it shows up within the home as everything from "ghost flushes" at the toilet, to sinks that simply won't drain properly. (The upcoming sidebar explains more about ghost flushes; it also tells you and how to rid your house of their spooky presence!)

Leaves, trash, tennis balls, and even bird's nests can find their way into your vent pipes and clog things up pretty quickly.

Because clearing vent-pipe blockages can be a real pain in the you-know-what, these preventive steps can help you.

Getting rid of blockages

Unfortunately, the best place to clear a blockage in a vent pipe is from the roof.

Working up on the roof can be a dangerous task, to say the least. So, you may want to have this job done by someone who has experience working up high. If you feel confident about performing the work yourself, be sure that the roof is dry, wear rubber-soled shoes, and use a safety harness to prevent yourself from falling off the roof should you slip. (See Chapter 5 for more tips on working on the roof.)

Dealing with clogs

You'll need a flashlight, a plumber's snake, and a garden hose. Use the flashlight to shine a bright light down the vent pipe to look for leaves, nesting materials, or other debris you may be able to remove from above. Then try the following:

>> **Remove any items you can reach.** For those items you can't remove from above, run the plumber's snake down the vent pipe.

>> **Feed the end of a garden hose down the vent pipe and have someone on the ground turn on the water.** Listen carefully for water backing up and a sudden whoosh when the weight of the water forces the clog into and down the drain.

You can also feed the hose down into the vent pipe as you would a plumber's snake to dislodge a clog that's not solid enough to dam water.

Putting preventive measures in place

One of the most effective means of preventing plumbing vent-pipe blockages is with the use of vent-pipe screens. These nifty devices fit snugly onto the top of vent pipes and prevent blockages from animals, insects, and debris such as leaves. You can find these screens at hardware stores, home centers, plumbing wholesalers, and online.

THE CASE OF THE GHOST FLUSH

Imagine enjoying a calm evening at home. But just when you think you're all alone, the unexpected sound of a toilet flushing startles you. Has an intruder taken a bathroom break while scouring your home for valuables to pilfer? Before you panic, consider the phenomenon known as "ghost flushing." There are two possible explanations for this eerie occurrence.

Firstly, if the flush valve (the flapper at the bottom of the toilet tank) is worn, water may slowly drain out, triggering the toilet to flush and refill autonomously. Secondly, if the ghost flush coincides with using the bathtub or shower, a blocked vent is likely the culprit. Showers and toilets are often connected to the same vent pipe, and if it becomes obstructed, water moving down the sewer line creates suction. When the clogged vent can't draw in enough air to offset the rising negative pressure, the toilet effectively becomes the ventilation intake port. Case solved!

Avoiding Problems with P-Traps

The *p-trap* is that strangely curved pipe that you see beneath any sink in your home. Actually, a p-trap can be found at every single plumbing fixture — whether you can see it or not. If you can't see it, you can be sure it's inside the fixture (as it is with toilets), beneath the floor (in the case of showers and tubs), or inside the wall (for washing-machine drains).

The name of this special piece of drain comes from the letter of the alphabet that it resembles, and also from the fact that it actually traps water. Essentially, the trap holds enough water in its curved base to act as a "water door," preventing unpleasant waste and sewer gases from backing up into the home.

Unfortunately, the trap's water-trapping ability extends to hair, grease, debris, and soap scum. This makes a p-trap the number-one location of clogs in the sewer system. If the p-trap becomes only slightly clogged, then you experience slow drainage in the fixture. Oh, you say the toilet is the place where all the clogs occur at your house? The toilet has the largest p-trap of any fixture in the home. Had to pull any toys out of yours lately?

You can prevent drain clogs by being careful about what you put in the drain and by performing monthly preventive cleaning, as explained in the earlier section, "Keeping Your System Clog-Free." But if these measures don't work and you experience slow draining in your fixture, try cleaning the p-trap to avoid a full-blown blockage. You need the following:

» 1 small plastic bucket

» 1 rag

» 1 large pair of pliers or a pipe wrench

» 1 portable light

Before beginning, remove everything from under the sink so that you have ample room to work. Then follow these steps:

1. **Position the plastic bucket directly under the p-trap.**

2. **Using the pliers, remove the two coupling nuts that attach the trap to the sink tailpiece and to the adjacent wall fitting.**

   If the nuts are plastic, you may be able to loosen them with just hand pressure. If the nuts are metal and won't budge, or if they simply fall apart when you try to move them, it's time to purchase a replacement trap.

3. **Clean the interior of the trap with a large nylon bottle brush.**

   Make sure that all the parts are completely clean inside and out. A piece of debris lodged between a drain washer and the drainpipe can cause a leak.

4. **If you discover that the trap is clean and clear (and not the reason for the clog or slow draining), then insert a small retractable drain snake directly into the drain or, if the p-trap has been removed, directly into the pipe in the wall.**

   Work the snake in and out while rotating the handle clockwise.

5. **Reassemble the trap.**

   Make sure that each washer is properly seated. Twisting can be a real problem. Don't over-tighten the connections. At first, the coupling nuts should be no more than hand-tight. If a leak persists, continue to tighten a little at a time until the leak disappears. If increased tightening doesn't do the trick, chances are that the washers are dirty, twisted, or defective. Try again!

If cleaning doesn't solve your p-trap problems, call a plumber or sewer-and-drain specialist who has the expertise and proper tools to get things flowing freely.

TIP

If all the drains in the home are running slowly, the main sewer line may be the problem. Skip all these steps and go straight to the plumber.

Determining Your Sewer System's Fall

If you repeatedly have drainage problems, and you've determined that all waste lines, vents, and p-traps are clean and clear, then the *fall* (the downward slope of the pipes), or actually the lack of fall, could be the problem.

One thing you don't want is a sewer system that looks like a set of roller-coaster tracks — up and down, up and down. Sewers work best when the waste lines slope downhill. In fact, they don't really work very well at all otherwise.

The National Plumbing Code requires sewer lines to fall (slope downward) at a rate of ⅛ inch per foot (which equals 1 inch every 8 feet). I'd argue that the fall should be as much as ½ an inch.

REMEMBER

Getting the fall right is a balancing act. Too little and the waste won't move down the pipe. Too much and the flowing liquids speed up and abandon the solids. Orphaned solids come to a stop in the pipe and build up into clogs.

If fall is an issue, call a plumber to correct the problem. I don't recommend major sewer work as a DIY project.

Maintaining Your Septic System

If you live in a rural area or have vacation property in the middle of nowhere, you're no doubt familiar with the form and function of a septic system. (See Figure 9-4.) In brief, a septic system is your very own on-site sewage treatment facility. It's used primarily where access to a municipal sewer system is neither available nor economically practical. A septic system is out of sight and is odorless (when properly maintained).

A septic system is reasonably maintenance-free. The waste flows in, where it meets "good bacteria" who go to work breaking down solids and then sending them to the *leach field*, (the underground area where all of the sewage drainpipes are located). A well-constructed, properly maintained tank could last indefinitely. However, the leach field will most likely require some treatment or, rarely, replacement after about 15 to 20 years of service.

Following a few simple rules — like not using too much water and not depositing materials in the septic tank that bacteria can't decompose — should help to make a septic system trouble-free for many years. But don't forget that the septic tank does need to be cleaned out when too many solids build up.

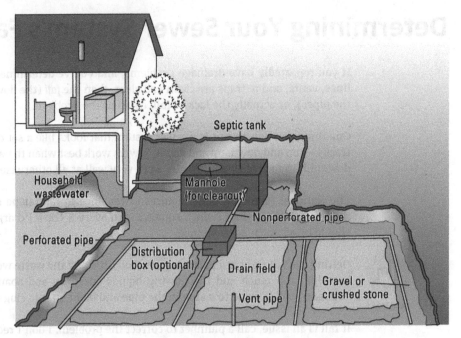

FIGURE 9-4:
Parts of the septic system.

Being careful about what goes in

Be mindful about what you and your family put into your septic system. It doesn't take much to upset the delicate biological balance within the tank that keeps the good bacteria working to break down waste. You can extend the life of a septic system by watching everything that's introduced to the system.

REMEMBER

Keep in mind the following recommendations:

>> **Too much water can upset the delicate biological balance within the tank, thus defeating its ability to work wonders.** Moreover, discharging more water into the system than it can handle can cause it to back up — not a desirable occurrence.

>> **Don't use excessive amounts of any household chemicals.** You can use minimal amounts of household detergents, bleaches, drain cleaners, and other household chemicals without stopping the bacterial action in the septic tank. But, for example, don't dump cleaning water for latex paintbrushes and cans into the house sewer.

>> **Don't deposit coffee grounds, cooking fats, non-biodegradable wipes, disposable diapers, facial tissues, cigarette butts, and other**

non-decomposable materials into the house sewer. These materials won't decompose, will fill the septic tank, and will plug the system.

TIP

Use a high-quality toilet tissue marked "safe for septic" that breaks up easily when wet. One way to find out if your toilet paper fits this description is to put a handful of toilet tissue in a fruit jar half-full of water. Shake the jar, and if the tissue breaks up easily, the product is suitable for the septic tank.

>> **Avoid dumping grease down the drain.** It may plug sewer pipes or build up in the septic tank and plug the inlet. Keep a separate container for waste grease and throw it out with the garbage.

WARNING

According to the Environmental Protection Agency, because of the presence of significant numbers and types of bacteria, enzymes, yeasts, and other fungi and microorganisms in typical residential and commercial wastewaters, the use of septic-system additives containing these or any other ingredients is not recommended.

Also, watch out for septic tank additives! While some manufacturers of these products suggest they can break down septic tank sludge, eliminating the need for pumping, the Environmental Protection Agency (EPA) warns against their efficacy. Studies indicate that these additives often fail to significantly impact the bacterial populations within the tank. Septic tanks inherently harbor the necessary microbes for efficiently breaking down household wastewater pollutants. The most reliable method to maintain proper functionality and ensure years of service from septic systems remains periodic pumping. For more information, visit www. epa.gov/septicsmart.

Cleaning and pumping your septic tank

If solids have built up in your septic tank, it needs to be pumped to remove the solids. With a little care about what is going into the tank, this won't happen often. But when it does, solids need to be removed to restore the function of your personal sewage plant.

How often you need to have your septic tank pumped also depends on the size of the tank, the volume of wastewater, and the number of people in your household. A small tank (500 to 750 gallons) would be pumped every 3 to 5 years; a medium-sized tank (750 to 1,000 gallons) every 7 to 8 years; and a tank that is 1,500 gallons or larger might need to be pumped every 10 to 12 years. If the history of tank pumping is unknown, have a septic pro open the tank lid for inspection.

IN THIS CHAPTER

» Keeping your heating system happy

» Ventilating your home from top to bottom

» Maintaining your air-conditioning cool

Chapter **10**

Heating, Ventilating, and Air-Conditioning Systems

I can describe heating, ventilating, and air-conditioning (HVAC) with just four words: *hot, cold, in,* and *out.* Or, more specifically: heating the interior when it's cold outside; cooling the interior when it's hot outside; drawing fresh air into your home to moderate temperatures and humidity; and venting moist, smoky, greasy, or stinky air from inside to outside.

And this brings us to the paradox of HVAC: These seemingly simple processes actually rely on some complex technology. As a result, there are very few maintenance tasks that don't run the risk of damaging the furnace, the air conditioner, or you! But the tasks that *can* be done by a DIYer are easy and non-threatening. I'm confident you can do them without difficulty or danger — and they'll make a huge difference in the efficiency, performance, and life of your system, whatever kind it is.

Making Friends with the Monster: Your Furnace or Boiler

Most grown-ups would never admit it, but they're terrified of their furnace or boiler. These are big, complicated, fire-breathing pieces of machinery. But your heating system is actually less mysterious and scary than you think. It heats up air or water, and then moves hot air, water, or steam around the house. It's really that simple. In this section, I tell you what you need to do to maintain your heating system for maximum comfort and efficiency.

Identifying the types of heating systems

To help keep things clear, it's good to know what kinds of heating systems you have and the fuels they use:

>> **Forced-air systems use furnaces and are most commonly fueled by natural gas.** These systems heat air and distribute it throughout your home via a series of ducts.

>> **Hot-water or steam systems use boilers to heat water or steam, which is circulated through your house via piping to radiators.**

>> **Electric heat is typically provided by baseboard heaters and is the most expensive way to heat a house.** These heaters are mounted in individual rooms, and each runs off its own thermostat.

>> **Heat pumps are a highly efficient form of electric heating system that essentially reverses the refrigeration cycle used by air conditioners to create and distribute heat.**

TIP

If I asked you what that machine is called that heats your house, you'd probably say a furnace. That's right about 75 percent of the time. If your home is heated by forced air, you'd have a furnace, but if it's heated by hot water, you'd have a boiler. It's helpful to know the difference, especially when it comes to understanding the type of maintenance each system needs.

Looking at forced-air heating systems

In a forced-air system, air is heated as it passes through the furnace. (See Figure 10-1.) A blower and a system of ducts move the warmed air throughout the house, and then cooled air is sucked into return ducts back to the furnace. Your forced-air system needs to be regularly maintained to keep it running safely at peak efficiency.

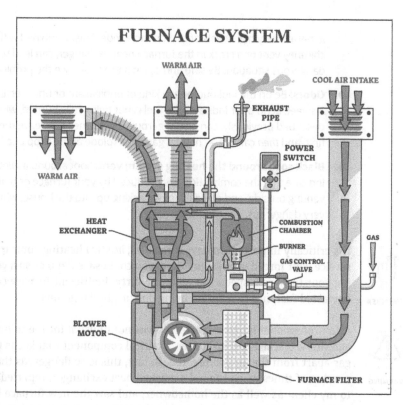

FURNACE SYSTEM

WARM AIR

COOL AIR INTAKE

EXHAUST PIPE

POWER SWITCH

WARM AIR

HEAT EXCHANGER

COMBUSTION CHAMBER

BURNER

GAS CONTROL VALVE

GAS

BLOWER MOTOR

FURNACE FILTER

FIGURE 10-1:
Standard forced-air heating system.

REMEMBER

The parts of your furnace and their locations may be different from the illustrations in this book. For specifics on your furnace, consult the owner's manual that came with it. If it's not available, you'll probably find it on the manufacturer's website, or you can just do a Google search for the brand, model number, and manual.

Inspecting and servicing a forced-air furnace

Forced-air furnaces most commonly run on natural gas or propane. As the fuel burns, it leaves combustion deposits behind that need to be cleaned. That's why it's important that it be inspected, cleaned, and serviced by an HVAC pro every year before the heating season begins.

Besides the annual service, here are some things to watch for that indicate you may have a problem.

>> **Flame color:** A furnace flame that is yellow or orange rather than blue, or flickering rather than steady indicates a combustion problem. The orange flame is a sign that the gas is not being completely burned, which can

generate very high levels of carbon monoxide. This, combined with a blocked chimney vent or a crack in the furnace heat exchanger, can lead to a very dangerous situation. Be safe and call in a pro to service the problem.

>> **Odors:** Be on the lookout for any kind of unpleasant or unexpected odor. A sweet, acrid odor indicates the fuel is not being fully burned, which, as described previously, can be dangerous. If you smell gas, leave the building first, and *then* call 911 — natural gas can explode at the drop of a hat.

>> **Black soot around the heating system vent:** Soot around a vent can indicate that the combustion gas produced by your furnace or boiler is not venting outside, and could even be backing up into the house, which could be very dangerous.

REMEMBER

It's critically important to have a *qualified, licensed* heating contractor inspect and service your forced-air system. Sure, you could save $200 or so a year by not having your furnace inspected at all, but a dirty, inefficient furnace costs you plenty in wasted fuel, not to mention being downright dangerous.

WARNING

As a professional home inspector, it was not unusual for me to inspect a furnace and find a cracked *heat exchanger*, a critical component that keeps the combustion gas apart from the air you breathe. In fact, this is so dangerous that I can recall a number of times when I found a cracked heat exchanger, reported it immediately to my client as well as the homeowner, and saw the new furnace being delivered while I was still on the job finishing the inspection! Plain and simple, dangerous defects like this will not be found without a qualified set of eyes looking for them and can become a danger to you and your family.

Replacing the filter

The easiest furnace-maintenance task is replacing the filter. During the heating season, you should replace your furnace filter every month. If an air conditioner is part of the same system, you should change the filter every month year-round.

The most basic filter, typically fiberglass or pleated fabric, is designed to take dust, dirt, pollen, lint, carpet fibers, and pet hair and dander out of the air, which keeps your home cleaner and keeps allergies at bay. Without all that stuff in the airflow and inside the unit, the blower motor lasts longer, and other parts of the heating system work better. The filter also prevents the air-conditioner evaporator coil (hidden within the unit) from becoming clogged — that's a good thing, because when the evaporator coil is clogged, the air conditioner's efficiency is reduced, the compressor life is shortened, and your utility bill runs sky-high.

LET'S CLEAR THE AIR ABOUT FILTERS

Regularly changing the filters in your forced-air system is step one in maintaining indoor air quality, and you can go several steps above and beyond by incorporating a whole-house air cleaner. It's a smart upgrade to consider when it's time to replace your current system, and I know homeowners who can tell the difference after having one installed.

If your home has a forced-air heating and cooling system, using a top-quality air filter is a must. Go for a MERV rating of 6 to 8, or 11 if your family is prone to allergies. MERV stands for Minimum Efficiency Reporting Value and is a rating for filters that describes the size of the holes in the filter that air is allowed to pass through. The smaller the holes in the filter, the higher the MERV rating and the efficiency.

Another option is a whole-house air cleaner. Installed by an HVAC pro, whole-house air cleaners are part of forced-air systems, virtually eliminating such airborne contaminants as dust, pollen, pet dander, and bacteria. Today's systems are so good that they can trap virus-size particles and can help you to breathe easy in your home.

To replace the most common type of furnace filter (about 1 inch wide with a cardboard frame), follow these steps:

1. **Locate the filter slot.**

   You can usually find the filter near where the cool air enters the furnace — in the cold-air return duct, or at the entrance to the blower chamber. Although it is redundant, sometimes you'll find filters in both locations — typically a washable filter at the furnace and a replaceable fabric filter at the return duct (often located on the wall or ceiling somewhere in your home; see Figure 10-2).

2. **Slide out the old, dirty filter.**

   You may have to jockey it back and forth a bit. Slide it right into a trash bag to avoid spilling any of the trapped dust it contains.

3. **Open the new filter and locate the airflow arrows on the side.**

4. **Position the filter so that the airflow arrows point toward the blower.**

5. **Slide in the new filter, being careful not to dent, deform, or tear the cardboard frame.**

   Some filters have straps or brackets that you'll need to secure in order to hold the filter in place.

6. **Check to make sure the filter is snugly in place and all the way in its slot.**

FIGURE 10-2:
Replacing a dirty HVAC filter at a ceiling return register.

The Toidi/Adobe Systems Incorporated

Cleaning the blower compartment

The blower is a large "squirrel cage" fan (refer to Figure 10-1) located inside the furnace that pushes air out through the ducts to the registers throughout the home. The blower also draws air through return registers into the return ducts and into the unit to be reheated or re-cooled and recirculated. An HVAC pro will clean the blower as a part of the system service, but you can do it yourself if things look dusty. Here's how:

1. **Before you do anything, turn off the power to the unit.**

   A service/emergency switch may be mounted on the furnace or near it. If you can't find the switch, turn off the power at the circuit breaker or fuse box.

2. **Open the access panel on the front or side (if it isn't already open) to change the filter.**

   You may need a screwdriver or socket wrench to do this.

3. **Use a vacuum cleaner with the upholstery brush attachment on it to remove any dirt, lint, and dust bunnies you find.**

4. **Replace the access panel, making sure it's in correctly and tightly closed.**

5. **Turn on the power to the unit.**

WARNING

Whenever you're poking around inside your forced-air unit, be careful not to disturb any of the small wires inside the unit. Most systems have low-voltage controls, so you can't get zapped, but if you inadvertently dislodge a control wire, the system may not come back on.

Getting your ducts in a row

Ducts are square or round metal tubes in the ceiling, walls, and/or floors that transport air from the furnace to each room in the house. A leak in a duct can allow massive amounts of heat into the attic, crawlspace, or basement. Keeping the ducts tightly sealed ensures that all the expensive heated air coming from the furnace gets to where it belongs.

Leaks aren't the only issue with ducts, though. Even with a serious commitment to filter replacement, the insides of ducts eventually accumulate a coating of fibers, lint, dirt, allergens, mildew, grease, and even bacteria.

CHECKING THE DUCTS FOR LEAKS

If you have access to your ducts, checking for leaks is easy:

1. **Follow each duct from the furnace to its termination, paying special attention to the joints between segments.**

2. **Look for fuzz that has been forced through joints and feel for warm air coming through gaps.**

   You may need to pull insulation away from the joints and visually inspect them. Dark stripes in the fiberglass insulation are a telltale sign of a duct leak below the insulation. Other big leak locations are around the *boot* (the piece where the duct penetrates your wall, floor, or ceiling).

TIP

If you really want to identify how leaky your ducts are, bring in a pro to perform a duct pressure test. This test involves pressurizing the entire duct system, which determines how much of your heated or cooled air is being wasted. A duct pressure test usually runs in the neighborhood of $250 to $500, depending on the size of your home and where you live.

SEALING LEAKS

If you find any leaks during your inspection, seal them:

>> **If your leak is in the duct section seams, seal it with metal UL 181 duct tape.** The key difference between UL 181 tape and just about every other duct tape you've ever used is that the UL 181 adhesive doesn't dry out. (UL 181 refers to the UL standard under which this tape is manufactured and should be clearly printed on the tape.)

» **Alternatively, use an elastomeric duct sealant (available at most home centers or hardware stores).** When dry, the elastomeric duct sealant provides a rubbery, airtight seal at all joints and seams; it bonds flexible ducts to metal duct fittings.

» **You can also call in a heating pro to do the job for you.**

TIP

Keep your eyes open for ducts that are crushed or disconnected. I once did a home inspection and found an animal had wreaked so much havoc under a house that half of the ducts were disconnected and doing a great job of heating and cooling the crawlspace!

CLEANING THE DUCTS

Duct cleaning is a service frequently recommend by those in the business of duct cleaning. Shocker, right? On the face of it, it seems to make sense, which is why it turns out to be a pretty good business for HVAC pros. But the fact is that duct cleaning does not appear to prevent health problems, reduce dirt levels in the home, or improve efficiency. In fact, the Environmental Protection Agency (EPA) specifically states: "Duct cleaning has never been shown to actually prevent health problems. Neither do studies conclusively demonstrate that particle (e.g., dust) levels in homes increase because of dirty air ducts." (Search *duct cleaning* at www. epa.gov to find out more.)

Duct cleaning is not a typical cooling or heating service step and should only be done if there is mold in the ducts, vermin are living in the ducts, or the ducts are actually clogged. Anything more than that is likely a total waste of money. For a DIYer, vacuuming duct registers and staying on top of filter replacements is the best way to keep the air clean.

Troubleshooting uneven heating or cooling systems

Are some rooms in your home too hot, some too cold, and some just right? You need to fine-tune your system for maximum efficiency, minimum energy consumption, and even temperatures in every room. It's about airflow, dampers, and registers that help to control the airflow in the ducts.

Here's how to balance your central heating system:

1. **Start at the furnace unit and follow the main ducts outward, looking for small levers on the side; these are the handles for dampers.**

    When the handle is horizontal, the damper is fully open, allowing maximum airflow. When the handle is anywhere between horizontal and vertical, the damper is reducing airflow.

2. Put thermometers in the rooms in question, away from registers and cold-air returns, and place them all at about the same height from the floor.

3. Turn on the heat and open all the dampers, wait about an hour, and then check the thermometers.

   Is one room warmer than others? Is hot air roaring out of the register?

4. Partially close the damper in the duct that feeds that room by moving the handle one-third of the way between horizontal and vertical; wait an hour and recheck the room.

5. If the room seems cooler, you're done. If it doesn't, close the damper by another third, wait another hour, and check the room again.

   You also can fine-tune airflow by adjusting the register.

6. Repeat Steps 2 through 5 for each room until you have the temperature balanced.

   By the way, *balanced* may mean that the main living areas and bathrooms are warmer than the bedrooms, or vice versa. It all depends on what you prefer . . . or how cold your spouse claims to be.

7. After you've achieved balance, go back to the ducts and use a permanent marker to write a *W* (for winter) where the damper handle should be positioned for the heating season.

8. Repeat the process for the cooling season, except write an *S* (for summer) where the damper handle should be positioned.

TIP

In addition to regulating air flow through the registers, it's crucial to ensure that the return air flow remains unobstructed. *Return air* refers to the air that circulates into the return air ducts for re-heating or re-cooling. For rooms without their own return ducts, it is essential to have at least a ¾-inch gap under the door to the room. This undercut allows the return air to flow back to the HVAC system for the re-heating or re-cooling process when doors are closed.

REMEMBER

Aside from balancing your HVAC system, improving insulation, sealing drafts around exterior windows, doors, and through walls can go a long way towards restoring comfort in your home. Refer to Chapter 6 for tips on improving insulation and stopping drafts cold.

Looking at hot-water heating systems

Hot-water, or *hydronic,* systems use a gas- or oil-fired burner to heat a tank of water to near boiling, circulate it with a pump throughout the house to radiators or baseboard convectors, and then send the water back to the boiler to be reheated and make the round-trip again. (See Figure 10-3.)

WHEN TO REPLACE A FORCED-AIR FURNACE

How do you know when your furnace is on its last legs? When its old technology makes it unacceptably inefficient and expensive, that's when. In general, if your system is more than 15 years old, replacing it with a new Energy Star–rated system will save you money, prevent maintenance headaches, and keep you warmer and more comfortable. According to the EPA, Energy Star–rated furnaces are 15 percent more energy efficient than a conventional furnace. For more on the Energy Star program, go to www.energy star.gov.

Seems simple? Not so much, actually. As with forced-air systems, most maintenance tasks are beyond the skills of the do-it-yourselfer. Call in a qualified, licensed heating contractor to do an annual inspection and cleaning.

Hot Water Heating System

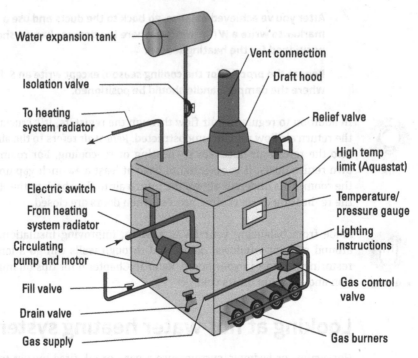

- Water expansion tank
- Vent connection
- Isolation valve
- Draft hood
- To heating system radiator
- Relief valve
- High temp limit (Aquastat)
- Electric switch
- Temperature/pressure gauge
- From heating system radiator
- Lighting instructions
- Circulating pump and motor
- Gas control valve
- Fill valve
- Drain valve
- Gas burners
- Gas supply

FIGURE 10-3: A hot-water heating system.

REMEMBER

Don't be penny-wise and pound-foolish. A dirty, inefficient boiler costs you far more than a service call. The serviceperson will catch little problems before they become big trouble, improve efficiency, and assure safe operation. And a neglected system will fail many years before a well-maintained one.

Gauging the pressure

Most hot-water systems have only a single gauge, located on the main unit, which measures pressure and temperature.

To monitor the performance of your hot-water system, keep an (occasional) eye on the pressure. Most hot-water boilers run at 12 to 15 pounds per square inch (psi) of pressure. If the pressure is lower or higher, something is wrong.

Low pressure most often is caused by a low water level. The system's automatic filling system should maintain the proper water level. But if yours doesn't, you can manually fill the boiler by opening the water feed valve on the incoming supply pipe. Just open the valve and keep it open until the pressure gets to 12 psi. Then call a professional.

Most hot-water systems today use a diaphragm expansion tank. High pressure usually is caused by too much water and too little air in the expansion tank — it's time to call an expert!

REMEMBER

Boilers must have a proper pressure-relief valve, located at the top of the unit. This important valve opens when the pressure reaches 30 psi — to prevent the boiler from exploding. If you ever see water draining out of the relief valve, chances are, the system is operating under excessively high pressure and should be shut down immediately — and stay shut down until it can be checked by a professional.

Bleeding the radiators

Bleeding radiators is sometimes necessary in even the best of systems. If you have a radiator in your system that just won't heat, chances are, it's air-locked. Bleeding the air out of the radiator relieves the pressure and allows the system to fill normally.

To bleed the radiators, look for a small valve at the top. When you've found it, rotate it about a quarter-turn counterclockwise and keep the screwdriver or radiator key in the valve. If you hear a hissing sound, that's good — it's air escaping. As soon as the hissing stops and you see a dribble of water come out, close the valve.

WARNING

Don't open the valve more than is necessary; hot water will come rushing out before you can close it. At the very least, you'll make a wet mess. At worst, you could be scalded. Don't forget to wear eye protection and rain gear when working with water that's under pressure.

Looking at steam heating systems

As with forced-air and hot-water systems (see the previous sections), it pays to have a professional, licensed contractor check your steam heating system every year. Not only will you save money in the long run through greater efficiency, but you'll also have peace of mind knowing that your system is operating safely. I cannot emphasize this point enough.

Making your own adjustments

Most adjustments to your steam boiler should be performed by a pro. But there are three important things you can do by yourself:

>> **Check the pressure gauge on a regular basis — every couple of days.** Make sure it's within the normal range of 0 to 15 psi (the lower the better). If it isn't, shut down the system immediately and call for service.

>> **Check the safety valve once a month.** As noted above, boilers must have a proper pressure-relief valve, located at the top of the unit to prevent the boiler from exploding. For steam boilers, the valve is set to open at 15 psi. If you ever see water draining out of the relief valve, chances are the system is operating under excessively high pressure and should be shut down immediately — and stay shut down until it can be checked by a professional.

>> **Check the water level once a month.** The water level should be visible in the gauge glass, preferably more or less in the middle of the glass tube. If the gauge glass is completely full of water, remove water from the system using the drain valve on the bottom of the boiler when it's cool, and add water by opening the valve on the pipe connecting the heating system to the plumbing system cold water piping.

TIP

Because steam systems occasionally need water added, consider adding an automatic water valve to your system if it doesn't already have one. The valve will monitor water levels and, if the system needs it, add water ever so slowly to avoid damaging the boiler.

Maintaining your radiators

You also can do a few things to keep your radiators working well:

>> **Make sure that every radiator slopes slightly toward the steam inlet pipe (the one that comes out of the wall or floor).** If one doesn't, slip a little ¼-inch-thick rectangle of wood under the feet at the vent end (as shown in Figure 10-4). This helps prevent those irritating knocking and clanging noises.

>> **Check the vents to make sure they aren't blocked.** Corrosion and paint can keep the vent from venting, and then air trapped in the radiator prevents steam from entering the radiator. If your vent is blocked or spits water, replace it. Your local hardware store probably carries vents. They simply screw off and on, so they're easy to replace.

>> **Check the position of the inlet valves.** The valves should be either all the way closed or all the way open. Unless it is a thermostatic valve (it will have a numerical scale marked on it) a partially open or shut valve does nothing to regulate the heat, and it causes knocking and clanging sounds.

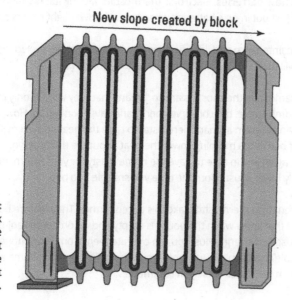

New slope created by block

FIGURE 10-4:
Place a block under the radiator to get the right slope and prevent banging.

TROUBLESHOOTING THERMOSTATS

Is your house too hot or too cool? Your problem could be the thermostat. Here are some potential causes:

- **It's in a bad location.** The thermostat shouldn't be located over or near any heat source, like a warm table lamp or fireplace. The limited warmth will prevent the thermostat from coming on, even while the rest of the room is cold.

- **It needs cleaning.** When older mechanical thermostats malfunction, those with lever-set temperatures and contact switches usually need cleaning only. To clean your thermostat, remove the cover and dust inside with a soft brush. To clean contacts, slip a piece of paper between them, moving the paper very lightly back and forth.

- **Its anticipator needs adjustment.** If your air conditioner or furnace cycles on and off too seldom or too frequently and you have a mechanical control, try adjusting the anticipator — usually a flat metal pointer on a scale. If heat starts and stops too often, move the anticipator a smidge higher. If it starts and stops too seldom, adjust it a tad lower. Wait a few hours to see if the adjustment was enough.

- **You need new batteries.** Electronic thermostats with digital readouts and keypads rarely fail. Just put in new batteries when the low-power light comes on.

With simple maintenance and light cleaning, thermostats, whether electronic or mechanical, will function best and as they should — for comfort.

Today's programmable thermostats are so "smart" that they will not only make your home more comfortable, but conserve energy and save money, too. How, you ask? Simple. You can program a smart thermostat to raise the heating system just before you get out of bed in the morning, lower the heat about the time everyone leaves the home, raise it again just in time to have the home toasty for your return after a long day, and finally lower it just about the time you snuggle into bed.

Smart home–enabled thermostats take this a step further. They feature built-in occupancy sensors that know when the house is empty and automatically adjust the heating or cooling to use less energy. Plus, you can operate them from your phone! Don't have a regular schedule? No problem. Just open your app before heading home and turn the heat up to warm the house while you commute!

Looking at electric heating systems

In an electric heating system, electrical resistance creates heat, which is most commonly radiated into rooms using baseboard units or radiant panels. Installations of electric heating systems hit their peak in the 1960s, when electricity rates were low. But today, the cost of electricity makes these systems very, very expensive to operate. If you have one, you're probably paying twice as much to heat your house as a neighbor with a gas-fired furnace or boiler.

Electric baseboard radiators are controlled by multiple thermostats, which are installed in each room or area they serve. While operating this kind of heat is very costly, adding electric baseboard radiators is often less expensive than extending your current heating system. That's why they're worth considering as a supplemental heat for an area where the main heating system doesn't reach, like a basement. Or, for where the need for the heat is limited, such as to warm a cold kitchen or bathroom floor. Nobody likes cold tootsies in the morning!

Systems like SunTouch (www.suntouch.com) offer roll-out or radiant heat panels that you can install under a finished floor. The heat operates via a smart thermostat app and can be programmed to run for short periods of time when floors are coldest, like first thing in the morning. Once installed, these systems, while costly to run, need very little if any maintenance.

About heat pumps

In addition to electric radiant heating systems, there's another type of electric heating system called a heat pump. I cover this in the air conditioning section the later section called "A Word About Heat Pumps." Read on to discover why these systems are inextricably linked!

Ventilation: Letting Your House Breathe

When I talk about ventilation, I'm actually talking about two different things: interior ventilation and structural ventilation. Proper interior ventilation is vital to the health and comfort of your family; it helps your home rid itself of moisture, smoke, cooking odors, and indoor pollutants. Good structural ventilation controls heat levels in the attic, moderates dampness in the crawlspace and basement, and keeps moisture out of uninsulated walls.

Locating interior ventilation

Kitchens, bathrooms, and laundry rooms are the biggest sources of moisture and odors. The secret to having a dry, stink-free home is to have two key exhaust units — a range hood and bathroom exhaust fans — each of which should be exhausted to the exterior.

Range hoods

Many kitchens have a range hood that doesn't actually vent to anywhere — it just "filters" and recycles stovetop air back into the room. But it's much better to get the greasy, smoky, steamy air outside, and that requires ductwork to an exterior vent.

So, if your kitchen is perpetually stinky, and the walls are covered with a thin film of grease, it's smart to pick up an exterior-venting exhaust fan.

TIP

If you just can't give up Mama's Special Sunday Fried Chicken and Homemade Hash Browns, you should know that airborne grease makes exhaust fans sticky, which in turn attracts dirt and dust. The key to preventing this process from getting out of control is regular cleaning:

>> **Clean the inside hood twice a year, or whenever it starts to look bad.** A household degreaser can help cut through the muck.

>> **Clean the filter in a range hood every couple of months or so (depending on how often or what you cook).** I clean our range hood filters in the dishwasher — works great! If your filter has charcoal pellets inside, you need to replace it annually.

>> **Clean the fan and housing every six months.** Lots of grease and gunk can build up on the fan housing and produce a foul smell. Use a spray-on nonchemical degreaser and a sponge to clean the housing. Rinse with fresh water and towel-dry.

Bathroom exhaust fans

Bathrooms generate huge amounts of moisture, causing chronic mildew in the shower, wallpaper peeling off the walls, or a lingering, funky smell. The solution is to install an exhaust fan with two important features:

>> **The exhaust fan should vent to the outside.** In many jurisdictions, the building code doesn't require this, but it's critical. That is, unless you think opening a bathroom window to vent steam on a winter day makes sense. Venting the exhaust fan to the attic is equally a bad idea. All that excess humidity can dampen insulation, making it less effective, as well as condense on the underside of the roof leading to decay of the sheathing.

>> **The ideal exhaust fan should run on a *humidistat,*** a switch that will keep it running until all the humidity is removed from the bathroom, or a timer switch that can be set to run the exhaust fan long enough to clear the humidity after a bath or shower (usually 15 to 20 minutes).

Pointing out structural ventilation

There are two kinds of structural ventilation:

>> **Passive ventilation.** This kind uses the natural airflow generated by convection (hot air rising, cold air falling) and is hands-down the best way to vent an attic.

>> **Active ventilation.** This kind uses fans to do the work.

To keep heat and moisture from roasting and rotting your home over time, you need adequate ventilation in the attic and crawlspace:

>> **Attic.** In the attic, passive ventilation creates an upward flow of air. Warm air rises and goes out through vent(s) near to, or at the peak of, the roof, drawing cool air through vents in the eaves or soffits. I recommend continuous roof and soffit ventilation. In this model, air enters at the soffits (the area below gutters and underneath a roof's overhang) and exhausts at the ridge. (See Figure 10-5.)

>> **Crawlspace.** In the crawlspace, where upward flow is impossible, passive *cross-ventilation* (the movement of air from one side of a space to the other) is created by placing vents on each exterior wall.

Ventilation — passive or active — won't work if insulation blocks the vents or if you don't have enough vents. Poor ventilation can result in an attic being damp and "tropical." Rot can develop in the wood framing and do great damage over time. Condensed water can soak insulation, making it ineffective and mildewed. Condensation from above and below can make its way into the house, ruining ceiling, floor, and wall finishes, and short-circuiting electrical wiring. If you notice that your vents are blocked, clear them immediately.

TIP

Building codes specify how much ventilation you need. As a general rule, you need to have 1 square foot of vent area for every 150 square feet of attic area or crawlspace. I think more is better.

TIP

You can use cardboard or prefab Styrofoam baffles to prevent insulation from blocking air flow from soffit vents. The baffles are easy to install. They fit between rafters where eave vents are located and are held in place with staples. When the baffle is installed properly, air passes over it and up the underside of the roof sheathing, and the insulation stays put!

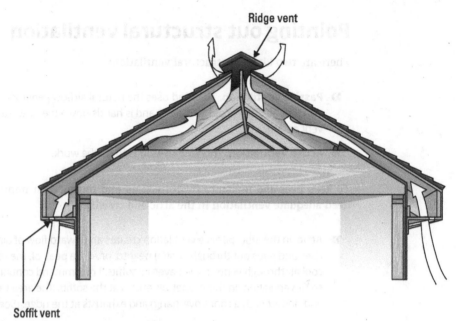

Ridge vent

FIGURE 10-5:
Continuous
ridge and soffit
ventilation.

Soffit vent

Crawlspace ventilation

If your crawlspace is damp, moist air can cause rot in the wood frame, attacking your home from below. Just like the attic (see the preceding section), a crawlspace needs a good flow of fresh air. If your crawlspace feels clammy, or you see mildew on the walls or structure, you need better ventilation in the form of *foundation vents*.

If you live in the humid southern United States, another option is to *not* use crawlspace vents and instead fully enclose the crawlspace. This technique is also known as *encapsulation*. It seals the dirt floor and foundation walls to prevent excessive moisture from leaking in and leaves the underside of the first floor open, allowing remaining moisture to permeate upward and mix with the house air.

WARNING

Extra vents are difficult to install and require special tools to cut through lumber, concrete block, concrete, stucco, and brick. Don't go poking holes in your foundation on your own — call a carpenter or masonry contractor to do the work. They have the know-how, tools, and experience to do the job right.

TIP

Does your crawlspace have a dirt floor? If so, the easiest way to reduce the moisture is to improve the grading and drainage outside your foundation walls. See Chapter 4 for step-by-step tips on how to do this yourself. In addition, add a plastic vapor barrier on crawlspace dirt floors.

TIP

If your basement has a window and it doesn't work, fix it! There is no substitute for natural light and ventilation. A little bit of sunlight throughout the day can create natural air currents that can help control moisture and odors.

Big or Small, an Air Conditioner Cools Y'all

When it comes to air conditioning (AC), people don't care *how* it works, just *that* it works. It's all about being cool. Fortunately for sweat-averse folks, AC technology has advanced tremendously in recent years. And, even better, the energy efficiency of central-AC equipment has improved along with it. In fact, if you have an AC unit that is more than 15 years old, the Department of Energy says you can lower your electric bills and improve your energy efficiency by investing in new equipment.

The efficiency of window units has also improved a great deal, as has the performance of AC/heat-pump units. With all this new technology, are there any maintenance tasks a do-it-yourselfer can do? Not very many.

Maintaining a central air-conditioning system

Homeowners can help take care of a central-air system just by changing the furnace filters monthly, and periodically hosing off the fins of the exterior *condensing unit* (that's the large unit that sits outside and blows hot air) to remove dust and debris. It's also smart to keep landscaping trimmed back at least 12 inches away from the condensing unit, to allow it to cool properly.

TIP

The most important thing you can do to maintain your central air-conditioning system is to have it professionally serviced every spring! Service techs will do things like clean and lubricate parts and check refrigerant levels to find out if the system is cooling properly.

Regular maintenance aside, if you're getting to know your service technician a little too well because of frequent and repeated repairs, it's time to replace your system. According to the Department of Energy, if your air-conditioning system is 15 or more years old, you should replace it with a new, significantly more energy-efficient Energy Star–rated model.

A WORD ABOUT HEAT PUMPS

A heat pump is a versatile system capable of both heating and cooling a home. While resembling a central air-conditioning system, it stands out by having the ability to *reverse* the refrigeration cycle to provide warmth during winter. To visualize this, consider a window air conditioner that blows cold air inside and hot air outside; now, imagine flipping it around to have hot air blowing inside. That's essentially how a heat pump operates!

Similar to central air conditioners, heat pumps require annual maintenance and frequent filter changes, but are more cost-effective than electric resistance heat (see "Looking at electric heating systems" earlier in the chapter).

However, it's crucial to be aware of some key points about heat pumps.

- **Climate consideration:** Heat pumps were originally designed for moderate temperatures, where winters are brief and freezing conditions are limited. Despite this, advancements in heat pump technology have expanded their applicability to colder climates.

- **Thermostat functionality:** Heat pump thermostats are programmed to engage the heat pump if the temperature difference between the set temperature and the room temperature is 2 degrees or more. Beyond this threshold, the heat pump triggers an internal "emergency" electric resistance heat system, leading to increased electricity costs.

- **Usage tips:** To avoid activating the expensive electric heat, it's advisable to set your thermostat and leave it be. Continuously adjusting the thermostat can lead to frequent triggering of the electric heat, resulting in higher electricity bills.

Replacing a central air-conditioning system is not a do-it-yourself project. Contact a qualified heating and air-conditioning contractor who will be able to discuss the various decisions you have to make when purchasing and installing a new system.

Among these considerations is size. In the past, the general rule for sizing a central air-conditioning system was 1 ton of air-conditioning capacity for every 600 to 800 square feet of living area. Today, sizing an air-conditioning system takes into consideration many factors and is far more complex.

REMEMBER

When it comes to central air-conditioning, bigger isn't necessarily better. An oversized unit will cycle on and off frequently, which prevents the unit from delivering even temperatures throughout the home. Another disadvantage to an oversized unit is that it won't run long enough to adequately remove excess humidity, resulting in a cold but clammy environment. What's more, an oversized unit will experience increased operating costs. Conversely, an undersized system will run much longer than it should and will likely never do an adequate job of cooling your home.

To help consumers understand and compare the energy efficiency of residential air conditioners, the U.S. Department of Energy established minimum efficiency standards for air conditioners. Every unit is given an efficiency rating, called a *seasonal energy-efficiency rating* (SEER). The higher the SEER number, the more efficient the unit, and the lower the cost to provide a given amount of cooling. Today, the mid-range SEER for a new ENERGY STAR–qualified central air conditioner is 15 to 18. Ultra-efficient models have a SEER of 19 to 22. (*Note*: Window AC units are exempt from the SEER requirements — instead, look for an EER [energy efficiency ratio] rating of 10 or higher.)

How to test a central air conditioner

If your air conditioner appears to run longer than it should or just doesn't cool the house well, there's an easy way to determine if it needs servicing. To do this test, you'll need two pocket thermometers or refrigerator thermometers. Here are the steps:

1. **Lower the temperature for the air conditioner to 60 degrees or so.**

   The idea here is that the unit should run continuously.

2. **Locate the return register for your HVAC system.**

   It's usually centrally located in the home and is where the house air flows back into the ducts to be re-cooled.

3. **Hang one of the thermometers in the middle of the register to measure the temperature of the return air.**

4. **Locate a supply register (where the air comes out) that has a strong flow.**

5. **Insert the other thermometer here to measure the temperature of the supply air.**

6. **Let the system run for about 10 minutes, then take note of both temperatures.**

   If the difference between the return and supply air is between 12 and 20 degrees, the system is cooling adequately. If it's less than 12 degrees, the system is probably low on refrigerant, and needs to be serviced. (By the way, this test also works for window air conditioners, although if those are low on refrigerant, it's probably time to replace them.)

Choosing a mini-split ductless air conditioner

Right there in size between a central air-conditioning system and a window air conditioner is a category of HVAC appliances called "ductless mini-split air conditioners." These utilize a wall-mounted blower inside your home that's connected to a small compressor outside your home via refrigeration lines. (See Figure 10-6.) Mini-split systems are available to provide just cooling, or as a heat pump that provides both heating and cooling. In the last several years, the popularity of these systems has soared for a number of reasons, including their quiet, efficient operation and the fact that they don't require ducting to be installed throughout your home.

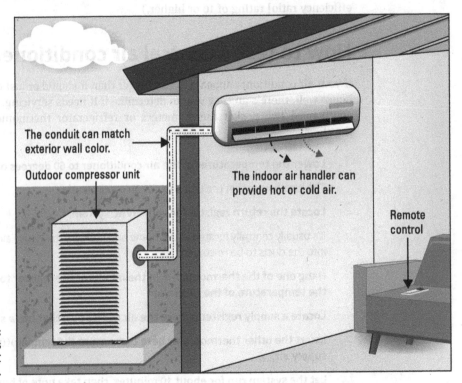

The conduit can match exterior wall color.

Outdoor compressor unit

The indoor air handler can provide hot or cold air.

Remote control

FIGURE 10-6: Ductless mini-split HVAC system.

Choosing a window air-conditioning unit

As with a central AC system, there's not much you have to do to maintain a window air-conditioning unit:

>> **Clean the filter on the interior face every month.** Unplug the unit. Pull off the front panel and remove the filter or slide the filter out the side. Next, wash the filter gently in a mild detergent, rinse, and then dry.

>> **Clean the condenser coil fins on the exterior face at least once a year.** Gently vacuum or brush the fins and then straighten any bent fins with a comb.

TIP

Got a 10-year-old window air conditioner? Throw it out! A new unit will be far more energy efficient. But don't buy just any air conditioner; get one that works efficiently — one with an Energy Star label, one that does all it can to help you keep your electric bill in check. Also, you'll want to do the following:

>> **Buy the right capacity unit.** Measure the length and width of the room you want to cool. Compare your room's size with the size that the air conditioner is recommended for.

>> **Get a unit with an energy-saving thermostat that cycles the unit on and off.**

>> **Make sure you get a three-speed fan (*high* to cool the room quickly, and *medium* or *low* to maintain the temperature).**

>> **Choose a model with a timer to turn the unit on before you get home.**

4

Inside Home Sweet Home

Chapter **11**

Walls and Ceilings

I t doesn't take much to mess up a wall or ceiling. Drywall is more designed to be decorated than durable. Dings, dents, cracks, and nail pops happen. However, too often repairs to walls and ceilings look good initially, but six months later they're back. In this chapter, I'll share tips to repair the most common maladies, so they don't happen again and again and again!

Life is hard on walls and ceilings. Luckily, most maintenance to these surfaces is well within your reach.

Cleaning Walls and Ceilings

You may not realize it, but everything in your kitchen is covered with a thin coating of grease and gummy dust. And your bathroom walls have their own coating of gunk, including hairspray, cleaning products, and stuck-on dust. And don't forget crayon marks on bedroom walls and handprints and ugly smudges galore everywhere else.

You can wipe away fingerprints, crayon, pen marks, dirt, and dust from walls, trim, and doors with almost any household cleaner and a damp cloth. If your house is relatively new, make a bucket of soapy water and wipe the walls and ceiling with a damp sponge. If your house is older, you need something that cuts through the accumulated crud, like TSP, which removes greasy dirt like nothing else. Short for *trisodium phosphate*, TSP is sold in powder form in most home centers and hardware stores. It's also a good choice to clean surfaces before painting. Mix up a bucketful according to the label directions, wipe down the walls and ceiling, and then rinse thoroughly with clean water.

TIP

Wiping down walls and ceilings may sound like a monumental task, but it gets a lot easier when you use a foam-rubber sponge mop. Mix up a cleaning solution in a bucket, then dip the mop, ring it out, and away you go. This method works for most smooth walls, but not for textured surfaces like popcorn ceilings. Gravity being what it is, it's best to wear a hat and start with ceilings and then move on to walls. You can wrap a towel on the mop head to dry the surfaces as you go. Remember to use as little water as possible and turn off the electric circuits to the rooms you are working in until everything is clean and dry.

Dealing with Drywall

Chances are, the walls and ceilings of your home are made of drywall (also referred to as wallboard, gypsum board, or Sheetrock). Drywall is both easy to damage and easy to repair.

Drywall is subject to two kinds of damage: gouges and hairline cracks. Gouges are usually caused by accident — by you, moving furniture, doors that fling open too far, or (no matter how many times you ask them not to) kids playing ball in the house! Hairline cracks are usually caused by movement in the foundation or framing of your house, which is normal. The frame of your house expands and contracts with the seasons, as temperature and humidity levels change.

Repairing small cracks

Got a small crack? Fill it with a flexible silicone caulk. The silicone flexes as the crack widens and narrows with normal house movement. Caulking is easy — just follow these steps:

1. **Buy a fresh tube of silicone caulking (the paintable kind).**

2. **Use a caulking gun to spread a thin bead of the caulk into the crack.**

3. **Wipe the excess from around the crack with rubbing alcohol.**

4. **Let the caulk dry.**

5. **Coat the repair with primer.**

   Don't skip this step or you'll end up with a permanently goofy-looking, non-matching area.

6. **Repaint, as necessary.**

WARNING

Remember the movie *Groundhog Day*? That'll be you if you fill a crack with drywall joint compound or spackle. Spackle's brittleness allows the crack to come back year after year.

Filling bigger cracks

Bigger cracks require a different kind of maintenance. Here's what you need:

» 6-inch taping knife

» 10- or 12-inch taping knife

» 1 square piece of plywood or a plastic mud pan

» Drywall joint compound

» Fiberglass drywall tape (not paper tape)

» 220-grit sanding mesh and a drywaller's sanding block

Here's how to stop that crack dead in its tracks:

1. **Clean out the crack so there are no loose "crumbs."**

2. **Put a blob of compound on the plywood or mud pan.**

   This step makes it easy to load compound onto the knife.

3. **Cut a length of fiberglass tape a few inches longer than the crack you want to repair and apply the tape to the crack.**

   Fiberglass tape is a mesh-like material with a self-adhesive surface, making it easy to position over the crack, and easier to use than paper tape.

   If the crack is really crooked, cut the tape in short lengths so that you can follow the line as closely as possible.

TIP

4. **Apply a thin coat of compound over the tape and smooth it with the 6-inch taping knife, making sure to feather the edges.**

   Let the patch dry completely (usually overnight).

5. **Apply a second, smoothing coat using the 10- to 12-inch taping knife, again making sure to feather the edges.**

   Let the second coat dry completely.

6. **Apply a third (and, with luck, final) coat using the 10- to 12-inch taping knife, again making sure to feather the edges.**

   Let the third coat dry completely.

7. **Sand the patch until smooth.**

8. **Apply a coat of good-quality primer.**

9. **Paint to match.**

Filling holes like a pro

Joint compound alone is not enough to fill any hole larger than a quarter. You've got to put something into the hole or onto it and then use compound to make it smooth and invisible.

Repairing small holes

Holes that are too large to fill with compound but are no more than three or four inches across can be patched with a precut stick-on patch and some joint compound. The idea is to take a peel-and-stick patch made of stiff, perforated metal mesh, place it over the hole, and then cover the patch with two or three coats (or more) of compound. (See Figure 11-1.) Here's the more detailed explanation:

1. **Cover the hole with the stick-on patch.**

   Use scissors to trim the patch so that it's about an inch larger than the hole.

2. **Smear and then smooth the compound over the entire area, feathering the edges.**

   Here, less is more. A thin layer of compound at a time is the big secret. A thick layer is difficult to sand, shows up on the wall as a bump, and may develop cracks.

3. **Let the compound dry completely, and then sand it lightly.**

4. **Smooth a second layer of compound over the patch, and let it dry completely.**

   Finish the project with a third coat of compound and allow it to dry completely. A fourth coat or "touch-up" coat may be required for a truly invisible patch.

5. **Sand, prime, and paint.**

Patching Small Holes in Drywall

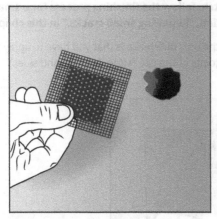

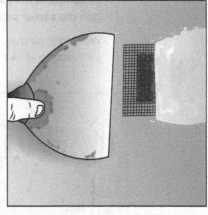

FIGURE 11-1:
For small hole repairs, use a self-sticking mesh patch.

Step 1: Cut the patch wide enough to overlap the hole by 1-inch on all sides and apply over the hole.

Step 2: Spackle over the patch using 3 thin coats. Then lightly sand, prime, and paint.

Repairing large holes

Holes that are too big for a metal patch require a slightly different technique. For these holes, you have to make a patch using a chunk of drywall. The easiest way to make this kind of repair is to use drywall clips. These little metal wonders straddle the edge of the hole and create a series of little "shelves" along the back edge of the hole, providing screw-backing for a cut-to-fit patch. Follow these steps:

1. **From a piece of scrap drywall, cut a square or rectangular patch large enough to completely cover the hole.**

2. **Hold the patch over the hole and trace its outline with a pencil.**

3. **Use a utility knife or drywall saw to cut away everything inside the penciled outline.**

   When cutting into a wall, watch out for wires and pipes! If you're unsure, some electronic stud finders offer the added ability to detect metal pipes and electric wires.

WARNING

4. **Install drywall clips on all sides of the hole (no more than 8 inches apart) and secure them using the screws provided with the clips.** See Figure 11-2.

5. **Insert the patch into the hole and drive screws through the patch into the clips.**

6. **Snap off the temporary tabs of the clips (the ones that extend beyond the face of the wall).**

7. **To complete the patch, follow the finishing process for a smaller patch (see the earlier section, "Repairing small cracks," in this chapter).**

   With larger patches, the only difference is that you have to apply fiberglass joint tape on all four joints of the patch (top, bottom, and sides).

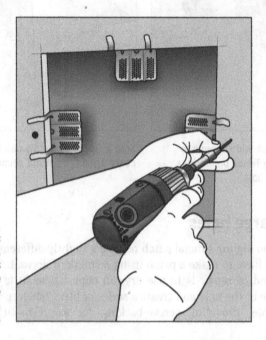

FIGURE 11-2: For larger holes, use drywall clips to secure the patch, then tape seams, spackle, prime, and paint.

RE-CREATING TEXTURE

If your walls have a textured surface, you need to re-create that texture on the patched area. Here's how.

- **For a swirly finish:** Place blobs of compound evenly throughout the patched area, and then swirl away! Try to duplicate the swirls on the rest of the wall. You can use almost any implement that will duplicate the original pattern (a drywall knife, a paintbrush, a roller). Personally, I like to use a wallpaper adhesive brush; it's wide and rough, and with a twist of the wrist, it creates a nice swirl pattern.

- **For a flattened-bumps finish:** Use spray texture in a can. DAP recently released *2in1 Wall & Ceiling Spray Texture*, including Orange Peel, Knock Down, and Popcorn textures. Each product features a multi-directional nozzle that allows the user to apply the texture evenly to any surface, right-side-up or upside-down! To find out more, go to www.dap.com/ and do a search for "spray texture."

Tackling truss uplift

If your home has been plagued by constant cracks at several joints where the walls and ceiling meet, then you may have more than a simple drywall-patching problem. You may have *truss uplift*. Truss uplift results when moisture content differences exist between the upper (rafter) and lower (ceiling joist) chords of wood trusses. (See Figure 11-3.)

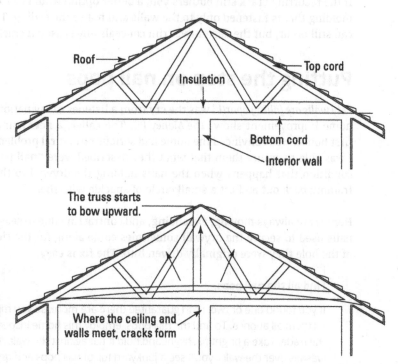

FIGURE 11-3:
Truss uplift can cause gaps between walls and ceilings.

Moisture content differences are typical when one chord is cold and the other chord is warm. For example, the bottom chord of a truss surrounded by a well-insulated attic will be warmer than its cold rafter counterpart. The expansion of the top chord of a truss exerts an inward force on the bottom chord, which causes it to bow upward and lift away from the tops of interior partitions (hence, the term *truss uplift*).

TIP

According to the American Wood Council, trusses are made up of "chords" and "webs." The three sides of the triangle that make up a truss are called chords. The webs are wood pieces connecting the top and bottom chords.

Most importantly, truss uplift falls under the "annoying but harmless" category of home maintenance. There is no surefire means of preventing truss uplift. Repairs to eliminate the cracks at the ceiling-to-wall connection would require a pretty big project. (You'd need to remove all the ceiling drywall fasteners within 18 inches of the adjacent interior partition from each of the trusses, and then repair the enormous hole you created, so definitely not worth it!)

If the recurring crack still bothers you, a better option would be to install a crown molding that is fastened only to the walls and not to the ceiling. Thus, movement can still occur, but the decorative trim conceals any seasonal cracks.

Putting the stop on nail pops

"My walls are falling apart!" was the cry from a listener to my nationally syndicated home improvement show, *The Money Pit*. The caller, a new homeowner in their first house, was convinced the home had serious structural problems. Fortunately, I was able to assure them that what they described were "nail pops," a cosmetic condition that happens when the nails holding the drywall to the home's wood framing back out and lift a small circle of spackle with them.

Homes are always moving, expanding, and contracting due to seasonal shifts. The nails used to secure the drywall sometimes come along for the ride and back out of the hole they were originally driven into. The fix is easy.

1. **Find all the nail pops.**

   If you found one or two, I can guarantee there are more, so you might as well fix them all at once. To find the nail pops, employ this home inspector's trick of the trade. Take a bright flashlight and hold it flat against the wall. As the light washes over the walls, you'll see a junkyard full of nail pops and drywall seams (which is why I never recommend using anything other than flat paint on walls or ceilings. Add a sheen and you see all the defects.). As you find a nail pop, mark it with a small piece of painter's tape.

2. **Stop the nail from moving.**

   There are two ways to do that.

   Take a drywall nail, distinctive because of its black color and wide head, and drive the new nail into the wall next to the loose nail, being sure to overlap the head of the original nail. This will hold it in place and prevent further movement.

   As an alternative, you can also remove the original nail and replace it with a drywall screw, which will never pull out.

With both methods, make sure you've driven the nail or screw in deep enough to create a dimple in the wall.

3. **Apply one or two coats of spackle over the dimpled area. Then sand, prime, and paint.**

Plastering: More Trouble than You May Want

Older houses have plaster walls and ceilings with "rock" lath or wood lath for a base. Rock lath (1930s-1960s) is drywall in small sheets nailed to wall framing. Wood lath (pre-1930s) consists of parallel wood strips. These thin strips of wood were installed on the wall framing with gaps between them, which the original plaster was squeezed through, creating "keys." Once the plaster dried, the lath held it securely in place.

If your plaster walls are in good condition, you can fix cracks and holes using patching plaster. But if your walls or ceilings are sagging and have big holes, you've got a big job ahead of you.

Fixing small cracks and holes

Cracks and tiny holes in plaster are slightly more difficult to patch than wallboard — not because the damaged area is harder to fill, but because prepping the surface requires more work to remove a hundred years' worth of paint and wallpaper that's accumulated. Once this is done, you can proceed. Refer to the earlier section, "Repairing small cracks," in this chapter, and take a little extra time to match the finish.

Dealing with sagging and other big problems

As plaster ages and the house shifts, the ceiling plaster can loosen and sag. Finding a sag is easy. You can confirm your diagnosis by pressing against suspect areas with the flat of your hand. If the plaster feels spongy or gives, a repair is in order.

WARNING

If a sagging ceiling area is not fixed, it can suddenly let go, with a huge potential for damage and personal injury. Plaster is very heavy and can leave a dent in the floor, or in YOU, if it falls. Don't wait for this to happen.

For minor sagging in a small area, you can reattach the plaster to the lath using long drywall screws fitted with plaster washers. (*Plaster washers* are thin metal disks through which drywall screws are threaded and then driven through the plaster into ceiling joists, wall studs, or lath.) This screw/washer combination pulls the loose plaster tightly against the framing, effectively fixing the sag and stabilizing the area.

REMEMBER

Be sure to proceed cautiously, tightening each screw/washer gradually while applying firm pressure against the plaster with your free hand. This ensures a gradual and snug fit to the framing.

If the sagging is severe (more than 1 inch away from the lath), or if the sag covers a large area, you've got a much bigger problem. Crumbling plaster tends to become a chronic issue. A sag in one place often indicates potential sagging in multiple spots over time. When that happens, the best option is either to remove all the plaster and replace it with drywall or leave the plaster in place and add a layer of drywall on top.

I've remodeled homes both ways and prefer to cover old plaster walls with drywall. Tearing out plaster creates one heck of a dirty, dusty mess, and the original wood studs are never as flat as new walls due to the original plaster compensating for inconsistencies. Although covering old plaster walls with drywall requires additional steps, such as extending electrical outlets and switch boxes to accommodate the thickness of the drywall, the effort is worthwhile, ultimately producing a better result.

Interior Painting: Doing the Job Right

Nothing freshens things up like a new coat of paint. But, like anything, there's a right way and a wrong way to do the job. In this section, I walk you through the steps for painting. Follow my advice, and you're sure to be pleased with the results.

Prepping makes perfect

You've bought your paint, you've got new brushes and rollers, you've spread out the drop cloths, and you've opened up the stepladder. You're ready to paint.

Whoa! Stop right there! If you want your paint job to last, you can't skip the most important step: surface preparation. The real secret to a beautiful, long-lasting paint job is getting the walls and ceiling really clean and perfectly smooth.

CHOOSING THE BEST DROP CLOTHS

Drop cloths come in two primary materials: heavy plastic and canvas. While many consumers may choose plastic, professionals prefer canvas for specific reasons. Plastic, being slippery, tends to allow paint drips to spread widely. Conversely, canvas quickly absorbs drips and possesses enough weight to remain stationary, preventing it from shifting under a ladder.

For best results, strike a balance by using plastic to cover items susceptible to paint damage, such as furniture or other belongings. However, when it comes to covering floors, it's smart to consistently opt for canvas.

REMEMBER

Painting is hard work. If you fail to properly prepare the surfaces you'll be painting, your paint may not go on smoothly, or even peel off a short time later. Preparation means the difference between a long-lasting paint job and one that you have to redo long before you're ready:

1. **Prepare the room.**

   Make sure you do the following:

   Remove lamps, irreplaceable knickknacks, and as much furniture as you can, and then push whatever is left to the middle of the room.

   Remove anything attached to the walls, including pictures, window treatments, and switch and outlet plates.

   Take off all the window and door hardware.

   Cover every inch of everything — floor, furniture, and radiators — with canvas or heavy-plastic drop cloths.

2. **Clean the surface (see the earlier section, "Cleaning Walls and Ceilings," in this chapter, for details).**

   REMEMBER

   If you have mildew on a wall, you need to kill it and cover the remaining stain with a stain sealer primer made to hide stains. (See MY Easy All-Surface Mildew Remover (Chapter 20) for more tips on killing mildew.)

3. **Prepare the surface.**

   To prepare the surface, you need to do the following:

   Fill nail holes, cracks, and other imperfections with patching compound.

   Scrape any loose or flaking paint on windows, sills, and woodwork. (See the nearby sidebar, "Removing paint from woodwork," for more information.)

Sand patches and any bare areas on windows, sills, and woodwork.

Lightly sand or use a deglosser to knock down the shine on glossy trim. (A *deglosser* is essentially liquid sandpaper; it etches the existing finish so that the new paint can stick better.)

Lightly sand walls if they're uneven, brush-marked, or bumpy.

Fill gaps between the trim and the walls (especially along the baseboards and door trim) with caulk.

4. Clean again.

Vacuum the room to remove sanding dust and paint flakes (don't forget to do the windowsills and trim). Then wipe down everything with a tack cloth or barely damp rag. (A *tack cloth* is a piece of cloth that is coated in a sticky [tacky] substance so that dust and particles stick to it.)

5. Mask the windows.

Use wax paper or a layer of thin plastic taped to the windows to prevent paint splatters on the glass.

TIP

When masking windows, walls, or trim, use "painter's" tape. It's specially formulated to be less adhesive, which means it will be easier to remove and will cause less potential damage when peeled off.

Now you're ready to gather your supplies.

REMOVING PAINT FROM WOODWORK

For most woodwork, a putty knife and sandpaper remove loose flakes. But if your woodwork has 37 layers on it, try a scraper. I recommend you start off by using a scraper designed specifically for moldings. If that doesn't work well, or if you're a little low on elbow grease, try an electric heat gun or chemical stripper. Heat guns soften the paint so that it can be scraped away. Strippers also soften the paint for easier scraping. Be sure to ventilate the area where you are working to avoid the fumes.

Never use a propane torch to remove paint. Dangers include risks of scorching wood, vaporization of lead in old paint, and the very real fire risk by ignition of bird/rodent nest material often found behind thin siding or woodwork.

Scraping, sanding, or using a heat gun is not an option if the paint contains lead. Be safe, not sorry. Your local hardware store or home center carries a special test kit that will tell you if lead exists. The test takes only minutes, and you're always better off taking the time to check.

If your paint contains lead, and it's not peeling or flaking, your best bet is to simply give it a TSP wash and apply a fresh coat of primer and finish. If the paint is in anything but pristine condition, or if you simply want it out of your home, it's best to hire a professional lead-paint abatement contractor to carefully remove the paint.

Gathering your paint and painting supplies

After you've scraped, sanded, filled holes, sanded again, and cleaned, the preparation phase is complete and painting can begin, right? Not quite yet. Not until you gather your paint and painting supplies.

Selecting a primer

Priming is an essential step in the painting process. Unfortunately, it's a step that too many impatient DIYers like to skip!

Think of primer as the glue that makes paint stick. It can cover a wide variety of surfaces and provides a perfect surface for the paint. If you fail to prime before painting, you may find that the paint begins to peel off shortly after the job was done. Primer can also help resist attack by moisture, fills small cracks, and smooths and seals the surface so that finish coats are more uniform and lustrous, as well as longer lasting.

TIP

In recent years, there has been a rise in formulations that integrate both paint and primer into a single coat. While these "paint and primer in one" products may appear to be a time-saving solution, my experience suggests otherwise. I've found that they don't seal surfaces as effectively as using a separate primer, and they also don't provide the same level of finish as a traditional top-coat. Applying products separately consistently yields superior results.

When you patch a spot or scrape down to bare wood, you create a rough, porous area that absorbs more paint than the area around it, creating an uneven gloss and an area that is slightly different in color than the surrounding area. Primer seals the area so this doesn't happen. A stain-killing primer also keeps mysterious dark marks, water stains, crayon, marker, and pen from bleeding through to the final finish.

If you can, use the same brand of primer and paint. Manufacturers formulate their paints and primers so that they work well together. In general, oil-based primers are the best for covering stains, but water-based ones work well for most everything else. If you are painting over very smooth and shiny surfaces, such as kitchen cabinets, it's helpful to use a special type of primer that's referred to as *high bond* — it's formulated to provide increased adhesion to the surface and helps assure the finish paint sticks.

Selecting a paint

Latex paints are the top choice for walls and ceilings. Don't let anyone tell you differently. They dry quickly and clean up with soap and water.

Unfortunately, as if latex paints aren't thin enough and wet enough to begin with, they can dry so quickly that brush marks and lap marks (also called *dry edge*, where a line left by the edge of the roller is visible) are hard to avoid. And, yeah, they don't stand up to scrapes and clunks as well as oil-based paints do. But the pluses far outweigh the minuses, particularly when you consider that latex paints contain no toxic solvents.

On the other hand, oil-based paints, while becoming more difficult to find due to ever-changing environmental regulations, are still the best choice for doors and trim. They dry slowly, giving brushstrokes time to disappear. They also dry to a very hard, durable finish. However, cleanup requires solvents and, as oil-based paints dry, they release volatile organic compounds (VOCs) into the air. (For the sake of the environment, when purchasing oil-based paint, be sure to look for a low-VOC product. Low-VOC paints contain fewer toxic chemicals.)

Fortunately, improvements in the chemistry behind latex paints are continuing to enhance their durability. Recently, for example, I took on a cabinet painting project using Sherwin Williams Emerald Urethane Trim Enamel and was impressed with the finish and toughness of the final surface.

Buy the highest-quality paint you can afford — unless you like to paint. If you use poor-quality paint, you'll probably need to apply more than two coats — plus, you get to paint again in just a few years. Why not do the job right the first time?

How much paint should you buy? Measure the area (square footage) of your walls and ceiling, look on the can of paint to see how many square feet it can cover, and divide your room square footage by that amount. You can do the same thing for the trim. Most paint covers 400 square feet per gallon.

Getting the right painting tools

When you're getting ready to paint, you need the following supplies.

>> **A trim brush:** A 2-inch brush for painting door trim and other wide moldings.

>> **A sash brush:** A 1½-inch angled brush made for detail painting of windows and narrow trim pieces.

>> **A roller:** A fabric-covered hollow cylinder (typically 9 inches long) that fits over a metal roller frame. You use a roller when you want to paint a large area, like a wall; you use paintbrushes for the detail work. The *nap* (length of the fabric) varies depending upon the desired finish. In general, use a short nap for smooth surfaces and a long nap for rough surfaces.

When buying a paintbrush, consider the following:

>> **The handle should feel good in your hand.** You're going to be holding it for a while.

>> **The metal piece that holds the bristles (called the *ferrule*) should be securely attached.**

>> **The bristles should fan out — not separate — when you press them against your palm.**

>> **The bristles should be smooth, straight, and have tiny split ends.**

>> **The bristles should stay attached when you lightly tug on them.**

>> **The brush should be appropriate for the kind of paint and surface that you want to paint.** For example, thick, fluffy rollers are for rough surfaces, and tight-nap rollers are for smooth surfaces. The kind of roller you need also depends on the paint and surface in question. Most paint manufacturers will list a recommended brush type and roller size right on the can.

Painting made easy

You've bought the right paint. You've got good brushes and rollers. The room is thoroughly prepped. Everything is covered up. It's time to actually paint.

A good paint job consists of three basic steps: priming, applying a first coat of finish paint, and applying a second coat of finish paint.

TIP

Before you do anything, stir the paint thoroughly. Paint looks better and lasts longer if all its components are mixed well from the start. Three minutes is a good amount of stirring time.

Always paint a room from top to bottom. The job will go faster — and turn out better — if you follow this sequence:

1. **Paint the ceiling, using a trim brush and a roller.**

   Using the trim brush, start from the edges and paint a 2- to 4-inch-wide strip that feathers out toward the middle of the room. Then paint the rest of the ceiling immediately with a roller, starting in a corner and painting across the narrowest dimension of the room.

2. **Starting when the ceiling is dry, paint the walls with a trim brush and roller.**

   Do one wall at a time. With a trim brush, cut in where the walls meet the ceiling, around the doors and windows, and along the baseboards. Use a roller for the rest.

3. **Paint the windows, using an angular sash brush, and, if you prefer, a smaller brush for the dividers.**

4. **Paint the doors, using a trim brush.**

   Work quickly but carefully. Paint all the edges, but not the hinges.

5. **Using a sash brush, paint the door and window trim — edges first and then the face.**

6. **Paint the baseboards, using a sash brush.**

   Protect the floor or carpet with painter's tape, drop cloths, or other protective material.

TIP

Here are a few more helpful hints to getting a great-looking paint job:

>> **Work with a partner if you can.** One of you can cut in the edges, and the other can follow along with the roller!

>> **Use plenty of paint.** Most do-it-yourselfers try to make a brush full or roller full go too far. If you skimp on the paint, you'll end up with a finish full of roller "tire tracks" and visible brush strokes.

>> **Two thin, wet coats of paint always flow better and, thus, dry smoother than one thick, dry coat.** Adding a bit of water to latex paint or thinner to oil-based paint will cause the paint to be thinner and wetter.

Cleaning up right

Latex paint cleans up with water. Wash the brush under warm water, making sure to work any paint out of the base of the bristles and the ferrule. Shake or snap the brush to get the water out, and hang it up to dry, bristles down.

TIP

Need a lunch break? No need to clean brushes or rollers you'll be continuing with. Cover your paintbrushes or rollers with plastic wrap to keep them from drying out. You can also cover and then store them in the fridge overnight, and they'll be ready to go (once warmed to room temperature) when you start again.

To clean up oil-based paint or primer, use paint thinner. Fill an old can or jar with enough thinner to cover the bristles and ferrule, and slosh the brush around, allowing the thinner to dissolve the paint. Remove the brush from the thinner and tap the ferrule firmly against the edge of a paint bucket (bristles pointing toward the inside of the bucket) to remove the thinned paint. Repeat this process until the brush is clean. It's a messy, stinky job. Luckily, you only need to clean your brushes once at the end of the job.

MY FAVORITE PAINT CLEANUP TOOLS

Painting projects are great, but the cleanup part? Not so much. However, with the right tools, you can make the cleanup a breeze and ensure your brushes and rollers last longer.

Painter's Multi-Tool: Available in various configurations, this tool serves multiple purposes. It helps pry open paint cans without damaging the rim and pierces holes in the rim to allow excess paint to drain back, ensuring a better seal and more uses. But its real magic for cleanup lies in the crescent-shaped cutout on the side. This feature is specifically designed to clean rollers effortlessly. Just swipe the tool across the roller, and you'll be amazed as paint gushes out, making it much easier to thoroughly clean the roller for its next use.

Paintbrush Comb: Over time, brushes can become stiff at the base because leftover paint wasn't completely cleaned out before storing them. The solution? A brush comb. This steel-tined comb can be inserted into the brush and used to loosen and flush out any paint that has collected deep within the bristles, ensuring your brushes stay in top condition.

(continued)

(continued)

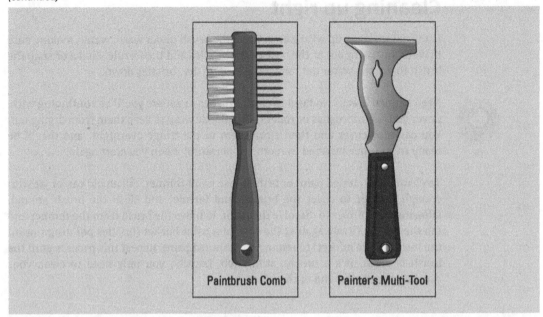

| Paintbrush Comb | Painter's Multi-Tool |

Storing leftover paint and making it last

When it comes to storing paint, success depends not only on how and where the paint is stored, but also the condition of the can. The enemy of storing paint is simply — air! The more air that gets into that can, the shorter the life of the paint. So, the seal is key to storing paint for the long run.

» **Use the brush to clean the seam as much as possible on the paint can, and use a rag to wipe the opposing seam on the lid.** Paint that dries in either area will prevent the lid from sealing completely.

» **Next, cover the open can with a piece of clear plastic wrap (like Saran Wrap).** This acts as a gasket and provides an additional level of seal protection, preventing air from getting into the can.

» **Place the lid over the plastic wrap and the can.** Tap it down using a rubber mallet to prevent dents and damage to the seam portion of the lid.

» **Lastly, store the paint can upside down in a cool place.** This prevents the possibility of any air seeping into the can.

Voilà! You've just doubled the life expectancy of your leftover paint!

Making Paneling Look Like New

Most houses more than 25 years old have at least one room with paneling. Believe it or not, paneling was very chic at one time, and it still has its place in Dad's den, the basement rec room, and rustic homes. There are three kinds of paneling: solid wood planks, plywood sheets, and faux-finished hardboard.

If you have solid wood or plywood on the wall, you can do a number of things to make it look like new. Cleaning is the easiest and most effective way to brighten the finish and should be done using a gentle cleaner like Murphy's Oil Soap.

If you're tired of the dark, woody look that paneling provides, but you like the texture of real wood, you can paint it. First, wash the surface with a solution of TSP (see the earlier section, "Cleaning Walls and Ceilings," in this chapter). When the surface is dry, prime it with an oil-based stain-killer primer. Finish the job with a good-quality latex paint.

TIP

If you're fed up with the paneling in your home and eager for a fresh look, you have two options: Remove it entirely or cover it with new drywall. Removing it is generally easier, provided the original paneling wasn't glued directly to the walls. To check, try gently prying a section of paneling away from the wall. If it's nailed on, that's great news — you can remove it and fill in the nail holes with spackle. However, if it's glued, attempting to remove it could result in stripping off the top paper layer of the drywall, which is difficult to repair. In such cases, covering the paneling with new drywall is likely the better choice.

Wondering about Wallpaper

Time is not kind to wallpaper: The edges peel and buckle, the adhesive gets tired and crumbles, bubbles develop, and the wear and tear of normal life starts to take a visible toll. Oh, and don't forget wallpaper patterns that become outrageously outdated. If replacement is in order, I can tell you how to easily remove what you have. But that doesn't mean that you have to rip it down. If it's still looking good and in style, I can help you repair everything else.

Removing wallpaper

If you've chosen to replace your wallpaper, you need to purchase a perforation tool (also called a "paper tiger"), which you'll find in the paint section of your hardware store, home center, or paint store. You'll also need to rent a wallpaper steamer. After you have these two tools, removal is a breeze:

1. **Use the perforation tool to puncture thousands (yes, thousands) of tiny holes into the surface of the wallpaper.**

   The perforations allow the steam to penetrate to the adhesive.

2. **Use the steamer to liquefy the adhesive, working from the top down.**

   Warm, liquefied adhesive flows downward and causes the lower portion of the paper to release more quickly.

3. **Gently pull the paper off the wall.**

   Don't be in a hurry. Patience works best with this process.

4. **Remove the rest of the adhesive that remains on the wall using more steam or a liquid enzyme adhesive solvent, which can be found in the paint and wallpaper section of your local hardware store, home center, or paint store.**

   For either, you'll need a large sponge to soak up the softened gooey mess that's left on the wall.

 If your wallpaper is looking dingy *and* it's washable, sponge it down with a solution of mild soap and cold water. Wipe with clean water and then wipe dry. (Be sure to test the colorfastness of the wallpaper in some inconspicuous corner before **TIP** you clean it.)

Read on to find out how to correct other wallpaper problems.

Fixing loose seams and clean tears

Got an edge that's coming unglued, a seam that's sticking up, or a clean tear? Here's how to fix it:

1. **Moisten the damaged area with warm water and *carefully* lift the softened wallpaper away from the wall.**

2. **Apply a thin coating of lap-and-seam adhesive (available at any wallpaper store).**

3. **Press the wallpaper back in place, matching it up exactly.**

4. **Roll the edge with a seam roller.**

   A *seam roller* is part of a wallpaper installation kit that you can find in your local hardware store, home center, or paint store.

5. **Sponge off any adhesive that squishes out with a barely damp sponge.**

Patching wallpaper

Got a stain or a big, ugly rip in your beautiful wallpaper? If you can find a matching leftover scrap, fix it this way:

1. **Cut a square or rectangular replacement piece that's a little bit larger than the damaged area, making sure to match the pattern exactly; then attach the patch to the wall with masking tape.**

2. **Cut through both the patch and the damaged wallpaper simultaneously using a utility knife (a process referred to as *double cutting*).**

   Don't make straight cuts. In fact, making a curvy, kidney-shaped cut is best, because a curved cut patch is just about impossible to see after it's finished.

3. **Put the replacement patch somewhere safe; then use a hot-water-soaked rag to dampen the damaged bit of wallpaper and peel it out.**

   If necessary, use a perforation tool and a coat of enzyme wallpaper-adhesive solvent to loosen things up.

4. **Apply another coat of solvent and sponge away any remaining glue on the bare spot; then clean the patch area with a clean, damp sponge and let dry.**

5. **Soak and soften the patch in a bath of warm water for about three to five minutes; when the patch becomes soft and pliable, apply a thin coating of adhesive evenly over the entire back.**

6. **Position the patch so that the pattern matches; then carefully smooth it down with a clean, damp cloth or a seam roller.**

7. **Sponge off any adhesive that squishes out.**

There you go — a fix that's nearly invisible to all eyes but yours.

Chapter **12**

Floors and Interior Doors

loors and doors are some of the hardest-working parts of any home. Floors take a pounding from foot traffic, which relentlessly grinds down the surface while simultaneously grinding in dirt. Doors get a daily workout as well, with the added stressor of seasonal swelling, shrinking, and sticking.

Fortunately, both floors and doors can be easy to maintain — if you know a few tricks of the trade! For example,

» A hardwood floor can be refinished using a simple floor buffer.

» Lipstick can be a really handy tool to have around when you need to adjust the lock on a door. (Read on to find out how.)

From refinishing floors to dealing with doors that don't close like they should, this chapter offers you a whole new perspective on how to maintain and improve the floors and doors in your home.

What's Underfoot? Flooring

While the floor framing and subfloor (which I cover in Chapter 4) provide the structural support for your floors, it is the "flooring" that delivers the durability and décor of the surfaces you see. Although some flooring can be reasonably inexpensive, really good, long-lasting flooring costs a bundle — making regular maintenance a must.

Vanquishing vinyl trouble

Odds are, you have sheet vinyl or vinyl tile *somewhere* in your house. After all, for decades, it's been the most popular flooring material for kitchens, bathrooms, and laundry rooms. It's popular because it's easy to care for. And that's good for you.

This is not to say that a vinyl floor won't ever have problems. Some problems are mainly cosmetic; others are more serious. Most vinyl flooring problems are not problems with the actual material but are the result of an issue with the floor structure below. As tempting as it may be, you can't just cover up these problems — you have to fix their underlying cause.

REMEMBER

These days, vinyl is largely falling out of favor as a preferred flooring choice. That alone makes it worth considering whether it's better to simply replace sheet vinyl with one of the low-cost, but super-durable vinyl plank alternatives that I cover in this chapter. But on top of this, fixing some vinyl problems can be complicated and, frankly, more work that they're worth. For these reasons, I'll provide remedies for the most common and easiest-to-address vinyl problems.

WARNING

Vinyl tile and sheet flooring manufactured prior to 1978 may contain asbestos. That's the year when the U.S. Environmental Protection Agency banned the use of asbestos in the manufacture of building products. When left alone, asbestos flooring poses virtually no risk of exposure, but when it's disturbed, it could release asbestos fibers into the air, which could be hazardous to your health. Therefore, be careful not to disturb old tile. If you opt for a new floor, you're almost always better off laying the new floor over the old one rather than exposing yourself and your family to the risks associated with removal. If you're not sure whether your floor contains asbestos, you can have it tested by a licensed testing lab.

Scuff marks

Use an art gum eraser (one of those grayish-tan ones like you used in school) or borrow a Pink Pearl eraser from your kid's school supplies. Just rub the mark and — *voilà!* — it disappears.

TIP

For tougher scuffs, use a little paint thinner on a rag to rub the spot clean. Be careful not to go nuts with the thinner — you could remove the vinyl's no-wax finish.

Persistent grubbiness

Before you know it, a vinyl floor can acquire a funky gray cast. This comes from infrequent or inadequate cleaning. Diligence is the key to avoiding this problem:

>> Vacuum or sweep regularly to remove abrasive dirt and dust.

>> Wipe up spills immediately.

>> Mop regularly with a damp mop and 1 tablespoon of white vinegar in 1 gallon of warm water. (No detergent!)

For the best results, work on a small section at a time and dry it before moving on to the next section. If the vinegar solution is left on for an extended period and allowed to air-dry, it can dull the finish.

REMEMBER

If regular cleaning doesn't keep the perma-dirt away, use a mop or sponge and a solution of warm (not hot) water and a few drops of liquid dish soap. Don't rub too hard. Rinse thoroughly with clean water.

Yellow discoloration

If the problem is a yellow discoloration, then you need to remove and reapply wax. However, don't remove the wax more than once a year — the chemicals in the remover are hard on the vinyl. When reapplying the wax, be sure to choose a product rated for floors as opposed to a paste furniture wax. Floor wax provides maximum protection without becoming dangerously slippery. Oh, and be sure that the wax that you use is the non-yellowing type — it'll say so on the container.

TIP

If the yellow discoloration is under a floor mat with a rubber backing, like the kind that people use in front of a kitchen sink, I've got bad news for you: all the scrubbing in the world won't take the yellow away! What you're seeing isn't a stain on the vinyl. Instead, it's a chemical reaction between the rubber and the vinyl. This reaction will turn the vinyl yellow, so the only solution is to replace the floor — or find a bigger mat to cover the stain!

No-wax vinyl floors require basically the same kind of care as the kind that requires waxing. Again, the secret to a long-lasting shine is keeping the floor clean. Stay on top of dirt and spills. And when you mop, use only a little white vinegar rinse and dry thoroughly.

Mildew and mold below the surface of the vinyl

If black, brown, or purple stains are visible just below the surface of the vinyl, the only way to remove the stains is to remove and replace the vinyl. These stains are mildew and fungus that are being fed by moisture from the crawlspace, basement, or concrete slab, or from water leaking beneath the vinyl from a source above it (shower, tub, sink, and so on).

REMEMBER

If you have moisture under your floor covering, you have to find the source and stop it. Check out Chapter 4 for information on how to solve a moisture problem in your crawlspace or basement and how to seal concrete. Check the various plumbing chapters in Part 3 to find out how to deal with pipe leaks.

Loving laminate

Laminate has been one of the most popular finishes for kitchen counters for nearly half a century. Starting with only an image or pattern of the desired floor, manufacturers figured out how to sandwich that image between a base layer for rigidity, and a clear coating for durability. Over the last 20 years, that same technology was used to create laminate flooring, which became one of the hottest products to hit the flooring market in decades. Harder than vinyl and water resistant, it has the ability to match virtually any wood flooring or even ceramic tile pattern with uncanny accuracy.

WARNING

Laminate flooring is certainly durable, but it does have one big weakness. While the flooring is water-*resistant*, it is not water-*proof*. One incident of an overflowing sink, bathtub, or washing machine backup, and the seams will allow water to soak into the base layer and swell. Once that happens, there's no fix. Be mindful of any excessive water that lands on your laminate floor! Quick cleanups are key to avoiding ruining the floor.

REMEMBER

Even though laminate flooring has a harder finish, it can still scratch and dent, and the surface can wear and lose its luster. But by staying on top of a few basic maintenance tasks, you can preserve and protect your laminate floor.

The first thing to keep in mind with laminate (and many other types of flooring) is to avoid abrasive cleaners. It also means keeping your floor free of dirt, one of Mother Nature's most natural abrasives. Door mats, gliders under chairs, and frequent vacuuming are the easiest ways to avoid wear and tear. Next, damp-mop the floor with clean water. As you mop, keep changing the water to avoid re-depositing dirt on the floor. Never use wax cleaners, polishes, or abrasives like steel wool or scouring powder.

TIP

You can fix scratches and dents using specially designed repair sticks or fillers prepared by the flooring manufacturers. If you need such a fix, contact the manufacturer to find out what's available. If you can't locate an exact match, keep in mind that you can often mix two colors for a perfect blend. Just choose one that's slightly lighter and one that's slightly darker than the color of the spot you're trying to match.

Repairing ceramic tile

Got ceramic tile on the floor? Need to know how to care for it? Turn to Chapter 13 and read about caring for tile countertops. It turns out that everything I describe there works well for the floor, too. If you want to install a new tile floor, you need a different book; try *Home Improvement For Dummies*, by Gene and Katie Hamilton (Wiley Publishing).

If you're dealing with a cracked tile, the solution may not be quite as simple. The first thing to know about tile is this: tile doesn't bend! Most tiles crack because the base they were installed on is weak and has allowed the tile to flex and crack. The bigger the tile, the more important it is to make sure that your base is solid. If you discover a cracked tile, press gently on the area around it. If you detect a significant amount of flex in the floor, you'll need to improve the structural support in that area. (See Chapter 4 for tips.) If the floor seems solid, then the cracked tiles can be removed and replaced, or reglued if the tile is simply loose.

Need to replace a cracked tile or two and don't have any extras from the original installation? You've got options:

>> Shop local tile stores or go online to find replacement tiles that match.

>> Remove a tile from a less conspicuous area like inside a closet, and use that tile as the replacement.

>> Purchase a tile in a color that would complement the current tile. For example, if the tile is white, choose a nice blue for the accent pieces, or use unique hand-painted tiles for the accents. With this option, you'll need to remove more perfectly good tiles to make room for the complementary tile pattern. I've used this trick a lot over the years and am always surprised at how often my guests think the pattern was always there and compliment the tile floor design!

If you want your ceramic tile floor to stay looking good, never, ever use an abrasive cleanser on it. It literally sands off the finish on the tiles. Check the labels of the products you use — you'll be surprised by how many contain abrasives.

Keeping hardwood happy

Solid hardwood floors have long been considered the most desirable flooring to have in any home. They became very popular in the 1950s and continue through today. Typically made from oak, these floors have a strength and durability paralleled only by their natural, organic beauty. Real estate agents will often attest to the value that hardwood floors add to a home. Buyers find hardwood floors to be a very desirable feature and are often willing to pay more for homes with hardwood than homes without.

WHERE THE WILD THINGS ARE: BAMBOO

Bamboo has become popular because it's renewable and inexpensive, and it lasts a long time. To keep bamboo in good condition, do the following:

- Make sure the floor remains free of dirt and dust by using a broom, a dry mop, or a soft brush attachment on your vacuum cleaner.

- When cleaning, avoid excessive water — use a slightly dampened mop.

- Never use abrasive cleansers or scouring pads on your bamboo. Just about any nonabrasive hardwood cleaner is suitable for use on a bamboo floor.

- Always read the instructions from the flooring manufacturer for best results, because some cleaners may void your warranty.

TIP

If your home has old, wall-to-wall carpet, there's a chance you're in for a happy hardwood surprise. Up until the 1980s, it was a common practice to cover solid hardwood floor with carpet! To find out what's under your carpet, pull up a corner in an inconspicuous area, like inside a closet or behind furniture. If you spot hardwood, you're in luck! Most of the time, you'll find the old carpet protected the floor for decades and some light refinishing is all that's needed.

Properly finished wood floors are, without a doubt, the easiest of all floor surfaces to keep clean and looking good. But like any floor, hardwood floors can be damaged by the dirt and grit brought in from outside. This grit is like sandpaper rubbing across the floor over and over again. In some cases, it can literally cut right through the floor's finish!

REMEMBER

Keep grit off the floor. Use walk-off mats at all exterior doors to help prevent dirt, grit, and sand from getting on your wood. Laying down throw rugs or small sections of carpet just inside the entrances is a good idea.

In addition, I recommend the following for maintaining your wood floors:

- ▶▶ Vacuum frequently to keep abrasive dirt to a minimum.

- ▶▶ In kitchens, use area rugs at high-spill locations and at workstations such as the stove, sink, and refrigerator.

- ▶▶ Avoid ultraviolet light damage to finishes by installing window tinting or draping large windows.

- ▶▶ Put fabric glides on the legs of your furniture to prevent scratching and scuffing when the furniture is moved.

>> Wipe up spills immediately and then wipe dry.

>> Clean using a not-very-damp mop and an oil soap solution, and then immediately wipe the floor dry.

If a floor is waxed, occasional buffing helps renew the shine and remove scuff-marks that may appear in the wax coating. If the shine can't be renewed in heavily used lanes, occasionally re-waxing these areas may be necessary. You may be able to go a year or longer between waxing if you've properly cared for your floor.

For more information on how to care for or repair your wood floor, contact the National Wood Flooring Association at 800-422-4556 or go to www.nwfa.org.

CAN HARDWOOD FLOORS BE REFINISHED?

Yes. In fact, they can be refinished multiple times over the course of their lives. That process requires sanding off the old finish using a giant machine called a floor sander, which is armed with just about the roughest sandpaper you'll ever see. Because of the bulk of this machine and the other tools that are necessary to do a great job, sanding and refinishing a hardwood floor is best left up to a professional.

However, there's another totally DIY option. If the floor finish is simply worn, and there aren't any excessive dings, dents, or deep scratches, the floor can be lightly sanded and refinished using a floor buffer and a sanding screen, which you can rent from most home centers. Here's how:

1. Remove all furniture from the room.

2. Vacuum the floor thoroughly, and then damp-mop it to make absolutely sure no dirt is left behind.

3. Rent a floor buffer with medium-grit sanding screens. These will stick to the bottom of the floor buffer and lightly sand the old floor finish. The buffer will take off just enough of the old finish to get it ready to accept a new coat of polyurethane. This approach is far easier and much less likely to damage your floor than using a floor sander.

4. Slowly and methodically, buff-sand the entire space you're refinishing. Note that you may need to hand-sand the perimeter of the room and any other areas you can't easily access with the buffer.

5. Once you're done with the buffer, vacuum and damp-mop the floor once again to pick up dust or dirt left behind.

(continued)

(continued)

6. Now it's time to apply the floor finish. I highly recommend using oil-based "satin" polyurethane for a low-luster finish. While water-based urethane is available, it's not nearly as durable a finish.

7. When applying the finish, start by using a brush to apply the finish to the room's perimeter. For the main body of the floor, it's best to use a *lamb's wool applicator* — a thick, cloth-like pad attached to a wood block and handle just wide enough to use with a standard paint roller pan. To apply the finish, just dip the applicator into the finish and mop it on the floor. Remember, you'll need to stay off the floor for as much as 24 hours to allow for proper drying, so plan ahead and work your way out of the room.

Going for engineered hardwood

Engineered hardwood floors offer the beauty of natural hardwood without some of the limitations. Engineered floors are made in layers, with only the uppermost layer being solid hardwood. The lower layers provide structural and dimensional stability, meaning they won't warp, twist, or swell like solid hardwood. Best of all, these floors have a super-durable factory-applied finish that stands up incredibly well to wear and tear.

Because engineered hardwood floors have a very thin surface, they must be meticulously maintained. To keep engineered hardwood floors in good condition, make sure to remove dirt and dust daily with a broom, dry mop, or soft brush attachment on your vacuum cleaner. If an engineered floor gets dings, dents, or deep scratches, it can be touch-sanded and refinished, but it can't be deep-sanded.

REMEMBER

When cleaning any wood flooring, avoid excessive water. Use a slightly dampened mop and never use abrasive cleansers or scouring pads on a hardwood floor (engineered or not). Most engineered flooring manufacturers offer an approved cleaner. Never use a cleaner on an engineered floor that has not been approved by the manufacturer.

Keeping carpet clean

TIP

The most effective method of keeping carpeting clean — and making it last a long time — is to vacuum it regularly. In fact, manufacturers recommend vacuuming three or more times per week, and daily in high-traffic areas.

The quality of your vacuum makes a difference. An upright vac does the best job of removing deep-down dirt, but a canister vacuum with a beater-bar attachment (the spinning brush built into the vacuum's carpet head) will also do a good job.

The motor must also be powerful enough to create enough suction to remove the dirt, sand, and debris that is ground into the carpet. Beater brushes must be kept free of lint, fuzz, and threads. The suction port and hose should be checked regularly for suction-robbing blockages and the bag or dust receptacle should be changed/emptied frequently to ease the flow of air through the vac.

Why all this emphasis on vacuuming? Because soil is your carpet's biggest enemy. Carpets wear out because foot traffic grinds embedded dirt into the carpet fiber. And vacuuming is the best way to reduce the dirt that works its way into the carpet.

TIP

Aside from regular vacuuming, the best way to keep your carpet clean and reduce wear is to place welcome mats outside every exterior door, and rugs on the inside to catch any leftover grit before it gets farther into the house. Finally, it really pays to have everyone remove their shoes when they come into the house.

But what do you do when little Nina spills some sticky, red juice in the living room? Give her a big hug, tell her that you love her, and then spot-clean!

Spot-cleaning carpets

Most of today's carpets are made with a factory-applied stain guard. As a result, a small amount of water and a drop of vinegar or club soda will typically get out a stain. Use a clean, white, dry cloth. Don't scrub — blot.

REMEMBER

The most common mistakes people make when they try to spot-clean are over-scrubbing and using too much water. Scrubbing destroys carpet fibers. Excess water gets below the carpet into the pad, which leads to mildew and a funky smell.

Over time, especially after numerous carpet cleanings, the factory-applied stain guard provides little stain protection. Although a host of stain repellants are on the market, your best bet is to have an after-market stain guard installed by a professional carpet-cleaning and -dying company.

If stains persist, there are a million carpet-cleaning products you can use. Just be sure to follow the directions on the label to the letter.

Cleaning entire carpets

Sooner or later, your carpet will need to be cleaned. Some people like to do the job themselves, while others would rather leave the job to a professional. The pros use a variety of methods, including dry powder, foam, and steam (hot-water extraction). Most do-it-yourself carpet-cleaning machines use the hot-water extraction method: A hot-water-and-detergent solution is sucked out of a reservoir, sprayed on the carpet, and immediately extracted with a powerful vacuum. The machines aren't difficult to use — they're just loud.

If you go the DIY route, here are a few tips that will help you be a carpet-cleaning success:

>> Before you head off to the home center to rent a machine, you need to know what your carpet is made of in order to select the right cleaning solution.

>> Before you start, test the solution on an out-of-the-way spot to make sure it won't leave a stain of its own or bleach the color out.

>> Read the instructions on the machine and on the detergent. Follow them exactly. This is no time to ad-lib.

>> Don't make the mistake of using too much water or too much detergent. Excess water creates mildew, and excess detergent stays in the carpet and attracts dirt like a magnet.

>> Open the windows (or turn on the air conditioning) and use a powerful fan to help speed the drying process. The quicker you get the moisture out of the carpet, the better.

Professional carpet cleaning costs less than you think. In fact, the cost of renting a machine and buying carpet-cleaning solution may not be much less. Plus, the truck-mounted extraction machines that pros use are way more powerful than any machine you can rent, so they get more dirt out and leave less moisture in.

Re-stretching/Re-attaching carpets

If you've ever seen wall-to-wall carpet installed, you may have noticed that very few nails (if any) are involved. That's all due to the *tackless system* — handy strips of wood attached to the floor around the perimeter of the room. Installers stretch the carpet and use the tack strips to hold the carpet in place. This works well, for a long while. But ultimately, carpet can become stretched out, and bunch up, usually in high-traffic areas. Not only does this look unsightly, but it can also be a definite tripping hazard.

The good news is that carpet can be re-stretched and re-attached to that same tack strip. It's not a difficult job but it does require a handy tool known as a *carpet kicker* that installers use to grab and stretch the loose carpet toward the wall, where they'll then trim the excess. Intrepid DIYers can rent a kicker and do the project themselves, but for the rest of us mere mortals, re-stretching carpet is a job best left to the pros.

De-stinking smelly carpet

Time, home life (especially cooking), and pets can make carpets stinky. You may not notice anymore, but anyone who comes into the house probably does. If your carpet has picked up a funky smell, you can try a commercial carpet deodorizer or you can go to the pantry and arm yourself with a natural alternative. Here's a simple guide to a) making your own natural carpet deodorizer and b) actually using it:

1. **Gather your ingredients.**

   You'll need baking soda, salt, and dried mint leaves or lavender buds.

2. **In a mixing bowl, combine 2 cups of baking soda with ½ cup of salt.**

   Baking soda is excellent for neutralizing odors, and salt enhances the deodorizing effect.

3. **Thoroughly mix the two ingredients, then add ¼ to ½ cup of dried mint leaves or lavender buds, adjusting to your preference.**

   These herbs not only provide a pleasant scent, but also enhance the deodorizing power.

4. **Vacuum your carpet to remove most of the dirt.**

5. **Evenly sprinkle the prepared mixture across your carpet.**

   Using a mesh strainer or sifter can help distribute it more uniformly and prevent clumps. Pay special attention to areas with strong odors or high foot traffic.

6. **Allow the baking soda, salt, and dried herb mixture to sit on your carpet for at least 20 to 30 minutes.**

   This gives it ample time to absorb odors and freshen up the carpet fibers.

7. **After the waiting period, vacuum your carpet thoroughly.**

   Be sure to vacuum the entire area to remove all the baking soda, salt, and dried herbs.

And just like that, the carpet funk will disappear and be replaced by a fresh and inviting scent!

Dealing with Interior Doors

While you may think of a house as a relatively stable structure, it's actually not. Homes are always expanding and contracting, primarily due to changes in weather that allow temperature and humidity to impact your home. When the house moves, the door frames and doors shift — sometimes moderately and sometimes excessively. This cycle of movement occurs every winter and every spring, making door repair an ongoing maintenance issue. To make matters worse, interior doors contain several components that have a habit of failing.

Mastering common door-maintenance tasks

Whether it's a swinging door, a bypass, or a bifold, doors (or their individual components) eventually begin to wear or shift. When this happens, they rattle, won't close, and/or won't latch or won't open. It makes no difference whether the door is solid or hollow, wood, fiberglass, or metal; the typical repairs are usually treated in exactly the same way.

If your exterior doors are giving you problems, check out Chapter 6.

Adjusting a sticking door

The most common door problem is *sticking* — when the door grabs the frame, making it hard to open or close. Sticking is caused by seasonal house movement or house settlement. If the amount of grab is slight, the easiest solution is to sand the door. Hand-sanding or machine-sanding will do the trick. To find the spot where the door sticks, close the door slowly and keep a close eye on where the door starts to rub up against the frame. After identifying that spot, mark it with a pencil or piece of masking tape so you know where to sand.

TIP

The best way to hand-sand a door is to wrap a piece of sandpaper around a wooden block about the size of an index card. This will give you better control over the sandpaper and make it easier to keep the block on the door edge you're trying to sand.

WARNING

Too much sanding can prove to be a problem. If the original problem was caused by seasonal shift and the door moves the opposite way during the next season, you may find the resultant gap to be an eyesore. Sand only enough to provide clearance for the door, and apply a coat or two of paint to touch up the spot you sanded.

Repairing a door that closes by itself

Doors that close by themselves (ghost-closing — probably Casper) can be repaired easily. Here's how:

1. **Remove one hinge pin (any one you like).**

2. **Take the removed hinge pin out to the sidewalk and lay it on the concrete.**

3. **Tap it once with a hammer to bend it slightly — 10 or 15 degrees. (See Figure 12-1.)**

4. **Put the hinge pin back in the hinge.**

   The door that once had a mind of its own will never be a problem again.

Bent

FIGURE 12-1: Reforming a door hinge.

After

Before

Straight

I've made this repair many times, and it works beautifully.

Repairing a loose hinge

Doors are heavy, and hinges are small. After years of use, hinge screws can loosen. You know what happens: You have to lift on the knob to get the door to close. Here's why: The screw strips the wood and becomes loose in its hole — and that's when the hinge starts to flop around. You can elect to use a longer screw to make this repair, or you can do what I do and fix the stripped screw hole. The repair can be made with toothpicks — it's easy:

1. **Find the loose screws and remove them.**

2. **Use a few toothpicks dipped in wood glue to fill the stripped screw holes in the door or frame. Push as many of the glued toothpicks into the hole as possible and tap them into the hole with a small hammer — gently now.**

3. **Wait for the glue to dry completely.**

4. **Cut away the excess toothpicks and reinstall the old screw(s).**

Cutting to accommodate carpet

When new carpet is installed, some companies cut the door bottoms for you so that the doors can open and close easily. (This also allows return air to flow back into your furnace or air-conditioning system. You'd be surprised by the amount of air that will travel through the small space between the bottom of a door and the carpet.) If your installers don't cut the bottom of the door for you, you can do it yourself. Follow these easy steps:

1. **With the door closed, mark a line along the entire length of the bottom of the door.**

   An easy way to do this is to lay a ruler on the carpet along the bottom of the door and use that to trace the line you'll cut.

   Generally, I prefer to cut the door bottom about 1 inch off the carpet. However, the amount of space you create under the door is a matter of both preference and function. If the goal is to just clear the carpet, a minimal cut makes sense. However, if your home has forced-air heating and cooling, the space under the door provides a way for the air to get back to your home's return air inlet (unless the room has its own return). In that case, you'll need at least a full inch to provide enough clearance for that to happen.

2. **Remove the door by removing the hinge pins.**

3. **Place the door on a flat work surface or a couple of sawhorses.**

4. **Use a utility knife to make a cut along the pencil line; then place duct tape just above the cut/pencil line.**

   The slice made with the utility knife and the duct tape prevents damage to the door during the cutting process. Without these preventive measures, the cut line can easily chip and splinter.

5. **Use a saw to cut off the bottom of the door.**

TIP

Be sure to mark the bottom of the door you're cutting very clearly before taking the door off the hinges. Once it's removed, you'd be amazed how much the door top looks like the door bottom, and you wouldn't want to cut the wrong side by mistake! *(Just sayin' — don't ask me how I know!)*

Working with different types of doors

Standard swinging doors (flush-mount doors) all end up needing the same types of repairs to resolve sticking, swinging shut with no help, and not latching properly. After you've repaired one flush-mount door, you can repair them all. This isn't so much the case with other types of doors that have different mounting devices and unusual hinges or tracks. In this section, I cover the most common problems with other types of doors.

Bypass and bifold doors

Bypass and bifold doors ride on tracks and are often derailed. To fix this common problem, do the following:

>> **For bypass doors:** These sliding doors are often used for closets. Hold the door at about a 15-degree angle into the room and then engage the rollers into the track.

>> **For bifold doors:** Unlike bypass doors which remain parallel to the door's opening, these bifold doors "fold" inward to a room. Simply press downward on the roller at the top of the door and then align it with the track above. Once it's aligned, simply release the roller, and watch it pop into the track.

If your bypass or bifold doors are not closing evenly with the wall opening, they are easy to adjust. For a bypass door, loosen the screw that attaches the wheel to the door. This will allow you to raise or lower the wheel as needed to assure alignment. For bifold doors, loosen the screw holding the top pin in the top track. Slide the pin closer or further from the door jamb until the door lines up with the opening as it closes.

Pocket doors

This style of door is appropriately called a *pocket door* because, when in the open position, the door neatly slides into a void space in the wall. A pocket door glides on rollers that hang from a track mounted on the frame above the door.

Old-fashioned pocket doors always seemed to fall off the track. That doesn't happen with the newer doors. However, you may need to adjust the height of the doors because of changes in the floor covering. The procedures for doing this vary, depending on the manufacturer and model of the door, but here are some general guidelines:

1. **Remove one of the split headers that hide and trim the roller track.**

Beneath the rollers, you'll find a hanger with an adjustment bolt and nut or screw.

2. **Use a thin-end wrench or a screwdriver to turn the nut or screw to raise or lower the door.**

To clean dust from the tracks, use a vacuum. Lubricate the rollers with spray silicone lubricant.

Silicone lubricant keeps the hardware locks functioning unless they become very dirty. In that case, remove the lock or lever and clean them in mineral spirits. Spray a coating of silicone on the interior parts; then reassemble.

Turning knobs, locking locks, and latching latches

With all this talk about door adjustments, you may be thinking there's not much else that could go wrong with the proper operation of a door. But there is! When doors move, door hardware goes along for the ride. In fact, doorknobs, locks, and latches need more maintenance and attention than the doors themselves. Here are the most common causes of door that won't close, latch, or lock.

Dirty doorknobs

Barring a damaged finish, just about the only problems you'll have with doorknobs and sliding door latches are (1) screws that loosen and (2) collected dirt that jams up the mechanism. Doorknobs themselves rarely fail, and cleaning and lubrication can solve most problems.

When a doorknob, key lock, or sliding-door latch begins to stick intermittently, or when it isn't operating as smoothly as usual, it's probably gunked up with dirt. When this happens, using a spray lubricant like WD-40 can easily solve the problem. Apply the WD-40 to the door latch and door bolt, and between the handle and the door, then open and close the door handle and lock to work it in. Then wipe away any excess.

Someone told us your screws were loose

You reach for the doorknob, and as you grip it, you notice that it's shifted from its original position. You can see where the trim ring and the paint don't line up. You try wiggling the knob in hopes that it won't move, thinking to yourself that if it doesn't, further attention on your part won't be required. Hey, sooner or later, you'll have to deal with it. The nice thing is that the maintenance is unbelievably easy.

To solve the problem, tighten the screws that hold the knob in place. Often their location is pretty obvious. Usually, they can be found at the interior trim ring, although on some hardware, the screws are hidden. To tighten the screws on these models, do the following:

1. **Using the blade of a small screwdriver, depress the small push-button release found in the shaft of the knob to pull the knob away from the door.**

    The push button is usually located on the underside of the knob shaft.

2. **Remove the knob and pop off the trim ring by applying pressure to a small spring lever located at the inside edge of the trim ring.**

    Alternatively, pry it off with a screwdriver. The screws — two of them — will be directly beneath the trim ring.

3. **Tighten the screws snugly in place and replace the trim ring and the knob.**

First time around, the process may confuse you slightly. After that, you'll wonder how anything so simple ever avoided your attention.

TIP

You can keep key locks lubricated with graphite powder, but it can be a bit messy, and there's a chance that using too much could temporarily jam the lock. However, there is an easy and inexpensive alternative: Rub a pencil onto your key. Then push the key into the lock. The lead, which is actually a graphite compound, will transfer to the lock and lubricate it. It really does a great job.

The strike plate

When is a plate big enough to hold a door closed, but not large enough to hold your lunch? When it's a strike plate, that's when. If you just laughed, then you know that the *strike plate* is the small metal thing attached to the door frame that interlocks with the latch on the doorknob when the door is closed. The strike plate is so named because it's what the latch "strikes" as the door is being closed.

The strike plate actually serves three purposes:

>> Its curved outer edge helps to gradually depress the latch as the door closes.

>> It acts as a shield preventing wear and tear to the doorframe.

>> When interlocked with the latch, it holds the door snugly to the frame. With some strike plates, this function is adjustable.

One of the major causes of door (and window) misalignment is house movement. Actually, if a house didn't move, there would probably never be a need to realign its doors. However, until homes stop shifting, doors will have to be tweaked one way or another, and the process will often have to include adjusting the strike plate to realign it with the door latch.

Closing the door just enough for the latch to lay on the outside edge of the strike plate can give you a good idea of why the latch isn't interlocking with the strike plate. The latch must rest centered between the top and bottom of the plate. If the latch is lower than center, the plate must be lowered. If the latch is higher than center, the plate must be raised.

Lipstick to the rescue

TIP

Here's an easy way to figure out exactly where the latch is missing the strike plate. Grab a lipstick — yep, just regular old lipstick! — color the end of the latch with a coat of the lipstick, then close the door repeatedly. The lipstick will transfer to the strike plate and show you exactly where that bolt is hitting. This same trick works for aligning a deadbolt. Just color the end of the deadbolt with the lipstick, close the door, and then close the deadbolt a few times. Once you open the door, you'll see exactly where the problem is.

Most often, the adjustment needed is extremely minor. Place a chisel into the hole in the strike plate. To lower the strike plate, hold the edge of the chisel against the bottom of the hole and tap downward on the chisel with a hammer. One light blow is all that it usually takes to move the strike plate enough to clear the bolt. Hold the chisel against the top of the opening and lightly tap upward with the hammer to move the plate up. Keep in mind that if the strike plate has to be moved more than 1/8 inch, the door may have to be adjusted instead. In some cases, you may need to adjust both the door and strike plate.

Two screws hold a strike plate in place. Slam a door often enough and the screws will definitely come loose, resulting in a door that wobbles when closed. First, try tightening the screws. If they're stripped, which is often the case, do the following:

1. Remove the screws and the strike plate.
2. Dip a few toothpicks in glue.
3. Fill each hole with as many toothpicks as will fit.
4. When the glue has dried, cut off the excess toothpicks with a utility knife.
5. Reinstall the strike plate.

   No more wobble!

Loving your locks

In addition to making sure that your locks are securely fastened to the door, you also need to clean and lubricate them to keep them in good working order.

To remove the lock so that you can clean it, first unscrew the screws holding the faceplate on the inside knob and remove the knobs. Then remove the screws in the latch plate and remove the latch bolt assembly. The latch is that part of the door hardware that fits into the strike plate on the door frame when the door is closed. Clean the latch bolt assembly with mineral spirits. Lubricate the assembly with silicone spray, and then reinstall the lockset.

Chapter **13**

Cabinets and Countertops

Kitchen and bathroom cabinets take a beating. Day in and day out, their doors and drawers are opened and closed many, many times, which gives hinges, door catches, and drawer guides a real test.

That much use, and that kind of abuse, is tough on cabinets. Frequent cleaning to remove dirty, oily handprints and greasy buildup can go a long way toward keeping your cabinets looking great. However, as the wear and tear gets worse, you'll eventually need to kick it up a notch. Luckily, most of the time, all you need to do is repaint, refinish, repair scratches and dings, repair a drawer-glide, or adjust hinges. Projects like these are all well within the skill set of a beginning DIYer.

Countertops are pretty tough. They can be made of *plastic laminate* (a thin layer of plastic glued onto a wood-composite base), solid surface (solid plastic or solid acrylic), ceramic tile, stone (such as granite, quartz, or marble), or wood butcher block. Each surface requires different care; when they're damaged, they need different cures to repair and protect their surfaces and extend their life span.

In this chapter, I show you the ins and outs of both cabinets and countertops and also walk you step-by-step through the to-dos needed to keep them working well and looking great.

Cleaning Kitchen Cabinets

Kitchen cabinets are magnets for grease, food bits, spills, and moisture. This slimy crud builds up, making them look dingy and dirty. As the paint or varnish on the cabinet wears, the wood beneath can become stained or even damaged.

If your cabinets aren't terribly nicked up or scratched and the drawers and doors still work well, then all they may need is a little TLC. In fact, a good cleaning could be just the trick to make their surfaces look new again.

If your cabinets are painted wood, metal, laminate, or vinyl-covered, you can clean them with warm, soapy water and a sponge:

1. **Gather your supplies.**

   You'll need two buckets, Murphy Oil Soap, two cleaning rags, a sponge, and a couple of towels to dry the cabinets as you go.

2. **Empty your cabinets.**

   This is also a good time to toss anything that's past its prime and reorganize what's left.

3. **Mix the cleaner.**

   In the first bucket, mix the soap and warm water (as hot as you can stand). Follow the instructions on the soap to determine the ratio, but generally, the mix is ½ cup of Murphy Oil Soap per gallon of water. In the second bucket, just add plain warm water.

4. **Work from the top down.**

   Starting with the wall cabinets, dip your cleaning rag in the soap solution and start gently rubbing the cabinet door. Then open the door, wipe around the frame, and lastly, clean the inside of the cabinets.

TIP Use only as much water as necessary. Getting the cabinets too wet can cause them to swell or become otherwise damaged.

5. **Rinse as you go.**

   Once you've thoroughly cleaned the cabinet inside and out, dip the second rag in the clean water and use it to wipe away any remaining soapy water or grime. Then dry the cabinet with the towel and leave the door open to let it air-dry further.

6. **Repeat the process for all the wall cabinets and then the base cabinets.**

   For larger cabinets, work them in sections so that no cabinetry is left wet longer than necessary.

Something Old Is Something New: Refinishing Your Cabinets

Kitchen cabinets must stand up to years of heavy use. A constant cycle of opening and closing wears out their finish, pots and pans scratch them, and hinges and handles wear out. But while replacing kitchen cabinets can be a time-consuming, expensive, and difficult task, refinishing them is not. Plus, there's a big bonus: Painting kitchen cabinets can deliver stunningly colorful results!

TIP

If your cabinets could use a little pick-me-up, but they don't quite need to be refinished, replace the drawer pulls and door handles. Nothing perks up your cabinets — and your mood — like new hardware!

Getting your cabinets ready for refinishing

Before you paint your cabinets, there's much work to be done to get them ready. If you don't prepare properly, your paint finish will look bad, and likely even peel. Follow these steps for a factory-like finish:

1. Remove the cabinet doors and drawers, being sure to label them so that you can get them back in the right place.

TIP

Here's a helpful method for labeling cabinet doors: Start by taking a photo of your kitchen cabinets and printing it out. Number each door on the printed photo. Then, write the corresponding number on the back of each cabinet door, underneath where the hinge is located, and cover it with a small piece of painter's tape. You can proceed to paint the door, covering the tape as well. When you're ready to reattach the doors, simply peel away the tape to reveal the door number and refer to your photo to remember where each door belongs.

ONE SMALL BUDGET, ONE HUGE SUCCESS

My wife and I recently bought a home, and judging by the appearance of the solid birch cabinets, it seemed like the kitchen hadn't been remodeled since the 1960s! Despite their vintage look, I was impressed by the sturdy construction, which was so solid that it showed very little wear and tear, despite the fact that had those cabinets been a person, they'd be nearing social security eligibility! To refresh the kitchen, we decided to paint the cabinets and update the countertop, which cost us approximately $700. Since then, friends and neighbors who have stopped by have complimented us on our "new kitchen." Hey, we won't tell them if you won't!

2. **Remove the drawer pulls, door handles, and hinges.**

3. **Wash all the cabinet surfaces and the drawer and door surfaces with a mild solution of trisodium phosphate (TSP), a heavy-duty all-purpose cleaner, or other heavy-duty cleaner and wipe them dry.**

4. **Lightly sand all the surfaces you plan to paint using 220-grit sandpaper.**

   The goal is not to remove all the paint or varnish, but to create a uniform surface for the new finish. So don't go nuts — just get it smooth.

5. **If you're painting, fill all nicks and blemishes with wood filler. Let dry and then sand flush to match the rest of the cabinets.**

6. **Vacuum the cabinets, drawers, and doors using an upholstery brush.**

7. **Wipe down the cabinets with a tack cloth or a soft cloth dampened with mineral spirits.**

TIP

You'll find it helpful to lay out as many doors or drawers at a time as possible when you paint them. If the weather's good, you can work outside — just be ready for the occasional leaf, blade of grass, or other wind-driven element to land squarely on your freshly painted surface. If available, working in a garage or basement is ideal.

Steps for cabinet painting perfection

With prep complete, your cabinets are ready to paint. Follow these steps:

1. **Cover everything with canvas or heavy-plastic drop cloths.**

   Use painter's tape to protect countertops where they meet the cabinets and to create a paint/no-paint edge between the cabinets and the walls.

2. **Apply a primer.**

   My preference is to use an oil-based primer for maximum adhesion to the smooth and often shiny surfaces of cabinets. However, I have also had good success with "high bond" latex primers, which are designed to provide solid adhesion to cabinets, tile, and even glass.

   If you're making a big change in color, have the primer tinted at the paint store to closely (but not exactly) match the finished color.

3. **Once the primer has dried, you're ready to apply the top coat to your cabinet frames, doors, and drawers.**

   For this, I'd recommend a gloss or semi-gloss paint, which gives cabinets a finished look and makes them easy to clean. As I describe in Chapter 11, while oil-based paint is preferred for cabinetry, I completed a cabinet painting project using Sherwin Williams Emerald Urethane Trim Enamel and was impressed with the finish and toughness of the final surface.

Gravity counts, so when painting cabinets, be sure to work from the top down.

TIP

The quality and type of brushes are crucial factors in achieving a satisfactory paint job. Using a low-quality brush can result in an unattractive finish on the painted surface. For latex paints, it's best to use a high-quality synthetic brush, while for oil-based paints, a natural or "china bristle" brush is recommended. Purdy brushes are a reliable choice — they are well made, reasonably priced, and can last for years if properly cleaned and stored after each use. For more guidance on maintaining your paint brushes, refer to my tips in Chapter 11.

4. **Cover the drawer bodies with plastic and mask the edges of the drawer bodies where they meet the fronts.**

5. **Repeat Steps 2 and 3 for the doors and drawers.**

6. **Replace the hinges, pulls, and handles.**

TIP

You can make your old grungy, grimy hinges, pulls, and handles look new again by soaking them overnight in a mild solution of dishwashing liquid and warm water — about 1 tablespoon to 1 quart of water. Mix the solution in a plastic bucket and allow the hardware to soak overnight. Use a nylon-bristle brush to get into the nooks and crannies, rinse, and towel-dry. Use a fine metal cleaner and polish such as Flitz to remove stains and blemishes and provide a protective finish.

Maintaining your cabinets

After you have your cabinets looking good (whether you're starting with new cabinets, you've just cleaned your cabinets, or you've painted them), you still need to do some tasks on a regular basis to keep them looking good and working well in the future.

Once a year, do the following:

>> **Tighten drawer pulls and door handles.** Don't over-tighten them. One-quarter turn beyond snug should do the trick.

>> **Lubricate and adjust the hinges.** Don't go crazy — a drop of fine machine oil is plenty.

REMEMBER

Less is more when it comes to lubrication.

>> **Lubricate and adjust the drawer slides.** A little squirt of WD-40 works well on metal guides. Use beeswax or paraffin if your drawers have wooden guides.

>> **Remove finger smudges.** Try spray cleaner first. If that doesn't work, try a vinegar-and-water solution (one part vinegar to three parts water). If all else fails, put a small amount of mineral spirits on a rag, and use that to wipe off the smudges.

Counter Intelligence: Cleaning and Caring for Your Countertops

In the kitchens of our parents, laminate countertops were the norm. You may know them by one of their popular brand names (such as Formica or Wilsonart). While plastic laminate countertops served our families well for many generations, today there are many far more durable and attractive countertops to choose from. It's these that I'll focus on next. Plus, for those who are still stuck with laminate countertops, I'll share an amazing finish that can transform those relics into stone, granite, or marble masterpieces.

Cleaning tile countertops and backsplashes

Ceramic tile has long been a popular option for kitchen countertops and backsplashes. But while the tile is durable and easy to clean, the grout is the weak link.

Grout is a magnet for moisture, dirt, grease, and the wide variety of spills that happen on these workhorse surfaces. In Chapter 8, you'll find my best advice on maintaining tile surfaces, wherever you find them. As for kitchen countertops and backsplashes specifically, keep the following in mind:

>> **Clean regularly:** Wipe down the countertops and backsplashes regularly with a mild detergent and warm water. Avoid using abrasive cleaners or scouring pads as they can scratch the surface of the tiles.

>> **Avoid harsh chemicals:** Steer clear of harsh chemicals such as bleach or ammonia-based cleaners as they can damage the grout and discolor the tiles over time.

>> **Seal grout:** Make sure the grout between the tiles is properly sealed to prevent moisture from seeping in and causing mold or mildew growth. I recommend a silicone-based sealer, reapplied every one to two years.

>> **Clean stains quickly:** Spills and stains should be cleaned promptly to prevent them from setting into the grout or tiles. For tough stains, you can use a mixture of baking soda and water or a commercial grout cleaner.

>> **Avoid impact:** Ceramic tiles can chip or crack upon impact, so be cautious when placing heavy objects on the countertops and avoid banging pots and pans against the tiles.

Caring for super solid surfaces

You probably know this easy-to-care-for countertop material by one of its brand names — Corian, Avonite, and a number of others — but the generic name for it is *solid-surface countertops*. Plain and simple, solid-surface countertops require little care and are virtually impossible to permanently damage.

Because these countertops are made of a nonporous plastic or plastic-like material, soap and water are all you need to keep them clean.

TIP

Got some light scratches, stains, or scorched spots? The first thing you should do is go to the manufacturer's website and find the care-and-repair instructions. Then follow the steps to the letter, using the exact materials recommended.

If all you want to fix are light surface scratches or stains, you can do the repair with a lightly abrasive cleaner like Soft Scrub and some elbow grease. If that doesn't do the job, use an abrasive sponge (such as a Scotch-Brite pad) to *lightly* "sand" the surface smooth. Don't press too hard, and make sure that the area remains wet while you work to reduce the chances of creating new scratches.

WARNING

Don't attempt this repair if your countertop has a high-gloss finish — the repaired area will not be glossy anymore.

Things get dicier if you have deep scratches, burns, and deep stains. The best answer is to call in a pro to resurface the area (and maybe the entire countertop). The next best answer, if you're feeling bold, is to *lightly* hand-sand the area using 400-grit wet/dry sandpaper. Keep the area wet while you work. Don't get carried away. Do *not* use a power sander — you'll ruin your countertop.

REMEMBER

The manufacturer of your countertop probably offers a repair kit. If you need to undo some self-inflicted imperfection, read the manufacturer's instructions and do exactly what they tell you to do.

Protecting marvelous marble

Whether in sheets or pieces, marble is an elegant surface. Unfortunately, it's unbelievably soft. Many folks think that marble is a type of stone. It isn't — it's actually petrified calcium (old seashells) and can be easily damaged. A spill of orange juice, a few drops of hair spray, or a splash of your favorite alcoholic beverage is all it takes to damage marble.

If you see a circle on the counter where the juice glass once was, you can count on the fact that the spot has been permanently etched. You can hire someone to polish etched areas, but a better — and cheaper — solution is to keep alcohol and even the mildest acids away from marble.

Despite your best efforts, you may end up with a stain. Here's a neat trick that you can use to clean stained marble: You'll need half a lemon and a dish of table salt. Just dip the lemon into the salt and rub the marble. Thoroughly rinse with fresh water and towel-dry. You'll be amazed by how well it works. (If you can't get your marble clean with this trick, you probably won't get it clean at all.) While we're on the topic, this trick also removes tarnish on copper pans!

Sealer goes a long way toward preventing damage. Choose a high-quality, food-grade sealer, and apply it (and reapply it periodically) exactly according to the manufacturer's instructions. You can find a marble sealer at most hardware stores, home centers, or marble fabrication shops.

Caring for granite countertops

Granite is one of the hardest stones. In my opinion, there is no surface that is as durable or as easy to maintain as granite. Ten years later, it shines as beautifully as the day it was installed.

All it takes to remove coffee or tea stains from granite is some warm water on a cloth or paper towel. Hot pots have no effect on granite, and cold granite is an absolutely perfect baker's surface.

To maintain your granite, simply do the following:

>> **Keep it clean by wiping with a damp cloth.** Easy enough.

>> **Apply a clear, penetrating sealer with a clean, soft, cotton cloth at least once a year (twice a year for kitchen counters).** The sealer prevents cooking oils, grease, and other materials from being absorbed into the granite; these substances can cause discoloration and act as a hiding place for bacteria.

You can find a granite sealer at most hardware stores, home centers, or granite fabrication shops.

Caring for quartz countertops

If you have quartz countertops, you're in luck. These are among the most beautiful and durable countertops available. Maintenance is simple and can prolong their lifespan while keeping them looking pristine. First, it's essential to clean up spills quickly to prevent stains from soaking in. Use a gentle cleanser or mild soap and warm water to wipe away spills. Avoid abrasive cleansers or scouring pads, as they can damage the surface.

Regular cleaning is key to preserving the beauty of quartz countertops. Simply wiping them down regularly with a soft cloth and a mild detergent will help remove any dirt or grime buildup. Avoid using harsh chemicals or acidic cleaners, as they can dull the surface over time. For tougher stains or dried-on spills, a mixture of water and vinegar or a specialized quartz cleaner can be used, followed by a thorough rinse with water.

Countertop Conversions: Transforming Your Old Countertop into a Stone, Granite, or Marble Masterpiece

When it comes to choosing the perfect material for kitchen countertops, marble, granite, and engineered stone are all popular options. Each material has unique characteristics and aesthetic appeal, making it a sought-after choice for home-owners looking to enhance the beauty and function of their kitchens. But while the biggest obstacle to these materials is their high cost, countertop coatings developed by Daich Coatings provide DIYers with the opportunity to achieve these same surfaces without the hefty price tag.

Daich countertop coating products can be applied over a wide variety of materials, including old laminate, wood, concrete, tile, or MDF (medium density fiberboard). I've used these products twice, once creating a stunning granite countertop and then again, a natural marble countertop. In both cases, the resulting countertops were beautiful and provided a durability very similar to the natural material.

Whether you're tired of the same old kitchen or bathroom countertop, or the countertop has seen better times, Daich Coatings Countertop Kits offer three distinct options for marble, granite, or stone finishes. Each one is cost-effective, realistic-looking, and easy to achieve in a single weekend. Find out more at www.daichcoatings.com.

Chapter **14**

Appliances

The kitchen is the entertainment hub of most homes. If you doubt this, just throw (or go to) a party — and watch where everyone congregates. The nicer and more inviting the kitchen, the more crowded it is. The sleek, beautiful appliances you find in the kitchen certainly add to the attraction.

In this chapter, I'll share specific tips and ideas for the safe operation, maintenance, and longevity of the incredible array of marvelous and ingenious conveniences that make the kitchen the heart of the twenty-first-century home. Plus, life gets stinky if your washer and dryer decide to take a timeout. I'll explain how to keep these key components working at peak performance.

Safety First

When it comes to maintaining and repairing appliances, you *must* respect the power of, and potential danger posed by, the natural gas in the pipe and the electricity in the wires. Always use extreme care when working inside any appliance. In the following sections, I give you the most important safety information you need when it comes to gas- and electric-powered appliances.

CLEANING IS JOB ONE

The life span of most major household appliances can be severely shortened by neglect and, on the flip side, greatly prolonged by simple care and basic preventive maintenance. And that maintenance mostly centers on, you guessed it, cleaning. Fortunately, a few simple household ingredients, plus a little elbow grease from time to time, will keep your appliances sparkling, operating efficiently, and one step ahead of unexpected breakdowns.

When it comes to choosing a cleaner to use for the different tasks, you have two choices:

- **You can use commercial cleaners.** If you do, make sure they're mild and nonabrasive; harsh cleaners can damage the glossy surfaces you're trying to clean and preserve.

- **You can use easy-to-make, non-caustic, homemade cleaning solutions.** You'll be surprised by how powerful simple dishwashing soap, baking soda, vinegar, lemon juice, and salt can be — and how much better than chemical cleaners they are for you, your appliances, and your home environment. (Chapter 20 shares recommended recipes for homemade cleaners.)

Regardless of the cleaner you use, keep these points in mind:

- **All cleaners work best when left to sit for a while.** Generally, the tougher the stain, the longer you let it sit to work. This is especially true when you use a disinfectant, which needs to stay on the surface long enough to kill the germs. This is known as the contact or "wet" time and will be listed in the disinfectant's instructions.

- **If you're using commercial cleaners and solvents, always read the label for the manufacturer's usage directions and special warnings.** These warnings can range from potential health hazards to potential discoloration and surface damage.

- **Always wear rubber gloves, protect your eyes with glasses or goggles, and have plenty of ventilation when using any type of cleaner — whether store-bought or homemade.** Even though many homemade cleaning solutions are made with natural products, they still contain mild acids that can sting and burn your eyes and skin. Commercial products can be even more dangerous and highly volatile due to caustic components and chemical ingredients that can sting, burn, and give off vapors.

The owner's manuals for your major appliances are filled with valuable information for day-to-day operation, safety, and preventive maintenance. If you can't locate your manual, you'll very likely be able to find it online. Just do a Google search for the exact model number of your appliance and download it to a folder on your computer.

Keeping your gas appliances safe

If you grew up around natural gas appliances, you've probably smelled a whiff or two over the years. But what you are smelling isn't actually the natural gas, but a foul-smelling additive called *mercaptan*. Natural gas actually has no odor, so mercaptan is added to help you sniff out leaks and stay safe.

WARNING

If you smell gas, move quickly: *First*, leave immediately. *Then*, once you are outside and away from the house, call 9-1-1 to report the leak.

First responders will shut off the main gas valve for the house and ventilate any remaining gas. Don't even use the phone or flip a light switch. Even the tiniest spark can ignite a massive explosion. Always get outside before calling for help.

Staying safe when using your electric appliances

Large electric appliances like ranges and ovens are powered by their own dedicated circuit breaker inside your home's main electric panel and are designed to protect against electrical shocks and fire. That said, with any electric appliance, be wary of unusual sounds or smells. If you ever hear a funny buzzing sound or smell burnt rubber, this means something inside your appliance is sparking or *arcing* (electrical shorting). Unplug the appliance immediately and call a technician.

WARNING

At this point, anything you do will be dangerous, so stop and call a professional.

Caring for Your Cooktop

Cooking can be messy. Splatters, drips, boil-overs, and spills happen. And as a result, the cooktops in many homes (including yours?) have burnt-on food, hardened mystery globs, and a few thoroughly blackened rigatoni under the burners. In this section, I give you detailed information on cleaning and maintaining your cooktop.

Cleaning up the cooking crud

For day-to-day surface cleaning of the range or cooktop, a wet, wrung-out cloth or sponge will do the job — if you wipe up spills immediately after the meal. If you don't get to a spill right away, a general, all-purpose cleaner, like the All-Purpose, Handy-Dandy Cleaner (featured in Chapter 20), will cut through the crud. For tougher, cooked-on spills, you need a cleanser with a little more oomph, like the DIY Cleanser Scrub (also in Chapter 20) or a commercial cleaner that cuts through grease. Let the cleaners sit for a while to soften those really tough stains and hardened spills.

WARNING

No matter how burnt on, dried up, or crusty your cooking crud gets, never, ever, *ever* use an abrasive cleaner. You'll scratch the glossy surface, and it'll look lousy forever.

Whatever cleaner you use, do a thorough job. Look for nooks and crannies where crud and crumbs gather. Make sure you remove that grease film from all glossy or shiny surfaces. (You can use full-strength white vinegar or lemon juice for that.) Remember to wipe off the burner elements (when cool) and the grates. Heck, put the grates in the dishwasher every now and then. And don't forget the knobs! Pull them off and wash them in warm, soapy water. Air-dry the knobs thoroughly and completely before replacing them.

Maintaining your electric range and cooktop

There are several kinds of electric ranges and cooktops, and what you can repair and replace depends on the type you have. Here are the three types of electric ranges and cooktops.

WARNING

Before doing a deep clean of any electric appliance, be sure to unplug the appliance or turn it off at its circuit breaker.

>> **Plug-in burners:** Most electric ranges and cooktops have plug-in burners, which tend to collect grease and moisture down at the tips where they go into the power receptacle. This buildup leads to minor arcing that slowly increases and eventually ruins the burners. To prevent this problem, remove the plug-in burners and carefully clean the surfaces and tips with a damp rag or stiff nylon brush. If those don't do the trick, use a soapy steel-wool pad.

WARNING

Never fully submerse plug-in burners in water. Even though the metal prongs may appear to be fully dry, trace amounts of moisture usually remain on the plug-in tips and electric receptacles, which contain porcelain, an extremely porous material that absorbs water. The result: You've brought water and electricity together for a potential electric shock — and a serious zapping.

TIP

Most ranges have two 6-inch and two 8-inch interchangeable burners. When removing them for cleaning, always mark their origin so you can put them back in exactly the same receptacle.

>> **Fixed-unit burners:** Another kind of electric burner, the fixed unit, is hard-wired and generally lifts up for cleaning underneath. The advantage to this type of burner is that the tips never corrode or burn out from dripping grease, so you don't need to concern yourself with that possibility.

>> **Glass top electric ranges:** With just one flat surface, glass top ranges are the easiest to clean. First, make sure the range has cooled down completely. Then, use a non-abrasive cleaner specifically formulated for glass surfaces, a soft sponge or cloth, and, if needed, a scraper designed for **glass cooktops,** and not the one you used for last weekend's painting project! Apply the cleaner generously onto the cooled surface, focusing on any stubborn stains or spills. Let it sit for a few minutes to loosen grime, then gently scrub the surface with the sponge or cloth in circular motions. Wipe down the surface with a clean, damp cloth to remove any remaining cleaner residue, and you're done!

TIP

Always keep lightweight, inexpensive aluminum drip pans under the heating elements to prevent grease, liquids, and burnt pasta from getting into the works of the range. Besides keeping a spill from shorting the burners, they also increase the efficiency of the burners by reflecting heat upward. (That's why they're shiny!) The added benefit of using these aluminum drip pans is that they're disposable! Once they get dirty, just remove them and replace. And if the stove's original drip pans need a cleaning, just soak them in hot, soapy water or run them through the dishwasher.

Keeping your gas range and cooktop in tip-top shape

Gas burners need a little TLC, too. Very little. Cleaning and maintenance is easy — and much safer than cleaning and maintaining electric burners, because you don't have to deal with electricity.

Cleaning removable gas burners

Take out removable gas burners periodically, and clean them with a stiff nylon brush, using baking soda and hot water to keep the *ports* (gas jet holes) clean. You can remove most burners simply by lifting them out of the opening in the cooktop; you don't need any tools. If you aren't sure whether your burners are the removable type, refer to your owner's manual.

WARNING

Never use any kind of soap or put your removable gas burners in the dishwasher. The chemicals in soap and dishwasher detergent trigger corrosion on burner housings, which are made of aluminum.

Cleaning nonremovable sealed gas burners

You'll know if you have a sealed gas burner: the drip pan that surrounds each burner is anchored securely to the cooktop, or the cooktop is one big piece with indentations surrounding the burners. For these types of burners, the only components that can be removed for cleaning are the *burner cap* (which evenly distributes the flame) and the *burner grate* (the part that rests above the flame, on which you put the pots). Both just lift off.

1. **Start by cleaning the burner caps with a small brush and a solution of ¼ cup of baking soda and 1 quart of warm water.**

   Be sure to thoroughly wipe the burner caps clean and remove all water from the gas jet port openings — first with a soft cloth, and then using a hair dryer to remove all moisture, if necessary.

2. **Tackle the burner grates.**

   You'll need to up the ante when it comes to cleaning burner grates. Use an all-purpose cleanser scrub (like the DIY Cleanser Scrub — see Chapter 20) to clean these components. Dry thoroughly afterwards.

Cleaning the connector tube

Between the burners is a connector tube (technically called a *flash tube*) with an opening and a pilot light or electric spark igniter. This tube is where the gas is actually ignited and carried or drawn to each burner. If you notice that one flame jet shoots farther out than the others, then the openings are partially blocked and need cleaning. In most cases, this configuration is part of the burner assembly and can be cleaned the same way as the burners (see the preceding sections).

TIP

When it comes to gas burners, remember this adage: "Blue is beautiful. Orange is awful." A proper gas flame burns clear and blue. If yours burns yellow and orange, it probably is starved for air; the burners should be cleaned with a wire brush.

Opening the Door and Rolling Up Your Sleeves: The Oven

Whether your oven is gas- or electric-powered, it's going to get dirty. Really dirty. That's just how it is. And cleaning your oven will be a drag, so just take a deep breath, roll up your sleeves, and do the job right. In this section, I'll tell you how, as well as fill you in on two other oven maintenance tasks: checking the temperature control and replacing the oven light.

Cleaning your oven

Aside from saving you embarrassment when company comes calling, a clean oven operates more efficiently by providing more even heating. A dirty oven can also prevent the door from sealing properly, which allows heat and smoke to escape.

Cleaning the interior

You can clean oven interiors with commercial cleansers, steel-wool soap pads, or the People-Friendly Oven Cleaner (see Chapter 20 for the recipe). (*Note:* Don't use commercial cleaners on self-cleaning ovens; for details, see my discussion of self-cleaning ovens toward the end of this section.)

TIP

Here are a couple of tips to make oven cleaning easier:

>> **To loosen up tough, baked-on spills, preheat the oven to 200 degrees, turn off the heat, and then put a bowl of ammonia in your oven overnight.** This strategy works well as long as you don't mind the smell of ammonia in your kitchen the next day.

>> **To make oven cleaning easier, you can remove the door.** Just open the door 8 to 10 inches and try lifting the door up and out. Most ovens have special hinges that allow the door to lift right off. You can then clean deep into the oven interior without stretching over the lowered, open oven door. You also can comfortably clean the glass and inside surface of the door on top of a towel spread out on the countertop.

TIP

If the wire oven racks are severely caked with food spills, put them in a plastic trash bag, add some ammonia, and seal the bag well with a twist tie. Leave the bag outside overnight, and then hose the racks off, hand-wash them, or run them through your dishwasher.

Here are some specific tips for the various types of ovens.

>> **Electric ovens:** In electric ovens, you find two heating elements — one for broiling (above) and one for baking (below). In some models you can lift the bottom bake element for easier cleaning of the bottom of the oven. (If you're in the market for an oven, look for this handy feature.)

WARNING

Many people believe that they can simplify oven cleaning by lining the bottom of their electric oven with aluminum foil to catch spills. This is a no-no! A layer of foil causes an electric oven to heat unevenly. It also shortens the life of the element by causing it to superheat in certain locations.

>> **Gas ovens:** Like most ovens, the bottom of the gas oven is the object of most cleaning attention. Remove the bottom panel of a gas oven by lifting it out or by removing a couple of screws that hold it in place. Doing so lets you work on it in a deep sink or bathtub. It also enables you to inspect and clean the gas burner.

Over time, the bottom panel of a gas oven can become corroded or cracked. If this happens, you can replace it. Just get the proper part from the manufacturer or your local appliance parts dealer. Remove the old piece and put in the new piece. *Voilà!*

Uneven heating, poor baking, or an odor of gas when the oven is on are telltale signs of a clogged burner. Your best bet to determine how the burner is working is to turn it on with the bottom panel off. If the flame isn't continuous along both sides of the burner, some of its holes are likely clogged. To set your burner free, turn off the oven control and carefully use a narrow, stiff wire — such as a large paper clip or coat hanger — to clear the clogged holes. Works every time!

After the gas burner is clean, check to make sure that it's burning efficiently — with a steady, blue, 1-inch cone, and an inner lighter-blue cone of about ½ inch. Adjusting the air shutter controls the air mixture and, in turn, the color of the flame. Consult your owner's manual for specific information on how to adjust the burner flame in your gas oven.

>> **Self-cleaning ovens:** Never, never, *never* use commercial oven cleaners on a self-cleaning oven. They can pit, burn, and eat into the special porcelain surface. The result? When you reach the normal 850- to 900-degree level for self-cleaning, you can actually pop chunks of porcelain as large as 6 inches across off the oven walls. Instead, let the intended high-heat action turn food spills into carbon, which all but disappears with complete combustion, and then wipe up any minor dust-like ash residue with a damp cloth, paper towel, or sponge when the oven cools.

The least ideal moment to run a self-cleaning oven cycle is just before you need it most, such as the night before Thanksgiving or any other holiday gathering where the oven takes center stage. These cycles subject the oven to intense heat, reaching temperatures between 800 and 900 degrees, which can put significant stress on the appliance. If your oven is prone to breakdowns, it's more likely to occur during this demanding cycle, leaving you in a bind. Imagine the challenge of scrambling to find a local supplier of a 20-pound roasted turkey to feed the crew you've invited over for the big celebration!

Manufacturers recommend removing the racks during the self-cleaning process to prevent them from turning brown. To clean these racks, use the process mentioned earlier in this section. (I strongly recommend that you consult your owner's manual for specific information on how to use your self-cleaning oven.)

Using the self-cleaning feature will automatically lock the oven door, which will stay locked to let the oven cool for a time after the three hour self-cleaning cycle has ended. When the cycle is running, don't be alarmed if you notice a flame-up or smell something burning. The oven is just doing what it's supposed to do. If you're really worried, just shut the oven off. The lack of oxygen in the closed and sealed oven and diminishing heat level extinguish any burning in a matter of minutes.

You can clean the area surrounding the oven door gasket with any type of mild abrasive, such as the DIY Cleanser Scrub (see Chapter 20) or a commercial silver polish. Use a wide spatula or paint scraper to lift the gasket edge up to prevent rubbing up against it and possible fraying.

>> **Continuous-cleaning ovens:** These ovens have a special rough-texture porcelain interior. Spills gradually burn off as you use the oven. A speckled surface helps hide foods while they burn off, but these ovens may not always look clean in the process.

Combusted foods tend to remain on the oven walls. To avoid this situation as much as possible, always wipe up large spills — especially sugary or starchy foods — as soon as the oven cools. These models work best on greasy spills.

WARNING

Never use harsh abrasives, scouring pads, or commercial oven cleaners on continuous-cleaning ovens. These cleaners damage the special lining. Gentle cleaning by hand with baking soda and warm water works best.

Cleaning the window glass

Ammonia and commercial window cleaners that contain ammonia are great for cleaning browned and discolored oven-window glass. You can also use mild abrasives and scouring pads for tough spots.

Cleaning behind the range

Occasionally you may want to clean and vacuum the back of your range and the areas behind, on either side of, and below it. On the back of a range is a metal panel that can be removed (by a professional) for service or repair. You can clean dust and grime off this panel, but don't remove it yourself.

To clean behind the range, pull it away from the wall. If the range is electric, the cord should be long enough for you to move the appliance out and then unplug it. Gas models should have a flexible gas line that enables you to pull out the appliance.

Today, most new ovens are sold with a tip-over bracket that prevents the oven from tipping should a small child climb on an open oven door. If your oven doesn't have such a bracket, it'd be smart to pick one up. Tip-over brackets are easy to install and can prevent a serious injury to an adventurous child.

Don't move a gas range that has a rigid gas pipe — instead, call a service professional.

To avoid damaging flooring in front of an appliance when moving it, turn an old piece of carpet upside down and place it under the appliance, or use an appliance dolly or an appliance skid pad (both available from an appliance service company).

Checking the oven temperature control

A poorly calibrated temperature control can make it virtually impossible to conform to heating instructions on recipes. Thus, you end up with a dish that is either under- or overcooked. Yikes!

To check the accuracy of your oven's temperature control, put an oven thermometer on the middle rack. Set the thermometer for 350 degrees and heat the oven for 20 minutes. Write down the temperature. Check three more times at ten-minute intervals, noting the temperatures. The average temperature should be within 25 degrees of 350.

If you find that the temperature is off, you can recalibrate the temperature control.

For analog controls, remove the oven temperature knob and do one of the following:

>> Loosen the screws and turn the movable disk on the backside. One notch usually represents 10 degrees.

>> Turn the adjustment screw inside the hollow shaft clockwise to lower the temperature, counterclockwise to raise it. If it requires more than an eighth of a turn or is off by 50 degrees or more, have a new temperature control installed by a qualified professional.

For digital controls, consult the owner's manual (for your oven) for instructions on how to perform the recalibration.

If after you've recalibrated the temperature control, your oven still fluctuates or bakes unevenly, then chances are good that your thermostat is faulty. Your best bet is to leave thermostat installation to a pro.

Replacing the oven light

When the oven light burns out, turn off the power at the circuit breaker, remove the glass shield, and, using gloves or a dry cloth, unscrew the old bulb. Replace it with a special 40-watt appliance bulb that can stand extreme temperatures (or consult your owner's manual for the recommended bulb).

Cleaning Your Range Hood

Although it's a simple appliance, the range hood has an important job: It removes excess moisture and smoke produced by cooking. The most important range-hood maintenance task is cleaning.

Remove and clean the metal mesh filter(s) that keep grease from getting into the ductwork. Soak the filters in a sink full of hot water and liquid dish detergent. Then rinse them clean with very hot water. You can also clean mesh filters by running them through a short cycle in a dishwasher. At least once a month (more often if you cook and operate the vent and fan frequently), inspect the filters for grease buildup. Replace worn or damaged filter screens with new ones.

With filters removed, wash the range-hood interior with an all-purpose cleaner (like the All-Purpose, Handy-Dandy Cleaner featured in Chapter 20) or try warm water and liquid dish detergent.

REMEMBER

Range hoods can be vented (ducted to the outside) or unvented which captures and runs exhaust through a filter. Cleaning is just as important for unvented hoods. Clean these hoods and replace their charcoal filters according to the manufacturer's recommendations.

Microwave Maintenance

When it comes to a microwave oven, your job is to keep it clean, use it properly, and call a pro or replace it when it begins to act up.

Here's why keeping the inside of your microwave clean is so important: Stuck-on food particles eventually turn to carbon and cause arcing, which, in turn, can etch interior surfaces and could even compromise the seal around the door. Always wipe up spills promptly. Keep the interior of the oven and the area surrounding the door clean, using a damp sponge to catch spills and splatters as they occur, or an all-purpose cleaning solution for spills that have been left over long periods of time.

REMEMBER

Never use a microwave oven for anything other than what it was designed for — cooking and heating. And only use microwave-approved containers and dishes.

TIP

Given the relatively low cost of microwave ovens and high cost of service repair technicians, it's usually not worth having a failing microwave oven repaired. Unless the oven is still under the manufacturer's warranty, my advice is to replace rather than repair it.

ARE APPLIANCE SERVICE CONTRACTS WORTH IT?

Appliance service contracts, or extended warranties, are popular additions when you purchase major appliances like refrigerators, dishwashers, and clothes dryers. They offer repair and maintenance coverage beyond the manufacturer's warranty. Consider the following to determine if extended service contracts make sense for you.

- **Coverage clarity:** Before committing, understand both the manufacturer's warranty and what the service contract covers. Make sure it includes potential damages and part availability for repairs.

- **Appliance repair reputation:** Assess if the appliance warrants such coverage. Consider its repair frequency and cost compared to replacement. Review my sidebar, "Repair or Replace? How to Decide," later in the chapter to determine life expectancies of major appliances.

- **Hidden costs:** Be aware of deductibles and additional service fees. Understand the financial implications of each repair or potential contract cancellation.

- **Convenience:** Check if service technicians come to your home or if you need to transport the appliance elsewhere. Consider the continuity of service if you relocate.

- **Provider reputation:** Check review sites to determine the reliability of the company offering the service contract. Avoid contracts from companies with limited history, as recourse may be limited if they go out of business.

So, do extended warranties ever make sense?

Yes, if you understand the terms and assess the risks. In my experience, extended warranties only make sense if you prefer predictable repair costs. However, for most new household appliances, manufacturer warranties often suffice due to low repair incidence.

Cleaning Your Dishwasher

What's the single most important dishwasher maintenance task? Easy! Keep the interior clean. Doing so keeps all the hoses and passages clear, which, in turn, lets the machine operate freely and washes your dishes better.

The best way to clean the interior is with citric acid. Use pure citric-acid crystals, which you can find online or in grocery stores and drugstores. Fill your main soap cup and then run the empty dishwasher through a complete cycle. The crystals clean everything, including the unit's interior, racks, hoses, and water ports. Then, once a week, add 1 teaspoon of the acid crystals to your soap for general maintenance.

TIP

Commercial dishwasher cleaners offer a convenient way to maintain the cleanliness of your machine. These cleaners usually come in tablet form or as a liquid in a special dispenser. You simply run them through an empty dishwasher, and they release a cleaning solution throughout the cycle.

REMEMBER

Here are some other tasks you can do to keep your dishwasher washing dishes:

>> **Use the right amount of soap.** Too much will lead to a residue buildup that's hard to remove.

>> **Run your dishwasher at least once a week.** This keeps all the seals moist and prevents leaks and eventual failure.

>> **Clean the dishwasher filter weekly.** You'll find the filter located below the spray arm. Review your manual to find out how to remove it. An old toothbrush comes in handy here to remove hard-to-reach bits of food.

>> **Periodically wipe the area around the seals.** This prevents soap scum buildup, which can cause a leak, as well as bacteria growth, which can produce nasty odors.

Cleaning Your Fridge and Freezer

Refrigerators are usually the largest appliance in the house, and they have many components to keep clean. You've got the exterior, the interior, the freezer, water lines, drain lines, and coils to worry about. Not that the maintenance they require is difficult — you just have to stay on top of it to make sure the fridge does a good job of keeping everything cold.

REMEMBER

Temperature-wise, keep the food compartment set between 34 and 40 degrees, and the freezer compartment at about 0 degrees. Generally, refrigerator and freezer controls should always be set midway initially, and then adjusted up or down as needed.

Taking care of the condenser coils

The most important thing for any refrigerator is to keep the condenser coils clean. The coils are usually located at the bottom of the refrigerator behind a removable grille; on some older models, they're located on the back of the refrigerator. Air passing over these coils is what cools the refrigerator, and if they're dirty, the unit has to work harder to do its job.

To clean the coils, first unplug the refrigerator. Remove the grille by grabbing both ends and pulling gently. Use a vacuum cleaner with a brush or crevice attachment to get as far into and under the unit as possible (being careful not to force access, which can bend condenser tubing and the thin metal coil fins). While the grille is off, also remove the refrigerator drain pan and wash it.

TIP

Typically located inside your refrigerator is an electric heater power switch. It controls small electric heaters that keep the outside of the cabinet from sweating. Only turn the switch on when it's humid and you see moisture beads. When both the weather and your refrigerator are dry, turn this switch off to save energy costs. The electric heater also helps prevent rust and nasty mold buildup.

Cleaning the gasket

The chilled air inside a refrigerator is kept there primarily by a gasket at the perimeter of the door. In good condition, it provides a good airtight seal. However, it can get tired and worn, or hard, and also is a prime candidate for mold. Here's how to take care of it:

>> **Every six months or so, check the gasket to make sure it's in good condition.** How can you tell if your gasket is in good condition? Place a dollar bill between the gasket and the door jamb. If it's difficult to pull out, the gasket is okay. If it pulls out easily, you need to replace the gasket.

>> **Wipe the gasket every few months with a wet cloth, making sure to get all the surfaces and to go completely around the door.**

>> **As soon as you notice any mold around the gasket, remove it.** To do so, clean it with a solution of liquid chlorine bleach and water (4 tablespoons of

bleach in 1 quart of hot water), and scrub well with an old toothbrush. Afterwards, completely wipe off all residue with warm water and a mild, liquid dish soap.

>> **Always wipe off any food or liquid spills, drips, and runs from around the door and gaskets.** If you don't, they dry and become sticky, possibly ripping away the gasket when you open the door.

>> **If the gasket has pulled away in spots, stick it back down with a little contact cement.** Use a Popsicle stick to neatly smear a small blob of contact cement onto both the gasket and the door. Hold the surfaces apart for a minute or two for the contact adhesive to dry. Then press them together and hold them in place for 10 seconds and close the door.

Keeping the interior clean and fresh-smelling

To clean the interior of the refrigerator, first turn off the fridge (or unplug it) and remove all the food. Wash removable shelves and bins in the sink with liquid dish detergent and warm water. Wipe down the interior walls with an all-purpose cleanser or a solution of warm water and baking soda.

Maintaining inline water filtration

Most refrigerators offer automatic ice makers and water dispensers, which incorporate a filter to ensure clean ice and water. Typically, the only maintenance required is periodically changing the filter. Many units even have a warning light to alert you when the filter requires replacement. Replacement filters are readily available online. I suggest using a Sharpie to write the date of replacement on the filter and replace it at least annually. For detailed instructions on replacing the filter, refer to your owner's manual.

Prolonging the Life of Your Washer and Dryer

People tend to take their washing machines and dryers for granted — until they stop working in the middle of a load. You'd be amazed by all the technology inside your washer and dryer — in fact, so much technology is involved that you can't service many components yourself. Having to call a professional is okay, though — after all, the true battle for laundry-machine longevity is fought with basic cleaning and simple maintenance, and you can do all of that yourself.

Cleaning your washing machine

Over time and multiple wash loads, mineral deposits, lime, and soap build up inside your washer and can affect the pump operation. You can avoid this buildup by using citric-acid crystals to clean tub interiors. With the tub empty, use 1 cup of citric acid instead of laundry detergent, and run your machine through a complete cycle.

Here are other problems that you can fix with just a few tools and a little know-how (or a quick call to a professional).

>> **Rust stains inside the tub:** Temporary patch-ups on small nicks in the porcelain where rusting occurs can be made with a dab or two of enamel paint. A better solution is a porcelain repair kit made for bathtubs, available at your local hardware store.

>> **Lint-filled drain line:** If your water outlet hose drains into a laundry basin rather than a standpipe, cover the end with an old nylon stocking. Doing so collects 95 percent of all lint that otherwise would go into your sink's drain line. The nylon stocking filter also reduces splashing when the washer empties into the sink. When the stocking fills with lint, remove and replace it.

>> **Slow-running cold water:** Turn off the water inlet valves, remove the water hoses, and clean the small screen filters, which probably are clogged with mineral buildup and small debris. The fine mesh filters are usually at either end of the hose or on the back of the washing machine's water inlet port. If debris gets past these screen filters, it can damage the pump and lead to a costly repair.

TIP

If your washer is using rubber water supply hoses, consider switching to long-lasting braided stainless-steel hoses. They cost a little more but are far less likely to burst and are good insurance against what can be severe water damage caused by hose failure.

Keeping your dryer's lint traps lint free

Dryer lint is a big fire hazard. Plus, excess lint in the trap makes the dryer work extra hard, causing it to take forever to dry a load of clothes. To keep your lint traps lint free, do the following:

>> **Clean the lint screen thoroughly after every load.** If it's clogged with lint, the air won't circulate, the clothes won't dry, and the dryer will run far longer, which wears it out faster and wastes lots of energy dollars in the process.

>> **Remove lint that accumulates at the bottom of the housing that contains the lint screen.** Construct a mini vacuum hose attachment using a short piece of rubber hose, the cap to an aerosol can, and some duct tape. The cap acts as an adapter that fits over the end of a wet/dry vacuum hose. Make a hole in the center of the cap the size of the outside diameter of the hose. Insert the hose snuggly into the hole and attach the two with duct tape. Attach the cap to the end of a wet/dry vacuum and insert the hose into the filter housing until it reaches the bottom. (See Figure 14-1.)

FIGURE 14-1:
Removing
lint from inside
the machine.

Taking care of the dryer vent

The dryer vent transports hot, damp air from the dryer to the outside of your house. Without it, your house would be very hot, excessively humid, and covered in a light coating of lint. The problem: All dryer vents slowly fill with lint, which impedes or blocks airflow (making the dryer inefficient) and creates a significant fire hazard. A couple of times a year, take a few minutes to clean the dryer vent. A clean vent is a happy vent.

The easiest way to clean a dryer vent is with a dryer vent brush. It's the mini version of a chimney-sweep brush and has a round brush at one end with a flexible handle that can make negotiating curves a breeze. You can find these brushes at most hardware stores. Use it in combination with a vacuum, and your vent will be lint free! (I like the Gardus LintEater Rotary Dryer Vent Cleaning System, which is available at a wide variety of home centers and hardware stores.)

In addition to cleaning the dryer vent, periodically remove the flexible accordion-type exhaust hose (located between the back of the dryer and the vent at the wall or floor) and vacuum it. Better yet, don't bother cleaning the flexible vent (especially if it's vinyl). Throw it away and replace it with a metal duct. It won't clog nearly as much, and it's a more efficient vent, making your clothes dry faster.

TIP

Most dryer manufacturers do not recommend using plastic flexible hoses for venting. This is because the pleats found in flexible hoses, whether made of metal or plastic, create air turbulence, leading to reduced airflow. Additionally, moisture tends to accumulate in these pleats, which attracts and traps lint. Opting for a smooth metal vent is ideal, and it should follow the shortest route with the fewest elbows to the exterior of your house. Even a single 90-degree elbow creates resistance equivalent to adding 20 feet of straight duct, so minimizing turns is key to efficient venting.

Knowing what to do when the dryer suddenly stops

If you suddenly have a dead electric dryer, it may have burned its thermal fuse — a totally fixable problem and much cheaper to fix than buying a new unit. The thermal fuse is a built-in safety mechanism that works only one time; after it goes off, a service technician has to fix it before your dryer will operate again.

TIP

You can prevent the dryer from burning its thermal fuse by never opening the door in mid-cycle without first turning the dial to the air-dry mode or advancing the timer to shut off the heater. If you stop in mid-cycle, the red-hot heaters allow heat to collect inside the unit until it triggers the thermal fuse.

REPAIR OR REPLACE? HOW TO DECIDE

As the saying goes, all good things come to an end, and for appliances, that usually means at the least convenient time. When that happens — and it will happen — you need to decide whether it's worth the expense to repair your broken-down machine or just buy a new appliance and start again.

To make the call, you need to consider the following factors.

- **Type of appliance:** Larger, more costly appliances are usually more cost-effective to repair. Lower-cost appliances like disposals or microwaves are rarely worth repairing unless they're under warranty.

- **Age of the appliance:** The older the appliance, the more likely it is to break down again.

- **Cost of the repair:** Lower-cost repairs make sense for appliances of any age. Spending big on an old appliance is risky.

- **Risk of repetitive repair:** This varies with the age of the appliance, but generally, the older it is, the more likely it is to need ongoing repairs that might exceed the cost of appliance replacement.

A lot to think about? You bet! That's why some years ago, I developed a chart to provide a handy guideline to compare appliance age, repair cost, and the risk of future breakdowns to determine if you'll get a return on your investment.

(continued)

(continued)

Appliance Repair vs. Replace

Appliance Risk of Failure	Estimated Cost*	Age Range		
		Low Risk	Medium Risk	High Risk
Refrigerator	$1,000 - $2,500	up to 8 years 40%	8 to 14 years 30%	16 years & up 20%
Range	$600 - $1,500	up to 15 years 30%	15 to 25 years 20%	26 years & up 10%
Dishwasher	$500 - $1,200	Up to 10 years 40%	10 to 15 years 30%	16 years & up 20%
Built-in-Microwave	$500 - $1,800	up to 4 years 20%	4 to 10 years 15%	11 years & up 10%
Food Waste Disposer	$200 - $500	up to 1 year Replace**	1 to 2 years Replace**	2 years & up Replace**

Notes:
* Estimated cost does not include installation
**Unless under warranty, disposers are never cost effective to repair.

IN THIS CHAPTER

» **Mastering the basics: masonry versus prefabricated fireplaces**

» **Knowing key components for a safe fireplace: firebox, damper, flue, and spark arrestor**

» **Preventing disaster: the importance of chimney inspections and cleanings**

» **Picking the perfect wood for efficiency and safety**

» **DIYing fireplace maintenance: from crack patching to damper care**

Chapter **15**

Don't Get Burned: Fireplaces

Before the convenience of modern heating systems, the fireplace or wood stove stood as the primary source of warmth in homes. Despite the efficiency and ease of operation that today's heating systems offer, the warmth of a crackling fire still captivates homeowners, making the fireplace a welcome feature in any dwelling.

However, maintaining a wood-burning fireplace involves more than just aesthetics; it's essential for safety and efficiency. Failing to maintain your fireplace can lead to problems ranging from relatively minor (smoke in the house) to catastrophic (a chimney fire).

In this chapter, you'll find out about fireplace and chimney maintenance, focusing on keeping your wood burning clean and safe. From understanding the different styles of fireplace construction, to cleaning chimneys, fixing cracks, and cleaning soot from the brick face of smoky fireplaces, you'll get to know what to do — and what not to do — to keep your system in tip-top shape.

Keeping Your Fireplace Clean and Safe

Whether you're cozying up on a winter evening or simply admiring the flickering flames, a well-maintained fireplace provides both comfort and peace of mind.

There are two basic styles of fireplace construction: masonry and prefabricated metal (also called *zero clearance*). The different fireplace styles operate in essentially the same fashion:

>> Each has a *firebox* (the place where you burn the wood), a *damper* (the door that resides between the firebox and the chimney), a *flue* (chimney), and a *spark arrestor* (a screen atop the chimney that prevents sparks from getting into the air).

>> Each is typically outfitted with a mesh screen and glass doors.

>> In each type of fireplace, the hearth and fireplace face can be constructed of brick, stone, or another decorative finish.

Here are the key differences between masonry fireplaces and prefabricated metal fireplaces:

>> **A masonry fireplace** is custom-built of bricks and mortar. The firebox is constructed of firebricks, and the flue consists of bricks or a clay or terra-cotta liner. Firebricks and the mortar that surrounds them are made to withstand extreme temperatures.

>> **A prefabricated metal fireplace** is factory built and installed on-site. The metal box contains firebrick panels (see Figure 15-1), called *refractory brick panels,* that line the sides, back, and bottom of the firebox. The flue for a prefabricated fireplace consists of a metal pipe that is concealed by a chimney constructed of plywood or another siding material.

However, when you use your fireplace — as a secondary source of heat during winter or simply for its aesthetic qualities — keep in mind that a poorly maintained fireplace can spell disaster.

WARNING

Failing to maintain your fireplace properly can lead to a chimney fire. Chimney fires occur when combustible deposits on the inner walls of the chimney ignite. These explosive deposits, called creosote, are a natural byproduct of combustion. A fire hazard exists if ⅛ to ¼ inch of creosote (or more) coats the inner walls of the chimney — built-up creosote is a time bomb waiting to go off. Remember: A chimney fire can literally level your house.

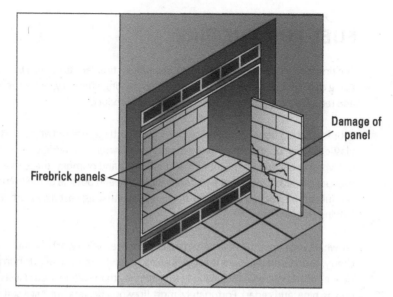

Damage of panel

Firebrick panels

FIGURE 15-1:
A prefabricated
metal fireplace.

One thing stops creosote from becoming a problem: a fireplace inspection and sweeping by a professional chimney sweep at least once a year or after burning one cord of wood — whichever comes first. More frequent cleanings may be required, depending on the type of wood burned, the type of appliance, and the frequency of use. In general, an older, uncertified wood stove, or any appliance that is used frequently, requires more than one cleaning per year.

TIP

Prefabricated metal fireplaces require more frequent cleaning due to their tendency to burn cooler. This lower temperature allows for a greater accumulation of combustion deposits on the interior surface of the fireplace flue. Additionally, although wax logs offer a convenient way to start fires rapidly, their usage should be limited as they can leave stubborn waxy deposits inside the flue, which can be challenging to clean.

According to the National Chimney Sweep Guild (www.ncsg.org), a national trade association composed of chimney sweeps, a visual inspection is all that is normally required for most chimneys. In the case where a visual inspection is neither possible nor adequate, many chimney sweeps are equipped to do more elaborate inspections with a video camera and monitor, referred to as a *Chim-Scan*. A Chim-Scan costs more than a visual inspection, but it reveals more and better information about the condition of your chimney — which is especially important when the integrity of the flue is in question due to age or damage from an earthquake or chimney fire.

FUEL FOR THE FIRE

The first step to having a healthy, well-maintained fireplace is to burn the right fuel. Being choosy about what you burn improves heating efficiency, helps the environment, and reduces the amount of creosote your fires produce.

Your fireplace is not an incinerator! Don't burn garbage, treated or painted wood, plastic, rubber, or any other non-recommended material. In addition to causing an unfavorable buildup on the interior of the firebox and chimney, these materials also produce noxious fumes that pollute the air (inside and outside of the home). Being careful about what you burn is the first line of defense against a catastrophic house-leveling chimney fire.

So, what's best to burn? Oak, hard maple, madrone, hickory, ash, walnut, locust, apple, cherry, peach, and plum are the top-burning hardwoods. Hardwoods burn longer and cleaner with less creosote buildup in the chimney than softer woods (such as willow, poplar, pine, and cedar). Fortunately, most firewood dealers don't sell softwoods and recommend hardwoods.

Seasoning is of equal importance when shopping for wood. Unseasoned (green) wood won't burn well due to its high moisture content. When it burns, it often sizzles and pops and gives off steam. Dry, seasoned wood ignites and burns much more easily, and it causes fewer problems with condensation and creosote.

WARNING

During my two decades as a professional home inspector, I often encountered cases where well-intentioned homeowners sought out chimney sweeps to inspect their chimneys, only to be alarmed by claims of imminent danger. However, many times, these claims turned out to be exaggerated or even unfounded, with the chimney sweep seemingly motivated by a desire to upsell unnecessary repairs. I refer to such unscrupulous contractors as "panic peddlers." If you ever find yourself facing a costly emergency repair declaration from a contractor, it's wise to seek a second opinion from an unbiased professional, such as a professional home inspector, to ensure the legitimacy of the situation without any conflicts of interest.

Staying on Top of Fireplace Cracks

In a masonry fireplace, firebrick is used to construct the firebox. Refractory brick panels line the firebox of a prefabricated metal fireplace. In both cases, the bricks and fireclay mortar are designed to withstand extreme temperatures. However, over time, the brick, mortar, or panels can crack and crumble, creating a serious fire hazard.

Here's what you need to do to address these problems:

>> **If a brick in a masonry fireplace cracks,** you need to patch it. (Head to Chapter 4 for instructions.) If the brick is crumbling, have it replaced with a new firebrick embedded in refractory mortar.

>> **If the mortar joints in a firebox are crumbling,** then chisel out the old mortar and replace it with new mortar. (See Chapter 4.) This process, known as *tuckpointing,* is the same one you follow to replace or repair mortar joints in any brick structure. The only difference is that in a firebox, you must use *refractory mortar,* which is specially designed to withstand extreme temperatures.

>> **If the integrity of most of the firebrick and mortar in the firebox is in question,** then have a qualified chimney sweep or masonry contractor inspect it. If replacement is in order, the job is best left to a pro.

>> **If a panel of a prefabricated metal fireplace develops extensive cracks or is beginning to crumble,** then replace it with a new panel. This is a job that most do-it-yourselfers can handle: Simply remove the old panel by unscrewing the screws that hold it in place and install the new panel; it should fit snugly against the adjoining panels. When replacing a rear panel, remove the side panels first. Refractory mortar is not generally needed, because the corners are designed to fit snugly against one another.

TIP

To make the job of finding a replacement panel easy, jot down the fireplace make and model number. (You can find these numbers on a metal plate just inside the opening of the firebox.) Give this information to the manufacturer or an installing dealer. Although replacement panels are often a stock item, a special order may be required, which can take from a few days to a couple of weeks. Don't use the fireplace until a full and final repair has been made.

Note: Repairing minor cracks and mortar joints in prefabricated metal fireplaces must be completed in strict accordance with the fireplace manufacturer's specifications and so may not be suitable for DIYers to do.

Dealing with the Damper

The damper is a steel or cast-iron door that opens or closes the throat of the firebox into the flue. It regulates draft and prevents the loss of heat up the chimney. To start a fire, you must have the damper in the full-open position.

Often, a damper becomes difficult to operate or sticks in one position. One of the most pervasive causes of a stuck damper is rust, often caused when rainwater enters the chimney through a faulty or nonexistent chimney cap (see the section, "Arresting sparks and other hazards," later in this chapter).

You can clean a dirty or rusty damper with a wire brush along with a lot of elbow grease. Wear safety goggles, work gloves, a hat, and old clothing. Then, with the wire brush in one hand and a flashlight in the other, use the brush to remove soot and rust buildup. (See Figure 15-2.)

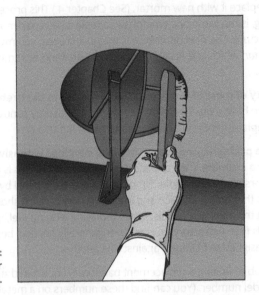

FIGURE 15-2:
Cleaning your damper.

If, after cleaning the damper, it still sticks, apply a rust-and-corrosion-penetrating oil (let it sit overnight for maximum effectiveness) or WD-40 to help dissolve the rust and corrosion at the damper's hinges.

When the damper is operational, work it back and forth while applying a high-temperature lubricant at all the joints and moving parts. When it's clean and in good working order, spray-paint the damper with a black, high-temperature paint to prevent future rusting.

TIP

Fireplaces without dampers or with faulty dampers can be retrofitted with new dampers. Unlike the style of damper located immediately above the firebox, a retrofit model is mounted at the top of the chimney and is operated by a long thin cable with a chain handle at the bottom.

Caring for the Outside of Your Chimney

Although caring for the inside of your fireplace, chimney, and damper is important, don't forget the outside. A chimney can be an exposed vent pipe (typical with pre-fabricated fireplaces), a framed enclosure that is covered with siding (called a *sided chase*) that houses the flue pipe, or a masonry chimney. Brick chimneys in particular are fully exposed to the weather and need regular attention to key areas.

Maintaining the flashing and flue pipe

The chimney travels from the inside of the home to the outside either through an attic and roof or out a wall. The point where the chimney exits the structure is a primary source of leaks. (See Figure 15-3.) Thus, you should water-test the flashing that surrounds this location using a garden hose, to make sure that it's in good condition and leak-free. (Turn to Chapter 5 for instructions on how to use a water hose to discover leaks.)

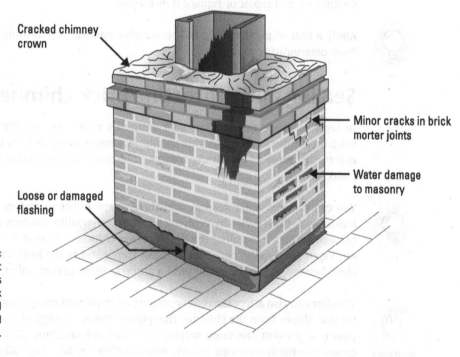

Cracked chimney crown

Minor cracks in brick mortar joints

Water damage to masonry

Loose or damaged flashing

FIGURE 15-3: The most common places where brick chimneys need repair and maintenance.

Another potential problem area is the metal vent pipe. It can be attacked by rust, and the joints can become loose. To maintain the metal pipe, do the following:

1. **Use a wire brush to remove the rust.**

2. **Prime and paint the rusted area with high-temperature paint.**

3. **Use a screwdriver to tighten screws at all connections.**

4. **Install new self-tapping sheet-metal screws at locations where screws were previously installed and worked loose. (*Self-tapping screws* are ones with their own built-in drill-bit tips.)**

Remove an existing screw and use it as an example when purchasing replacement screws.

Masonry fireplaces have a unique flashing detail called a *masonry counter flashing*, which is a secondary piece of flashing that covers the primary flashing. The counter flashing has a slight lip that's inserted into a mortar joint and then either mortared or caulked into place. Water-test the caulking or mortar annually (see Chapter 5), and repair or replace it as needed.

Apply a coat of paint to help hide otherwise unattractive flashing and prevent it from deteriorating too rapidly.

Sealing and protecting brick chimneys

In regions where the weather gets unusually cold, I've actually seen unsealed brick on chimneys crumble. This condition, known as *spalling*, occurs when water enters the pores of the brick, freezes, and then expands, causing the brick to break apart.

You can prevent water seepage and the damage to bricks and mortar caused by freeze-and-thaw cycles by applying a coat of top-quality masonry sealer to all the brick or stone surrounding the fireplace and chimney. Be sure the sealer is listed as "vapor permeable"; otherwise, it can trap water in the bricks and cause more frost damage. Apply the sealer with a pump garden sprayer, roller, or brush.

Weather can also affect the *chimney crown*, an important component made of mortar that slopes from the chimney flue pipe to the outer edge of the brick. Its purpose is to prevent rain from seeping into the brick structure. As time passes, the crown inevitably develops cracks, necessitating repairs. Typically, this involves filling the cracks with a high-quality sealer. However, in cases where the crown is severely deteriorated, broken, or loose, it's essential to opt for complete removal and replacement.

Arresting sparks and other hazards

A *spark arrestor* is a cage-like device with a solid cap, which is secured to the top of the chimney. (See Figure 15-4.) It prevents sparks and ash from escaping and causing a fire on the roof or on other potentially flammable substances. It also keeps squirrels, birds, and raccoons from nesting in the chimney. Nesting materials can cause a serious safety hazard; plus, the animals' droppings pose health risks, because diseases may be transmitted through fecal matter.

The solid cap — usually metal — prevents rainwater from entering the chimney. Rainwater can cause significant damage to the interior of a chimney by combining with the creosote to produce an acid that breaks down the flue lining and mortar. Rainwater also causes the damper to rust.

If your chimney doesn't have a spark arrestor, install one. If your chimney already has one, make sure that it's in good condition (no holes in the mesh and no rust or deterioration on the cap) and securely fastened to the top of the chimney. If you find holes (or if you accidentally make a hole or two while trying to remove rust with a wire brush), try patching the holes before replacing the entire unit. The method used to patch the spark arrestor screen is similar to the process used when patching a window screen, except that you use galvanized wire mesh rather than window screen material. (See Chapter 6 for more information.)

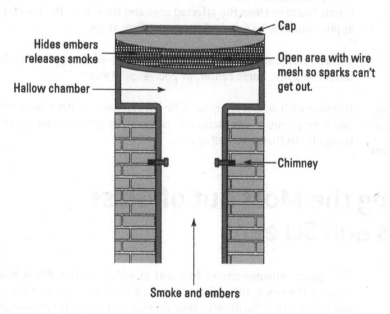

Hides embers releases smoke

Cap

Open area with wire mesh so sparks can't get out.

Hallow chamber

Chimney

Smoke and embers

FIGURE 15-4: Arresting chimney problems with a spark arrestor.

You can patch a rusting chimney cap using a small piece of galvanized sheet metal that is slightly larger than the damaged area. Attach the patch by pre-drilling a small hole and then using self-tapping screws to secure the patch in place. If rust is a problem, see Chapter 19 for tips on how to remove it. After it's clean and repaired, paint the spark arrestor to prevent future rust and to slow deterioration.

Cleaning a Soot-Covered Brick Fireplace Face

Smoky soot can make an otherwise handsome brick fireplace face look tired and decrepit. To reduce the effect of these combustion deposits, regularly vacuum the brick face and hearth, and periodically wipe them down with a damp sponge. To prevent smoke from staining your fireplace face, elevate the fire by adding a layer or two of firebrick at the bottom of the firebox.

If the hearth is heavily soiled, then it's time for a more serious cleaning. All you need is a 10 percent solution of muriatic acid. (That's one part muriatic acid to nine parts water. Add the acid to the water, not the other way around.) Use a bristle brush to clean the affected area and rinse with fresh water. More than one application may be required for extra-dirty areas.

You can buy muriatic acid in the swimming-pool supplies section of your local hardware store, home center, or pool-supply store.

WARNING

Working with acid is dangerous. Be sure to wear rubber gloves and safety goggles and have plenty of ventilation. Plus, carefully protect floors, furniture, and anything else in the surrounding area.

Making the Most out of Glass Doors and Screens

A fireplace exhausts smoke in a sort of siphon action. When heat begins to rise through the stack, the siphon continues to draw air from within the house. The end result is that the draw in your fireplace can actually remove warm air from the home, leading to *increased* heating costs!

To offset the potential heat loss, do the following:

>> **Install glass doors.** Glass doors act as dampers when the fireplace isn't being used. When closed, they'll reduce the amount of warm air that is drawn out of the home, into the fireplace, and out the chimney.

>> **Add outside air ducts to the inside of the firebox.** Outside air ducts — also known as *combustion air ducts* — are required in the construction of all new fireplaces and can be retrofitted into existing ones. Outside air ducts supply fresh air to the fire, so it won't draw heated air from your house.

TIP

The exterior side of combustion air ducts is typically covered by a protective screen to deter birds and other animals from building nests. Periodically check these ducts to make sure they're clean and free flowing.

Cleaning glass fireplace doors

TIP

Here is a neat trick that keeps glass fireplace doors clean and neat year-round:

1. **After the doors have cooled, spray them with glass or window cleaner or your own mixture of vinegar and water.**

2. **Spray a clean, soft cloth until a wet spot is created.**

3. **Dip the wet spot into the fine gray ash left by your last fire and rub the ash onto the dirty surface.**

   The ash fills the microscopic pores of the glass, thus reducing the surface tension and making it easier to clean than ever before.

4. **After the ash has dried to a haze, buff the glass clear with a clean, dry cloth.**

Oven cleaner also works well for cleaning smoke-covered glass doors.

WARNING

Make sure to wear rubber gloves and eye protection, have plenty of ventilation, and follow the manufacturer's instructions when working with oven cleaner.

Giving sluggish glass doors a pick-me-up

If your fireplace doors are operating less than smoothly, some cleaning, a little lubrication, or a slight adjustment usually fixes the problem.

Most doors can be raised and lowered or adjusted from side to side using a screwdriver or a small open-end wrench. Make a small adjustment and open and close the door until it operates smoothly. Lightly lubricate tracks, hinges, and other moving parts with a high-temperature lubricant (available from most fireplace dealers).

REMEMBER

Because not all doors are alike (some are swinging, others are bi-fold), your best bet is to refer to the owner's manual for specific information on how to adjust the doors. If you're unable to find the manual, visit a local fireplace shop.

Screening out sparks

A fireplace screen is essential for a safe fire. The mesh screen prevents sparks from flying onto the carpet or flooring in front of the fireplace and causing a fire.

Some screens are freestanding, others are bolted to the fireplace face, and still others are an integral part of the glass-door system. Most screens include a metal rod. As the screen and rod become dirty, the screen becomes increasingly difficult to operate. To keep the screen gliding smoothly, periodically vacuum the top of the screen and rod using an upholstery attachment, and then wipe with a damp sponge followed by a touch of high-temperature lubricant.

Just as with every other surface near the fireplace, the screen can develop a buildup of soot and oils from combustion. Rust can also be a problem. Although many cleaning products can cut the grease, some screens are just too dirty to be cleaned this way. If yours happens to be the latter, try either of the following solutions (both are best performed in a bathtub or outdoors):

>> **Use oven cleaner.** To get rid of rust on the screen, first remove as much rust as you can with a wire brush. (**Remember:** Make sure to wear eye protection and gloves, and work in a well-ventilated area; outdoors is good.) Next, apply a light coat of oven cleaner to the entire surface of the screen. Allow the oven cleaner to do its thing, and then rinse thoroughly with fresh water. After the screen has dried, paint it with a heat-resistant, matte-black spray paint. Doing this every few years keeps your fireplace screen looking like new.

>> **Use ammonia.** Remove the screens from the fireplace and place them in a large, plastic trash bag. Pour in 1 cup of ammonia, seal the bag, and allow it to sit overnight. The ammonia takes all the elbow grease out of cleaning the screens. Remove the screens, rinse, and paint.

IN THIS CHAPTER

» Keeping your home and family safe from fires

» Warding off carbon-monoxide poisoning

» Keeping your natural-gas lines leak free

» Looking at electrical safety

» Tightening up on security

» Making sure your garage door is safe

Chapter **16**

Maintaining Your Home-Safety Systems

I n the following pages, you'll learn time-honored, proven safety practices blended with a host of new innovations, and the very best of today's most advanced technology. When all these measures are used together, they provide layers of safety and security for your home.

Using Smart Strategies for Fire Prevention

According to the U.S. Fire Administration, over 353,000 house fires occur each year, leading to nearly 3,000 deaths. Cooking is responsible for 42 percent of these reported incidents. In short, fire poses the leading household hazard, continuing to endanger homes and lives.

These common-sense strategies can help you avoid the most common causes of house fires and keep your home and family safe.

>> **Cooking accidents:** Unattended cooking, overheating oil, grease fires, and leaving cooking appliances on can lead to kitchen fires. Always stay present while cooking, keep flammable items away from heat sources, and handle hot oil and grease with caution.

>> **Unsafe heating systems:** Poorly maintained furnaces, space heaters near flammable materials, and lack of tip-over switches are dangerous. Have your heating system serviced annually, use fireplace spark screens, and maintain a clean chimney to prevent fires.

>> **Faulty wiring:** Signs like flickering lights, tripping circuit breakers, or blown fuses indicate electrical problems. Fix or replace damaged cords, avoid overloading outlets, and use appropriate light bulbs to reduce the risk of electrical fires.

>> **Flammable liquids:** Improper storage or handling of gasoline, propane, or cleaning solvents can lead to fires. Store hazardous liquids safely (away from heat sources and children, for example) and exercise caution when using combustible materials near flames.

>> **Careless fireplace use:** Failure to use spark screens or clean chimneys can cause serious fires. Dispose of fireplace ashes safely, away from your home, as they can remain hot and reignite if not handled properly.

By being aware of these common fire hazards and taking proactive steps to prevent them, you can significantly reduce the risk of a house fire.

Shopping for smoke detectors

Smoke detectors are among the least expensive, and best, form of protection you can buy. A working smoke detector *doubles* your chances of surviving a fire!

REMEMBER

For minimum coverage, have at least one smoke detector on every level of your home and in every sleeping area. Alarms can also be added to hallways outside every bedroom, the tops and bottoms of all stairways, and often-forgotten places such as basements, attics, utility rooms, and garages.

When shopping for smoke detectors, consider the following:

>> **Smoke detectors use two types of detection technologies: ionic and photoelectric.** Ionic detects slow, smoldering fires. Photoelectric detects hot, flaming fires. The best detectors have "dual" technologies to cover both types of fires.

>> **Battery-operated smoke detectors are inexpensive and easy to install.** All true, but the need to constantly replace batteries annually makes maintenance a hassle. Instead, look for newer detectors with "10-year batteries." These batteries are built-in and designed to run for a full decade. After that, just replace the detector and start again!

>> **AC-powered smoke detectors, permanently wired with a backup battery, are commonplace.** One big benefit of AC-powered smoke detectors is that they are "interconnected," meaning that when one detector triggers an alarm, all the detectors throughout the house alarm as well.

>> **Some "smart" battery-powered detectors on the same Wi-Fi network also have the ability to be interconnected.** When one goes off, they all go off, plus an alert is sent to your phone.

Regardless of which type of detector you have, follow these tips to maintain it properly:

>> **Once a month, test detectors.** All smoke detectors have a test button, which, when pushed, causes the alarm to sound. Also, most detectors have either a blinking or solid light that glows to let you know that the alarm is getting power. If the alarm doesn't sound, replace your batteries, or replace the detector with one of the new 10-year detectors described earlier.

>> **Replace the batteries at least once per year.** Unless you have newer detectors with 10-year batteries, get in the habit of replacing the batteries when daylight saving time begins in the and fall, especially because more home fires happen once the heat is turned on!

>> **Brush or vacuum the alarm to keep dirt and dust out of the mechanism.** Do this at least four times per year — more often if you live in a dusty area. Never use cleaning sprays or solvents that can enter the unit and contaminate sensors.

>> **After ten years of use, replace smoke detectors.** At that point, a smoke detector has endured more than 87,000 hours of continuous operation, and the internal sensors probably have become contaminated with dust, dirt, and air pollutant residues.

Choosing the right fire extinguisher

Most fires start small. If you have a working fire extinguisher on hand, you may be able to easily and quickly put out a fire. Experts recommend having one fire extinguisher for every 600 square feet of living area, including the kitchen, garage, and basement.

Fire extinguishers are classified A, B, or C based on the type of fire they can put out:

>> **Type "A"** is for ordinary fuels like wood, plastics, or cloth.

>> **Type "B"** is for flammable liquids.

>> **Type "C"** covers electrical fires.

For the best protection, purchase a multi-purpose extinguisher with a "BC" or "ABC" rating for typical home use, and check its pressure gauge regularly. Some older extinguishers can lose pressure over time so make sure yours always shows as "Full."

TIP

Using a fire extinguisher is thankfully not something you will need to do regularly. But if you're faced with a fire emergency, remembering this handy acronym will help you know what to do: PASS.

>> **P**ull the pin.

>> **A**im at the base of the fire.

>> **S**queeze the handle.

>> **S**weep the base of the fire from side to side, starting with the closest edge and working away from yourself.

Preventing Carbon-Monoxide Poisoning

Carbon monoxide (CO) is the leading cause of poisoning deaths in the United States. This deadly gas is invisible and odorless, making it difficult to detect. It's produced by the incomplete combustion of various fuels such as gasoline, kerosene, propane, natural gas, oil, and even wood fires. Inhaling CO in your home can quickly be fatal, leading to death within minutes or hours depending on the concentration in the air.

The symptoms of CO poisoning vary depending on its concentration. At low levels, individuals may experience flu-like symptoms such as shortness of breath, mild nausea, and headaches. Moderate levels can cause headaches, dizziness, nausea, and light-headedness, while high levels can lead to unconsciousness and death.

These symptoms are often mistaken for common illnesses, making it difficult to identify CO poisoning. Additionally, CO is absorbed into the bloodstream, causing confusion and making self-diagnosis even more challenging.

CARBON-MONOXIDE CRISIS AVERTED

A few years ago, during a home inspection, I discovered a blocked chimney due to a nest. This blockage prevented the heating system's exhaust gases from escaping, leading to CO-laden gases venting into the house. This situation was immediately reported to the homeowners, a husband and wife expecting a child. The wife had been feeling unwell but attributed it to her pregnancy. CO poisoning was identified as the cause, and once corrected, the situation returned to normal.

TIP

One telltale sign of mild CO poisoning is flu symptoms that go away when you're outside your home in fresh air.

WARNING

Even with a garage door open, carbon monoxide can quickly leak into a house and poison the residents. Never warm up your car, run a generator, or cook with a charcoal or gas grill inside or even near your garage.

Maintaining carbon-monoxide detectors

Carbon monoxide wafts through a room like a bad odor — only you can't smell or see it. That's why having a working CO detector in your home is critical. The Consumer Product Safety Commission recommends every home with fuel-burning appliances of any kind be equipped with a least one CO detector for every level of the home as well as outside sleeping areas.

Place your CO detectors anywhere from 14 inches above the floor to eye level, but never where there is a draft (such as near a window, doorway, or stairwell).

TIP

CO detectors can be battery operated, hard-wired, *or* mounted directly in an electrical wall outlet. If you use a unit that plugs into a direct power source, make sure it also has an independent battery backup to provide protection during power outages.

Your CO detector should have a digital display with memory that indicates and records a problem, even when it's too small to trigger the alarm. A normal low level of CO in a home is zero. However, even a low reading — such as 25, 30, or 35 parts per million — indicates a problem that could escalate.

The care and maintenance of CO detectors is basically the same as for smoke detectors with regard to cleaning and frequent testing. (See the section, "Shopping for smoke detectors," earlier in this chapter, for more information.)

Spotting sources of carbon monoxide

Typical sources of CO in homes include malfunctioning gas furnaces, space heaters, gas stoves, water heaters, clothes dryers, and improperly vented fireplaces. Additionally, using a gasoline-powered generator indoors or too close to the home, using a gas or charcoal grill indoors (or in the garage) for cooking or heating during power outages, and running a car in the garage or carport where exhaust fumes accumulate and can enter the home pose real dangers. To avoid exposure to CO, do the following:

» Once a year, have your heating system, vents, chimney, and flue inspected (and cleaned if necessary) by a qualified technician.

» Follow manufacturer guidelines for use of space heaters.

» Make sure that your fuel-burning appliances are always vented. (See Chapter 10 for more information on heating systems. Chapter 15 tells you all about chimney and flue inspections.)

» Never, ever run a generator, gas or charcoal grill, or any other fuel-burning appliance, near or inside your home, or even your garage.

Keeping Your Natural-Gas Line Safe

Of all emergency preparedness efforts, gas lines deserve extra consideration — both in the event of natural disasters and for day-to-day living. If not properly maintained and installed, natural gas may be the most potentially dangerous feature in your home. Negligence and carelessness can result in gas leaks, which can cause instant flash fires and devastating explosions.

TIP

Gas lines must be properly installed, monitored, and maintained to prevent these catastrophes. Here's how:

» **Protect your gas meter.** An exposed gas meter is always susceptible to damage or being dislodged by contact. For protection from housework and gardening, and to keep gas meters that are located near driveways and sidewalks from being hit, place two heavy metal pipes in concrete (much like you would set a fence post) in front of the gas meter. Make sure the pipes are set wider than the meter, so as to protect both the front and sides of the meter from impact.

Don't pour concrete or put asphalt around the rigid gas line that comes up out of the ground leading to the meter. This pipe must remain in soft and pliable dirt to safely ride out any seismic activity or other impact. Also, embedding gas lines in concrete or asphalt can make it difficult to detect a gas leak that forms underground.

>> **Keep the gas-line shut-off wrench handy and easily accessible in a gas emergency.** Attach the wrench to the main line at the shut-off valve with a piece of chain and a hose clamp. If you ever have to close the main gas valve, you only need to rotate the bar on the valve one-quarter turn, so that it runs across the gas line (closed) rather than parallel to it (open).

>> **Inspect all gas-line connections in your home.** Those leading to appliances, furnaces, and water heaters should only be a flexible, corrugated stainless steel or a new epoxy-coated flexible connector. You should see a shut-off valve where the flexible gas line meets the solid gas pipe.

TIP

Have you ever smelled "gas"? That distinct odor is not natural gas but rather *mercaptan,* an additive with a strong scent added to natural gas for easier detection. If you smell gas or suspect a leak, a simple test can help pinpoint the location. Create a solution with 25 percent liquid dish soap and 75 percent water. Apply this mixture to the suspected area and look for bubbles forming. If bubbles appear, indicating a gas leak, evacuate the premises immediately and contact emergency services at 9-1-1.

>> **Call 811 before you dig.** The FCC has designated 811 as a federally man-dated phone number in order to consolidate all local "Call Before You Dig" numbers, making it an important service to be aware of. Underground lines, such as gas, electricity, and water, are typically just a few feet or less beneath the surface around your home. Accidentally hitting one of these lines can lead to inconvenience or serious danger. That's why, before digging a ditch, installing a fence post, planting a tree, or any other activity that disturbs the soil, you should dial 8-1-1 to access the national 811 call center. They will arrange for technicians from major utilities to survey your property and mark the location of these lines, all at no cost to you.

WARNING

If the possibility of striking a utility line doesn't prompt you to dial 8-1-1, the potential financial consequences might. In numerous states, failure to adhere to this procedure can lead to substantial fines and costly damage that you'll be held accountable for. So, don't hesitate to make that call!

Shining a Light on Electrical Safety

Your home's electrical system typically doesn't require regular maintenance, but certain signs indicate potential electrical issues that can be hazardous:

>> Habitually flickering or dimming lights

>> Outlets or switches that are warm to the touch

>> Burning odor from outlets, switches, or electrical panels

>> Repeatedly tripping circuit breakers or burning out fuses

These symptoms may indicate loose connections or overloaded circuits, posing a fire risk. Properly installed circuit breakers or fuses that correctly match each circuit's wiring provide the best protection. For instance, #14 copper wire handles 15 amps, while #12 copper wire handles 20 amps. If the breaker or fuse is too large, the wire can overheat, leading to a fire. This issue is more common in older homes with fuse boxes, as fuse sockets are often interchangeable.

TIP

If your home uses a fuse panel, have an electrician check the wiring size for each fuse and label the panel with the correct size for each circuit. The next time a fuse blows, check that notation and be sure to replace it with the correctly sized fuse.

WARNING

For the inexperienced DIYer, electrical work can be a serious hazard to both the wannabe electrician and the home itself. It's surprisingly easy to install electrical wiring incorrectly, rendering it unsafe. To be safe, leave most electrical work to a qualified electrician.

Avoiding Shocks and Sparks

GFCIs (Ground Fault Circuit Interrupters) and AFCIs (Arc Fault Circuit Interrupters) are electrical safety devices designed to protect against electrical hazards. Each serves a separate purpose.

GFCIs are designed to protect against ground faults, which occur when electrical current leaks from a circuit and flows through unintended paths, such as through water or a person. Typically installed in "wet locations" such as bathrooms, kitchens, garages, and exteriors, GFCIs constantly monitor the flow of electricity in a circuit. If they detect even a small imbalance in the current, they trip the circuit to prevent electric shock.

AFCIs are primarily designed to detect and prevent arc faults, which are electrical sparks that can occur when wires are damaged or frayed, potentially leading to electrical fires. AFCIs monitor the electrical current flowing through a circuit and quickly trip the circuit if an arc fault is detected, cutting off power and preventing a potential fire hazard.

Both GFCIs and AFCIs can be installed as outlets or circuit breakers and, when correctly implemented, can protect an entire circuit. These devices play critical roles in preventing electrical accidents in homes and other structures. Adding either to your home is a wise upgrade for safety.

TIP

GFCI and AFCI receptacles and breakers have test buttons. Be sure to test each one in your home once a month. If the test doesn't trip the breaker, have an electrician investigate, and replace the GFCI or AFCI immediately.

Maintaining Your Burglar Alarm

Not all household dangers come from the inside. Common-sense home security steps, along with a DIY or professionally installed alarm system, can help. Here are some key maintenance tasks to keep your system in optimal condition.

>> **Regular testing:** Test your burglar and fire alarms monthly to make sure they are functioning correctly. Follow the manufacturer's instructions for testing procedures.

>> **Regular battery replacement:** Replace batteries in your alarm system regularly, typically once a year or as recommended by the manufacturer. A low battery can compromise the effectiveness of the alarms. This is particularly important for systems incorporating wireless sensors.

>> **Cleaning and dusting:** Keep the alarm sensors and detectors clean and free of dust or debris. Use a soft brush or cloth to gently clean the sensors to maintain their sensitivity.

>> **Check wiring:** Periodically inspect the wiring of your alarm system for any signs of damage or wear. Loose or damaged wiring can affect the system's performance and reliability.

>> **Update software:** If your alarm system has software or firmware, keep it up to date with the latest version provided by the manufacturer. Updates often include improvements and bug fixes for better functionality.

TIPS TO KEEP THE BAD GUYS AT BAY

A few simple guidelines can make your home as tight as the proverbial bug in a rug, affording you greater safety while you're home and when you're away:

- **Check all window and door locks to make sure that they're locking properly.** Use deadbolts on all exterior doors and check that window latches all lock properly.

- **Add crossbars to secure sliding patio doors to deter forced opening.** A crossbar is a horizontal metal bar attached to the interior of the sliding patio door frame (usually midway up the door) and abuts the sliding door, preventing it from being opened.

- **Trim back any shrubbery and bushes near windows and doors.** Overgrown landscaping can provide cover for a burglar's work-in-progress.

- **Add outdoor security lighting with a motion detector on/off control.** Burglars like to work in the dark. Don't let them! Motion-activated lighting stops that from happening.

- **Secure your garage door.** When leaving home for an extended time, insert a large stove bolt through one of the side track holes to prevent the door from being slid open.

- **Never hide a house key in an obvious location.** Even amateurs know most favorites, like under doormats, in flowerpots, and inside fake rocks.

- **Close drapes and shades when you're out.** The goal is to prevent burglars from seeing that you're gone.

- **Use timer switches on lights.** These simple devices cost only a few dollars each, yet can create the appearance of activity inside your house 24 hours a day.

REMEMBER

Before installing an alarm system, it's crucial to check with local law enforcement about any restrictions or special ordinances. Many police departments advise against dialer-type alarm systems that automatically call them when activated. These systems often result in false alarms, diverting police resources from other important duties.

TIP

A better alternative is to have your alarm monitored by a central reporting service, which is now available for both DIY and professionally installed systems. This way, if there is a false alarm, the police or sheriff won't be automatically summoned, saving you from potential false-alarm fees.

Navigating the Ups and Downs of Automatic Garage-Door Opener Safety

Garage doors are heavy, and they can close quickly, posing a danger to anyone or anything that happens to be under them when they come down. To address this safety issue, garage-door openers must be equipped with a monitored non-contact safety reversing device or safety edge that stops and reverses a closing garage door, such as the following.

>> **An electronic-beam sensor that is installed at either side of the door opening:** When the beam is broken, the door stops and reverses itself.

>> **A pressure-sensitive electronic rubber strip that attaches to the bottom of the door where it makes contact with the floor:** When the strip comes into contact with an object, the door automatically stops and reverses itself, avoiding injury or damage to property.

In addition to extending its life, monthly inspection and testing of the automatic opener can prevent serious injuries and property damage. Careless operation and allowing children to play with or use garage-door opener controls is dangerous and can lead to tragic results.

A few simple precautions can protect your family and friends from potential harm. These tests are particularly important after any repairs or adjustments are made to the garage door or opener:

>> **Test the force setting of the garage-door opener, by using one of your hands to hold up the bottom of the door as it closes.** If the door doesn't reverse, the force is excessive and needs adjusting. Check your garage-door owner's manual — it explains how to adjust the force sensitivity.

>> **Test the reversing mechanism and the pressure-sensitive rubber strip.** Place a 2-by-4-inch block of wood flat on the floor in the door's path before lowering the door. If the door fails to immediately stop and reverse when it strikes the wood, disconnect the opener and use the door manually until the system can be repaired or replaced.

>> **Test the electronic beam sensor.** Place a bucket or some other big object in the beam path and start lowering the door. The door should not move. If it does, it needs to be repaired immediately.

>> **Test the non-contact safety device.** Lower the door and temporarily block the beam. The door should stop and reverse immediately. If it doesn't stop, it needs to be repaired immediately.

MAINTAINING YOUR GARAGE DOOR

Here are some common maintenance tasks that you can perform to keep your garage doors operating smoothly:

- **Visually inspect the garage-door springs, cables, rollers, and other door hardware.** Look for signs of wear and frayed or broken parts. Most minor repairs, such as roller replacement, can be performed by a handy DIYer, while more complicated tasks should be handled by a garage-door service technician.

- **Periodically lubricate the rollers, springs, hinges, and tracks.** Use spray silicone, lightweight household oil, or white lithium grease according to the instructions in your owner's manual.

- **Periodically test the balance of the door.** Start with the door closed. Disconnect the automatic-opener release mechanism so that the door can be operated by hand. The door should lift smoothly and with little resistance. It should stay open around 3 to 4 feet above the floor. If it doesn't, it's out of balance and should be adjusted by a professional.

WARNING

Never stand or walk under a moving door. Don't let children play "beat the door." Keep transmitters and remote controls out of reach of children and teach them that these devices are *not* toys. The push-button wall control should be out of reach of children (at least 5 feet from the floor) and away from all moving parts. The button should always be mounted where you can clearly see the door in full operation.

REMEMBER

As with all mechanical components in a home, an automatic garage-door opener requires periodic maintenance to ensure safe and efficient operation. One of the best resources for garage-door maintenance is the owner's manual.

WARNING

Garage-door springs and related hardware are under high tension and could cause severe injury if they were to break and fly off. To stay safe, close the garage door, then thread a sturdy wire through the spring, tied off at each end. This way, should the spring break, it will slide back on the wire, and not fly off forcefully, potentially causing serious injury.

TIP

If you don't have an owner's manual for your garage-door opener, you can usually find it online. Just search Google using the brand and model number.

5

Out in the Great Wide Open

IN THIS CHAPTER

» **Keeping concrete drives, paths, and patios clean and looking good**

» **Repairing concrete steps**

» **Painting and staining concrete**

» **Cleaning masonry and stone**

Chapter **17**

Walkways, Patios, and Driveways

oncrete is an amazingly durable building material that's been around for centuries. MIT researchers reported that reinforced concrete was first used by the Romans to build the famous Pantheon almost 2,000 years ago! Fortunately, our concrete needs for today's home are a lot less complicated. Foundations, patios, driveways, and walks are the most common places concrete is used in a house. But despite its durability, concrete needs basic maintenance and repair to last.

Although concrete bears the brunt of the traffic around most homes, masonry (brick and stone) is often used instead of, or in addition to, concrete for paths, patios, and walkways, or as a decorative element on homes. Because concrete, brick, and stone are similar in composition, the materials and techniques used to clean and preserve one of them can, more often than not, be used to clean and preserve the others, so I've put them together in this chapter.

Whether your garage floor is concrete or your patio is brick, cleaning, repairing, and sealing make them look good and last a long time.

Cementing Your Relationship with Concrete

This may come as a surprise to you: Your sidewalk, driveway, patio, and paths are not made of cement. Instead, they're made of concrete, which contains cement — Portland cement to be exact. Basic concrete is a mixture of rock, sand, and cement. In combination with the oxygen in water, the rock, sand, and cement bond together to make good old-fashioned concrete. You know, the stuff with cracks — the cracks you're always trying to patch.

The following sections explain how to perform common concrete maintenance and repair tasks.

Cleaning off grease and oil stains

You probably let your vehicle rest in a garage, carport, or driveway when you're not driving it. Depending upon the mechanical condition of your vehicle, oil and grease spots soon begin to decorate the concrete in these areas. If this situation sounds familiar, you'll be pleased to know that I have a clean-up formula for you — a pair of formulas actually, depending upon the severity of the stains. In any case, wait until the area is shaded to prevent the cleaning solution from drying out too quickly.

Plan A: TSP concrete cleaner

TSP, or tri-sodium-phosphate, is a heavy-duty cleaner and degreaser. Depending on the strength of the mixture, it is useful for a wide variety of applications. For this project, you'll need the following:

>> A nylon brush or stiff-bristle broom

>> A mixing bucket

>> TSP (tri-sodium-phosphate)

TIP

You'll find TSP at your nearby home center or hardware store — usually in the paint aisle as TSP also makes a great solution for cleaning walls before painting. When using TSP, always wear eye protection and other safety gear as specified by the TSP manufacturer.

To use TSP, follow these steps:

1. **Mix 1 part TSP with 6 parts water.**

2. **Apply the solution to the stain and let it soak in for 15 to 20 minutes.**

   Reapply as needed during this time to keep the stained area saturated.

3. **Scrub the stain with the brush, being careful to avoid splashing the liquid.**

4. **Rinse the area thoroughly with clean water.**

Plan B: Muriatic acid

If Plan A (see the preceding section) doesn't do the trick, then it's time to bring out the big gun — muriatic acid. Make a solution of 1 part muriatic acid to 9 parts water, adding the acid to the water (not the other way around).

WARNING

Working with muriatic acid is dangerous! Wear eye protection, put on rubber gloves to protect your hands and arms, and make sure that there's plenty of ventilation. Do *not* attempt this project when children or animals are present.

After you carefully mix the acid solution, follow these steps:

1. **Pour the solution over the area and work it in using a nylon scrub brush or stiff-bristle broom.**

   Be careful not to splash — you don't want to damage the surrounding area or spray the solution back on yourself.

2. **Flush the entire area with fresh water after the solution has stopped fizzing — about ten minutes.**

   More than one treatment may be necessary for those stains that only professional race-car drivers can appreciate.

By the way, just before you clean your concrete is the perfect time to get that leaky engine fixed!

Cleaning up mildew

Mildew is a type of fungus or mold that can grow on virtually any material inside and outside of the home. Dormant mildew spores are in the air almost everywhere, and all they need to develop and prosper is a warm, damp environment, which they often find on your concrete.

To keep your concrete fungus free, here's a foolproof formula developed by the U.S. Department of Agriculture's Forest Products Laboratory. This recipe works well on concrete and a wide variety of (non-colorfast) painted or washable surfaces, inside or outside.

To use this all-surface, easy mildew remover, follow these steps:

1. **Add 1 quart liquid chlorine bleach to 3 quarts warm water.**

2. **Add ⅓ cup of liquid dishwasher detergent.**

   Even though this solution is mild, make certain to wear safety goggles and rubber gloves, and have plenty of ventilation.

WARNING

   Use ammonia-free detergent. You never want to mix bleach with ammonia because the combination of the two creates a lethal gas.

3. **Apply the solution to the affected areas using a brush or broom.**

   Be careful not to splash the solution, as the bleach will stain anywhere it lands.

4. **Leave the mixture on for 15 minutes, long enough for the solution to soak into the affected area.**

   You'll start to see the black or green stains turn white, but don't let it dry.

5. **Rinse the entire area with fresh water.**

TIP

Sunlight is the most effective natural mildewcide. To slow the re-growth of mildew on your concrete surfaces, prune and trim trees that shelter these surfaces. Proper cleaning helps fight the battle against mildew, while taking preventive steps helps win the war!

TURNING UP THE PRESSURE CLEAN

When tough stains aren't the issue and you just want to give your concrete a good once-over cleaning, a pressure washer is a fast and effective cleaning tool that can cut hours off otherwise time-consuming projects.

If you're thinking about purchasing a pressure washer, consider these three key factors.

Water pressure: How much pressure you need your pressure washer to deliver depends on the type of job you're going to be doing. The basic light-duty pressure washer (1300 to 2000 PSI) is 30 times as powerful as a garden hose but a good choice for cleaning concrete, boats, cars, and siding. Medium-duty (2000 to 2600 PSI) is good for cleaning grease and grime. Heavy-duty (2700 to 4000 PSI) is what you need if you want to strip surfaces for repainting.

Gallons per minute: The larger the GPM, the more surface area a pressure washer can clean. A higher GPM flow rate can clean a larger area faster.

Price: Pressure washers range in price from a low of $200 to more than $2,000.

Using a pressure washer can be a satisfying experience, especially as you witness dirt and mildew vanish. However, be cautious not to use excessive pressure, as it can damage the surface being cleaned. Most pressure washers come with a range of nozzle tips designed for different surfaces. Opt for the mildest nozzle tip when cleaning concrete to avoid causing damage.

Patching cracks

Aside from sprucing up the exterior appearance of your house, repairing cracks and holes in concrete also prevents water damage and improves safety. Cracks in concrete can allow water to travel deeper into the concrete you're trying to preserve, where in winter it will freeze, expand, and worsen the crack you're trying to fix! Furthermore, cracks, potholes, and uneven concrete are notorious causes of nasty falls.

Frequently, extensive or severe cracks in concrete are the result of a soil condition that needs attention. For example, an inordinate amount of water from an overflowing gutter or poorly positioned downspout can flood the soil beside or below a path or foundation. This could cause the soil to expand and the concrete to crack. All the cosmetic crack repairs in the world won't correct a drainage problem like that, one that probably will result in more severe damage if left uncorrected. Address excessive moisture due to over-watering or poor drainage before making any crack repairs. Standing water, mold- and mildew-laden walls and siding, cracks in walks and walls, and leaking basements are telltale signs of poor drainage.

After you take care of any long-standing drainage needs, turn to Chapter 4 for instructions on patching concrete using one of my favorite products — vinyl concrete patch.

This process will both etch the concrete surface, providing traction as well as remove most stains. However, if the surface is heavily stained, more than one treatment may be necessary.

AVOIDING SLIPS AND FALLS ON CONCRETE

If your concrete is clean, but it's still slippery when wet, applying an anti-slip sealer can restore traction to the surface. Daich Coatings (www.daichcoatings.com) makes a product called *TracSafe* that adds traction and the option of a decorative color coat to any concrete surface.

It's also possible to add traction to a smooth concrete surface by etching it with muriatic acid. While this is effective, be advised that working with muriatic acid is dangerous! Wear eye protection, put on rubber gloves to protect your hands and arms, and make sure that there's plenty of ventilation. Do *not* attempt this project when children or animals are present.

To etch concrete with muriatic acid, mix 1 part muriatic acid to 5 parts water, adding the acid to the water (not the other way around). Note that very hard and very smooth concrete might require a stronger 1 part acid to 3 parts water solution.

After you carefully mix the acid solution, follow these steps:

1. **Pour the solution over the area and work it in using a nylon scrub brush or stiff-bristle broom.**

   Be careful not to splash — you don't want to damage the surrounding area.

2. **Flush the entire area with fresh water after the solution has stopped fizzing — about ten minutes.**

TIP

Got a small crack in a highly visible place? Using a masonry drill and a tube of clear or gray silicone caulk, you can easily mix up a concrete patching compound that will leave the crack virtually invisible. Follow these steps:

1. **Gather some concrete dust from your driveway.**

   Find an out-of-the-way spot in your cracked patio or step, such as just below the grade. Place a small, flat, metal pan underneath where you plan to drill. Use a masonry drill bit to drill a hole in the hidden area and collect the dust coming out of the hole.

2. **Apply a bead of caulk to the top of the crack you want to repair.**

3. **While the caulk is still fresh, sprinkle the masonry dust over the crack and work it into the caulk with your finger.**

4. **Sweep away the excess dust and — *voilà!* — no more crack!**

Sealing concrete

Concrete is quite porous and acts like a sponge. When temperatures drop and concrete is wet, it can freeze, causing cracking and *spalling* (chipping). Rock salt used to melt snow is another primary source of deterioration of concrete.

TIP

When selecting ice-melt for sidewalks and driveways, make sure the product is labeled "safe for concrete." Calcium chloride and magnesium are generally considered safe for concrete. Rock salt (sodium chloride) is not — and will leave you with a sidewalk full of pock marks that will need to be filled come spring.

You can minimize this damage by periodically sealing the concrete with an acrylic or silicone-based concrete and masonry sealer. A liquid concrete sealer prevents water absorption by filling the pores of the concrete. A concrete sealer lasts for six months to a year, depending upon the quality of the material, surface preparation, and climate.

TIP

When selecting the sealer, be sure it's labeled "vapor permeable." This type of sealer allows moisture in the concrete surface to evaporate and minimizes the risk of spalling.

You apply concrete sealers with a brush, roller, or pump garden sprayer. Before you begin, clean the concrete using the concrete cleaning tips mentioned earlier in this chapter.

Painting your concrete

Paint remains a popular finish for concrete porches, patios, paths, garages, carports, and basements. Painting concrete is a great idea — if the paint will stick to the concrete. You can increase the stick-to-itiveness with thorough cleaning and prep, but there are certain conditions — such as moisture — that are particularly important to manage. Moisture wicking up from below the concrete can prevent even the best of finishes from sticking.

TIP

You can determine whether moisture is a problem by taping a 1-foot-square piece of plastic (like a garbage bag) or aluminum foil to the concrete. Leave it there 24 hours, and then remove it. If a damp spot appears where the plastic was placed or there is condensation on the underside of the plastic, paint won't stick. If that happens, you'll need to delay your project until the concrete dries out. You can speed the process along by using a fan or dehumidifier.

Looking at types of concrete paint

Three basic types of paint are available for concrete.

>> **Acrylic latex paint:** Latex paint is the most widely used. It has excellent adhesion properties, allows water vapor to escape (prohibiting blistering and peeling), and is the most user-friendly to apply because it cleans up with water.

>> **Oil-based paints:** Oil-based paints are still a favorite for porches and patios. They offer a harder, shinier, and more abrasion-resistant finish. The challenge here is that oil-based paints are becoming less and less available as regulations change to foster use of more environmentally friendly products.

>> **Epoxy:** Epoxy is the most durable and longest-lasting paint, and my top choice for painting concrete. Epoxy paints generally consist of two parts which, when combined, create a chemical reaction that results in an above-average bond and highly abrasion-resistant finish. Most epoxy finishes also include "color flakes" that add a subtle design to the newly painted floor, which helps hide dirt. In addition, a clear epoxy finish is often used on top of the color coat, to provide a high-gloss, attractive finish.

Doing the job right

Don't be in a hurry to paint freshly poured concrete. For best adhesion, let the concrete cure for 60 to 90 days before painting. Existing concrete is ready to go when you are.

Here are the step-by-step instructions:

1. **If necessary, remove any flaking, peeling paint on previously painted surfaces, using a chemical remover, sandblaster, or mechanical abrader.**

2. **Clean the surface.**

   Grit, grease, oil, and other contaminants inhibit the paint from sticking. (For cleaning instructions, see the concrete cleaning tips earlier in this chapter.)

TIP

   If you have rust stains on your concrete, try using a phosphoric acid cleaner, which will remove a wide variety of stains, including rust.

3. **Lightly etch the surface using a 25 percent solution of muriatic acid.**

   Etching helps the paint stick better. Simply pour the solution onto the concrete, spread it out evenly, and let it stand for approximately 15 minutes. Then flush the entire area with water. (See the sidebar, "Avoiding slips and falls on concrete," for more information on working with this acid.)

4. **Using a medium-to-long-nap roller and a nylon/polyester brush or paint pad to cut in the edges, apply concrete floor paint using the method required by the type of paint you choose.**

   Latex paint: Most latex concrete floor paints are designed to be applied directly to raw concrete. Apply a first coat as a primer and a second coat to get a full and uniform finish.

   Oil-based paint: These paints should be applied over a coat of oil-based concrete or masonry filler/primer (thin the primer slightly using mineral spirits to enhance the penetration and improve the bond). (**Note:** You can apply an oil-based paint over an existing oil finish, as long as the existing finish is clean and has been de-glossed with TSP or a similar liquid paint de-glosser.) After the primer dries, apply the finish coat. Use mineral spirits for cleanup.

   Epoxy paint: Epoxy typically comes in two parts that you mix together prior to application. Follow the mixing instructions carefully to make sure the epoxy is ready to use. The mixture creates a chemical reaction that makes the finish bond with the concrete for a long-lasting, durable finish. When working with epoxy finishes, timing is key — once mixed, the epoxy will have a limited "working time" before it starts to harden. If you have a large area to paint, work it in sections; first apply the epoxy finish, then spread the color flakes and let that area thoroughly dry before moving on to the next section.

TIP

Sprinkling color flakes on to wet epoxy can be tricky. To get an even coating, it's helpful if you can walk on the epoxy. Here's a pro trick to allow you do to just that without leaving footprints: wear golf shoes! The cleats in a turf shoe leave small dots on the wet epoxy finish, which will fill in as the epoxy dries.

Resurfacing deteriorated concrete

Over time, concrete walkways, patios, and driveways can wear down and become unsightly. This often happens due to the use of rock salt as a de-icer, which can corrode the concrete, leaving shallow holes. Another common issue is homeowners attempting to patch old concrete with more concrete or mortar. This never works because new concrete simply won't stick to old concrete and usually separates over the first winter, leaving you back where you started.

Fortunately, there are products specifically designed for resurfacing concrete. These products are designed to adhere to old concrete, with amazing holding power. One of my favorites is Re-Cap Concrete Resurfacer, made by QUIKRETE. I've witnessed tests of this product where engineers repaired an old concrete surface, then tried to make it separate. The grab power was so strong it actually *pulled the old concrete apart* while remaining securely bonded to the repaired surface!

If your concrete isn't damaged but looks worn or dated, another option is to recoat it with a product designed to replicate stone, terrazzo, or granite surfaces. Some years ago, a friend of mine resurfaced her porch using Daich Coating's Terrazzo Decorative Concrete Resurfacer (www.daichcoatings.com). It adhered well and has proved to be a durable and attractive finish that's lasted for years.

Repairing concrete steps

Patching broken or crumbling concrete steps enhances the appearance and safety of your home for a fraction of the cost of new stairs. And the best part is that it's a task that most do-it-yourselfers can handle with ease.

As the weakest point of construction, the step's edge is most vulnerable to damage. Expansive soil, freeze and thaw cycles, and deterioration from salt and traffic are a few causes of crumbling concrete stairs.

REMEMBER

Crumbling steps frequently result from what were once small cracks that were not tended to. You can prevent most of the damage to steps by caulking, which allows the concrete to expand and contract yet prevents moisture from entering the area.

To repair broken concrete stairs, you need these supplies:

- Masonry hammer
- Masonry chisel
- Safety goggles
- Mixing container
- Shovel
- Garden hose
- Concrete finishing trowel
- *Wooden float* (a wooden trowel used to tamp and work the concrete into place)
- Small piece of ¾-inch plywood to act as a form board
- Concrete bonding agent
- Ready-to-mix concrete patch material (or epoxy patch material)
- Metal trowel
- Tarp or plastic sheeting
- 1 quart of clean motor oil or concrete form-release oil
- At least four bricks (more may be needed)

Follow these steps to get your steps feet-worthy:

1. **Remove the loose and crumbling concrete with a masonry hammer and masonry chisel. (Be sure to wear safety goggles!) Then sweep up all the debris and clean the area with the strong spray of a garden hose.**

   Isn't it just like a home fix-it expert to suggest breaking something the rest of the way before making a repair? It seems paradoxical, but to successfully repair a concrete stair — or anything else made of concrete — you must first completely remove all loose pieces and make sure that what remains is solid.

2. **Paint the raw patch area with a concrete bonding agent and allow it to set up for about 15 minutes.**

   The bonding agent is a glue that helps the new patch material adhere to the old, cured concrete.

3. **Cut a scrap piece of plywood equal to the height of the step and a few inches longer than the damaged area at either end.**

   You'll set this form board flush against the face of the step to hold the concrete patch material in place until it's fully cured.

4. **Apply a light coat of clean motor oil or form-release oil on the surface of the form board facing the concrete to prevent the form from sticking and damaging the patch when removed.**

5. **Place the form board flush against the face of the steps for a smooth patch.**

   The bottom of the form board should fit flat against the top of the step below.

6. **Use several bricks to hold the form boards firmly in place. (See Figure 17-1.)**

7. **Mix the concrete patch material according to the label directions.**

   Vinyl concrete patch and polymer cement are the most popular concrete patching products because they're easy to use and they blend well with the old material — although more expensive, epoxy patch material is the best money can buy. The consistency of the patch material should be loose, but not runny.

8. **Using the wood float, pack the material firmly into the area, being sure to eliminate any air pockets.**

   The butt end of the float works great for this.

9. **Remove excess patch material with a wooden float and finish the patch to match the surrounding concrete with a metal concrete trowel.**

10. **When the material starts to set up (in approximately 10 to 30 minutes), cover it with a tarp or sheet of plastic.**

Doing so holds moisture in. If the material dries too fast, it may crack or not adhere securely.

Most exterior concrete surfaces have a slightly rough finish to prevent slipping when wet. The most common finish is the broom finish. After the patch has begins to set up, brush it lightly once (and just once) with a broom. Or, for a small patch, use a stiff paintbrush.

TIP

11. **Until the patch has completely dried (which can take up to a week), remove the cover once a day and spray the patch with a fine mist of water and then replace the cover.**

Leave the form board in place during the drying process to reduce the prospect of damage resulting from form board removal or foot traffic.

12. **Complete the job by carefully removing the form boards, stakes, and bricks.**

Getting Things on an Even Keel

If you walk across your brick or stone path or patio and you feel as if you're on a ship on the high seas, chances are good that a little leveling is in order. Unlike a poured-in-place concrete path or patio that might need to be jackhammered out, a brick or stone patio is one big jigsaw puzzle embedded in a layer of sand. Consequently, this is a project that you can easily do yourself by selectively removing pieces of the puzzle, shoring up the sub-base, and reinstalling the pieces. The real beauty of this project is that it can be done a section at a time, and you can take as long as you want to complete your work. It's not like you have a slab of wet concrete that must be finished before it dries hard as a rock! A few tools and a little time and it'll be smooth sailing.

Leveling settled brick patios and walkways

Leveling and resetting a brick patio is slow, heavy work. Fortunately, it's not a complex project — just one that takes time and effort to do right.

You need the following:

- » Chalk
- » Crayon
- » Small pry bar
- » Shovel
- » Hand tamper
- » Rubber mallet
- » 4-foot level
- » Measuring tape
- » Broom
- » Crushed limestone
- » Coarse sand
- » Fine sand

When you have these items, follow these steps:

1. **Use chalk to mark out the settled area.**

2. **Starting in the middle of that area and working toward the edge, use a small pry bar to remove the whole bricks and stack them neatly nearby.**

3. **Number any partial, cut bricks using a light-colored crayon.**

   Don't use chalk — it'll rub off and make resetting a nightmare.

4. **When all the settled area's bricks are removed, explore what's underneath.**

   You should find sand. And under that you may find crushed limestone or compacted gravel. But it's more likely that you'll find dirt or clay underneath.

5. **If you find dirt or clay that's wet or loose underneath the brick, dig it out until you find solid earth.**

6. **Fill the now-low areas of the bed with crushed limestone and compact it thoroughly using a hand tamper.**

   Your wrists and hands will never be the same!

7. **Use a level to see where the top of the reset bricks will be; then use more crushed limestone (tamp it down good!) to fill the bed until there are 3 inches between the bottom of the level and the top of the bed.**

   Most patio bricks are 2 ¼ – 2 ½ inches thick, and you want to leave room for 1 inch of sand underneath.

REMEMBER

8. **Add 1 inch of sand, and then double-check that you still have a bit more than 2 inches for the bricks.**

9. **Reset the bricks you removed earlier, working from the middle outward. Be careful to maintain the original pattern.**

   Be sure to put them in straight down to avoid jamming sand between them and messing up the spacing. Whack each brick hard a couple of times with a rubber mallet to make sure they're securely set.

10. **Sweep fine sand into the joints to fill the gaps and to lock the now-level bricks in place.**

    Save some sand to sweep in after the next rain.

TIP

Leveling and resetting stone paths

The process for fixing a sinking, uneven brick sidewalk or stone path is the same as it is for a settled patio (see the preceding section). However, in my experience, you're more likely to find just dirt underneath. My advice when you find no stabilizing stone/sand base: Pull the entire thing up and start fresh with a proper substrate. That way you won't have to fix it again in two years . . . and then every two years after that.

Sealing an asphalt driveway

Few home-maintenance projects are easier than sealing an asphalt driveway. Mostly you need a strong back to maneuver the big, heavy buckets of sealer.

You need these supplies:

>> Putty knife

>> Broom

>> Clean and sturdy stirring stick

>> Squeegee or roller

>> Hose

>> Asphalt caulk

>> Asphalt patch

>> Asphalt sealer (latex)

When you've gathered everything you need, follow these steps:

1. **Check the weather forecast to make sure the temperature will stay above 50 degrees and there'll be no rain for the next 36 hours.**

   Cool temperatures and excessive moisture interfere with adhesion and drying.

2. **Remove debris from any large cracks using a putty knife, and thoroughly sweep the entire surface with a push broom.**

3. **Fill all cracks more than ¼ inch wide with asphalt caulk.**

   You need to use asphalt patching material to patch bigger cracks. Smaller cracks can be filled by the sealer. If the crack is deep, use *backer rod*, a foam tube inserted into the crack to about a half inch below the surface. This prevents wasting sealant that would otherwise fall deep into the crack.

4. **Prepare the surface by spraying it with water to remove any dust. Clean oil spots using one of the methods described in the section, "Cleaning off grease and oil stains," earlier in this chapter.**

5. **Allow the driveway to fully dry.**

6. **Get the sealer ready.**

   Drag the big, heavy buckets of sealer onto the driveway. Without opening them, flip them upside-down to allow the heavier goop to sink toward the top; then flip them back, crack them open, and stir thoroughly with a sturdy, clean stick. Put the lid back on the now-stirred sealer and drag one of the big, heavy buckets of sealer to your starting point.

7. **Pour out only as much sealer as will coat about 20 square feet (you'll figure out how much that is pretty quickly); then use the roller or squee-gee to spread the coating across the driveway using overlapping strokes.**

   REMEMBER

   Two things to keep in mind as you apply the sealer:

   - Stir the sealer as you apply it to ensure its consistency.
   - A thick coat is not better than a thin coat.

8. **Keep dragging the big, heavy buckets around and doing 20 square feet at a time until you're done.**

   Be careful not to slop sealer onto the sidewalk or street.

9. **Let the sealer dry for at least 24 hours, and preferably 48 hours.**

   During the drying time, stay off the driveway. Put the empty buckets at the end of the driveway to prevent visitors from driving on your freshly coated and very, very handsome driveway.

Mastering Masonry Maintenance: Cleaning, Repair, and Sealing

So far, I've talked about cleaning and repairing concrete walks, patios, driveways, and other horizontal surfaces. But aside from the masonry we walk on, brick, stone, and stucco are often used on the exterior walls and foundations of our homes. These can be structural or decorative, but when it comes to cleaning, repairing, and sealing, the techniques and materials used are the same. I tackle this next.

Dealing with stress cracks

Stress cracks typically occur in mortar joints rather than within the actual brick or stone. If stress cracks in mortar are the problem, see Chapter 4 for the lowdown on tuck-pointing.

If the problem is a cracked or broken stone or brick, you can remove it by chiseling out the mortar surrounding it. With the mortar out of the way, the brick or stone will have room to expand and can be broken up easily using a cold chisel and a small sledgehammer. Just insert a new brick or stone into the hole to replace the one you removed. Then finish the job by mortaring around the brick or stone for a solid fit. Another option is to leave the cracked brick or stone in place due to the difficulty of finding a matching replacement.

TIP

When a new mortar patch dries and doesn't match the existing shade or color, have a small amount of latex paint color-matched to the existing mortar. Use an artist's brush to paint the new mortar joints. No one will ever know where the existing material ends and the new work begins — including you!

Cleaning your masonry

The most common masonry-cleaning problems are the following.

>> **Fungus, moss, and mildew:** One quart of household liquid bleach mixed into 1 gallon of warm water, applied with a stiff-bristle brush, usually takes care of these unsightly problems. (Don't forget to rinse the solution off with clean water.) However, sodium hypochlorite, the active ingredient in bleach, may not dissolve large masses of these types of growths. In such cases, scrape off as much of the crud as you can with a broad-bladed putty knife (or wire brush); then scrub on the killer mixture.

TIP

When trying to eliminate fungus, it's the bleach that does the job — not the elbow grease. Make sure you give the bleach a good 15 minutes or so to work before scrubbing and rinsing away. If not, fungus spores will remain and can grow back quickly.

>> **Oils, soot, and mineral residue:** Oils, soot, and white, powdery mineral residue pose a slightly more difficult problem. They're embedded more deeply than moss or mildew into the pores of the masonry. You need a solution of 1 part muriatic acid to 9 parts water to get rid of this hard-to-remove crud. Add the acid to the water and apply the solution; allow it to set for about 15 minutes; then use a bristle brush to clean the affected area and rinse with fresh water. (If soot is the problem, head to Chapter 15 for ideas on how to get rid of it.)

>> **Paint:** When it comes to removing paint from masonry, you have several options — sandblasting, wash-away or peel-off paint removers, hand or electric wire brushing, muriatic acid washing, and pressure washing. Sandblasting and wire brushing are labor-intensive and messy, while paint removers can sometimes create more mess than they remove. Instead, consider using a pressure washer. You can rent a commercial pressure

washer for around $75 per day. It's easy to use, keeps mess to a minimum, and doesn't require extensive chemical knowledge.

However, be cautious, as a pressure washer used too aggressively can harm the masonry. Choose your pressure washer tips carefully, avoiding those that create a narrow stream. Prolonged use in one spot can "carve" into the masonry, removing more than just the paint! For softer old brick or stone surfaces, a chemical stripper like Peel Away (refer to Chapter 15) is your best option.

Applying a sealer

Applying a sealer can minimize brick or stone damage from salt air and severe weathering. It can even work to prevent *efflorescence* — mineral salt deposits left behind when water evaporates. Just as you would with concrete, you need to thoroughly clean your brick and stone before applying a sealer. See the section, "Sealing concrete," earlier in this chapter, for information on what you need to perform this task. Be sure the sealer you select is "vapor permeable," meaning it will let moisture evaporate out of the masonry rather than trapping it inside, where it can freeze and cause damage to the stone or brick.

IN THIS CHAPTER

» **Preserving and protecting wood structures**

» **Performing a deck safety check**

» **Fixing up fencing and posts**

» **Avoiding termite troubles**

» **Making retaining walls last**

Chapter **18**

Decks, Fences, and Retaining Walls

Eventually, everything on the planet deteriorates. However, some building materials last longer than others. For example, stone, brick, plaster, and concrete (discussed elsewhere in this book) last a long time and require little or no maintenance. On the other hand, wood and wood-based composites must be regularly maintained and protected with paint or a preservative to achieve lasting quality. Why? Because wood is highly susceptible to damage caused by moisture and the sun's ultraviolet rays, whereas the other building materials aren't nearly as fragile.

So, given wood's need for maintenance, why is it used in building construction? Simple: Wood is beautiful, available, very inexpensive (compared to all the alternatives), and really easy to work with!

In this chapter, I'll walk you through how to handle wood's shortcomings and prolong the life and natural beauty of your wood structures.

REMEMBER

Chapter 5 explains how to care for wood siding. This chapter focuses on other outdoor wood structures. Although you use many of the same principles and techniques to care for outdoor wood structures that you use to care for wood siding, the structures discussed here are more difficult to protect because each structure contains many pieces of wood, with each piece having more than one side exposed to the elements.

HOW MANY SIDES DOES A BOARD HAVE?

Ask this question to a few folks and you'll get a few answers. Most will say two, front and back. Others will say four, including front, back, and sides. But they'd all be wrong. The answer is six! Why is this important? Because when you paint, stain, or otherwise preserve wood, it's important to coat all *six* sides. If not, water will seep into the wood and the rot will begin.

Preserving Wood

Wood is wood and whether the wood is used for a deck, a fence, a gazebo, or a retaining wall, there is one common fact: Wood and water don't mix. When the moisture in wood reaches about 25 percent, organisms that cause decay "wake up" and start to break down the wood fiber, leading to rot. Fortunately, you can protect your wood structures in a number of ways, as the following sections explain.

Painting

A painted deck or fence can be beautiful, but painting can also be particularly difficult, and may not be the best choice. Unlike wood siding, decks, handrails, fences, retaining walls, and other complex structures expose several surfaces of each piece of wood to the weather. Some of the surfaces (such as the area between a fence rail and a fence board) are inaccessible and can't be protected, which makes it difficult to achieve a complete waterproof membrane and creates opportunities for paint failure.

Because of the chipping, bubbling, and splitting normally associated with painted decks and handrails, I'm reluctant to suggest painting. However, if you do decide to paint, do the following:

1. **Make sure that the surface is thoroughly clean and that the wood is dry.**

   Go to extremes to get the wood clean: pressure-washing, sanding, and detergent scrubbing. (Turn to Chapter 5 for cleaning instructions.)

2. **Remove all loose nails and replace them with exterior screws.**

   The screws will hold firmly and will never back out or loosen like nails. Set the screws just below the surface of the wood.

3. **Fill any other holes with a high-quality, exterior-grade putty.**

   While you're applying the putty, be sure to remove all excess putty to keep sanding to a minimum.

4. **Apply a high-quality polyurethane caulk at all joints.**

5. **Prime all bare areas and puttied spots with a high-quality primer.**

6. **Finish decks with a high-grade, exterior finish specified for floors, fences, or decks.**

   Handrails can be finished with a good-quality, exterior acrylic paint.

REMEMBER

Be prepared to re-caulk and touch up paint every year.

Applying a preservative

Another way to protect your wood surfaces is to use a high-quality, oil-based wood preservative — the same kind I suggest for exterior siding. (See Chapter 5.) Using an oil-based wood preservative with ultraviolet inhibitors keeps wood surfaces looking newer longer.

Unlike paint, oil doesn't lay on the surface; it penetrates deeply into the pores of the wood, preventing the attack of moisture from within. Oil also penetrates between joints and connections. With oil, there is no rigid surface layer (as there is with paint) that can bubble or split. However, oil eventually evaporates out of the wood, leaving it unprotected. If you use an oil preservative, you need to recoat your wood every 12 to 18 months.

If maintaining the natural color of your wood is important to you, applying a preservative can help, but preservatives are clear and won't help natural woods like cedar or redwood maintain those beautiful colors indefinitely. For that, stain is the best application, as explained next in the chapter.

TIP

Help force the oil or oil stain into the surface by going back over the entire area with a paintbrush or roller (called *back-brushing*). A natural-bristle paintbrush, also called "china bristle," is by far the best applicator for use with oil. Don't use a nylon paintbrush with oils, oil stains, or oil-based paints.

You can also make your own wood preservative at home. To do this, you need the following:

>> Boiled linseed oil

>> Mineral spirits

>> Pigment (the kind used to color paint)

>> *Mildewcide* (a pesticide that kills mildew; it's available at paint stores)

Mix equal parts of oil and mineral spirits. Then add pigment to the intensity you like, and stir in a package of mildewcide. (Follow the instructions for the mildewcide as if you were adding it to an equal volume of paint.)

When applying the preservative, don't put it on too thick. A little bit goes a long way. Don't forget to back-brush and wipe up any puddling. *Remember:* Oil and oil-stain puddles never dry. They turn into sticky, gummy messes that are nearly impossible to remove from your shoes.

REMEMBER

Even the clearest of finishes will slightly darken wood. To see how dark the wood gets, simply wet your thumb with a drop or two of water and press the wet appendage against the wood. The wet wood will look the same when oiled.

Staining

Exterior wood stain is my preferred choice for decks and fences. It combines the qualities of a wood preservative that penetrates deeply into the wood with a wide range of colors similar to paint.

TIP

Exterior wood stains are available in both oil- and latex-based formulas, although oil-based have become more difficult to find as more environmental regulators seek to reduce the release of harmful VOCs (Volatile Organic Compounds), which present risks to the environment. That said, while oil-based finishes have always provided the best long-term durability, the more environmentally friendly latex paints and stains have come a long way and now provide similar durability.

Stains come in three levels of density.

>> **Transparent stain:** Allows the natural grain and texture of the wood to be visible, offering UV protection and highlighting the natural color and grain. However, since it has no pigment, the natural color may fade over time.

>> **Semi-transparent stain:** Strikes a balance between color and the visibility of the woodgrain. Available in various colors, it enhances the wood's appearance while providing protection against weathering and UV rays. The color appearance varies depending on the wood's grain density, with harder grains appearing lighter and softer grains darker.

>> **Solid color stain:** Covers the wood's surface completely, offering long-term protection. Unlike paint, it still reveals the wood's grain and texture while providing excellent defense against moisture, UV rays, and other elements. Solid color stain is ideal for heavily used outdoor areas like decks and siding.

For exterior projects, solid color stain is always my go-to choice. When applied correctly, I've found that they last almost twice as long as semi-transparent stains and paints, while still showcasing the natural qualities of the wood.

TIP

Stains can be applied by brush, roller, or sprayer. If using a sprayer, you'll need to go over the stain with a brush or roller (known as back-brushing) to assure the best absorption.

Like all finishes, it's important to follow the manufacturer's instructions for prep. The wood needs to be clean, dry, and free of mildew.

REMEMBER

Always apply stain either early or late in the day when the wood is not in full sun. This gives the stain time to soak in before it dries.

PREVENTING A DECK COLLAPSE

Every summer, I hear about decks that collapse, causing serious injury or worse to party-goers who are oblivious to the danger under their feet. The cause is often the same: a deck that was not properly attached to the home. Before you host your next gathering, be sure to inspect your deck for the most common hazards. Here's a list recommended by the North American Decking and Railing Association (www.nadra.org).

Check for split or decaying wood: Examine various areas of the deck, including the ledger board (a common source of deck failure) where it attaches to the house, support posts, joists, deck boards, railings, and stairs. Pay close attention to damp areas as well as spots regularly exposed to water or in contact with fasteners.

I recommend using an ice pick or screwdriver to test the wood's integrity. If it easily penetrates ¼ inch, breaks off without splinters, or feels soft and spongy, decay may be present. Look for small holes indicating insect activity.

Inspect flashing: Flashing directs water away from critical areas where the deck meets the house, preventing moisture buildup and serious rot. Make sure the flashing is intact and properly installed. Replace any damaged sections to prevent water intrusion.

Check for loose or corroded fasteners: Tighten loose fasteners and secure popped nails. Avoid relying solely on nails for the ledger board. Lag bolts or carriage bolts

(continued)

(continued)

provide the strongest attachment. Replace rusted or corroded fasteners with rust-proof stainless steel fasteners to prevent wood deterioration. A stable deck should not sag, sway, or move during testing.

Sturdy stairs: Verify the stability of railings, handrails, and stairs. Ensure they are firmly attached and free from decay. Clear stairways of potential tripping hazards like planters or décor.

Secure railings and banisters: Secure railings, especially for elevated decks. Spindles should have no less than 4-inch spacing, and railings should support at least 300 pounds in any direction.

Repeat this inspection at least once per year, and have any needed repairs completed promptly. For even more deck safety recommendations, check out the www.nadra.org website.

Cleaning Your Wood Structures

Always keep a wood surface free of any debris. Leaves, pine needles, and dirt hold water and accelerate rot. An occasional sweeping is all that's required. You can also give your wood surfaces — oiled (clear finish), oil-stained, or painted — a good scrubbing using the following formula:

>> ½ cup liquid chlorine bleach (if moss is present)

>> 1 gallon hot water

>> 1 cup powdered laundry detergent, ammonia free, as ammonia and chlorine bleach can form a caustic reaction

Add the bleach to the water, and then add the detergent.

WARNING

Although this solution is mild, be sure to wear gloves and eye protection.

Work the solution into the surface with a stiff-bristle broom or a nylon brush. After scrubbing the surface, completely rinse it with water.

REMEMBER

If you plan to refinish the wood after cleaning, allow the wood to completely dry before applying the finish. After it's dry, countersink any nail heads that rise above the deck's surface, or replace them with exterior screws.

TIP

If you find a rotting or severely cracked wood decking board, here's a simple way to avoid replacing it. Gently pry up the board, flip it over, and nail it back down. Since the underside hasn't been exposed to years of sunlight, it should be in nearly perfect condition, just like when it was first installed!

TIP

To get a composite-wood deck to last longer, simply keep it clean. Cleaning in spring and fall will reduce the chance for mold. Contact the wood-composite manufacturer to find out what cleaners it recommends. Some manufacturers suggest a household degreasing agent for oil and grease stains and good old household bleach for mold. In the absence of a proper cleaner, a mild detergent always works.

For more-extensive cleaning measures, read on.

Pressure-washing

A thorough cleaning with a pressure washer (which you can rent from a paint store or tool-rental company) saves a lot of elbow grease and makes those hard-to-get-to areas, like handrails and trellises, easy to clean. Pressure-washing natural wood that has turned gray can help remove discoloration and can bring the wood back to its natural color.

WARNING

A pressure-washer can be a fun and effective tool to use. It cuts through dirt, mold, and mildew and brightens surfaces with startling speed. But don't get mesmerized by the magical transformation. If you use too much pressure, you'll easily damage the wood you are trying to preserve. Choose the gentlest setting and keep your head in the game!

Using a wood brightener

Severely neglected, dirty, tannin-stained, or oil-stained wood may require washing with a wood-brightening product. Look for one that contains oxalic acid. Wood brightener is typically used after cleaning a deck but before staining it. Brighteners open up the pores of the wood, increasing the absorption of wood stains, and even bring out the color.

WARNING

Apply the product with a nylon brush in accordance with the manufacturer's instructions. Wear protective clothing, rubber boots, gloves, and safety goggles to avoid injury.

Tightening Loose Rails, Fence Boards, and Fence Posts

As fences age, it's common for fence boards, rails, and posts to become loose, or to decay. If left unrepaired, fences can sway in the wind and weaken, eventually requiring more expensive repairs. However, fence repairs are relatively straightforward and can prevent costly damage.

WARNING

When repairing a fence, be sure to use hot-dipped galvanized (not electro-coated galvanized) nails or exterior-rated construction screws. Regular shiny, non-coated nails can completely rust away in as little as a year or two.

When a fence post begins to rot at the base, the fence it supports is usually not long for this world. While replacing a rotted fence post is always possible, it's a big project. Instead, *fence-post repair brackets* offer an easier option.

You can find two styles of fence-post repair brackets: straight and off-set. As explained next, the straight brackets presume your fence post has been set in concrete and was driven into the void left by the rotted post. With the off-set bracket, the damaged post is secured by the bracket and a new concrete footing dug a few inches from the original post hole. Straight bracket is the more common repair method and is explained next. However, the off-set bracket works just as well, except that you basically are detaching the post, discarding the rotted base of the post, trimming off any remaining rot from the detached post and attaching the relatively undamaged part of the post to the bracket and then resetting the post in the ground inches away from the rotted base.

REMEMBER

Not every post can be reused. If the rot at the post base extends more than 8 or 10 inches above the concrete pier that holds the post in the ground, then the post should be replaced.

Also, for straight bracket repair, there must be at least 3 inches of concrete between the edge of the fence post and the outside edge of the concrete pier. If the pier is damaged, the off-set fence-post repair bracket should be used instead.

To repair a fence post using the straight-bracket approach, you need only a few items:

>> 1 small block of wood

>> 1 piece of scrap 2-by-4, about 6 inches long

- » 1 pair of straight fence-post repair brackets
- » Hammer
- » Flat pry bar
- » Shovel
- » Sledgehammer
- » A few screws, or a handful of size-10d, hot-dipped galvanized nails

Just follow these steps:

1. **Brace the fence with the 2-by-4 to hold it in a plumb position until the repair can be completed. (See Figure 18-1.)**

   Holding the fence in an upright position, wedge one end of the 2-by-4 into the landscape and nail the other end of the brace to the fence near the post to be repaired. Don't drive in the nail all the way. The brace is temporary, and you'll have to remove the nail after you've made the repair.

FIGURE 18-1:
Installing a fence
repair bracket.

2. **Using the hammer and/or the flat pry bar, remove any fence boards that cover the area to be repaired.**

   Use the block of wood to buffer the blow of the hammer, which reduces the chance of damaging a fence board.

3. **Shovel the dirt away, exposing the base of the post and the top of the concrete pier.**

WARNING

   Sweep the area clean so that you can clearly see the outline of the post in the concrete. Attempting to drive a fence-post repair bracket in the wrong location can easily bend the bracket.

4. **Use the sledgehammer to drive in the brackets.**

   As you drive the bracket into place with the sledgehammer, it crushes the post and wedges itself into the post hole in the concrete. The first bracket usually goes in pretty easily. However, the second one is more difficult to install because the first bracket usually uses up all the available space between the rotted portion of the post and the pier. Be prepared to apply more force to each blow of the sledgehammer to properly seat the second bracket.

5. **Bolt, nail, or screw the brackets into the post.**

   Because the brackets are tightly wedged between the pier and the post, the way in which you attach the bracket to the post usually is not terribly important. However, where substantial post damage exists, use bolts.

6. **Replace the fence boards, remove the temporary brace, and cover up the concrete pier with the dirt you had swept away earlier.**

Congrats. You've just saved more than $300 on a post replacement.

GRAVEL POWER: SECRET TO ROT-FREE FENCE POSTS

Almost all wood fence posts set in concrete will eventually rot, usually at ground level. Pressure treated in-ground posts rated "ground contact" last the longest but ultimately replacement may still be needed. Concrete retains water like a sponge, leading to constant saturation and post decay. However, there's a proven method I've used for years that avoids these issues. Instead of concrete, I set the post using packed gravel. Here's how:

1. Dig a post hole to the required depth (typically 2 - 3 feet).

2. Add a shovel or two full of gravel to the bottom of the hole.

3. Place the 4-by-4 post in the hole and move it up and down a few times to pack the gravel.

4. Begin adding more gravel around the post, periodically tamping it down using a tamping bar or a 2-by-4.

5. Check the post for level and adjust by adding more or less gravel as needed. You'll find you have a lot of control here. Adding gravel and tamping the right side of the post moves the post to the left, and visa-versa.

6. Continue adding gravel and tamping until you're within an inch or two of the top of the hole, then cover with soil.

The surprising strength of posts set this way is remarkable. Once set, they're incredibly sturdy and difficult to move, without using any concrete. You can also continue building your fence without waiting for concrete piers to dry. But the biggest advantage is that because gravel drains well, the posts are less likely to rot. I have wood posts set this way that have lasted 25 years!

Straightening Sagging Gates

A sagging wooden gate is a nuisance at best, and at some point makes the gate hard to open or impossible to latch. The solution lies in installing a *gate repair kit*, which includes a cable with corner mounting brackets and a turnbuckle, which helps keep the gate square. These kits are commonly available in most home centers and hardware stores. Once installed, they allow you to easily adjust the tension of the cable, raising or lowering the gate as needed.

The kit contains the following:

- >> Two metal corner brackets with mounting nails

- >> Two lengths of wire cable with galvanized metal U-bolts, which are used to attach one end of each cable to one of the corner brackets and then the other end of each cable to the turnbuckle

- >> A galvanized metal turnbuckle

Here's how it works:

1. **Attach a metal bracket to the upper corner of the gate (on the hinge side).**

2. **Mount another bracket diagonally at the lower corner of the gate on the latch side.**

3. **Attach cables to each corner bracket and then to the two ends of a turnbuckle. (See Figure 18-2.)**

As you tighten the turnbuckle, the latch side of the gate rises. As you loosen the turnbuckle, the latch side of the gate drops.

WARNING

This system won't work if the upper bracket isn't placed on the hinge side of the gate.

FIGURE 18-2:
Giving your
gate a lift.

Termite Troubles: Keeping Your House Off the Menu

Termites love two things: wood and plenty of time to devour it. Termites can make quick work of the wood in your home's structure, and every hour adds up to more extensive, expensive damage.

Be aware of two types of termites.

>> **Subterranean termites:** These live in the ground and travel up into your house to feed. If their path crosses into daylight, they'll construct "mud tunnels," which are tubes of dirt or sand that they travel through to avoid daylight and to stay moist. Treatment to get rid of termites involves applying an undetectable termiticide to the soil at the foundation perimeter, which the termites pass through and then take back to the nest.

>> **Drywood termites:** These termites actually nest in your home. They're common to the southern United States and much more difficult to extermi-nate. To rid a home of drywood termites, it often has to be "tented," wherein a tent is literally placed over the entire house and then filled with a gas that permeates every nook and cranny, eliminating the problem.

Since subterranean termites are much more common in the far southeastern and southwestern United States and easier for homeowners to spot, here are a few signs to help avoid infestation or catch them early enough to avoid damage.

>> **Inspect to detect:** Look for mud tunnels constructed on exterior or interior sides of foundation walls or across wood floor framing. (See Figure 18-3.) A good way to find damage early is to inspect the area above the foundation wall to look for tunnels. Another trick is to tap each wood floor joist with a large screwdriver, which was always my favorite tool for termite detection! If it sounds hollow or breaks through a damaged joist, you'll need an exterminator.

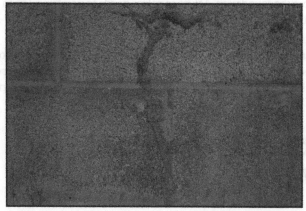

FIGURE 18-3: Termite mud tunnels on a house foundation.

Photo by USDA Forest service

>> **Examine the walls:** If your home is built on a concrete slab, you won't have exposed floor joists. In that case, hold a bright flashlight flat with your interior walls and look for depressions in the walls that look a lot like veins just below the surface. Termites are crafty excavators and will tunnel into drywall, eating the paper surface but not the paint that covers it!

>> **Spot the swarmers:** Termites don't spend all their time underground. At certain times in the year, usually warm spring days with recent rainfall, winged adult termites will "swarm," flying out of an underground nest in search of new places to form colonies. While frightening, this doesn't mean your home is in for an infestation — it's more of Mother Nature's way to make sure the colonies survive.

>> **Use smart firewood storage:** Avoid storing firewood near your foundation. Instead, use a firewood rack and keep it at least 20 feet from the house. Keep fence slats and any wood trim around your house up off the soil. Remove all wood, cardboard, and paper from crawlspaces and basement floors. If storage is necessary, make sure it's off the floor surfaces to avoid attracting insects.

The same advice applies to garage floors. I can't tell you how many times I found termite infestations in a garage where the termites seemingly found their way through 4 inches of concrete on their way to a tasty treat of 2-by-4s holding up the house!

>> **Avoid moisture:** Termites love moisture, so take steps to keep your house dry. Keep gutters and downspouts clear to ensure that water drains away from the foundation. Adjust sprinkler heads to point away from the foundation.

If you suspect termites have invaded your home, have a professional exterminator treat the home's foundation with a termiticide and pick up a service contract that includes a yearly inspection to make sure termites haven't returned.

Extending the Life of a Wood Retaining Wall

A wood retaining wall often doesn't get noticed until it begins to topple. They're considered temporary, but you can improve their life expectancy by keeping the wood as dry as possible with strategic drainage. To keep your retaining wall dry, follow these steps:

1. **Dig a 6- to 12-inch-wide trench between the retaining wall and the hill it supports.**

   The trench should go to the bottom of the retaining wall.

2. **Line the bottom and both sides of the trench with landscaping filter fabric.**

3. **Place 6 inches of drain rock over the burlap in the bottom of the trench.**

4. **Install a 4-inch perforated drainpipe (perforations down) over the first layer of rock.**

   The drainpipe should *daylight* (come out of the ground) at some point beyond the end of the retaining wall. If possible, extend the pipe so that it drains directly into the public storm-drain system. Be sure to maintain a slope of at least ¼ inch per foot to keep things flowing.

5. **Fill the rest of the trench with drain rock to within 6 inches of the top of the dirt being retained.**

6. **Cover the rock with a layer of landscaping filter fabric and cover that with 6 inches of soil.**

   Make sure that the support posts are not in unnecessary contact with any soil and that the surrounding earth is graded to shed water away from the posts and retaining boards.

Once a year, clean the wall and post with soap and water, and apply a fresh coat of oil-based wood preservative (see the section, "Applying a preservative," earlier in this chapter).

TIP

If you're replacing a rotted wood retaining wall or building one from scratch, interlocking retaining wall blocks are a much better choice. Made of concrete with an attractive decorative surface, they're designed to be stacked at a slight offset, leaning towards the hill. Like a wood wall, drainage should be provided between the wall and the hill it is supporting, but once installed, the wall needs virtually no maintenance.

IN THIS CHAPTER

» **Preventing rust**

» **Removing rust**

» **Repairing rust damage**

Chapter **19**

And Then There Was Rust

ust, the reddish-brown crust that forms on materials that contain iron, is caused by low-temperature oxidation in the presence of water. To maintain metal over very long periods of time, all you have to do is control rust. Fortunately, rust can be removed from metal year after year, layer after layer, without causing appreciable damage to the structural value of the metal. This is the main reason why metal is such a good buy in the long run.

Note that although rust can't be prevented entirely, you sure can slow it down. In this chapter, I'll share how to remove rust from metal surfaces and prevent it from coming back.

Painting Tactics to Defeat Rust

Barbecues, patio furniture, grills, handrails, and lawn and garden equipment are just a few of the many metal finishes around the home that are susceptible to damage by rust.

Aside from its ugly appearance, left untreated, rust can bring any of these finishes to an early demise and lead to other damage. Rust also presents a safety issue.

A rusted-out screw in a handrail or the rust-ravaged leg of a garden chair could lead an unsuspecting guest to a nasty fall. Rusty outdoor power equipment leaves the operator particularly vulnerable because a rusted bolt could act as a projectile. Remember Superman and that speeding bullet? That could be you if you let rust have the upper hand.

Painting can shield a metal surface, and, therefore, prevent oxygen and water from forming damaging rust.

Choosing your primer and topcoat

Before you get down to painting metal surfaces, you need to know a few things about the primer and paint you choose.

A good paint job always begins with a high-quality primer. In this case, the primer should be made specifically for metal. Paints containing certain pigments — zinc and iron oxide, for example — adhere to metal much more effectively than other types of paint.

Choose a topcoat that matches the type of primer you use. For instance, if you use an oil-based primer, opt for an oil-based finish coat. This combination provides excellent abrasion and weather resistance. It's also advisable to stick with the same paint brand throughout the process. Manufacturers ensure their paints and primers work seamlessly together, eliminating the need to switch to a different brand.

For surfaces that get hot, like grills, metal fireplaces, firepits, wood stoves, heaters, or furnaces that reach temperatures above 200 degrees, use a specialized enamel paint called "high heat." This type of paint is specifically formulated for items that get too hot to touch.

TIP

Keep in mind that some high-heat paints may emit fumes the first time they're heated, but this odor dissipates quickly and only occurs initially.

Applying the paint

One coat each of a high-quality primer and a high-quality oil-based topcoat is all that should be required. You can apply the primer and topcoat using a brush, roller, paint pad, or sprayer.

TIP

The first step for painting metal isn't painting — it's prep! Cleaning, removing existing rust, and wire brushing or sanding the surface are all important steps that will ensure that the primer and paint adhere and last a long time. Check out the section, "Stripping Off Rust," for my step-by-step tips on how to remove rust.

When applying an oil-based paint, use a natural-bristle brush. Synthetic brushes made from nylon or polyester work perfectly well with latex paints, but are too stiff for use with oil-based paints, and often cause brush marks — not to mention loose bristles — to remain in the finished product.

For small projects, using canned aerosol spray paint is the best way to go. It's far easier to use than a paint sprayer and offers the ability to handle intricate surfaces as well as a wide variety of projects.

TIP

If you've ever picked up a can of spray paint you stored from a prior project, it can be frustrating to find that the tip is clogged, and the remaining paint is wasted. To avoid this, the solution is to clear the tip before storing the paint. Simply turn the can upside down and spray it for a moment until air flows from the tip. This action blows out any residual paint that could dry and cause clogging, readying the can for your next painting project!

PICKING THE PERFECT PAINT SPRAYER

If you have a big paint project to tackle, or one that is extremely detailed, a paint sprayer can be a handy and efficient way to get the job done. You have two types of paint sprayers to consider:

Airless paint sprayers: While traditional paint sprayers used by professional painters are powered by a large-forced air compressor, airless sprayers are more DIY friendly. They use a high-pressure pump to atomize the paint into a fine mist, which is then sprayed evenly onto the surface. Airless sprayers can handle a wide range of paint types, from latex and acrylics to oil paint, stains, or sealers, making them versatile for different painting needs. However, while airless sprayers can be a quick way to apply paint to a large or detailed surface, the time it takes to set up the sprayer and clean it when you are done is significant. Plus, for projects like railings, they tend to waste as much paint as they apply.

HVLP (High Volume Low Pressure): These paint sprayers draw paint from a hand-held reservoir and deliver it at lower pressure levels than airless sprayers. HVLP sprayers provide a more accurate application of paint with less waste and are a good choice for detailed work like spray-painting metal patio furniture. Before using an HVLP sprayer, be sure to check the manufacturer's recommendations for the tip size needed for the paint you are applying. Thicker paint needs larger spray tips, and failure to have the right one results in clogs that will frustrate you and delay the project!

Paint sprayers can speed up the painting process and offer advantages for detailed work. But as I've shown here, each type has tradeoffs that can quickly eliminate the convenience you counted on.

For a do-it-yourselfer, using a paint sprayer offers several advantages. Spray-painting works well on intricate designs and is smoother (without brush marks). However, you do need to take several precautions when spray-painting:

>> **Follow the necessary safety precautions.** Be sure to wear eye protection and a respirator. And never spray-paint in an area where flames or sparks could ignite volatile vapors.

>> **Mask off surrounding areas with plastic, paper, or canvas to avoid damage by overspray.** Don't try spray-painting on a windy day unless, of course, your neighbor's car needs a paint job. Just be sure they're pleased with the color.

>> **If you're using a spray rig, use a tip that's compatible with the paint to avoid putting too much paint on at once.** Tip sizes vary in accordance with the type of paint being used (oil based, water based, lacquer, and so on). Each type of paint has a different viscosity and, therefore, must be sprayed through a different-size tip.

>> **Avoid paint runs by applying several thin coats rather than one heavy one.**

Protecting your metal with paint helps prevent rust as much as it can be prevented. However, as paint is chipped or scratched, and as it oxidizes with time and the elements, its effectiveness as a rust barrier diminishes. Eventually, moisture can make its way through the paint to the metal's surface, and rust results. To extend the life of your paint job and the protection it provides, touch up chipped and scratched areas immediately.

Stripping Off Rust

The real secret to dealing with rust is to remove as much of it as possible before trying to apply a new finish. (You can read about applying a new finish in the preceding section.) Depending upon the level of detail in the item you're painting, removing rust can be a tedious process that requires lots of elbow grease. In the end, your goal is to remove the rust down to bare metal. The following sections explain how.

Step 1: Removing rusted fasteners

When stripping a fixture of rust, you need to remove any rusted screws and fasteners — which is sometimes easier said than done. That's because rust can act as a bonding agent and cause the fasteners and the metal structure to "freeze together" and become one.

Here are some ways you can remove rusted fasteners:

>> **Saturate the fastener with penetrating oil.** The oil helps dissolve a small amount of the rust and acts as a lubricant to help free up some frozen connections.

Don't count on using penetrating oil to remove rust. Penetrating oil breaks down a certain amount of rust, but it isn't considered a good rust remover.

REMEMBER

WARNING

>> **Use heat to remove the fastener.** A heat gun or propane torch causes a stubborn nut to expand and break loose from the bolt.

If you plan to use heat to remove a fastener, be sure to first wipe off any lubricant or cutting oil you may have applied because the combination can cause a fire.

>> **Use a drill and a hacksaw.** When all else fails, drilling out the fastener or cutting it free with a hacksaw or reciprocating saw usually does the trick.

Step 2: Getting rid of the rust

The various methods (and tools) you can use to remove rust — wire brush, sandpaper, flexible sanding sponges, solvents, and so on — fall into two general categories: those that rely on elbow grease and those that rely on chemical reactions. The following sections have the details.

WARNING

Whichever method you choose, be sure to wear protective gloves (to prevent metal splinters) and safety goggles (to prevent eye injuries caused by flying metal particles).

A little bit (or a lot) of elbow grease

Sandpaper, sanding tape, flexible sanding sponges, steel wool, and nylon scouring pads all work well and can be especially useful when working on tubing or twisted and curved material.

TIP

Sanding cord (industrial-strength dental floss) is a must when working around hard-to-access decorative elements, such as those you might find on a railing. As with sandpaper, sanding cord is available in a variety of grits.

RUST-OLEUM HAD A FISHY START

By now, you've probably figured out that removing rust can be hard work. That's exactly what sea captain Robert Fergusson thought back in 1921. Fergusson noticed that fish oil prevented rust from forming on his ship's metal deck. Working with a chemist, Fergusson developed one of the world's first rust-preventive paints and Rust-Oleum was born! Rust-Oleum has long been my go-to for metal painting projects. I like the way it adheres to metal surfaces old and new, and also protects and preserves them for years to come. Find out more at www.rustoleum.com.

In those situations where there is more rust than elbow grease can handle, I recommend the addition of a little power. A wire brush or wire wheel attached to a drill can make simple work of stripping rust. A bit of fine finishing with sandpaper or steel wool helps remove any residue that may remain.

WARNING

Using a wire brush or especially a wire wheel attached to a drill can be dangerous. Be sure to use a full-face mask or safety goggles to protect your eyes from wires that can fly off the brush or wheel.

Using chemical removers

Some rust simply can't be sanded or scraped without resulting in damage to the fixture. When dealing with this kind of rust, use a chemical rust remover or dissolver. These products contain ingredients that will chemically break down rust.

Rust-removal products containing gelled phosphoric acid, such as Naval Jelly, work best. You either brush the gel on (with a cheap paintbrush) or spray it on, and leave it there for 15 to 30 minutes for best results. Then simply rinse the chemical off with fresh water and dry it immediately. (*Remember:* Raw, wet steel begins to rust in minutes.) More than one application may be required, depending upon the severity of the rust.

WARNING

Again, safety first. Be sure to wear rubber gloves and safety goggles, and have plenty of fresh ventilation when you're working with chemical rust removers.

Step 3: Repairing damage to the surface

Badly pitted areas can be filled with a patching compound in the same manner that wood is repaired. The difference with metal is that the patching compound must be specifically made for use with metal. Metal expands and contracts at a much different rate than wood does. A metal patch such as Bondo (often sold in auto supply stores) is designed to expand and contract the same way that metal does. You apply a metal patch much like you apply spackle to wallboard when you're filling a nail hole: Simply apply the metal patch using a putty knife, allow it to dry, and sand off the excess.

After you've removed the rust and repaired any surface damage, you're ready to prime the metal. Do so within 24 hours to prevent the formation of new rust. (See the earlier section, "Choosing your primer and topcoat," for tips on priming and finishing a metal surface.)

When All Else Fails: Converting Rust

Although I strongly recommend removing rust, there may be areas where this is simply impossible. If you can't dissolve or scrape off rust, then you have another alternative: You can convert it.

Rust converters are a specialized type of primer that neutralizes and stops rust. You apply rust converters directly over rust in the same way that you apply any other primer. The converter chemically combines with the rust, changing the rust to an inert byproduct. After the converter has cured, you can apply a fresh coat of paint directly over the converter.

One major disadvantage of using a converter in lieu of removing the rust is the likelihood of an uneven finish. The best way to guarantee a top-notch finish is to scrape, grind, patch, and sand the rust until it's smooth.

6 The Part of Tens

Make your own cleaning solutions.

Master ten maintenance skills.

Explore your smart home future.

Chapter **20**

Ten Cleaning Solutions You Can Make at Home

n the days of old, our ancestors didn't buy cleaners for every surface imaginable. They made their own using commonly available household ingredients. If you'd like to go the DIY route, these tried-and-true recipes for homegrown cleaning solutions are easy to make, non-caustic, and work.

All-Purpose, Handy-Dandy Cleaner

You can use this All-Purpose, Handy-Dandy Cleaner to clean and freshen just about any surface. It works especially well for day-to-day cleaning of range tops and cooktops. Just mix up the following ingredients:

» 1 teaspoon borax

» ½ teaspoon washing soda

» 2 teaspoons white vinegar

» ¼ teaspoon dishwashing liquid

» 2 cups hot water

Washing soda is essentially turbo-charged baking soda. The technical name is sodium carbonate. Washing soda is a highly alkaline compound that makes a great all-purpose cleaning product and is often used as an additive to laundry detergent and other cleaning products to produce superior results.

You can replace the washing soda with baking soda and use lemon juice instead of white vinegar, depending upon what you have lying around the house. Just keep in mind that washing soda and lemon juice are a bit stronger than baking soda and white vinegar.

TIP

The secret to most cleaning formulas is hot water. It helps the various ingredients blend.

DIY Cleanser Scrub

This formula for DIY Cleanser Scrub is especially suited for cleaning up baked-on spills on glass or porcelain ranges and cooktops when you would normally pull out the cleanser. Start with the following ingredients:

>> ¾ cup borax

>> ¼ cup baking soda

>> Dishwashing liquid to moisten

Combine the two powders and moisten them with just enough dishwashing liquid to create a gooey paste. You can use all borax or all baking soda if you want, depending upon what you have around your house, but just keep in mind that the concoction won't be quite as strong without the borax. For a more pleasing and lingering aroma, add ¼ teaspoon of lemon juice.

Gentle Glass Cleaner

My Gentle Glass Cleaner works well for cleaning the glass shelving in your refrigerator, glass cooktops, and the windows in range and oven doors. You need the following ingredients:

>> 2 tablespoons ammonia

>> ¼ teaspoon dishwashing liquid

- » ½ cup rubbing alcohol
- » Hot water

Mix the ammonia, dishwashing liquid, and rubbing alcohol, and then add enough hot water to make 1 quart of cleaner. If you prefer, you can avoid the smell of ammonia by using white vinegar or lemon juice. However, these optional concoctions will cause the formula to be slightly less powerful.

TIP

For super-duper window cleaning — especially in cold weather when windows are extra dirty — add 1 teaspoon of cornstarch to the formula to boost your cleaning-and-sparkling horsepower.

Natural Carpet Freshener

Steam-cleaning carpets can be a pretty big project, but a quick vacuuming with this natural carpet freshener can deliver fragrant results and stave off more frequent deep cleans. Here's what you'll need:

- » 2 cups baking soda
- » ½ cup salt
- » ¼ to ½ cup mint leaves or lavender buds

In a mixing bowl, combine the baking soda and salt; then add the dried mint leaves or lavender buds to the mix and stir well. The baking soda will help neutralize odors, while salt helps to enhance the deodorizing effect and the herbs add a pleasant scent.

Once the mix is ready, vacuum your carpet to remove most of the dirt. Then sprinkle the mixture evenly across your carpet. Pay special attention to areas with strong odors or high traffic.

Leave the baking soda, salt, and dried herb mixture on your carpet for at least 20 to 30 minutes. This gives it time to absorb odors and freshen up the fibers. Then, just vacuum your carpet thoroughly. And with that, the funk will be all gone and replaced with a fresh, pleasant scent!

People-Friendly Oven Cleaner

This People-Friendly Oven Cleaner is a safe alternative to those conventional, caustic oven cleaners. You can also use it to clean barbecue grills and grungy pots and pans. Start with the following ingredients:

>> 2 teaspoons borax or baking soda

>> 2 tablespoons dishwashing liquid

>> 1¼ cups ammonia

>> 1½ cups hot water

Mix the ingredients, apply generously to spills, and let the solution soak for 30 minutes or as long as overnight. Loosen tough spills with a nylon scrubber, and then wipe up with a damp sponge.

Super-Duper Disinfectant Cleaner

The Super-Duper Disinfectant Cleaner works well anywhere you would use a store-bought disinfectant, such as on appliance pulls and handles; the inside face of the refrigerator where the gasket is seated; the refrigerator drip pan; counters and cutting boards; and around the opening of your clothes washer. It works especially well on all surfaces of a trash compactor — inside and out.

Mix the following ingredients and then scrub:

>> 1 tablespoon borax or baking soda

>> ¼ cup powdered laundry detergent

>> ¼ cup pine-oil-based cleaner or pine oil

>> ¾ cups hot water

For kitchen countertops, backsplashes, and the like (where there is a lot of area to cover), you can dilute this mixture with more hot water to get more coverage.

Cola Concrete Stain Remover

Use the Cola Concrete Stain Remover on all concrete where the surface looks like the floor of your neighborhood car repair shop. You need the following ingredients:

>> A small bag of cat litter

>> A few cans of cola beverage (diet or regular)

>> 1 cup liquid chlorine bleach

>> 1 cup powdered ammonia-free laundry detergent

>> 1 gallon hot water

Completely cover the grease or oil stain with a thin layer of the cat litter and grind it in with your shoes. When the mess is completely absorbed, sweep up and discard the cat litter. Cover the stain that's left with the cola beverage, and use a bristle brush to work the liquid into the affected area for about 15 to 20 minutes or until the cola stops fizzing. Don't let the area dry out — use fresh water to rinse away the cola. A gray stain will be left. Add the detergent and bleach to the hot water, and scrub away the gray stain.

WARNING

Although this solution is mild, be sure to wear gloves and eye protection when you work with it.

Easy All-Surface Mildew Remover

This Easy All-Surface Mildew Remover works great on painted or other washable surfaces and costs about one-fifth the price of its store-bought equivalent. Start with the following ingredients:

>> ⅓ cup powdered, ammonia-free laundry detergent

>> 1 quart liquid chlorine bleach

>> 3 quarts warm water

WARNING

Make sure the detergent you use is ammonia free. Mixing bleach with a solution containing ammonia can release a dangerous gas that's harmful to your lungs.

Pour the water into a bucket. Add the bleach to the water, and then add the detergent. While wearing rubber gloves, stir the concoction until the detergent fully blends into the solution. Pour some of the mildew remover into a spray bottle. Spray the remover onto any area where mildew exists and allow it to sit for five to ten minutes, but don't let it dry. You'll know that the solution is working when the black mildew stains turn white. Rinse all the surfaces very well with hot water and towel-dry.

WARNING

When you're working with this mildew remover, wear gloves and eye protection and make sure you have plenty of ventilation.

Foamy Drain Freshener and Cleaner

This Foamy Drain Freshener and Cleaner is great for bathroom and kitchen drains. Although it isn't meant to free badly clogged drains, it can freshen them and prevent clogging. Use this formula once a month for best results. Here's what you need:

>> 1 cup baking soda

>> 1 cup table salt

>> 1 cup white vinegar

>> 2 quarts boiling water

First, pour the baking soda into the drain, followed by the salt, and then the vinegar. The mixture will begin to foam. After a few minutes, pour the water into the drain. Let it stand overnight before using the faucet again.

WARNING

Be sure to add the ingredients in the recommended order. Adding the vinegar first followed by the salt and baking soda can actually create a clog.

Universal Roof-Cleaning Formula

Use this Universal Roof-Cleaning Formula when your roof gets dirty. The concoction also gets rid of roof algae and moss on your roof. You need these ingredients:

- >> 1 cup liquid chlorine bleach

- >> 1 cup powdered ammonia-free laundry detergent

- >> 1 gallon hot water

Add the bleach to the water and then add the detergent. Mix the ingredients until the soap granules dissolve. Pour the mixture into a garden sprayer. Apply the liquid onto the affected area, and keep it wet for at least 15 minutes. Use a broom to scrub the surface. Rinse with a garden hose.

TIP

For rinsing the roof, a pressure washer works best. Just be careful not to damage the roof with the force of the spray. Hold the spray tip back about 12 to 18 inches from the roof.

Chapter **21**

Ten (or so) Maintenance Skills You Need

ainting, caulking, lubricating, and testing are some common maintenance tasks that you'll eventually perform as a homeowner. In this chapter, I list ten or so universal home care to-dos and share a few basics that I hope will help you accomplish each task as quickly and as easily as possible without sacrificing safety.

Caulking

Caulk is the stuff you pump into a gap to make it airtight or watertight. Sounds easy enough — and it is once you get the hang of it. To caulk, all you have to do is make sure that the area to be caulked is clean and dry. Open the caulk, squeeze a bead into the gap or crack, wipe off the excess, and smooth the seam with a plastic putty knife or a credit card — I use my fingers. You can clean off the excess with water or the solvent recommended for the caulk being used.

There are many types and colors of caulk, and knowing which to choose is important.

Here are the most common types of caulk.

>> **Latex:** This is a good all-purpose sealant and adhesive for little projects where water protection isn't an issue. It's most popular among DIYers because it's paintable and cleans up easily with water. However, it does shrink and crack quite easily and doesn't deliver near the longevity of silicone caulk.

>> **Silicone:** This is the most durable caulk. Silicone is an excellent all-purpose sealant and adhesive. It's flexible and super long lasting. Not all silicone caulks are paintable, but you can find some that are.

Applying silicone caulk can be challenging because it tends to stick to your hands, making it difficult to achieve a smooth, even coat using your finger. However, there's a simple trick for this: dip your finger in liquid dish soap! The soap acts as a lubricant, allowing you to use your "finger trowel" effectively and create a smooth bead of caulk.

Aside from selecting the type of caulk, it's important to note that caulk is formulated for specific purposes. For instance, if you're caulking a window, choose an exterior caulk labeled for "window and door" use, as this formula includes UV protection. Similarly, for caulking your bathtub, opt for a "kitchen and bath" caulk that contains a mildewcide to prevent mold and mildew growth.

Regardless of which type of caulking you select, make sure that the surface you're applying it to is clean and dry — even if the caulk label claims it can be applied to wet surfaces.

Knowing How (and What) to Lubricate

A little lubrication can go a long way toward helping parts move more easily. Lubrication reduces stress on motors and equipment, which reduces operating cost and extends life. Here are some common lubricants and what they can be used to lubricate.

>> **Spray grease:** This is good for things like the rollers, gears, or the chain on your bicycle. Simply point and spray.

>> **Silicone lubricant:** This type of lubricant is good for sliding doors, sliding windows, and sliding screens, because it doesn't gum up. To apply silicone lubricant, clean the track and then point and spray.

>> **WD-40:** This lubricant is in a class by itself because it is actually a blended lubricant. According to the manufacturer, WD-40 is a "unique, special blend of lubricants." WD-40 also "contains anti-corrosion agents and ingredients for penetration, water displacement and soil removal."

>> **Graphite:** Use this to lubricate door hardware and locks. To use graphite lubricant, place the tip of the container against the keyhole and squeeze.

REMEMBER

Anything in your home that contains a moving part is a candidate for scheduled lubrication. If you aren't sure, contact the manufacturer and find out. The equipment you save will be your own!

Recognizing and Testing for Problems

You know that a smoke detector or carbon-monoxide detector with worn-out batteries provides absolutely no protection in the event of a fire. But did you also know that fire extinguishers can leak and lose their charge, rendering them useless in an emergency?

Many parts of a home's systems and components are designed to detect problems. Being aware and observant can help you avoid problems both minor and major. Here are a few to consider.

>> **Smoke and carbon-monoxide detectors:** Use the Test button monthly to check their operation. Replace detectors that are older than 10 years and opt for detectors with the new 10-year batteries.

>> **Fire extinguishers:** Twice a year, locate your fire extinguishers and read the pressure gauge. Every three years, replace your extinguishers.

>> **Water-pressure/temperature-relief valves:** Found on both water heaters and boilers, these valves are designed to open and leak water should the pressure become too high. If you spot these valves leaking, contact your local plumbing and heating contractor for a repair.

>> **GFCIs:** With an electrical circuit, it's important to ensure that your Ground Fault Circuit Interrupters (GFCIs) are operating properly. To check, simply press the Test button to be sure that the circuit is safe.

Many household devices are designed to be tested, so if something has a Test button, use it!

Not checking and testing a safety device can place you and your family in grave danger.

REMEMBER

Choosing the Right Tool for the Job

Nothing is more difficult than attempting a home-repair project without the proper tools. Can you spell "busted knuckles"? Not only is it important to have the right tool for the job, but that tool must be in good condition as well. A dull chisel, for example, can do more damage than good. A dull saw or the wrong saw for the job can break your back. (Did you know that there is a wrench made especially for reaching up behind the kitchen sink? Yep, it's called a basin wrench!)

So when you're tackling a job yourself, make sure you have the proper tools. Start by researching the project. Throughout this book, I tell you which tool you'll need for the job at hand. When you know which tools are needed, you can research what each one does. A handy neighbor or a knowledgeable hardware-store clerk can also be helpful.

What if you don't have or can't get the proper tool? Well, some projects are best left to contractors, especially when investing in the proper tools costs more than a professional repair.

Be cautious of bargain tools. A tool that breaks in your hand can hurt.

WARNING

Knowing Your Valves

Every home has a series of water valves. In the event of a plumbing leak, knowing where these values are and what they do can mean the difference between a minor clean-up and a massive repair.

Find and label the following valves, and make sure everyone in the house knows where they are.

>> **Main water valve:** This is the most important valve as it controls the flow of all water into your home.

>> **Washing machine valves:** If you still have rubber hoses going to your washer, you'd better get in the habit of turning the washer supply valves off between uses! Better yet, replace rubber hoses with the more durable steel-braided hoses and rest easy.

>> **Hose bib valves:** These valves control water flow to your outside faucets. They need to be turned off in the winter to avoid what could be a pretty major leak if the pipe were to freeze and break. After shutting the valve for the season, open the outside faucet to drain any water left in the supply pipe, and leave it open until spring.

>> **Icemaker valve:** This small water line could leak a heck of a lot of water if it were to break. You'll often find the icemaker valve in the cabinet beneath the kitchen sink or in a wall niche behind the refrigerator.

>> **Water heater valve:** This is your best friend if your water heater decides to leak. Turn the water valve off (along with the gas valve or electric circuit) to limit this leak to 40 gallons or whatever size your tank is.

>> **Humidifier valve:** You'll often find humidifiers in homes that have a forced hot air heating system to add moisture to the air. They can clog and leak if they're not maintained, which is when knowing this valve location comes in handy.

Painting

Painting provides a protective coating to a surface, preventing rot and deterioration and making for easy cleaning. Doing it right and doing it well couldn't be more important. Outside, the ultraviolet rays of the sun and water from rain, snow, and mis-directed sprinkler systems can destroy the home's exterior. A solid coat of paint looks good, but more important, it's a barrier between your home and Mother Nature. Interior painting is equally important to protect your home against everyday wear and tear. If walls and trim are beyond cleaning, it's time to paint.

Painting well requires two basic steps:

1. **Prepare the surface.**

   Preparation (sanding, caulking, and cleaning) constitutes 80 percent of a paint job, and it's key to a good final finish.

2. **Paint.**

TIP

   Use the best paint money can buy. The longer the paint lasts, the less often you'll find yourself with a paintbrush in hand. Plus, given that good paint lasts longer than not-so-good paint, and that prep is the most labor-intense part of the project, painting projects end up costing a lot less per year.

If you want more information on painting, check out *Painting Do-It-Yourself For Dummies*, by Katharine Kaye McMillan, PhD, and Patricia Hart McMillan (Wiley).

Knowing How to Shut Things Off

Aside from being able to quickly locate and shut off your main water valve as noted earlier in the chapter, having that same familiarity with gas valves and electricity supply can be critical.

>> **Electricity:** Every home typically has one main breaker that shuts off all the electricity. You need to know where the main breaker (or fuse) is and how to shut the breaker off. In addition to the main breaker, it can be helpful to know what each individual circuit breaker controls. If these circuits are not already labeled, pick up a *circuit breaker finder*, a handy device that can help you easily trace every circuit in your home.

WARNING

   Never shut off a breaker when you're standing in a puddle of water.

>> **Gas:** Find out where the gas meter is on your property and what size wrench is necessary to turn it off. Most hardware stores carry the type of wrench needed for the gas meters in your neck of the woods. I suggest purchasing such a tool and tying it to the gas meter, so you won't have to go looking for it if and when an emergency arises. (**Note:** Modern gas-meter installations include an automatic earthquake shut-off valve.)

REMEMBER

Make sure every member of your household knows where all these items are located and how to turn them off. When in doubt, turn everything off. Some systems may be slightly difficult to turn on later, but it doesn't ever hurt your home to turn everything off in an emergency.

Venting Moisture from Your Home

Damp air, condensation, and steam are different forms of water that can damage your house. When any type of moisture attacks, metal rusts, mildew grows, wallpaper peels, and paint bubbles. Excess moisture can also lead to stale, unhealthy air and mold growth. That's why having good ventilation is crucial.

Start by installing a quality bath fan that vents outside, not into an attic or closed space. A powerful range hood is also essential for venting cooking steam, grease, and fumes. Ideally, ensure the range hood vents outside and doesn't just recirculate air, and remember to clean the filters regularly.

Attic ventilation is crucial, too. Moisture from the house rises to the attic and must be vented; otherwise, it can damage insulation and cause mold growth on the roof sheathing. Passive ventilation with ridge and soffit vents is preferable over an attic fan. This setup circulates outdoor air, keeping the attic cooler in summer and drier in winter when condensation is common.

For a vented crawlspace, ventilation is also necessary. Use a plastic vapor barrier on the floor and keep crawlspace foundation vents open in warmer months, closing them only during the coldest winter days.

Replacing Filters and Cleaning Sensors

Filters and sensors exist everywhere in your home. If I asked you to name a filter, you'd probably say "furnace filter," and you'd be right — the furnace filter is one of the most important of the bunch. But you have more filters.

Here's a list of the most common filters, and one sensor, and how often you should clean or replace them.

» **Furnace filter:** If your home uses the cheap, spun-fiberglass filters, they'll need to be changed monthly. That said, the air quality inside your home will benefit greatly from a better-quality filter. Look for a filter with a MERV

(Minimum Efficiency Reporting Value) rating of 11 or higher if sensitive to airborne allergens. Pleated filters are the best.

>> **Range-hood filter:** Clean every couple of months depending on how often you cook and how much frying you do. (More frying equals more frequent cleaning, because grease can build up and clog the filter.)

>> **Bath or laundry exhaust fan:** Clean every six months. (I know, the grate that covers the fan is not a filter per se, but a dirty cover can still wreak havoc with the system.)

>> **Refrigerator water filter:** Replace in accordance with the manufacturer's instructions. Besides, who wants dirty ice?

>> **Smoke-detector sensor:** Vacuum twice a year. Use your vacuum cleaner hose with a soft brush attachment.

>> **Whole-house water filters:** Change at least once a year. You may find that your water tastes better if you change the filter every six months. Filters trap debris and bacteria that can eventually affect the taste of water that passes through it.

>> **Dryer filter:** Clean it every time you use the dryer and clean the chamber that holds the filter at least once every three months. A long, skinny nozzle on the end of your vacuum cleaner hose is all it takes.

Checking On the Chimney

Nothing is as romantic as a crackling fire. And nothing can level your house faster than the explosion and raging fire from a creosote-laden chimney. Save the fireworks for the fairgrounds on the Fourth of July. Call a chimney sweep to thoroughly clean your chimney at least once a year or after every cord of burned wood.

Here are some chimney-related maintenance tasks you can do yourself:

>> Make sure the damper is in proper working order by ensuring that it opens and closes easily.

>> Keep birds' nests and other debris from blocking the spark arrestor atop your chimney.

>> If you notice missing mortar or loose bricks, don't use your fireplace until the cracks are repaired.

Tackling 10 Home Maintenance Tasks in Under 10 Minutes Each

Feeling like you have no time to take on home maintenance projects? Well, scratch that excuse! Many maintenance projects take literally 10 minutes or less to do. There's no reason you can't kick-start your Saturday morning by tackling one or two of these quick tasks every weekend.

1. **Test GFCIs monthly:** Ground Fault Circuit Interrupters (GFCIs) are crucial for electrical safety. They monitor electricity flow and trip if they detect even a small imbalance, preventing electric shocks. Testing is simple — just press the Test button on the face of the GFCI. If it works, you'll hear a "snap" as the breaker shuts down. Resetting restores power.

2. **Check sinks for leaks:** Fill your bath sinks with water until it reaches the overflow near the top. After a minute or two, release the stopper and let the water drain. Then, grab a bright flashlight and check under the sink for signs of leaks. Catching leaks early can prevent costly damage.

3. **Check toilets for leaks:** Leaky toilet flush valves (the rubber flapper at the bottom of the tank) can waste thousands of gallons of water and cause "ghost flushing." To test for leaks, remove the toilet tank lid, drop in a few squirts of food coloring, and wait 10 minutes. If the color appears in the bowl, the flush valve is leaking and needs replacement.

4. **Replace kitchen exhaust fan filters:** Most kitchen exhaust fans have either a cleanable metal filter or a disposable charcoal filter. Remove and clean or replace the filter monthly to ensure proper air flow.

5. **Lubricate locks and hinges:** Keep your doors operating smoothly and squeak-free by applying a few squirts of WD-40 into the locks and hinges.

6. **Replace your furnace filter:** For forced-air heating and cooling systems, changing the filter is essential for clean air and preventing clogs in the evaporator coil. This should be done once per month but can be done less frequently if you have a better-quality filter. Look for a filter rated MERV 11 for optimal performance.

7. **Clean and reverse ceiling fans:** Ceiling fans should be reversed seasonally for optimal airflow. They typically have a switch on the motor to change the direction. In winter, fan blades should pull air up from the floor, and in summer "push" air down from the ceiling. Cleaning the blades at the same time helps maintain efficiency.

8. **Test your smoke and carbon-monoxide detectors:** Monthly testing using the built-in Test button ensures they are functioning correctly. Vacuuming to remove dust is also important. Replace detectors over 10 years old and consider upgrading to models with 10-year batteries for convenience.

9. **Trim landscaping around air-conditioning compressors:** Maintain at least a 12-inch clearance around outdoor AC compressors to allow proper air intake. This prevents early compressor failure due to restricted airflow.

10. **Program your thermostat:** Utilize the clock-setback features on standard thermostats to adjust heating or cooling temperatures based on your schedule. Smart thermostats offer added convenience with motion detection and vacation mode for energy savings.

By dedicating just a few minutes each week to these tasks, you can ensure your home stays in top shape without overwhelming yourself with maintenance chores.

Chapter **22**

Ten Smart Home Products to Revolutionize Your Living Space

D
o you find yourself gazing with envy at the seamless integration of technology in your friend's smart home? That moment when they effortlessly control outdoor lights from their smartphone while the kids play in the yard or adjust the thermostat without leaving the comfort of their sofa?

If you've ever dreamed of transforming your living space into a smart haven, you're in luck! Today, the world of smart home technology is more affordable and exciting than ever before. With a reliable Wi-Fi connection and a smartphone, you can dive into the realm of smart home devices, creating a personalized and efficient living environment that caters to your every need.

For example, as I sat down in my office to write this story, I picked up my smartphone and asked Alexa to play "Bruce Springsteen music," which she gladly obliged, sending my request to the smart speaker, which was embedded into my smart smoke detector. Pretty crazy!

Let's explore ten innovative smart home products that can improve the way you experience and interact with your home.

Smart Speakers

Leading the charge in the smart home revolution are devices like the Amazon Echo and Google Home. These smart speakers are not just for playing music; they serve as the central hub for controlling a multitude of smart devices using voice commands. Imagine walking into your living room and simply saying, "Alexa, turn on the lights and play my favorite playlist," and watching as your space transforms into an inviting haven of comfort and entertainment.

Smart Thermostats

Say goodbye to manual temperature adjustments and hello to the Nest Thermostat and similar smart thermostats. These intelligent devices learn your heating and cooling preferences over time, creating customized schedules that optimize your energy usage and comfort. With remote control capabilities via smartphone apps, you can adjust the temperature from anywhere. Driving home from work on a chilly day? Just dial up the temperature in your house a few degrees before leaving the parking lot to arrive at a cozy and comfortable home.

Smart Lighting

Illuminate your home in style with smart lighting solutions that go beyond traditional switches. Smart switches and smart LED bulbs allow you to create custom lighting scenes tailored to different activities, whether it's a cozy movie night or a vibrant dinner party. With the ability to adjust brightness and color, and even schedule lighting routines, you can set the perfect ambiance while also optimizing energy consumption.

Smart Door Locks

Never worry about forgetting your keys again with smart door locks that offer convenient and secure access control. Whether you're welcoming guests or coordinating deliveries, smart locks allow you to lock and unlock your doors remotely using a smartphone app or keypad. Some models even offer advanced features like temporary access codes, making it easy to grant entry to trusted individuals without compromising security.

Smart Home Security Systems

Keep a watchful eye on your home with cutting-edge smart systems that bring together sensors, alarms, cameras, and monitoring services. Leading brands like SimpliSafe, ADT Pulse, and Deep Sentinel offer advanced functionalities such as real-time alerts, video surveillance, and customizable security zones. Devices like Nest Cam and Ring Video Doorbell enable remote property monitoring, alerting you to suspicious activity and enabling direct communication with visitors via the camera. Some systems even sync with smart speakers for effortless voice-controlled monitoring. With user-friendly smartphone apps, you can oversee and manage your security setup from anywhere, whether you're home or away.

THE APP-OCALYPSE IS OVER: ONE APP TO RULE THEM ALL!

If you're wondering how many apps you'll need to control all these smart products, that answer is just one! You can centralize control of your smart devices with smart home hubs like Samsung SmartThings or Apple HomeKit. These hubs act as command centers, allowing you to manage and automate various devices using a single app. From setting up routines and schedules to integrating third-party smart devices, smart home hubs offer convenience and customization options that enhance your overall smart home experience.

Smart Plugs

Transform ordinary outlets into intelligent hubs with smart plugs that enable remote control of connected devices. Whether it's turning on lights, fans, or appliances with a simple tap on your smartphone, smart plugs offer convenience and energy efficiency. You can also create schedules and automation routines to streamline your daily tasks and enhance your home's functionality.

Smart Water Valves

Protect your home from water damage with smart water valves that can detect leaks and automatically shut off the water supply. These proactive solutions not only prevent costly water-related disasters, but also provide real-time alerts via your smartphone, allowing you to take swift action and mitigate potential damage.

Smart Home Battery Solutions

Embrace sustainable energy solutions with smart home battery systems that store power from renewable sources or the grid. These versatile batteries not only provide backup power during outages, but also allow you to manage energy usage efficiently. With smartphone apps, you can monitor battery status, optimize charging cycles, and even participate in demand-response programs to save on utility costs.

TIP

Maintenance for smart home products is minimal but crucial. Always remember to update your devices to the latest software version. Additionally, it's wise to register your products with the manufacturer when you purchase them. This not only validates the warranty but also ensures that the manufacturer has your contact information to send software update alerts when needed.

Smart Heating and Cooling Systems

Upgrade to smart HVAC systems that offer proactive maintenance and energy optimization features. These intelligent systems can detect issues before they escalate, alerting you and your HVAC service provider to potential problems, and avoiding inconvenient breakdowns. By optimizing heating and cooling cycles based on your preferences and occupancy patterns, smart HVAC systems offer comfort, efficiency, and cost savings.

Smart Appliances

Bring connectivity to your kitchen and laundry room with smart appliances that offer remote monitoring and control. Imagine preheating your oven on your way home from work, checking the contents of your fridge while grocery shopping, or starting a load of laundry with a tap on your smartphone. Smart appliances not only streamline daily tasks but also enhance convenience and efficiency in your home.

Smart home products make it easier to improve and maintain your home. The best part about adding smart home products is that you don't need to go all in at once. Start with just one device and build on it. Smart home products will continue to get "smarter" and their capabilities are sure to expand as technology advances, so dive in!

Index

driveways
   importance of maintaining, 21–22
   sealing, 339–340
drop cloths, 239
dryers
   filters in, 384
   keeping lint-free, 295
   troubleshooting, 296–297
   vent of, 296
drywall
   cracks in, 230–232
   holes in, 232–234
   interior walls, 27
   nail pops in, 236–237
   truss uplift in, 235–236
drywood termites, 354–355
ductless mini-split air conditioning, 224
ducts
   cleaning, 210
   insulating, 118–119
   leaks in, 208–210
   pressurizing, 209
   sealing, 209–210
   vacuuming, 210

E

Easy Mildew Remover mixture, 187–188
efflorescence, 62–63, 342
electric appliances, safety and, 282–283
electric heating systems, 216–217
electric water heater
   cleaning, 156–158
   thermostat, 158
electrical safety, 318–319
electronic-beam sensors, 321
energy audits, 113
Energy Savers, 113
ENERGY STAR certification, 130
epoxy, 332, 333
epoxy-based grout, 183
etched marble, 276

exhaust fan
   covers on, 384
   filters in, 385
expanding polyurethane spray foam, 120, 123–124
expenses, 13–15
extended warranties, for appliances, 292

F

fall checklist, 41–42
falls, avoiding on concrete, 330
fasteners
   on decks, 347–348
   rust on, 362–363
faucets, 165–167
   aerator, 166
   polishing, 166–167
fences, 22, 343–357
   applying preservative to, 345–346
   cleaning, 348–349
   painting, 344–345
   repairing rotted fence post, 350–353
   staining, 346–347
   straightening sagging gates, 353–354
   termites in, preventing, 354–356
   tightening loose boards and posts, 350
fiber cement, 107
fiberglass, 163
fiberglass doors, 131
fiberglass insulation, 112
fiberglass screens, 127
fiberglass showers, 180
fill valve, 168
filters
   cleaning, 224
   dryer, 384
   forced-air heating systems, 206–208
   furnace, 207, 383, 385
   kitchen exhaust fan, 385
   range-hood, 384
   refrigerator water, 384
   whole-house water, 384

frost-heave, 100
fungus
  efflorescence, 62–63
  on masonry, 341
furnace, 204
furnace filter, 207, 383, 385

G

galvanized pipes, 141
galvanized plumber tape, 145
garage doors
  automatic, 321–322
  securing, 320
garbage disposals, 192–194, 293
gas appliances, safety and, 281–282
gas fireplaces, 30–31
gas forced-air furnaces, 206
gas meters, 382
gas water heaters, 148, 154–156
gaskets
  in refrigerators, 292–293
  in toilets, 175
gates, straightening, 353–354
gauge glass, 214
generators, 316
GFCIs (Ground Fault Circuit Interrupters), 317–318
ghost flush, 197
Glass Cleaner, Gentle, 370–371
glass shower doors, cleaning, 180–181
granite counters, 276
graphite, 379
graphite powder, lubricating, 267
gravel, around fence posts, 352–353
grills, 316
Ground Fault Circuit Interrupters (GFCIs), 385
grout
  cement-based, 183
  cleaning, 182–183, 274
  epoxy-based, 183
  replacing, 183
  sealing, 182, 274
  staining, 183

gutters, 19, 64–65
  cleaning, 101
  guards for, 102
  protection systems for, 101–102

H

hammer tacker, 116
handles
  cleaning, 273
  maintaining, 273
handrails, 345
hardwood flooring, 255–257
  under carpet, 256
  engineered, 258
  refinishing, 257–258
heat exchanger, 206
heat pumps, 25–26, 204, 217, 222
heat tape, 117, 142
heating systems
  electric, 216–217
  forced-air, 204–211
    blower compartment, cleaning, 208
    ducts, 209–210
    replacing filter, 206–208
    servicing, 205–206
    temperature regulation, 210–211
  hot-water, 211–214
    pressure, gauging, 213
    radiators, bleeding, 213–214
  steam, 214–215
    adjusting, 214
    radiators of, 215
  types of, 204
  unsafe, 312
high gloss finish, on cabinets, 275
high-heat paint, 360
hinges
  cleaning, 273
  repairing, 263
holes
  in drywall, 232–234
  in plastering, 229–249

N

nail pops, in drywall, 229–249
nails, in outdoor wood structures, 344
National Chimney Sweep Guild, 301
National Plumbing Code
  sewer system fall, 199
  waste line, 194
natural-gas line safety, 316–317
NFRC (National Fenestration Rating Council)
    label, 130

O

oil stains, on concrete, 326–327
oil-based paint, 332, 333
Oven Cleaner, People-Friendly, 372
ovens
  cleaning interior of, 284–287
  lights in, replacing, 289
  temperature control, 288

P

paintbrush comb, 245
painter's multi-tool, 245
painting
  cabinets, kitchen, 271–272
  cleaning-up, 245
  concrete, 331–333
  exterior doors, 133
  outdoor wood structures, 344–345
  skills, 381–382
  steps, 243–244
  storing leftover paint, 246
  supplies for, 241–243
  surface prepping, 238–240
  wood, 106
paneling, 247
pans, copper, removing tarnish from, 276
PASS method of fire extinguisher use, 314
passive ventilation, 219
patching wallpaper, 249
patio doors, securing, 320
patios, 21–22

penetrating oil, 363
periodic tasks, 44–45
PEX tubing, 140–141
photoelectric smoke detection, 312
pinhole leaks, 139, 143
pipe-mounting straps, water hammer, 145
pipes
  clogging of, preventing, 191–193
  drain-pipe, 190
  freeze damage, 139
  galvanized, 141
  heating cable, 142
  insulating, 111, 142
  plumbing, 23–24
  soldering, 140
  vent, 190
plastering, 237–238
plumbing, 23–25
  bursting pipes, 142–144
  clogging, preventing, 191–194
  composite fixtures, surface maintenance, 164
  damaged pipes, 139–141
  deodorizing drains, 193–194
  drain-pipe, 189–190
  faucet, 165–167
  fiberglass, surface maintenance, 163
  high water pressure, 146–147
  pipes, 23–24
  porcelain fixtures, surface maintenance, 162–163
  private well, 160
  p-trap, 197–198
  re-routing, 118
  septic system, 199–201
    cleaning, 201
    items that damage, 200–201
  showers
    cleaning, 179–181
    glass doors of, 180–181
    tracks, 181
  softening water, 159
  stainless-steel fixtures, 162
  toilet, 168–179
    buildup, 171
    cleaning, 169–171

About the Author

Tom Kraeutler is a hands-on home improvement broadcast journalist and host of *The Money Pit*, America's largest syndicated home improvement radio show. The program airs on over 465 stations weekly, reaching millions of active home improvement enthusiasts nationwide. Additionally, he hosts *The Money Pit Podcast*, recognized among Apple Podcast's Best Home & Garden Podcasts of All Time.

Tom gained his expertise in home improvement through over 20 years of experience as a professional home inspector, learning how houses are put together, and how they fall apart! Since 1994, he has been a highly sought-after expert, providing straightforward advice, money-saving tips, and practical how-to guides to millions of Americans. He regularly appears on TV, radio, podcasts, online platforms, and major print media, sharing his expertise. Tom has been featured as a home improvement expert on numerous network and local television stations, including Fox, CNN, MSNBC, The History Channel, HGTV, and the DIY Network, making hundreds of appearances.

Tom served as the home improvement editor for AOL, and his work has been featured in *House Beautiful*, *Oprah*, *Smart Money*, *Reader's Digest*, and in hundreds of websites and newspapers across the nation. Together with his long-time co-host Leslie Segrete, Tom wrote *My Home My Money Pit: Your Guide to Every Home Improvement Adventure*.

Tom is a seasoned expert with a unique ability to combine encyclopedic home improvement knowledge with a comfortable and educational broadcasting style. This has earned him many loyal followers and led *Talkers* magazine to name Tom one of the "100 Most Important Talk Show Hosts in America."

Dedication

This book is dedicated to my mother JoAnn, my wife Sue, and our children Thomas, Sara, and Trevor, whose unconditional love and endless lists of projects make it possible for me to do this work.

Author's Acknowledgments

Life doesn't always flow in a straight line, and that was certainly the case with writing this book. My association with *Home Maintenance For Dummies* actually began back in 1999 when the For Dummies team reached out to me to ask if I'd be willing to sign on as the technical editor for the first edition of *Home Maintenance For Dummies*, written by James and Morris Carey. Because I had a career as a professional home inspector, the team felt I had the right skillset to review the content and offer suggestions for additional detail, clarity, and improvement. I knew James and Morris back then as hosts of the syndicated *On the House* radio show. At the time, I had just begun syndicating *The Money Pit Home Improvement Radio Show*, so although we were "friendly competitors," I certainly respected their program and experience and was happy to take on the project. Fast-forward to 2023, and Elizabeth Stilwell, acquisitions editor for the *For Dummies* line, asked if I'd be interested in writing the third edition, having no idea that I had worked on the original title. The moment felt like it was meant to be, and I was happy to accept the project. A lot has changed in the way we build and maintain homes over the last 25 years. This third edition builds on Carey's original work, with many updates, improvements, and additions to reflect those changes.

One of those changes is that today's young homebuyers are entering the homeownership market at a time when the nation is facing a dramatic shortage of skilled trade labor, making it harder than ever to find pros to fix things when they break or improve them before it gets that bad. On top of that, basic shop classes that were commonplace in middle and high school have almost all been eliminated. As a result, these first-time homebuyers are moving into homes that need ongoing maintenance and repair and yet literally don't know which end of the hammer to hold and can't find good pros to help when they need it. It is with this in mind that I set out to help those with a DIY spirit to take on these projects, building skills and confidence as their projects grow from simple tasks like painting a room to silencing a squeaky floor or fixing a roof leak.

It takes a team to build a house, and that was certainly the case with this book. Prior to my career in home improvement radio, I spent two decades as a professional home inspector, receiving training from one of the nation's most experienced and skilled inspectors, George Pettie. This background led me to recommend that George serve as the technical editor for this edition of *Home Maintenance For Dummies*. His extensive knowledge and meticulous attention to detail were both instrumental in crafting the highest-quality text possible and also deeply appreciated.

Finally, I'd like to thank both Elizabeth Stilwell, acquisitions editor, and Paul Levesque, senior project editor, for their valuable guidance and steady hand, helping to assure this latest edition would build upon the almost 25-year history of helping consumers maintain and care for their homes.

Publisher's Acknowledgments

Acquisitions Editor: Elizabeth Stilwell
Senior Project Editor: Paul Levesque
Copy Editor: Marylouise Wiack
Tech Reviewer: George Pettie

Production Editor: Saikarthick Kumarasamy
Cover Image: © Gorodenkoff/Adobe Stock Photos

Leverage the power

Dummies is the global leader in the reference category and one of the most trusted and highly regarded brands in the world. No longer just focused on books, customers now have access to the dummies content they need in the format they want. Together we'll craft a solution that engages your customers, stands out from the competition, and helps you meet your goals.

Advertising & Sponsorships

Connect with an engaged audience on a powerful multimedia site, and position your message alongside expert how-to content. Dummies.com is a one-stop shop for free, online information and know-how curated by a team of experts.

- Targeted ads
- Video
- Email Marketing
- Microsites
- Sweepstakes sponsorship

20 MILLION PAGE VIEWS EVERY SINGLE MONTH

15 MILLION UNIQUE VISITORS PER MONTH

43% OF ALL VISITORS ACCESS THE SITE VIA THEIR MOBILE DEVICES

700,000 NEWSLETTER SUBSCRIPTIONS TO THE INBOXES OF

300,000 UNIQUE INDIVIDUALS EVERY WEEK

# of dummies

Custom Publishing

Reach a global audience in any language by creating a solution that will differentiate you from competitors, amplify your message, and encourage customers to make a buying decision.

- Apps
- Books
- eBooks
- Video
- Audio
- Webinars

Brand Licensing & Content

Leverage the strength of the world's most popular reference brand to reach new audiences and channels of distribution.

For more information, visit dummies.com/biz

PERSONAL ENRICHMENT

9781119187790
USA $26.00
CAN $31.99
UK £19.99

9781119179030
USA $21.99
CAN $25.99
UK £16.99

9781119293354
USA $24.99
CAN $29.99
UK £17.99

9781119293347
USA $22.99
CAN $27.99
UK £16.99

9781119310068
USA $22.99
CAN $27.99
UK £16.99

9781119235606
USA $24.99
CAN $29.99
UK £17.99

9781119251163
USA $24.99
CAN $29.99
UK £17.99

9781119235491
USA $26.99
CAN $31.99
UK £19.99

9781119279952
USA $24.99
CAN $29.99
UK £17.99

9781119283133
USA $24.99
CAN $29.99
UK £17.99

9781119287117
USA $24.99
CAN $29.99
UK £16.99

9781119130246
USA $22.99
CAN $27.99
UK £16.99

PROFESSIONAL DEVELOPMENT

9781119311041
USA $24.99
CAN $29.99
UK £17.99

9781119255796
USA $39.99
CAN $47.99
UK £27.99

9781119293439
USA $26.99
CAN $31.99
UK £19.99

9781119281467
USA $26.99
CAN $31.99
UK £19.99

9781119280651
USA $29.99
CAN $35.99
UK £21.99

9781119251132
USA $24.99
CAN $29.99
UK £17.99

9781119310563
USA $34.00
CAN $41.99
UK £24.99

9781119181705
USA $29.99
CAN $35.99
UK £21.99

9781119263593
USA $26.99
CAN $31.99
UK £19.99

9781119257769
USA $29.99
CAN $35.99
UK £21.99

9781119293477
USA $26.99
CAN $31.99
UK £19.99

9781119265313
USA $24.99
CAN $29.99
UK £17.99

9781119239314
USA $29.99
CAN $35.99
UK £21.99

9781119293323
USA $29.99
CAN $35.99
UK £21.99

dummies.com

dummies
A Wiley Brand